The Psychoanalytic Study of the Child

VOLUME SIXTY-SEVEN

Founding Editors
ANNA FREUD, LL.D., D.Sc.
HEINZ HARTMANN, M.D.
ERNST KRIS, Ph.D.

Managing Editors
CLAUDIA LAMENT, Ph.D., and ROBERT A. KING, M.D.

Editors
SAMUEL ABRAMS, M.D.
A. SCOTT DOWLING, M.D.
ROBERT A. KING, M.D.
PAUL M. BRINICH, Ph.D.
CLAUDIA LAMENT, Ph.D.

Editorial Board

Samuel Abrams, M.D.	Steven Marans, Ph.D.
Denia G. Barrett, M.S.W.	Linda C. Mayes, M.D.
Paul M. Brinich, Ph.D.	Jill M. Miller, Ph.D.
A. Scott Dowling, M.D.	Wendy Olesker, Ph.D.
Karen Gilmore, M.D.	Mary Target, Ph.D.
Robert A. King, M.D.	Robert L. Tyson, M.D.
Rona Knight, Ph.D.	Fred R. Volkmar, M.D.
Anton O. Kris, M.D.	Judith A. Yanof, M.D.
Claudia Lament, Ph.D.	

To submit a new manuscript, please send it as an
e-mail attachment in MS Word to: CMLament@msn.com.
For those without e-mail, kindly direct queries by post or phone to:

Claudia Lament, Ph.D.
31 Washington Square West, PHA
New York, New York 10011
Telephone: 212-228-3082

The Psychoanalytic Study of the Child

VOLUME SIXTY-SEVEN

Yale University Press
New Haven and London
2013

*Copyright © 2013 by Claudia Lament, Robert A. King,
Samuel Abrams, A. Scott Dowling, and Paul M. Brinich.
All rights reserved. This book may not be
reproduced, in whole or in part, including illustrations, in any form
(beyond that copying permitted by Sections 107
and 108 of the U.S. Copyright Law and except by
reviewers for the public press), without
written permission from the publishers.*

*Anna Freud contributions reproduced by kind permission of the Marsh
Agency Ltd on behalf of the Estate of Anna Freud.*

*Yale University Press books may be purchased in quantity
for educational, business, or promotional use.
For information, please e-mail sales.press@yale.edu (U.S. office)
or sales@yaleup.co.uk (U.K. office).*

*Designed by Sally Harris and set in Baskerville type.
Printed in the United States of America.*

*Library of Congress catalog card number: 45-11304
ISBN: 978-0-300-19585-9*

A catalogue record for this book is available from the British Library.

*This paper meets the requirements of ANSI/NISO Z39.48-1992
(Permanence of Paper).*

10 9 8 7 6 5 4 3 2 1

Contents

SIBLINGS: NEW PERSPECTIVES

CLAUDIA LAMENT
   An Introduction   3
JULIET MITCHELL
   Siblings: Thinking Theory   14
ROSEMARY H. BALSAM
   Sibling Interaction   35
KAREN GILMORE
   The Theory of Sibling Trauma and the Lateral Dimension   53
JEANINE M. VIVONA
   Sibling Recognition and the Development of Identity:
   Intersubjective Consequences of Sibling Differentiation
   in the Sister Relationship   66
CLAUDIA LAMENT
   Three Contextual Frameworks for Siblingships:
   Nonlinear Thinking, Disposition, and Phallocentrism   84

WORK WITH PARENTS

KERRY KELLY NOVICK AND JACK NOVICK
   Concurrent Work with Parents of Adolescent Patients   103
SCOTT DOWLING AND CLAUDIA LAMENT
   Dialogue with the Novicks   137

CHILD PSYCHOANALYSIS

PAUL M. BRINICH
   Marianne Kris Lecture
   Weaving Child Psychoanalysis: Past, Present, and Future   149
AVA BRY PENMAN
   "There Has Never Been Anything Like a Classical
   Child Analysis": Clinical Discussions with Anna Freud,
   1970–1971   173

TRAUMA

LENORE C. TERR
 What Becomes of Infantile Traumatic Memories?
 An Adult "Wild Child" Is Asked to Remember   197
NANETTE C. AUERHAHN
 Evolution of Traumatic Narratives: Impact of the
 Holocaust on Children of Survivors   215

CLINICAL AND THEORETICAL CONTRIBUTIONS

ANDERS ZACHRISSON
 The Internal/External Issue: What Is an Outer Object?
 Another Person as Object and as Separate Other in
 Object Relations Models   249
OLAVI HÄMÄLÄINEN
 Commentary on Zachrisson   275
ETZIONA ISRAELI, ZEHORIT ASULIN-SIMHON,
AND RUTH SHARABANY
 The Interface between Cyberspace and Psychotherapeutic
 Space: Relationship Avoidance and Intimacy in Adolescent
 Psychotherapy   279
JOHN HITCHCOCK
 Acute Onset of the Sinking Feeling in the Elderly:
 A Case Report and Addendum to an Article Published
 in This Annual in 1984   298

INDEX   301

SIBLINGS

New Perspectives

An Introduction

CLAUDIA LAMENT, Ph.D.

FOR MANY YEARS, JULIET MITCHELL HAS BEEN HUNTING DOWN THE elements of a mystery: Why has there been no place for the topic of siblings in the psychoanalytic superstructure? Historically, the lateral dimension in psychic life was seen largely as a displacement from the more-important vertical, or parent-child, relation. The sibling relationship taken on its own merit has been a long time in the making. Notwithstanding the publication of numerous papers that address this imbalance, the subject of siblings sticks to the margins of theory. Mitchell's 2003 volume, with the fittingly direct title *Siblings*, demonstrated the fruits of her quest to parse this conundrum, and succeed she did. She extracted her central thesis from this book in her presentation at the Western New England Psychoanalytic Society Symposium in 2011. The paper, "Siblings: Thinking Theory," which stands as the centerpiece of this section, is an author-edited version of her presentation.

Her work uncovered several unanticipated interlocking clues: the penetrating and abiding structures of phallocentrism in Western societies, and psychoanalytic theories concerning the origins of hysteria. Her perusal of early psychoanalytic explanations placed its "truths" about hysteria within the parent-child dimension in pre-oedipal and oedipal iterations. Mitchell provides the following account: The hysterical girl—though true too of the rarer example of the hysterical boy—flaunts a fantasied position of owning the phallus to captivate the mother. This kindles a seductive intensity in the child in the hope that the arrival of

---

Claudia Lament, Ph.D., is Training and Supervising Analyst at the Institute for Psychoanalytic Education, an affiliate of the Department of Psychiatry, New York University Langone Medical Center. She is Assistant Clinical Professor in the Department of Child and Adolescent Psychiatry, the Child Study Center, New York University Langone Medical Center. She is also Senior Managing Editor of *The Psychoanalytic Study of the Child*.

The Psychoanalytic Study of the Child 67, ed. Claudia Lament, Robert A. King, Samuel Abrams, A. Scott Dowling, and Paul M. Brinich (Yale University Press, copyright © 2013 by Claudia Lament, Robert A. King, Samuel Abrams, A. Scott Dowling, and Paul M. Brinich).

a real penis will be forthcoming. All the while, the child also cleaves to an unconscious belief that it has been stolen away from her/him, leaving in its wake a profound sense of emptiness.

The late-nineteenth-century world-renowned neurologist Jean-Marie Charcot, having numerous male hysterics in his Parisian clinic, theorized an additional point of view: for him, the appearance of an environmental trauma was the designated culprit. Following his lead, Mitchell became curious about the idea of trauma in the hysteric and assembled the hysteric's symptomatology of always being both "too much there and insufficiently present—moving between grandiosity and psychic collapse" (2003, p. 7). Was there an unidentified trauma inherent in this outward picture? She cited King (1993) as noting the universal component of an "imitation of death," or annihilation in addition to the well-documented feature of the breakthrough of incestuous oedipal desire as typifying the hysteric's behavior. At this, the detective was as if struck by lightning: Mitchell drew together these two aspects—the fear of annihilation and the taboo of incest—and saw in them what she deemed fitting as the natural response to the arrival of a sibling. As she put it, for her, the oedipal rock shifted and behind it she found so many dancing and squabbling siblings. The imagistic vision of "dancing siblings" is intriguing as it summons up scenes of play, charming exuberance, and mutual loving exchange; yet, a closer look at Mitchell's thesis shows that the dance is more code for squabbling. Whimsical interlude is a veil for a darker psychic drama.

Through this vector, she not only argued that sibling arrival is a "trauma" that underpins the hysteric's disorder, but she also expanded the idea of sibling trauma as universal in its reach and inclusive of the only child's expectation that the sibling arrival is just around the corner. This awaited sibling engenders in its brother or sister profound love for someone who is "just like me" but who, at the same time, threatens the very uniqueness of the child and thus, is a replacement of oneself. Consequently, the child feels that his or her very being is not only under siege but, in fact, is annihilated. It is the task of humankind, Mitchell admonished, to surmount this developmental trauma or else remain mired in the seductive, provocative, self-aggrandizing, and histrionic displays that one observes in the toddler who must manage the fateful birth of the one who obliterates his or her personhood. If this is the case, namely, that sibling "trauma" is generalizable over all civilization, why has the role of siblings been occluded from its rightful place in psychoanalytic theory?

In the pages of this collection, readers will also discover an alternate perspective on Mitchell's view of siblingships as necessarily universally traumatic. Informing this difference in approach will be a conceptual overview of the developmental process and its continuous and discontinuous dimensions, as well as the roles of dispositional influences and gender biases as impacting the child's unique experience of this relationship.

Mitchell cited her second clue, phallocentrism and its deeply structured coordinates in the larger sociocultural context, as an important reason for the omission of the siblings vector from the psychoanalytic superstructure. The argument follows thusly: The ideal of fraternity is encoded in Western society as the brotherhood of men. Mitchell then charted the logic that holds that ideologies spawned by "brotherhood" structures are inextricably tied to patriarchies. She paused at this juncture to acknowledge how this privileged position of the patriarchy has exerted a deep and penetrating inflection on the social polity. Where taboos regarding incest and violence by parents toward children in vertically structured societies will naturally initiate the conditions for the creation of a social contract that binds and protects the biological relationship between parent and child, such societies also tend to fail to create a place where taboos form in like manner with their attendant social structures that care for the health of the sibling relationship. In effect, the hegemony of patriarchy—if blindly adhered to—will result in an abiding neglect of the vagaries of love and hate in siblinghood: The result of such a blinkered society is an unwitting carte blanche on incest and violence. Mitchell warned that the omission of the place of siblings in our cultural superstructure is a significant driving force that fuels our ignorance of the rampant extent of sibling abuse—and its displaced forms in love relationships and war—in Western society.

From here, it is hardly a stretch of the imagination to extend the argument that such phallocentric precipitates in our cultural milieu have created and perpetuated the vertical dimension of parent-child relations in psychoanalytic theory and clinical practice. Mitchell's sleuthing uncovered that conceptualizations surrounding femininity in analytic theory can be mapped easily onto those that surround siblingships. For example, sibling experiences reference emotions such as anxieties that are typically associated with females: annihilation, fears of loss of love, leaning on the other for confirmation, tendencies toward being the object of love as opposed to the active position as subject of loving relations. The feminine in psychoanalytic theory is cast as that which is different or as other: patriarchal matrices equate the normative with male and tend to expel that which is identified outside this grouping as feminine. The stability of the vertical ladder in theory substantiates this system of thinking by taking up all the space, leaving the sibling (as feminine) dimension at the corners.

In her 2003 volume, Mitchell brought some of these ideas to life in her example of the society of the Trobrianders in Melanesia, wherein the sibling dimension took precedence. Here, the anthropologist Bronislaw Malinowski (1927; 1929) discovered in the 1920s that theirs was a community highly sensitive to brother/sister incest and where, by Western standards, the usual parent-child axis was of secondary import: instead of its place on the promontory of the preferred social contract, the vertical dimension was situated in the lowlands, characterized only by its bond of affection in which any whiff of sexualized feeling was absent. The taboo against passions was located laterally. To uphold its tenets, young children were divided into sets wherein blood brothers and sisters were not allowed in the same group. In this "republic of children," as Malinowski referred to it, the children's social groupings were not adjudicated by adults but by themselves. Sexual exploration (in the absence of the biological siblings), experimentation of regulating violent feelings through play, and creating social bonds became the foundational fabric of their childhood experience. Thus, the taboo against sibling sex and violence found a natural buttress of support in the society's creation of social structures and community that were child-managed, without a trace of adult intervention!

As stated above, the topic of siblings has been addressed in the psychoanalytic canon, but in a manner best characterized as scattershot. Consequently, the drawing up of a cohesive, constellated perspective on the subject never came to fruition, which, had it happened, might have ensured its due place and integration within the metapsychology. Readers who wish to study the ebb and flow of this current will relish the introductory section of Rosemary Balsam's paper, which provides a flush and comprehensive compendium of contributions to this topic.

Of particular interest to the readership is her citation of this annual's publication of a section on "Siblings" in volume 38 (1983), which highlighted aspects of sibships that facilitated forward growth. The selection of this particular focus was the relative absence, at that time period, of a perspective that tracked the components of healthy and progressive development within the sibling experience. Two dynamic forces drew special attention: the nature of the relationships between parent and child, and, within the children themselves, the developmental capacities and preferences that helped shape the sibling experience. My own contribution in the present collection will accent and update this point of view.

Introduction

SUMMARIES OF THE CONTRIBUTIONS

The contributions in this section approach Mitchell's paper from contrasting contextual paradigms that open up the play of meaning across the contemporary psychoanalytic spectrum: Balsam's accent on intersecting vectors of both vertical and lateral axes and the use of the transference-countertransference matrix; Gilmore's attention to continuous features of growth and the consequence of the failure of discontinuities; Vivona's focus on issues of identity within siblingships along with its intersubjective dimension and its attendance to the ways siblings recognize and value similarities and differences between them; my contribution positioning siblings within the framework of nonlinear thinking, dispositional aspects of personality formation, and phallocentrism.

Rosemary Balsam acknowledges the clamorous petitions within our field that call for a postmodernist credo. Such tracts espouse the dimming down of the patriarchal Freudian parent-child axis, a fitting reflection of the tenor of our times: They cast a suspicious eye upon authority and rally the brothers and sisters toward alliance or war. Yet Balsam (as do our other contributors) refrains from stepping onto this bandwagon without looking back to its predecessor: She invokes both vertical and lateral dimensions in her report of her analysis of a woman with a sister. In so doing, she illuminates her position that juggling both dimensions provides rich and textured meanings to her patient's interior life. Balsam finds another anchor in her discussion of her patient in Mitchell's "Law of the Mother"—an ironic coinage that winks at Lacan's "Law of the Father." For Mitchell, the mother's law as writ upon the domestic scene is that she adjudicate the terms of sibling relationships with a fair and compassionate hand: mother's decision making is blinded to favoritism. One highlighted feature of mother's law is that she softens the sibling relationship by regulating emotional storms that flare among the sibling tribe and regulates bonds and fissures. Thus, it falls to mother to teach seriality to her brood: that is, that there is room for more than "me": there is "you" too and others as well. The matters that require arbitration in their base forms are incest and murder, but in daily life, they cover everything big and small in a child's domain. Should the mother consistently blink at her task or largely abandon it, the result can work serious consequences for children. The inevitable lack of assistance for unbridled emotion among siblings can promote problems along a spectrum inclusive of dysregulation and behavioral disorders. At worst, such neglect may result in covert or flagrant abuse.

In her presentation of the clinical data, Balsam draws upon Hans Loewald's use of the metaphor of theater as he sees helices of transferences superimposed one upon the other onto the analyst. Siblings make their appearances as do others, and Balsam maximizes this perspective. She takes us with her "onstage" as a player in her patient's drama; she shares her view of her patient's transferences and her own countertransferences as overlapping transparencies that, she proposes, reveal her patient's, her patient's sister's, and their mother's interior lives and their mutual interrelationships. For Balsam, the analyst's countertransference holds up a mirror to the past "as it really happened," both in terms of the external realities and the individuals' intrapsychic lives.

She takes the view that she discovered the mother's disturbance in her own countertransference reactions—here examined as the mother's failure to fairly parse the law that was hers to administer. Balsam holds the mother's perceived failing as the critical feature that accounts for the troubled sibling relations. This is a presentation that will undoubtedly elicit lively interest from our readership on several counts. First, its forward-looking interpretation in the clinical situation of the intersection between parent/child and sibling/sibling axes takes seriously Mitchell's invitation to widen our clinical viewfinder to include the world of those that reside beside one. At the same time, her clinical perspicacity succeeds in persuading that it does not make sense to throw the Freudian "vertical ladder" baby out with the bathwater. Secondly, her rich accounts from the workbench will tantalize interested parties toward further explorations in the area of constructions and reconstructions in the analytic field.

Karen Gilmore greets Mitchell's proposals with enthusiasm all around. Not only is it high time that the sibling dimension come into its own right as a profoundly shaping force in psychic life, but in particular, Gilmore gives special honors to Mitchell for the critical measure she has taken toward its integration into our overarching theoretical framework. Mitchell's quest to uncover why siblings have been omitted from theoretical discourse finds Gilmore pondering her own intriguing hypothesis: Perhaps it is the particularized "painful and powerful affects" linked to the sibling experience that has leveraged our preoccupation with the vertical, parent-child axis. Readers cannot be but taken by her further reflections on brutality and violence that typify sibships, more raw in their native qualities than what is structuralized into the vertical dimension. She concurs with Mitchell that "trauma" is an apt description for the child's experience of a sibling's birth.

Following Mitchell's focus on the toddler's experience of the newborn, Gilmore attends to the aspects of cognitive and psychological shifts that characterize developmental advance in this age group. The new baby's presence on the domestic scene may serve to upend the toddler's newly flourishing cognitive transformations and even flare her sensitivities to anger, hurt, and feelings of displacement. Gilmore thoughtfully wonders if such a congruence of external and internal pressures may propel the child toward pretend play at an accelerated clip. Gilmore then shifts the scene and situates the reader in a later epoch of growth; she brings to the reader's view the older youngster, one emerging into puberty and adolescence. Here she presents two cases of teenagers who carry with them the burdens of a continuous legacy of sibling trauma.

Adolescence retraces some of the same components that had emerged in early childhood, but at another level of organization: separation, identity, gender, differentiation, among others. Experimentation with fitting into the peer group and finding one's own place underscores sibling-associated issues. Perhaps even more important, Gilmore frames the physical transformations of adolescence, which demand that the young persons face their biological capacity for procreation with the possibility that they may repeat their own sibling trauma. Extending the point further, Gilmore alerts the reader to the parents' "re-edition" of their own sibling experience by identifying with one child as a former version of themselves while seeing in another child a version of a sibling. From this point of view, the transgenerational transmission of sibling trauma is a legacy destined for repetition in future generations.

Gilmore presents the reader with a view of disturbance that is housed inside a conceptual framework of linearity: The sibling "trauma" is destined for repetition. Readers will discover that the two adolescent patients Gilmore presents are also studied within this framework. The press of an experiential component from early childhood—in this case, sibling birth felt as "traumatic"—is tracked throughout sequential growth for both girls. Readers will find this perspective a valuable one. It highlights the continuous or linear aspect of the developmental process—the discontinuous or nonlinear aspect being the other coordinate—in one strand of the girls' forward trajectory and forces us to consider growth that has been hobbled by failures in discontinuity and change. Following in the footsteps of Mitchell's detective work, our readership may feel inspired to search for clues within the presenting data that point to factors that hijacked nonlinear growth and occluded transformative possibilities of reassembly of the girls' earlier perceptions of their siblings.

Jeanine Vivona takes the reader down another road, which highlights identity configuration within the sibling matrix, a fresh and innovative turn on this topic. She privileges a close examination of differentiation processes. As she defines them, they center on how one develops or even favors certain features or desires that are in contradistinction to a sibling's way of being and simultaneously how one suppresses those facets that are seen as similar. Using Jessica Benjamin's theory of "mutual recognition," Vivona expands the field of relationships within the sibship to investigate how children position themselves vis-à-vis one another and within the family itself. The interpersonal and intersubjective resonances of these will have their impact.

For Vivona, the central challenge for most children along the lateral axis is the problem of identity. She presents her thesis that processes of differentiation are a crucial means for a child to find her value, identity, and place with regard to her siblings and parents. For example, if a child perceives a sibling to have one particular characteristic, she may wish to distinguish herself from that sibling by putting forth to others a contrasting feature. How she is received in the world of her siblings—and *perceives* how she is received—will have reverberations upon her expectations of relationships with others outside the immediate family domain. Thus, Vivona warns, it is necessary to the child's sense of self to feel validated through her sibling's recognition of her difference and the means by which she carves out her place. Vivona takes it one step further: Another's recognition of one's self verifies a multiplicity of features facilitating the ownership of these within one's self. This has special relevance for the others who are beside one, because feeling legitimized or not by one's siblings will have particularized meaning for the position one has created on the lateral spectrum.

It is the stewardship of handling the rivalry and love for one's sister or brother that is at issue in finding one's place; namely, the child both wants to be victorious over her sibling and wants *not* to be victorious over her sibling. To tackle this paradoxical task is to embark on an ingenious strategy: Enlarge the scope of one's differences from the sibling and simultaneously play down one's similarities from that same sibling. In so doing, the child creates a unique position within the sibling relationship that ensures a singularity all her own while safeguarding that position from the other's aggression or envy. Not surprisingly, such a strategy is not uncommon in managing similar puzzles that appear with mother and father.

However, this game plan's long-term success is more apparent than real. If the child does not feel that the other—for the purpose of our primary focus, one's sibling—recognizes her differences along with her similarities, which Vivona remarks is a natural and inevitable occurrence, mutual recognition breaks down. In order to initiate a process of repair, it is necessary for one party to *surrender* (italics Vivona's) to the other's point of view in such a way that registers a valorization of the difference. The establishment of something new occurs, which is not owned by either individual but which becomes a shared perspective, or according to Benjamin, a *shared third* (Benjamin 2006). Readers will feel especially rewarded by Vivona's meticulous discussion in her bringing these proposals to the context of the consulting room by way of two striking case illustrations. Finally, the layeredness of Vivona's presentation gifts the reader with challenging ideas and questions about identity formation: To what degree must the support of the object (in this case, that of the sibling) be present as a requisite condition for one's feeling of legitimacy and wholeness? Apart from the role played by the environmental surround, by way of one's parents and siblings, are there other features that reside within the child herself—certain dispositional variants, strengths, or vulnerabilities, for instance—that strain or facilitate identity formation? The range of therapeutic strategies to address this issue are necessarily broadened by identifying influences that arise from internal as well as external sources. For example, promoting the transformational shifts that accompany new organizational growth within the setting of the child-analyst exchange can provide unexpected assistance to healthy identity development when the environmental surround fails to provide nurturing support.

My contribution takes the reader on an altogether different excursion. I place Mitchell's proposals as they are refracted through three lenses: nonlinear thinking, disposition, and an expansion of Mitchell's own interest in phallocentrism. I also locate the experience of sibling arrival within a developmental context that includes features of timing, birth order, and disposition as crucial variables in shaping children's reactions. In so doing, I bring another perspective to Mitchell's proposition of sibling birth as necessarily "traumatic" for all children. My alternative view does not delegitimize her argument that the sibling "experience," as I prefer to describe it, is generalizable to the population (including the only child) and should have a proper and integrated position within the metapsychological paradigm.

The nonlinear perspective considers the progressive hierarchical organizational changes that occur in the developmental trajectory. Yet there is a propensity in our field to place an accent on tracing the linear features of development and to reduce later forms into their earliest features. Such leanings and activities obscure how we assess the sibling experience as the child moves forward toward new platforms of growth. The progressive forces of development transform intrapsychic and cognitive structures, which produce discontinuities that cannot be reconfigured into their antecedent forms. I am interested in demonstrating how the sibling experience for any child will undergo profound changes over sequential stages of forward movement; otherwise, one observes a failure of discontinuous growth, a troubling occurrence.

Secondly, the role of dispositional features has been largely undervalued in psychoanalytic theorizing and clinical practice as an important source of influence in how children grow. Early on in our psychoanalytic history, Freud himself observed that this domain attracted few interested parties in favor of the more-popular focus on dynamically propelled components of intrapsychic life and their link with environmental forces. I take the position that particulars in disposition, such as differences and disharmonies in rate and timing of strands of growth, capacities in weighing love and hate, separateness and closeness, and regulation of affect states, will exert their press upon the nature of sibling interactions. Braided within such interactions is the question of how the intricacies of sibling interrelatedness exert a mutual effect upon each child's shifts into new organizational hierarchies. Finally, the experience of sibling arrival will be touched by these very features and at the same time will actively participate in the determination of a child's status on a continuum that spans trauma on one end and healthy adaptation on the other.

Thirdly, Western society's leanings toward phallocentrism have inflected psychoanalytic paradigms and theory, as Mitchell has described. Siblingship is treated as an aggressivized-male experience, as exemplified in the term "sibling rivalry." I take the view that such a linguistic form has become an embedded structure in culture that colors how we build meaning in favor of other perspectives that highlight affection or caring, for instance. On a sub-rosa register of awareness, such forms become structured in culture as "truths" that continuously recycle down through the generations.

Mitchell's far-ranging sleuthing among numerous domains—psychoanalysis, anthropology, sociology, psychology, literature, and her own personal reflections deserves our applause and high praise. She has created a space where dancing and squabbling siblings have become a legitimized faction all their own. She has also shown how a culturally encoded, gender-based bias has foregrounded the parent-child dimension at the cost of minimizing the effects of the sibling dimension and how each interacts with and affects the other. That all five papers in this section are written by women will not be lost on our readership. Among other narratives, perhaps the essays that follow will be understood by future psychoanalytic historians as the feminine voice within our sphere of influence that finally reevaluated the lateral dimension and its proper place in our psychoanalytic superstructure. In the pages that follow, readers will discover some of the reasons for the tight embrace of the vertical axis in our field. This steadfastness can be likened to the old and irrelevant costumes of a theater's lumber room that cannot be cast off for the draw of sentiment and the stubborn refusal to move forward. Herein these essays is a plea to create fresh interpretations.

REFERENCES

BENJAMIN, J. (2006). Two-way streets: Recognition of difference and the intersubjective third. *Differences* 17(1), 116–46.
KING, H. (1993). Once upon a text: Hysteria from Hippocrates. In *Hysteria beyond Freud*, ed. S. L. Gilman, H. King, R. Porter, G. S. Rousseau, and E. Showalter. Berkeley: University of California Press.
MALINOWSKI, B. (1927). *Sex and Repression in Savage Society*. London: Routledge and Kegan Paul.
——— (1929). *The Sexual Life of Savages*. London: Routledge and Kegan Paul.
MITCHELL, J. (2003). *Siblings*. Oxford: Polity Press.

Siblings

Thinking Theory

JULIET MITCHELL, M.A.

The paper argues for the development of a theoretical understanding of lateral relations, starting with siblings, along a horizontal axis. This would be autonomous but interactive with the vertical axis of parent-child.

THIS TALK IS FIRST AND FOREMOST A PLEA THAT WE MAKE SPACE for an analytical understanding of lateral relations along a horizontal axis, not instead of but in addition to the vertical, whose perspective is almost synonymous with so many of our disciplines. I start with sisters and brothers, "siblings," because they bear what anthropologists designate the "minimal difference from each other" and can be considered from a psychoanalytical point of view (though this is contested) to be the symbolic source of those that follow or succeed them: cousins, partners, wives, husbands, friends, and foe . . . I believe that this "minimal difference" is crucial also in psychoanalytical theory and therapy.[1]

Professor Juliet Mitchell, Fellow of the British Academy, is currently an Emeritus Leverhulme Fellow. She is also a Professor in the Ph.D. program in Theoretical Psychoanalysis, which she established at University College London; Emeritus Professor at the University of Cambridge; Founder-Director of the Centre for Gender Studies, Cambridge; and Fellow of the British Psychoanalytical Society and the International Psychoanalytic Association.

Earlier versions of this talk were given at University College London, University of the Witswatersrand, and Cambridge University, and one of these was published as "Psychoanalysis, Siblings and the Social Group" in *Psycho-Analytic Psychotherapy in South Africa* 19 (1), 2011. This is the only author-edited text of the talk as it was given in New Haven, Connecticut, at the Western New England Psychoanalytic Society Symposium in April 2011.

The Psychoanalytic Study of the Child 67, ed. Claudia Lament, Robert A. King, Samuel Abrams, A. Scott Dowling, and Paul M. Brinich (Yale University Press, copyright © 2013 by Claudia Lament, Robert A. King, Samuel Abrams, A. Scott Dowling, and Paul M. Brinich).

1. Freud's notion of "the narcissism of minor differences" can be seen as one psychological effect that results from this "minimal difference": Social amity is preserved through hostility to the closest neighboring group.

Here, my framework is the need to develop a place for siblings along a horizontal axis in our theoretical superstructure. A "sibling trauma" is the concept I propose as a starting point for the construction of such a position. There are many implications of a sibling trauma; here, after trying to establish its importance, I introduce its impact on both gendering and socialization.

THE THEORETICAL SUPERSTRUCTURE

When I came across sisters and brothers, "siblings," I had an experience common to many researchers in the field: One moment I hadn't noticed them; the next, they were everywhere. Why this surprise, why this sense of revelation of the obvious? This "then you didn't see them, now you do" is reflected in the way they are regularly presented as first found, and only then to have been previously missing—like reclaimed property you didn't know was lost. Looking back through the annals of psychoanalytic writings, they seem to have come up, been excitedly noticed with pleas for more exploration, and gone underground again. The good work has been dropped and later picked up once again rather than embraced and developed.

I argue that it is the effective absence of siblings in the theoretical superstructure that accounts for why the many observations of them go unnoticed by commentators. When this eventually does happen, it is as though they were a first-time discovery, because there has been no theoretical place where they could have been held in the meantime.

Freud (1893; 1905a; 1925) was fond of quoting his early mentor, Jean-Marie Charcot, to the effect that "theory is good; but it doesn't prevent things from existing" (1893, p. 13), thus apparently privileging observation over theory. However, Freud's work was also a notable example of the importance of the role of a possible theory, much as other scientists have addressed the issue. The astrophysicist Sir Arthur Eddington declared, "I hope it will not shock experimental physicists too much if I say that we do not accept their observations unless they are confirmed by theory."[2] One can, after all, observe different things from one week to the next without being able to make a relevant generalization. And this, I suggest, for psychoanalysis but also perhaps more generally, takes us to the heart of the matter: The obstacle to thinking about sisters and brothers is not in the observations but in the theory. Thus Freud wrote, "The great event of Hans' life was the birth of his

---

2. *Address to the Annual Meeting of the British Association for the Advancement of Science*, 11 September 1933 (in Kaempffert 1933, p. 13).

sister when he was exactly three and a half" (1909, p. 10), and then from this observation about a sister, Freud proceeded to develop his emerging theory of the vertical castration complex—not without reason—but without taking on board what might be a distinct meaning of the little sister, the object of Hans' agonizing jealousy and the threat to his sense of his own existence.

In suggesting that siblings need to be an autonomous aspect of the theory, I do not have anything very grandiose in mind. A theoretical construct will need to find that the experience of them is generalizable—something we all experience—if it is to play a role in the construction of the unconscious aspect of the human psyche. In the clinical context, psychoanalysis works through the particular case of an individual patient with his or her own unique history. The various individual histories are "accidental" in the sense of what happens to fall to one's lot. Where these varied and specific histories touch down on the general, we have the raw material of what can come to constitute the theory of psychoanalysis.

Freud (1905b) first believed that the many stories of paternal seduction had caused the widespread hysteria of his nineteenth-century patients, male as well as female, himself as well as others. He then realized that however extensive such abuse was (and is), it was not everybody's lot. Actual abuse is accidental, an aspect of one's particular history. Distinct from this was the clinical observation that *everybody* desires incest with the mother. Unlike the stories of abuse that the patient could recollect, this observation of a general situation was not at first possible, because everybody has to repress this desire to such a degree that we have no knowledge of ever having wanted it; both the desire and the prohibition on it are unconscious. Unconscious processes are general: Everybody dreams; everybody, that is to say, manifests processes that are or have been unconscious, whether at one end as dreams, slips of tongue or pen, or as puns and jokes, or at the other end, as the symptoms of hysteria, obsessionality, paranoia, or schizophrenia.

If a horizontal axis is to have interactive but relative autonomy, then, within psychoanalytical theory it must address unconscious processes that are not simply derivative on the established vertical axis. My suggestion places a sibling trauma and the desires and prohibitions it unleashes as occurring between the stage of narcissism and the Oedipal stage. The defenses the individual produces will be distinctive—not the predominant projective identification of the pre-Oedipal nor the repression of the Oedipal, but productive nevertheless of unconscious processes. Making use of the work of Donald Winnicott, I would argue that these defenses are likely to be splitting and dissociation. If sibling relations do *not* independently produce unconscious processes, then no case can be made for their inclusion in the theoretical superstructure.

After he had split from psychoanalysis, Alfred Adler (1964) made sibling birth order a determinate of all psychic conditions. There is no doubt that birth order can be very important for one's psychic state, but it too is particular, accidental—what has fallen to one's lot. There can be general tendencies for the middle, eldest, or youngest child, but by definition, each of these cannot be generalizable to the human condition, only perhaps to many people in that particular position. Recovering a mass of individual stories will produce commonalities, but these, though forgotten, are not unconscious and therefore are not characterized by a different thought process—the "primary process" most easily perceived in the distortions of dream thinking. Ilse Grubrich-Simitis' elegant explanation of Freud's shift from the so-called "seduction theory" of trauma to the universal Oedipus complex, applies likewise to siblings' accounts: "Whereas the more conventional trauma model applied to the *pathogenesis* of a comparatively small number who had been sexually violated in childhood, the revolutionary drive model is concerned with the *psychogenesis* of everyone" (1994, p. 63).

As with most people, my own "discovery" of the importance of siblings came as a surprise. In retrospect, the context was this question of universality. For an unconscionable number of years I had puzzled about hysteria, in particular male hysteria. If everyone can be hysterical (as would seem to be the case), here again, the symptoms must be referring to a common, generic experience. Yet unlike other pathologies, hysteria was and is seen to have a gendered, hence specific, not generic population—women. It was male hysteria, therefore, that was the founding illness of psychoanalysis. But is this generic condition only the Oedipus complex or the pre-Oedipal relationship to the mother—the vertical axis? Hysteria is always a social relationship relying on the presence of others; these others are frequently peers rather than parents; mass hysteria is a peer phenomenon. Late in life Anna Freud had stated that there was something incomplete about our understanding of hysteria. One day pondering for the thousandth time this question and in particular the fact that the hysteric always claims an initiating trauma, the rock of Oedipus shifted slightly, and behind it were all these dancing and squabbling children. I went back and reread the case material: Sisters and brothers turned out to be everywhere. What were these siblings doing?

In Freud's theoretical superstructure, sisters and brothers are placed in the same category as mothers and fathers, and this amalgamation of parents and siblings is usually followed without concern. However, this is extremely problematic. It is true that sometimes sisters and mothers, brothers and fathers do stand in the same place—but by no means always. Being made to when they do not can lead to contortions as here in this account from Melanie Klein:

> [Gunther] vented his sadistic impulses towards the "bad" penis upon his brother, with whom he had also had sexual relations in early childhood, and at the same time he regarded him as the dangerous mother in whom were contained his father's penises. His brothers, it will be seen, were substitutes for both parents, to be more precise for the phantastic parent-imagos and it was towards them that he activated his relations to those imagos; for whereas he was devoted to his mother in real life and loved her much more than his father, he was possessed in phantasy, as we know, by imagos of the magical "good" penis (his father) and of the terrifying mother. (Klein 1932/1975, p. 268)

What we see here in Melanie Klein's account is a transposition from acute clinical observation into a theory that does not fit it or that ignores the most obvious element. Or again from Klein:

> I now made a venture and told Ruth that the balls in the tumbler, the coins in the purse and the contents of the bag all meant children in her Mummy's inside, and that she wanted to keep them safely shut up so as not to have any more brothers and sisters. The effect of my interpretation was astonishing. For the first time Ruth turned her attention to me and began to play in a different, less constrained, way. (Klein 1932/1975, p. 27)

If analyzing something is effective in therapy, it demands a place in the theory.

The Sibling Trauma

the case against: the "lonely only"

Infantile neuroses, particularly what was once known as infantile hysteria, are so regular as to be normative to the degree that they are often forgotten, even entirely overlooked. The "terrible twos" and the "dreadful threes" illustrate this contention. Looking again at these infantile illnesses, I realized that there was hardly an account of a child in psychoanalytical treatment in which the childhood illness had not originated with the birth of a sibling. The sibling prototypically arrives when the child is a toddler; it is the toddler who has the sibling trauma. However, there are of course large, indeed increasing numbers of children for whom the sibling does not arrive. If, as I claim, psychoanalytic theory is about the generic—what all humans have in common—then the "only," or for that matter, the "last" child must disqualify the notion of a universal sibling trauma. In fact, I want to argue that the toddler who does not have an actual baby following him or her proves rather than disproves the rule.³

The "only" child—the *fille* or *fils unique*, without a sister or brother—is the most obvious and always mentioned objection to a generic place for the sibling experience. In fact, from the psychoanalytic point of view, the "only" child is likely to have *more*, not fewer sisters and brothers than the child with siblings. They are more active in the thoughts and feelings, the unconscious and conscious fantasies, in the inner world of the "only" child than they are in those of its siblinged peers. The "only" child will ask What has happened? The "expected" one has not arrived. What have I done wrong? Six-year-old Erna was a patient of Melanie Klein's:

> Erna, who was an only child, was much occupied in her imagination with the arrival of brothers and sisters. *Her phantasies in this context deserve special attention, since, so far as my observations show, they have a general application.* Judging from them and from those of other children similarly situated, it would appear that an only child suffers to a far greater extent than other children from the anxiety it feels in regard to the brother or sister whom it is forever expecting, and from the feelings of guilt it has towards them on account of its unconscious impulses of aggression against them in their assumed existence inside its mother's body, because it has no opportunity of developing a positive relation to them in reality. This fact often makes it difficult for an only child to adapt itself to society. For a long time Erna used to have attacks of rage and anxiety at the beginning and end of her analytic session with me, and these were partly precipitated by her meeting the child who came to me for treatment immediately before or after her and who stood to her for the brother or sister whose arrival she was always awaiting. (1932/1975, p. 42; my italics)

The "only" child is concerned about its missing siblings because so far in human history everyone expects—yearns for and dreads—a sibling

---

3. Prophecy Coles asserts the opposite viewpoint: "What is different between an only child and a child with siblings is the *texture* of their inner world. By that I mean, there is much more 'noise' in the inner world of someone who has several siblings. In my experience, the inner world of an only child is quieter, their dreams are less populated by events with a lot of people and the transference experience is different" (2003, p. 6). If this is so, then I think that Coles is listening to the preconscious, "secondary process" story. Compare Klein's footnote to "Erna": "As Erna had no brothers or sisters in real life, her unconscious fear and jealousy of them which played such an important part in her mental life were only revealed through the analysis. This is once more an example of the importance of the transference-situation in child analysis" (1932/1975, p.42, n. 1).

to arrive after them. This is quite in spite of the fact of recent policies of one-child families in rapidly developing countries such as China, or of facts such as the demographic transition to nonreproductive populations of the economically wealthy Western countries or among the wealthy classes of the world (in India, Brazil, Ghana); the unconscious psyche takes a long time to change. And if we don't have blood siblings, some other kith or kin takes their place. Furthermore, the "only" child's experience is repeated to some degree in every "last" child who, though he or she may very well be preoccupied with its older kin, will wonder too and probably worry no less than the "only" child.

In her autobiography, Yvonne Kapp describes her experience when, at the age of ten, without explanation, her mother was mysteriously ill (in fact with appendicitis). Yvonne thinks her mother is having a baby and has not told her this:

> All this time some unborn brother or sister of mine had been lying under my mother's heart and she had never told me. I felt betrayed and, at the same time, a feeling I had never before experienced, an emotion so powerful and so violent swept over me that I thought it must destroy me. There was a strange tightening in my belly and a dreadful weight or terror and hatred of I knew not what.
>
> This anguish, now fastened upon me like some gnawing animal, was intensified by the blazing heat of those days from which, like the pain, there was no escape. *What I went through then, concentrated into little more than a few days, was a lifetime's savage and ungovernable jealousy of a younger sibling.* That torment remains in essence indescribable, but it poisoned every waking moment. I did not know, of course, that it was jealousy, but I did know that in some horrible way my feelings were shameful and this added an overwhelming sense of guilt to my burdened spirit. (2003, pp. 38–39; my italics)

Even when she has learned the true state of affairs, that her mother is not pregnant, she still cannot bring herself to say the word *baby*.

The nonarrival of a sibling for the "only" or "last" child is an "accidental" variation on the general theme. If something is general, then what does not happen is as significant as what does; it is merely its other side. Thus the arrival or expected but nonarrival of a sister or brother is what I call the sibling trauma.[4] It happens at the same time—is indeed another but very different aspect of what Winnicott (1971), with his enormous clinical experience above all with children, called the "trauma of separation."

---

4. For the sake of simplicity, in the next section I mainly write as though there is an actual sibling, as indeed there was in the case material I use.

Siblings

THE CASE FOR: THE VERTICAL "SEPARATION TRAUMA" AND THE HORIZONTAL "SIBLING TRAUMA"

Infancy is full of trauma—some generic, such as weaning or the various comings and goings of mothers. In traditional societies, weaning and hence renewed sexuality for the mother and a new conception would take place around the age of two, thus conflating the loss of the breast and the advent of the sibling. Until this very moment, the toddler has been the baby. The arrival of a new sibling means that the toddler instantly has its own identity obliterated. The new baby now lying in the place it occupied will be both narcissistically loved, as more of the toddler's self, and hated, as a replacement for itself. Speaking, eating, toilet training, walking are often abandoned; in order to get back its place, the toddler regresses to the babyhood that developmentally it was beginning to leave behind.

Joan was brought to the clinic of Donald Winnicott, who was then a pediatrician in training as a psychoanalyst:

> Joan aged two years five months, was an only child till thirteen months ago, when her brother was born.
>
> Joan had been in perfect health till this event. *She then became very jealous. She lost her appetite, and consequently got thin. When left for a week without being forced to eat, she ate practically nothing and lost weight. She has remained like this, is very irritable, and her mother cannot leave her without producing in her an anxiety attack.* She will not speak to anyone, and in the night she wakes screaming, even four times in a night—the actual dream material not being very clear . . .
>
> She pinches and even bites the baby, and will not allow him things to play with. She will not allow anyone to speak about the baby, but frowns and ultimately intervenes. When she was put in a welfare centre she worried a great deal, and, having no one to bite, bit herself, so that she had to be taken home again after three days.
>
> She is scared of animals.
>
> "If she sees the boy on the chamber she heaves until she is sick." If given chocolate she puts it in her mouth and keeps it there till she gets home, then she spits it all out again.
>
> She constantly prefers men to women.
>
> *The parents are exceptionally nice people, and the child is a perfectly healthy and loveable child.* (1931/1975, pp. 3–4; my italics)

Utterly normal or not, something traumatic is going on here. It is the new baby who turns what was an assisted development into a traumatic occurrence. In his later work, Winnicott (1971) refers to this occurrence as the "separation trauma," which indicates separation from the pre-Oedipal mother. There certainly is this separation, but it is a separation because another person who occupies what was the toddler's place preoccupies her: There is a new baby who, I argue, needs to feature in its own right. Without the new baby, the separation would be developmental; it is traumatic because of this actual (or expected) baby.

Despite all the preparation and the nine month's gestation, the new baby erupts onto the scene with a paradigmatic too-muchness that is traumatic. The toddler who was the baby one moment has to be the child the next. It is important to my argument that the sibling trauma, which occurs prototypically when a newcomer arrives or should arrive—that is, when the toddler is roughly two and a half, is indeed a "trauma" not just a "difficulty" of varying degrees.[5] A trauma has important psychic implications which a "difficulty" does not. Any trauma (an earthquake, a tsunami) is an excessive excitation coming from without, but in the case of a psychological trauma, the external impingement will be joined by a disturbing stimulus coming from within. The nature of the stimulus from within differentiates a trauma precipitated by natural causes from one that is brought about through other human beings. A psychological trauma will be urgently or compulsively repeated, often phobically avoided; it sets up an unconscious as well as a conscious response.

The traumatic experience of any sort is by definition violent. The quantitative strength of the excitation overloads the psyche. The protective barrier, a kind of psychological skin, is too weak to resist the blast. This weakness is particularly evident in the baby's early months, when the ego is only just coming into formation. The extreme helplessness of the human infant is a crucial factor. However, the experience of being filled with an overwhelming, unbounded, violent energy and an annihilated ego will be the same at whatever age the trauma occurs. Gradually with help, the ego is able to bind most of the raging energy—never entirely and sometimes not very well at all. There remains some identification with the violence of the traumatic experience, so that throughout life, rages that echo or repeat the experience will be added to already existent aggression and may erupt in personal violence or be channeled into socially legitimated killing. There can also be reaction formations against this violence.

The symptoms and expressions of trauma include nightmares, flashbacks, amnesia, disoriented personality, and prolonged irritability. There are rapid and unstable but near-total identifications with other people who substitute for the annihilated ego. The ability to form sym-

---

5. Volkan and Ast (1997), in their excellent *Siblings in the Unconscious*, refer to the experience as sometimes "difficult," sometimes "traumatic."

bols may collapse and speech become uncertain. Clinically, trauma is undoubtedly recognizable. How far does the sibling trauma accord with these accounts?

The external event is the arrival of the sister or brother; the internal stimuli are the illegitimate desires that are provoked by this external shock. These desires can be categorized as the wish for sibling incest and for sibling killing. My argument is that these cannot be assimilated only to the vertical axis of intergenerational incest and murder (the Oedipus complex). They are different and have different effects.

As well as the typical behavioral regression, with the toddler acting the babyhood that, cataclysmically, it has had to leave behind, the symptoms that occur at this juncture confirm that this is a trauma. Three that seem characteristic of the toddler are inarticulacy, identification, and what would seem to be an effect of its obverse—the irritability that arises if someone is excessively close. Prototypically, the sibling arrives when the toddler is mastering speech; it is a time when the frustrations of inarticulacy and inexpressibility occasion rage and despair. Loss of symbol formation characterizes trauma in general. Of the small child and its traumas, Freud (1939, p. 74) writes, "Impressions from the time at which a child is beginning to talk stand out as being of particular interest; the periods between the ages of two and four seem to be the most important. . . . (These traumas) relate to impressions of a sexual and aggressive nature, and no doubt also to early injuries to the ego (narcissistic mortifications)." The particular type of identification that is a response to trauma in general, I would argue, is inherent in the sibling trauma. This identification with the other person is made when the ego feels annihilated: The toddler is no longer who it was yesterday, no longer the family's or the mother's baby. Disorientated, where can the toddler locate itself?

> The mother said that there had been a great change toward ill health in the Piggle recently. She was not naughty and she was nice to the baby. It was difficult to put into words what the matter was. But *she was not herself.* In fact she refused to be herself and said so: "I'm the mummy. I'm the baby." She was not to be addressed as herself. She had developed a high-voiced chatter which was not hers. (Winnicott 1978, p. 13; Winnicott's italics)

The identification the toddler makes with the baby as opposed to the identification it makes with its mother develops into what the child analyst Charlotte Buhler (1935) called "transitivism," which characterizes children's relationships with each other: At this age a child will hit the right cheek of its playmate and instantly feel the blow on its own left cheek. There is thus a body mirroring that is echoed experientially: When the aggressor child says of the victim "He hit me," Jacques Lacan (1981), adopting Buhler's notion, claims therefore that he is telling a truth. In any case, this is an interchild relationship and thus on a horizontal axis. Transitivism indicates two are one; irritability protests against this excess proximity. Irritability, like an irritation on the skin, can be a response to the too-close presence of another person—later maybe in mind; here in actuality.

The new baby is who the old baby still is. If the new baby comes earlier, as with so-called "Irish twins" (within eleven months of each other) or later as with three-and-a half-year-old "Little Hans," in Freud's famous case history of infantile phobia (1909), or in the fantasy-expectations of ten-year-old Yvonne (Kapp 2003), then there will be some age-appropriate behavior as well as regression, such as Yvonne's devastating sense of shame at her feelings of the jealousy that didn't know its name. However, the traumatic nucleus of the experience will be referred to the typical time of two to two and a half years, through deferred or referred action. Unconscious processes do not know chronological time. The new baby will be the "same" but also the "other." Jealousy is the *modus vivendi* for the arrival of the "other," the one who is different but who should have been the "same."

The traumatic shock coming from outside is the advent of the new baby; the inner stimulus that joins it is the wish for narcissistic sexual union with one who is the same, and the simultaneous wish to murder one who is different. These desires have traumatic effects because the toddler will have been prohibited from carrying them out. The prohibition I call the "Law of the Mother" (Mitchell 2003). The toddler has to be prevented from trying to carry out its incestuous and murderous wishes, which need to be curtailed and transformed in some way or displaced into new and different forms. Later they will, for instance, be normatively transformed into conjugal love and fighting the enemy—one the province of women, the other of men.

THE SIBLING TRAUMA: GENDERING

I speak as a psychoanalyst, but the questions I bring to psychoanalysis always include thinking about gender in whatever field is being considered. So for instance we can ask: Does analyzing siblings tell us something important about the gendering of war or about psychological illness, social behavior, or creativity? In her empirical study in the U.K. of what she calls "sistering," the sociologist Melanie Mauthner (2002) claims to have found that a girl's femininity is constructed as much or more from her sister-sister relations as from her mother-daughter identification. If that is so here as elsewhere, where would I map it in the theory of psychoanalysis or any of the related disciplines?

The Oedipus complex, with its vertical before and after (the pre-Oedipal mother and the father of the castration complex), is the shibboleth around which the theory revolves. Does the dominance of verticality hide the horizontal? Does this skew our understanding of gendering? An interesting instance comes from a debate between the psychoanalyst Ernest Jones (1925) and the anthropologist Bronislav Malinowski (1927; 1929) in the 1920s over Malinowski's ethnography in the Trobriand Islands.

The main incest taboo in the Trobriand matrilineage was an extreme prohibition of sister-brother relations. However, Jones and Malinowski conducted a lively, indeed somewhat acrimonious debate over whether or not there was either no or several Oedipus complexes. The issue hinged on the nonacknowledgment/nonknowledge of the biological father and the paternal role of the "mother's brother." It thus omitted the main sister-brother incest taboo. Furthermore, the prevalent term the "mother's brother" stresses the vertical "mother" but ignores the horizontal "sister." The sibling relationship gives the sister some entitlement whether or not she is a mother. I would argue that wherever we are situated, this sister demands our attention.

In brief, my suggestion for the gendering of sibling relations is twofold. First, for the purposes of analysis, we need to distinguish lateral "gender" from vertical "sexual difference" (Mitchell 2007). Freud's still-radical theory of infantile sexuality (1905b) proposed that we separate sexuality and reproduction. Sexuality does not necessarily aim toward reproduction; the two are distinct. I have argued that Freud's concept of "sexual difference" should be kept to describe the later sexed reproductive position and our new concept of "gender" applied, as "gender diversity," to sexuality where sexed reproduction is not the psychological aim. The division is artificial; of course we are all both "gendered" laterally and "sexually differentiated" vertically. However, I think that a confusion of the two as "categories of analysis" (J. Scott 1986) has been a besetting problem since the introduction of the gender category at the inception of second-wave feminism.

For humanity, what is important is not a biological instinct that makes straight for its object. The human sexual drive is just a drive without an innate direction. Sexual difference (not my concern here) is enjoined as a nonnegotiable division following on the resolution of the castration complex; its subsequent identifications are modeled on the vertical axis—becoming parents. Sexual difference is about the child's future reproductive position; prefigured with the asymmetry of penis envy for girls and castration anxiety for boys, its realization is in puberty with the arrival of fertility. Except in matrilineages, it has nothing to do with siblings or with the horizontal axis.

The term *gender* should be applied to the lateral sibling position. Under gender, sisters and brothers are in identical positions, as both have the same murderous and incestuous wishes toward each other. Murder and incest are prohibited and potentially punished for both genders in identical ways—not differentiating the two, as does the castration complex.

Gender does not constitute the same problematic as sexual difference does. Where the trauma of the possibility of castration follows the "Law of the Father," forbidding maternal incest and patricide, the sibling trauma precedes the mother's prohibition on sibling incest and murder. We could say that in the first case, the law has priority, and in the second, the trauma. Where the father's law insists on sexual difference, the mother's focuses on the socialization of both children, in which gendering is an intrinsic part. One gender is not the condition of the other; although the girl/boy distinction is a universal, here there is more flexibility.

At birth, as far as we know, all cultures make their first distinction a categorical one that has been lying in wait for the newborn: It is a girl / it is a boy. This is what we can now call a "gender distinction." My suggestion is that this splitting into girl/boy at birth only acquires subjective meaning for the infant at the time of the sibling trauma when the next baby—the interloper the toddler observes and reacts to—is instantly assigned a gender; this new baby is not just a baby; it is a sister or a brother, a girl or a boy. I suggest the toddler gains access to its own gendered self through this "other." The baby whom the toddler thinks it is, or whom it wants to be, is gendered—thus the toddler itself gets an objective perspective on itself: It too must be girl or boy, unlike in its babyhood. Its own subjectivity as a child will always be acquired with this gendered meaning.

Freud claimed that there are two major questions that set the infant's mind to work under pressure from its need to get rid of the intruder. Both are the first and foremost questions in the quest for knowledge. They are: Where do babies come from? And: What is the difference between the sexes? Both questions refer to the new sibling. Perhaps rather anxiously, the toddler continues to hope that everyone can do and have everything: As babies come from people's tummies, the boy can give birth; the girl has a penis which is hidden or will grow. Despite the fact that privileges mostly accrue to one and not the other sex, in itself gender sexuality does not discriminate; the position of girl and boy is on a level.

Up the vertical ladder, to both the boy's and the girl's dismay, the "Law of the Mother" establishes that only mothers can give birth, and children of either gender cannot. One wants what the other has or will have, so this leaves the boy with womb envy and the girl wishing she could urinate so spectacularly or have the many social advantages enjoyed by boys; neither sex yet experiences the threat of castration. Neither is traumatized into gender acquisition. There is no absolute distinction, and it is not by chance that feminism got the concept of gender from the field of transgendering; unlike with reproduction, here lines can be crossed. Although for both genders there is the fantasy of parthenogenesis, which plays, I believe, a large part in creativity, this is the realm of sexuality, not reproduction—relatively fluid gender, not rigid sexual difference.

However, despite this continuing sameness and the bisexuality of gender, within the realm of gender there is also a distinction between the sexes. In order not to implode endogamously, societies enter into many and various modes of exchange. Within kinship systems, it is predominantly rights in girls not in boys that are exchanged between social groups; through this, sisters will have an additional position as wives. Rights in girls are exchanged so that they become wives as well as, but also independently from, their becoming mothers: You cannot have your brother sexually; you must have an outside husband (who will be, or become, a symbolic brother) instead. Differently, boys as a category are exchanged not so much in kinship rights as through labor contracts, which will include fighting. This gender differentiation happens to the people concerned in a lateral manner, on the horizontal, not on the vertical axis. It is fathers, however, who authorize exchange on a vertical dimension—giving away a daughter in marriage or a son to an apprenticeship with another man, but the people whose rights are thus exchanged are sisters and brothers. Of course women work and men become husbands. But it is not sexually differentiated mothers but gendered girls, not sexually differentiated fathers but gendered boys, who are moved in the contracts and circuits of kinship and labor. The separation of sexuality and reproduction that contributes to making Freud's *Three Essays on the Theory of Sexuality* (1905b) still so revolutionary a treatise can be seen even more clearly when we consider the illegitimate underside of kinship exchange: It is sisters, not mothers, who are sex-trafficked as slaves or sex slaves.

The response to this sibling trauma is then an important aspect of the social world that is constructed from the sibling relationship, and with it the sameness and the difference between brothers and sisters within the framework of gender. We have here a ground plan for an aspect of the psyche and a place where we can add intersibling relations into the larger theory. What does adding horizontality bring to the theory? I shall focus on the effects on the theory of this new place for the transition from the narcissistic, omnipotent baby-infant—"His majesty the baby" (Freud 1914, p. 91)—to the gendered, social child, girl or boy.

This sibling trauma is (to my mind) absolutely necessary. It is a trauma that must be resolved by socialization, for it marks a break between presocial infancy and social childhood and necessitates a rite of passage between the two (Mitchell 2006). Developmentally, the transition takes place, but to become someone new means losing the former position: This is invariably traumatic.

THE SIBLING TRAUMA: THE SOCIAL WORLD

Siblings are omnipresent in the observational material of psychoanalysis, particularly in child analysis. Where they are missing is in the theory, in the metapsychological superstructure. However, their putative position in the social world is accorded a place in the theory—and it is one that is distinct from the vertical axis of descent. Both at the micro level of "the nursery" and the macro level of human prehistory, siblings feature in their own right. Brothers can be found in the mythological explanation first offered by Freud in *Totem and Taboo* (1913) and favorably repeated by him at the end of his life in *Moses and Monotheism* (1939) (although no one else much liked *Totem and Taboo*, it is said to have remained Freud's favorite book). Having ganged up to kill the tyrannical *primal* father who had monopolized all the women, the brothers realized they must make a contract among themselves, not to kill each other and to share out the women among themselves. This fraternal alliance is considered to be the first *social* relationship.[6]

The emphasis of the social is on the contract among brothers; nothing is said of the relationship between the "contracted" sisters. Even if this is in some way a correct contention (as analyzing the castration complex was correct for Hans), it clearly must be a partial picture. The absence of women from the position of making the contract has

---

6. Above, I have suggested that fathers exchange their children; Freud makes brothers do their own exchanging. Below I suggest that both happen. The question is one for anthropology—but it is not likely to be answered, as in that discipline too, brothers are potential fathers. The work of Annette Weiner (1992) initiated for anthropology the kind of analytical distinction I am trying to draw for psychoanalysis.

to be as significant as the presence of brothers in making it (Mitchell 1974/2000).

Because for Freud the model for the social is the family, the horizontal relationship between the contracting brothers is subordinate to the vertical relationship to the father. Omitting the horizontal axis also limits our understanding of the vertical. The vertical affects the horizontal, but so too, the horizontal inflects the vertical. So, for instance, crucial to my thesis is a transposition of the vertical "Pre-Oedipal Mother" into a different vertical position occasioned by her role in socializing siblings; in a teasing reference to Jacques Lacan's (1981) "Law of the Father," I called this the "Law of the Mother," a law that emanates from a position rather than a person, one that above all acts on and between siblings. But also, as with brothers in Freud's myth *Totem and Taboo*, siblings can act and adjudicate between themselves without vertical interference, as is demonstrated by Anna Freud and Sophie Dann's (1951) pathbreaking account of a quasi-sibling group of concentration-camp children.

So instead of or as well as, Freud's gang of brothers and the social contract they make as a response to their murder of the father (*Totem and Taboo*), we can see the relationship of brotherhood and sisterhood as a response to the loss of the mother to the new baby. This loss is emblematized by the prohibitions against sibling murder and incest, the law that she institutes. This is a vertical law. But as well as vertical prohibitions, there is evidence that, as in the myth of *Totem and Taboo*, the brothers organize themselves. Here, however, we must add sisters and both identify them with and differentiate them from their brothers. Siblings, or brothers, do not just play a part in a social world; as with parents, they too are interactive in forging that social world.

When the sibling trauma occurs, the toddler's expectation is that the new baby will be an extension of him- or herself, the former baby. Traumatized by the fact that the toddler is not now the only baby (or even a "baby" at all), he or she makes an identification with the mother and with the new baby—both temporarily (and latently for all time); the ego of the toddler is nowhere. After trying for the impossibility of being in two places at the same time, hopefully helped to find a new position, the toddler's ego splits: he or she will be both baby and big girl / big boy—one moment regressed, the next the adult the child plans to be. The individual splitting of the ego in the response to the sibling trauma is necessary and normative and looks forward to the diverse and manifold splittings that characterize the social world: friend/enemy, young/old, white/black, child/baby, boy/girl . . . superior/inferior.

The new baby introduces the toddler to a threefold relationship, a triangulation of mother, baby, and toddler, as later, with the Oedipus complex, it will be mother, father, and child. Once it starts to disidentify with the mother, the mother can become the toddler's "object"; as such she is ripe for the child's Oedipal love. Once the toddler starts to disidentify with the baby, the baby will become the "other." The sibling relation, as it is transformed into a social one, does so on the cusp of this narcissistic identification of the baby as the same and then the discovery of the baby as "other-object."

Finding an object in psychoanalytic understanding is always a refinding of an object, someone who was there before in the preobject state of babyhood. In the case of the sibling, at first the object can only be the toddler's self as discovered in the transitivistic mirror image. In Freud's (1920, pp. 14–17) famous observation of his eighteen-month-old grandson, the baby mastered his mother's absence by throwing and retrieving a cotton-reel and then tried this on himself, appearing and then vanishing from a mirror. Looking at the baby sibling, the toddler sees the baby he or she was. Identification with the baby and then refinding him- or herself as the object in the baby is a double narcissistic whammy. At the same time, the toddler traumatically finds that this "other" is not the self. Caught in this impossible situation, the response to the baby as "other-object" is overwhelming jealousy. Unlikely as it sounds, I think it is this jealousy that facilitates the next stage, following the mother's law. Jealousy enables the move toward the psychic exchange of sociality—new friend for old baby?

Since Melanie Klein (1957), envy has had a good inning but somewhat at the expense of jealousy, with which it is often confused in our feelings but should not therefore be confused in our argument. Envy is binary; jealousy, triangular: One is envious of what someone has, jealous of the position that they are in or of where they stand. Acknowledging this other as "other" turns on jealousy: The baby stands where I want to be with the mother. I may be envious that the mother has a baby; I want one too. But it is the baby sibling of whom I am jealous. The hatred that just wants the baby out of the world—not to exist—can also be used in the key social institution of war. However, when it is recognized that the baby as "other" has come to stay, hatred can be replaced by jealousy; jealousy is a confirmation that this baby is another, an object to be rivaled. Jealousy is the repository for part of the murderous wish to get rid of the sibling; it is important to recognize both its normality and its energy. If recognized, jealousy can open the way to positive rivalry, competition, and creative struggle (Mitchell 2012); left unrecognized and unused, it will lurk as the green-eyed monster.

The narcissistic identificatory love for the baby who is the self can, via the transitivism of childhood, become the "we are as one" of adult couples. The splitting that is the response to the sibling trauma is a normative process and constitutive of social life. However, at its pathological end it characterizes psychosis rather than neurosis. The toddler has been called "mad" rather than "psychotic." Wilfred Bion claimed the baby really was mad; Donald Winnicott, that the baby was allowed madness. The trauma makes the toddler mad, but increasingly this is not allowed. The toddler is in transition: He or she has not yet fully taken on board what Lacan (1997) calls the "Symbolic," the full order of language that is human culture. It uses a "transitional" language, which is characterized by the search for understanding without as yet having grasped metaphor; it is not quite the same as what has been described as making "symbolic equations" (Segal 1957).

When Freud's grandson represented the comings and goings of his mother and then himself, he uttered his first pair of phonemes, which became contrasting words: ooo/aahh; *fort/da*, "gone"/"there." By the time the sibling arrives, these pairs have multiplied like the doubling of the toddler's self, which it saw in the baby that it had been. At the pathological end of the process we speak of the concrete language of the psychotic: Here in the verbal joy of the small child, I prefer to think of it as "literal" language. Bion (1974) describes a mother reentering a room to find her little daughter with her profiled face tenderly but firmly on the supine baby's tummy. The mother's inquiry elicits that, being a good girl, the daughter was doing as she had been asked and "keeping an eye" on the baby. To the adult this literal language is a source of new pleasure in the child, and children themselves seem to find their verbal similitudes comical. At the other end of the scale, we have schizophrenic puns; the deluded paranoiac jokes through his pain. But for the small child, the comical words or identificatory acts are early manifestations of sociability; small children produce pantomimes and play word games with each other; verbal teasers start and expand into latency. For the toddler, if there are other playmates, more children, the baby can be left to be a baby till another day.

The trauma of the sibling trauma is the invasion of something unknowable, psychically unprocessable. Only a rite of passage to a new state of being is possible. It is argued that, after his disillusion with the hysteric's story of abuse, Freud dismissed trauma from the metapsychology. In fact, never having entirely abandoned it, he brought it back into prominence when Nazism threatened. Ilse Grubrich-Simitis (1994) calls *Moses and Monotheism* "the book of the trauma." As the light went out, Freud argued (1937) that we must always remember a present pathology-producing conflict that replays in the infantile past, which had itself prefigured the later event. He argues too for a grain of "historical truth" in this earlier conflict. This is where I would place the sibling trauma, glimpsing in Freud's late insistence on historical truth, a part for the trauma's siblings to play in the theoretical superstructure. Arguing that we should make a "construction" in our therapies, a construction that needs to be part of a theory, Freud gave a pertinent illustration:

> If in accounts of analytic technique, so little is said about "constructions," that is because "interpretations" and their effects are spoken of instead. But I think that "construction" is by far the more appropriate description. "Interpretation" applies to something that one does to some single element of the material, such as an association or a parapraxis. But it is a "construction" when one lays before the subject of the analysis a piece of his early history that he has forgotten, in some such way as this: "Up to your nth year you regarded yourself as the sole and unlimited possessor of your mother; then came another baby and brought you grave disillusionment." (Freud 1937, p. 261)

Constructing, deconstructing, and constructing again a patient's plausible early history has been crucial to psychoanalysis. This construction has weighted vertical parent-child relations. Yet sibling relations are absent neither from psychoanalytic writings nor from the consulting room. Indeed, Freud's articulation of an emblematic analytic construction includes both mother and sibling: *"Then came another baby and brought you grave disillusionment."* This talk offers clinical practice a lateral lens through which to understand our patients both as children and as siblings. I suggest that the concept of a sibling trauma opens a place where we may place lateral relations along a horizontal axis within an expanded metapsychology. In its turn a theoretical habitus could contain the clinical observations and give them staying power.

REFERENCES

ADLER, A. (1964). *Problems of Neurosis*. New York: Harper & Row.
BION, W. (1974). *Bion's Brazilian Lectures 1: Sao Paolo 1973*. Brazil: Imago Editora.
BUHLER, C. (1935). *From Birth to Maturity*. London: Kegan, Paul, Trench, Trubner.
COLES, P. (2003). *The Importance of Sibling Relationships in Psychoanalysis*. London: Karnac.
FREUD, A., AND S. DANN (1951). An experiment in group upbringing. *Psychoanalytic Study of the Child* 6:127–68.
FREUD, S. (1893). Charcot. In J. Strachey, ed. and trans. *The Standard Edition of the Complete Psychological Works of Sigmund Freud*, vol. 3, pp. 7–23. London: Hogarth Press.

——— (1905a). Fragment of an analysis of a case of hysteria. In *Standard Edition*, vol. 7, pp. 1–122. London: Hogarth Press.

——— (1905b). Three essays on the theory of sexuality. In *Standard Edition*, vol. 7, pp. 123–246. London: Hogarth Press.

——— (1909). Analysis of a phobia in a five-year-old boy. In *Standard Edition*, vol. 3, pp. 7–23. London: Hogarth Press.

——— (1913). Totem and taboo. In *Standard Edition*, vol. 13, pp. vii–162. London: Hogarth Press.

——— (1914). On narcissism. In *Standard Edition*, vol. 14, pp. 67–102. London: Hogarth Press.

——— (1920). Beyond the pleasure principle. In *Standard Edition*, vol. 18, pp. 7–64. London: Hogarth Press.

——— (1925). An autobiographical study. In *Standard Edition*, vol. 20, pp. 255–70. London: Hogarth Press.

——— (1937). Constructions in analysis. In *Standard Edition*, vol. 23, pp. 255–70. London: Hogarth Press.

——— (1939). Moses and monotheism: Three essays. In *Standard Edition*, vol. 23, pp. 1–312. London: Hogarth Press.

GRUBRICH-SIMITIS, I. (1994). *Early Freud and Late Freud: Reading Anew* Studies on Hysteria *and* Moses and Monotheism. Trans. P. Slotkin, 1997. London: Routledge.

JONES, E. (1925). Mother-right and the sexual ignorance of savages. *International Journal of Psycho-Analysis* 6:109–30.

KAEMPFERRT, W. (1933). Star birth sudden, Lemaitre asserts. *New York Times*, 13 September, p. 13.

KAPP, Y. (2003). *Time Will Tell: Memoirs*. London: Verso.

KLEIN, M. (1932/1975). *The Psycho-Analysis of Children*. London: Hogarth Press and Institute of Psycho-Analysis.

——— (1957). Envy and gratitude. In *Envy and Gratitude and Other Works 1946–1963*, pp. 176–235. London: Hogarth Press and Institute of Psycho-Analysis.

LACAN, J. (1981). *The Seminar of Jacques Lacan, Book III: The Psychoses 1955–1956*. Trans. J. Miller and R. Grigg, 1997, pp. 29–43. New York: W. W. Norton.

——— (1997). *Écrits: A Selection*. Trans. B. Fink. New York: W. W. Norton.

MALINOWSKI, B. (1927). *Sex and Repression in Savage Society*. New York: Harcourt Brace.

——— (1929). *Sexual Life of Savages in North-Western Melanesia: An Ethnographic Account of Courtship, Marriage and Family Life Among the Natives of the Trobriand Islands, British New Guinea*. New York: Harcourt Brace.

MAUTHNER, M. (2002). *Sistering: Power and Change in Female Relationships*. Hampshire, UK, and New York: Palgrave.

MITCHELL, J. (1974/2000). *Psychoanalysis and Feminism*. London: Penguin.

——— (2003). *Siblings: Sex and Violence*. Cambridge: Polity Press.

——— (2006). From infant to child: The sibling trauma, the *rite de passage*, and the construction of the "other" in the social group. *Fort Da* 12, 35–49.

——— (2007). Procreative mothers (sexual difference) and child-free sisters (gender). In J. Browne, ed. *The Future of Gender*, pp. 163–88. Cambridge: Cambridge University Press.

——— (2012). The sublime jealousy of Louise Bourgeois. In Philip Larratt-Smith, ed. *The Return of the Repressed*. London: Violette Editions.

SCOTT, J. (1986). Gender: A useful category of historical analysis. *The American Historical Review* 91 (5): 1053–75.

SEGAL, H. (1957). Notes on symbol formation. *International Journal of Psycho-Analysis* 38: 391–405.

VOLKAN, V. D., AND G. AST (1997). *Siblings in the Unconscious and Psychopathology*. Madison, CT: International Universities Press.

WEINER, A. B. (1992). *Inalienable Possessions: The Paradox of Keeping-While Giving*. Berkeley and Los Angeles, CA: University of California Press.

WINNICOTT, D. W. (1931/1975). A note on normality and anxiety. In Winnicott, D. W. *Through Paediatrics to Psycho-Analysis*. London: Hogarth Press and Institute of Psycho-Analysis.

——— (1971). *Playing and Reality*. London: Brunner-Routledge.

——— (1978). *The Piggle: An Account of the Psycho-Analytic Treatment of a Little Girl*. London: Hogarth Press and Institute of Psycho-Analysis.

Sibling Interaction

ROSEMARY H. BALSAM, M.R.C.P. (EDINBURGH), F.R.C.PSYCH. (LONDON)

Sibling interactions traditionally were conceived psychoanalytically in "vertical" and parentified oedipal terms and overlooked in their own right, for complicated reasons (Colonna and Newman 1983). Important work has been done to right this, from the 1980s and onward, with conferences and writings. Juliet Mitchell's 2000 and, in particular, her 2003 books, for example, have brought "lateral" sibling relations forcefully to the forefront of insights, especially about sex and violence, with the added interdisciplinary impact of illuminating upheaval in global community interactions as well as having implications for clinicians.

A clinical example from the analysis of an adult woman with a ten-years-younger sister will show here how we need both concepts to help us understand complex individual psychic life. The newer "lateral" sibling emphasis, including Mitchell's "Law of the Mother" and "seriality," can be used to inform the older "vertical" take, to enrich the full dimensions of intersubjective oedipal and preoedipal reciprocities that have been foundational in shaping that particular analysand's inner landscape. Some technical recommendations for heightening sensitivity to the import of these dynamics will be offered along the way here, by invoking Hans Loewald's useful metaphor of the analytic situation as theater.

INTRODUCTION

FROM 1900 ONWARD, FREUD INTRODUCED THE CUTTING-EDGE IDEA that the oedipal situation ruled family psychosexual relations, governed

---

Rosemary H. Balsam is a Fellow of the Royal College of Psychiatrists (London); Associate Clinical Professor of Psychiatry, Yale Medical School; Staff Psychiatrist, Student Mental Health and Counseling, Yale University; and Training and Supervising Psychoanalyst, Western New England Institute for Psychoanalysis.

The Psychoanalytic Study of the Child 67, ed. Claudia Lament, Robert A. King, Samuel Abrams, A. Scott Dowling, and Paul M. Brinich (Yale University Press, copyright © 2013 by Claudia Lament, Robert A. King, Samuel Abrams, A. Scott Dowling, and Paul M. Brinich).

incest taboos, and—if unstable and unreliable—was in place in mental life to protect civilization and the propagation of the species. Parental relations to each child were patterned in that scheme as "vertical." Sibling "lateral" relations were seen more or less as a displacement of these vertical arrangements. In the new insights to the lateral sibling relations that Juliet Mitchell brings forward, destruction of the species becomes equally marked by these biopsychosocial forces. She says, "Why have we not considered that lateral relations in love and sexuality or in hate and war have needed a theoretical paradigm with which we might analyse, consider, and seek to influence them?" (2003, p. 1).

The historical pendulum of theory in psychoanalysis itself seems to swing between either stressing Eros as an instinct (Freud 1910) or some kind of preservation, or its classic opposer, the death instinct (Freud 1920) or some kind of destruction. Freud's portrait of the mind majestically, of course, calls for both forces of nature in conflict, in terms of the dual instinct theory. But Freud began chronologically with sex and procreation, and added by 1920, through life passages of war, frustration, and violence, the darkly seductive sway of the death instinct. As Elizabeth Young-Bruehl (2011) has noted about his followers:

> All Freudians were impressed with the emphasis that Freud put after 1920 on aggression, because everyone who survived the First World War realized that aggression and aggression against the self (masochism) had been underemphasized and undertheorized in psychoanalytic theory. But there agreement ended. And most subsequent psychoanalysts have either followed Klein and Lacan in elaborating the death instinct theory in various ways, or followed Hartman and Fenichel and others among the Ego Psychologists in repudiating the biological theory while accepting the idea that sex and aggression are fundamental drives. (Anna Freud stood diplomatically aside: speaking of sex and aggression as fundamental drives, but neither embracing nor rejecting the biological death instinct theory, which she felt called for confirming or disconfirming by empirical research.) (2011, p. 256)

The theoretical divide between vertical and lateral sibling dynamics could be seen as an echo of these theoretical debates and as a division of loyalties over the death instinct.

It is interesting that the recent emphasis on the lateral dimension has come from those not particularly involved with Freud's ego psychological structural theory, either theoretically or clinically. Juliet Mitchell, an academic and professor of psychoanalysis from the United Kingdom, whose feminist history includes very important Lacanian and Marxist rereadings of Freud, is a case in point. One of the first works that drew psychodynamic attention to siblings in the United States was coauthored by a research psychiatrist, Stephen Bank, and an academic professor of psychology, Michael Kahn (Bank and Kahn 1983). Other North American academic psychologists have seen recent value in the "laterality" dimension more than the vertical, such as Jeanine Vivona (2007; 2010), on its role in sibling differentiation, or Sue Kuba, whose 2011 book on sisters' roles in female development, surveys many analytic theories' deficits and then offers the solution of returning to the clinical drawing board of close listening to women's personal stories. Other recent work includes Joyce Edward's 2011 clinical and theoretically integrative account of sibling relations that comes out of her orientation to psychoanalytic psychotherapy from a social-work background. Prophecy Coles (2003), an English psychoanalytic psychotherapist, also writes on siblings but advances a rather dismissive notion that *all* psychoanalytic theory is predominantly autobiographical.

North American mainstream psychoanalysts who had a more vertical ego psychological orientation, in the 1980s nevertheless began to blend the lateral and vertical dimension of sibling dynamics (for example, Leichtman 1985). Volume 38 (1983) of this journal contained six articles about siblings. Pointing out that "To some extent, as in most clinical research, the attention has been given to what is 'noisy,' that is, what is associated with deprivation, conflict, or distortion," Solnit and his colleagues wished to use "data and theoretical propositions formulated during the Yale Longitudinal Study and the Psychoanalytic Study of a Family . . . [and] propose in these reports to examine the sibling experience with an emphasis on those aspects that promote growth and development" (Solnit 1983, p. 281). These child analysts were mainly influenced by Anna Freud (Solnit 1983; Neubauer 1982; Colonna and Newman 1983; Kris and Ritvo 1983; Provence and Solnit 1983). Later, Philadelphia child analytic colleagues of Mahler, Akhtar and Kramer in 1999, gathered contributors to their edited book from their Thirtieth Margaret Mahler Symposium, "Brothers and Sisters." Attention had been given to twins at least since the 1950s onward (for example, Burlingham 1952; Ainslie 1999; Levin 2010), the siblings of twins, and the siblings of sick or handicapped children (for example, Kennedy 1985; Lament and Wineman 1984; Safer 2003). Recent articles by other child analysts include Kieffer (2008), who reconciles aspects of Mitchell with Benjamin (1988). She sees a parallel between the unique condition of sibship that Mitchell points to in recognizing with agony that there are more individuals like oneself in the world and Benjamin's ideas about the establishment of "mutual recognition."

Social upheavals and academic postmodern outlooks have disrupted a mid-twentieth-century idealization of a "normal" heterosexual nuclear family that had continued aspects of Freud's day. Professional practice has altered also. Many articles have been written on how psychoanalytic practice has changed (for economic and psychiatric reasons), toward a "wider scope" of patients, people whose backgrounds and inner lives can prove markedly chaotic and fraught with aggression, boundarylessness, and sexual behavioral impulsivity. The psychoanalytic theories that have thus become popularized at the turn of the twenty-first century by lecturers, writings, conferences and journals in the United States have shifted away from the so-called "golden era" of a more-orderly, strictly "internal" ego psychology structuring of Hartmann, Kris, and Lowenstein (theoreticians who abhorred the death instinct), to a plurality of theory of mind that importantly includes much rage and explications of archaic and verbally unrepresentable mental states (for example, Bion, many South American and Italian theoreticians), at the forefront of which is Melanie Klein and her contemporary followers. Their stress on the persistence of early archaic aggression and forms of cannibalistic voracity have been appreciated as apt for the times and more-disturbed patients, as well as Klein's "de-scientific" (in contrast with Freud) views of an inner world organization that are less jarring to antibiological postmodernists, as expressing only two very simple (but intense) mentalized "positions," where if one is not in the paranoid lower register, the very best one can do is to exhibit a "depressive position" (linguistically, little to do with "depression"). The latter raw terminology today in our field, though, garners much more success than any talk of "attaining the genital stage," which suggested more practitioner interest in sex and procreation—in the older structural theory terminology, a name for the very best one could hope for psychologically, developmentally, and behaviorally.[1] To turn around an aphorism, human beings making war and *not* love seems closer to the tenor of contemporary analytic theory in 2013. The social times are favorable now to talk as much of vituperative "lateral relations" as "vertical relations," because they deemphasize the powerful and domineering internalized parents of Freud as the crucial dynamic in our postmodern world of suspicion toward authority. The replacement emphasis then is an inter- and intrapsychic interactional vigor that encodes fantasies like the wild grandiosity, violent behavioral hurtfulness, and brutal, loving competition in a vision of unbridled, overly powerful sibling strivings lacking steadying parental input. As Ju-

---

1. These two concepts, the depressive position and the genital stage, however, when studied closely, are not all that far from each other, partly because of Freud's and Klein's agreements about some kind of oedipal situation in internal life, and maturing capabilities of accessing preferably higher and less desirably lower levels of psychic integration (but for a good, detailed consideration, see Ellman 2010).

Sibling Interaction 39

liet Mitchell said of the origins of her current interest in siblings, which she feels she had previously overlooked, in an Internet YouTube video recording, ". . . I had been studying hysteria . . . and there was something that wasn't explained for me . . . and one day . . . suddenly . . . the central thing [in psychoanalysis] is the Oedipus complex, like a big rock in the middle of the theory, and suddenly this rock sort of shifted slightly, and there were these dancing, squabbling children behind it! And . . . 'Wait a minute, what are they doing?' And I went back and read not only my own notes . . ." and reread many other texts too, where she found that "siblings were just everywhere. . . . There is hardly a case history where the birth of a sibling, and the birth of a sibling after that isn't a major event which triggers some kind of dramatic reaction. . . ."[2]

Agger, who also appreciated siblings as overlooked, agreed earlier, "Commitment to traditional theoretical concepts inclines us to focus on parental transference figures within the oedipal helix" (1988, p. 7). Agger sees the problem of obscuring siblings in less-grand and sweeping terms than Mitchell and in more local theoretical and technical terms as countertransference avoidance in clinical psychoanalysis: "For some therapists, deviations from a psychoanalytic locus of concern . . . prevent the emergence of more obscure, drive-cathected layers of transference personae. Countertransference issues, inhibitions and anxiety regarding competition and incest, and lack of exposure in both training and personal analyses may cause therapists to overlook sibling interaction . . . in personality formation, neurosis, and treatment" (1988, p. 7). Another problem she pointed to is the sheer difficulty in teasing out overlapping and/or overdetermined mental representations. Kieffer (2008) suggests clinically that "sibling phenomena in the analytic encounter may be mutually disavowed because their acknowledgment and examination would threaten the hierarchical power structure that remains inherent in dyadic treatment." Szalita (1968) noted that postanalysis dissatisfaction was often linked to the person's first analyst having ignored sibling conflicts. Dent (2009a) experienced a kind of epiphany in hearing about the impact of siblings during discussions about the relevance of Mitchell's insights to A. S. Byatt's short story "The Chinese Lobster." Dent goes on to wonder interestingly about paranoia:

> Recognizing the depth and consequences of this [intersibling] fear has proved invaluable clinically. I've been struck by how many patients given to paranoid reactions grew up with a bullying or even brutal sibling. Further, I've noticed how often paranoid transference/countertransference dynamics seem to emerge out of lateral concerns—a fear that I'm

2. Mini-lecture: "Dr Juliet Mitchell on Siblings and Hysteria," UCL, May 26, 2010.

> making demands not out of any legitimate authority or purpose, but just because I can (I'm bigger; the patient is needier, etc.). Interpreting my role as that of an older sibling *pretending* to be a parent, whether out of insecurity or despotism, has proved quite useful. (Dent 2009a, p. 172)

Using Loewald's metaphor of theater for the analytic situation (Loewald 1975/1980; Balsam 1997) allows readily for the analytic development of sibling transferences, hence the news of laterality is telling but less startling to those exposed to his teaching. In addition to Loewald, as a candidate I was taught by those who contributed to the 1983 issue of *The Psychoanalytic Study of the Child* on the topic of siblings. Multiple transferences in the course of the analysis are played out and staged imaginatively, now externalized upon the pluripotential analyst, from the staging of scenarios within the patient's innermost life. Siblings are certainly players in this—as well as nannies, aunts, uncles, and teachers. But I agree with Mitchell and others that siblings have their own very special meanings indeed.

In the following case material I am particularly interested in the relationship of two sisters, born ten years apart, and in thinking about what Mitchell calls—with ironic apologies to Lacan's "Law of the Father" (1981)—the "Law of the Mother." Mitchell's "mother" regulates the severity of the original child trauma of being displaced by another sibling, by introducing the notion of family "seriality"—"there is room for you and me, a law which allows for one who is the same and different" (Mitchell 2003, p. 52). For Mitchell the mother is key to sibling bonding and subjectivity. Seriality is fostered by the mother who arranges for enough room for each child, in Mitchell's view. Thus, she concludes that the original sibling birth trauma that she perceives, of not just rivalry but of the older sibling's identity annihilation and hatred—resulting in, "I hate you, you are not me"—is actually a *precondition* for seriality. This is an interesting formulation and way of looking at what, from an ego psychological developmental perspective, or from a self psychological motivational systems theory perspective (Lichtenberg, Lachmann, and Fosshage 2010), might be considered one of the most important executive tasks of mothering. A father will also play a part in a child's individuation process in becoming a separate entity within the family, according to, say, Herzog (2001), who views the father's role even more significantly than the mother's role in helping the child separate not from the younger child, as Mitchell adds, but from the infantile aspects of the mother. I think that Mitchell's is an addition to the existent theory in considering the special (but I would not say exclusive) role of the mother in aiding the older child to separate from the baby as well as from the mother herself. The "Law of the Mother" as a theoretical abstract is naturally therefore an unconscious ideal. It *ought* to work that way, so that people could become perfectly individuated and be able to differentiate themselves from others clearly. In practice, of course, they often do not manage this state of separation so well.

CLINICAL ILLUSTRATION

Ms. Arlene A, a fifty-year-old married college professor, who had two grown children, initially told me how much, as an adult, she loved her ten-years-younger, divorced, childless sister, Lauren. There were just the two of them, and she was grateful for all Lauren, as a special aunt, did for her own children—presents at Hanukkah, gifts at Passover, family picnics in the mountains, sleepovers for the kids while Arlene and her husband went off for romantic weekends. She was a "roaring success," she said, as an aunt. (At the time my ears caught "roaring" with a question mark.) Her mother, she stated baldly, "was nuts." It was too bad, but that's the way it was. Her friends all agreed that their mother was "big trouble." It was so good to have at least her sister emerge as close, surviving this family mess. (Again my ears caught "this mess.")

Mother had never supported the patient's professional ambitions. All she wanted seemed to be for her to stay nearby and be her servant. Arlene had gone across the country to be educated to get far away from her. But the poor woman was limited, Arlene added, by her lack of education, and Arlene had totally forgiven her. (It is interesting, I thought, how some at the beginning of a possible analytic treatment wish they were at its end! This "forgiveness" is likely a forced foreconclusion, I thought. Arlene seemed a little too jocular and dismissive of the subject matter as she talked in these introductory sessions.) Father had not been much involved. He was always preoccupied by his successful importing business, but he had a bad temper. The mother loved doing crafts and painting, which the patient despised and could never get the hang of, being not at all artistic. Mother had said, "You're no good with your hands. You're all brain, so why bother?"

Lauren, the younger sister, these days owned a small art gallery. "So she liked painting, then?" I asked.

"I guess, but it was because she was no good in school," Arlene snapped irritably. (Had she not noticed this connection between Lauren's and Mother's shared interests? Or, I wondered, is it that she doesn't want me to have noticed? I noted her brief irritability.) She continued about how Lauren had done so poorly in school that she was very sorry for her, because her mean mother had always contrasted her negatively with Arlene, the brilliant scholar. Tearfully then, she confessed to me that she was far and away the favorite of both of her parents. Once into the four-times-per-week analysis, which she eagerly accepted, as she felt her problems were deeper than she had been able to reach in several psychotherapies she had tried, we had a chance to dwell with these family scenes.

We spoke at length of her guilt about this success and her guilt about outshining Lauren. I had transferential evidence to back up this internalization, due to her reactions to crossing paths in the waiting room with a student of her own who was doing poorly in school, and who was seeing a colleague in our suite. My patient was guilty about this student, comparing her own analysis favorably with this poor student's assumed once-per-week therapy. She was guilty that I favored her by offering analysis, whereas my colleague clearly had deemed this student not worthy of analysis. Many associations about Lauren emerged. Arlene had felt protective of and lovingly close to Lauren in this iteration.

Much material emerged about the birth of Lauren when my patient was just going into adolescence. She stressed the positive and empowering executive maternal stirrings of adolescence in herself toward her little sister. Mother had been delighted with her helpfulness with the new baby and had even said, "You'll be a wonderful mother someday." Arlene had glowed in the shining light of Mother's eye and the height of Mother's approbation for the very task that Mother prided herself on. These moments were all important within their relationship matrices, but not the whole story. So far, Arlene would seem to be suffering from a mild form of survivor guilt, comparing herself to Lauren, as the one who was picked for accolade for her superior "brains," and her potential as a "wonderful mother" . . . even if she had "bad hands."

I had noted to myself that Arlene's presenting complaint to me was that she was currently in subtle professional trouble, as she was complaining about a lack of ideas for writing, very late in giving editors promised assignments, and feeling ignored as a voice on her faculty. Her teacher evaluations were poor as well. Her mothering of her teenage girls was the most satisfying part of her life, and her marriage, she consistently said, was fine, with many incidental portraits of feeling supported by her husband. *So what had happened to the originally joyful schoolgirl in Arlene? I thought. Or what in the story did not yet add up?*

In among the loving positives of this sibling bond were my first clues that there were too sharply perceived contrasts in this family between these sibs. Because Arlene had dismissed the mother's psyche as "nutty" and denigrated her consistently, I wondered privately if she were dismissing Lauren's intellect, too, and that her stress on how good she herself was at school might be defending her against a more-complex view of her relations with her sister. According to Arlene, in this first version of the family tale, she was the clear favorite. But how did young Lauren end up sharing the same interests as the mother, if she had been, indeed, so lowly in her eyes? The story about how favored Arlene was in her mother's imagined eyes became more textured.

THE RHYTHM OF SIBLING INTIMACY

Lauren had had an early childless divorce, and Arlene had been much more sympathetic than the parents about it. It was at that time she felt especially close to her—but the "closeness" and its quality were relative states of mind about Lauren when the longer-term trajectory unfolded. The rhythm of sibling intimacy was actually one of extreme closeness followed by extreme distance. On further analysis, aspects of this sisterly sympathy over the divorce involved also schadenfreude—a hidden triumph, the malicious pleasure in another's failure, which is particularly characteristic of sibling rivalry encoded into ambitious strivings. The ambivalent threads within this sibship relation came into view.

As the analysis progressed over a few years, other issues in Arlene's life and associations took precedence. One day I drew to her attention that she talked little about Lauren again, after initially talking of how important she was. Arlene tearfully now revised the story, saying that she often had felt alienated from her. Lauren had a terrible temper, just like Father, and by keeping their conversation "light" she could manage to keep anger at bay. To an analyst's ear, the relationship sounded as if Arlene were walking on eggshells most of the time, alert to minimizing tension in case Lauren would "lose her cool" or "yell." She could "get crazy," Arlene said. "I don't talk to her much anymore, especially since I've been so preoccupied here with the problems in my own life and struggling with my lack of creativity in work."

THE DRAMA AND STAGING OF SCENES FROM THE "LAW OF THE MOTHER"

I started working with her on the sharp contrast in the opening and mid-phase accounts of her relations with her sister.[3] It emerged how angry Arlene had been in our opening phase, when I had said that "*she*" (Lauren) liked painting. Arlene was still angry. (Now this was familiar from other scenarios.) My patient was characterologically devoted to "being and looking cool." It usually took her at least a month to realize

---

3. Transferentially here, I was moving back and forth in the roles of each sister, as well as occupying maternal space (where the "Law of the Mother" fits in).

she had been angry, hurt, disappointed, or let down. "Never forgive and never forget"—but above all, "look like it doesn't matter" was a central part of her style of hoarding insults.

More deeply into this "family dinner table" scene of her anger with me, I began to take on the cloak of her mother to her. It was "clear," she whimpered, that I preferred Lauren, otherwise why would I have emphasized that *she* liked painting? It was also "clear" from the watercolors on the walls of my office that I myself was an artist. That meant to Arlene that I had *really* said in the consultation sessions several years ago, "*You* don't like doing creative things," and between those hurtful lines, "What's *wrong* with you, anyway?" The latter interaction became an important pivot in the negative transference. Gradually there emerged the absolute certainty that I disliked her. Always there was a direct comparison with someone else—mostly my other patients. She would ingeniously twist a question into an accusation, and an interpretation into a hurtful exposure of her lacks.

A few vivid contemporary stories of Lauren emerged. The parents, now growing old, wanted to move out of their large house. Suddenly the two siblings seemed to be at each other's throats, with my patient giving pained accounts of Lauren's "yelling" at her about how greedy she was, while she was tearfully convincing me that all she'd done was to ask whether this or that beautiful vase was appropriate for their new small home.

Arlene was representing herself to me as a victim of young Lauren's aggression in this pained interaction about who wanted the beautiful parental vase more, in much the same way as I experienced myself as a victim when earlier she had been railing against my maternal "accusation" that Lauren was more talented artistically than she. As many of these conversations were in detail, I was persuaded that in her awareness of herself in the original family home, in asking her sister about the vase, Arlene may have no more felt *consciously* accusatory than I had when making my statement about how Lauren must "like to paint."

As I viewed this transferential experience and many similar interactions as involvement in Arlene's projective identifications, I told the patient that I could see how she felt like a victim and misunderstood by Lauren when they were around their parents, as her reaction bore a similarity to my own reaction when she surprised me with telling about how hurt she'd been when I noted that Lauren liked to paint, in contrast to her. I too had felt "innocent," but it had had so much more meaning to her. Arlene was interested in this and recognized the pattern. Could it be, she wondered suddenly, if Lauren *felt* similar to her, and hurt by implied criticism, when I had seemed to accuse her of having no painting talent? Maybe Lauren felt hurt, and imagined she had no right to want the vase, for example? Arlene spoke of the possibility of a role reversal, where I was like her, and she like Lauren. At that point she shed further light by bringing in much more material about the mother and how she managed their frequent fights in childhood—and even now. These materials are the substance of what Loewald has called "the fantasy character of the analytic situation" (1975/1980, p. 352). Mother would say to Arlene in the aftermath of observing (and participating in) Arlene fighting with Lauren, "Your sister's so crazy. Don't believe a word she says; I don't." The gratification of virtue in Arlene's victimhood was thus enhanced. Arlene illuminated that even as she'd raged at me, there was a part of her from time to time that was observing herself with amazement. It was as if she were several people in fantasy joining in argument and counterargument. One voice was saying, "You're *accusing* me, you crazy woman!" Another said, "You're nuts; she's only asking a question!" Another said, "But you know she (Mother/analyst) doesn't say what she means; she *really* means you've got poor taste and aren't at all artistic or creative!" Invoking the mother between the two sisters in my own fantasy of this impassioned back-and-forth filled in the missing links. Sometimes I was the mother, letting Arlene know subtly how much I preferred Lauren—the painter just like me—to her. Other times in the scene I was the mother who was supposed to play my appointed part in this drama by making amends, cozying up to Arlene, sympathizing with how victimized she was by her wicked sister, who should be dismissed as "nuts." When I was in the drama as if in maternal position of playing out a strong preference for young Lauren (the painter just like me, as Arlene had designated me earlier in the analysis), Arlene would feel compelled to seek far under the surface of my mind to find "the *real* truth" in this battle among Mother and both siblings. If only that truth were out in the open, and expectedly and especially hateful of her, because of all her aggression, fantasied destructiveness, and guilt, only then she thought she could feel "safe."

How myriad are the ways to seek out individual forms of imagined "safety"! It is as necessary to analyze a patient's conception of inner "safety" as it is to attend to the more-obvious routes of inner rage or destructiveness. It seemed that in that analytic encounter, for Arlene at times, nothing was what it seemed, and words and tonality could not be trusted. Verbal interchange was a kind of "Alice Through the Looking Glass" communication experience. At times, her insistence on my malignant motives was so strong, and she was so insistent that she *knew* without a doubt that I thought her not to have an ounce of special writing talent (as a displacement from painting, which was closer to her heart) that I once had a fantasy that I myself had gone "nuts" and must be unaware of my hatred toward and despising of her. I realized then that I was angry about how helpless I felt to analyze her shaky self-esteem while she was so sure I held her in contempt.

ROLE OF CONSTRUCTION AND RECONSTRUCTIVE FANTASY IN THERAPEUTIC ACTION

We now reached a potential reconstruction of the inner world of Arlene as including her possible versions of the inner world of her mother. My part in this co-construction was based on the shifting transferences to me and my reactive countertransferences in the sessions. For Mother, when one girl was "in" her good graces the other was "out." Mother's "out" was so utter and complete that each little girl filled up the gaping emotional space with agonizing fantasies or familial spoken criticisms of her own deficits. Each child individually interpreted in her own terms the reasons for Mother's exclusion and banishment of each of them. Neither, of course, attributed her exclusion outside her own narcissistic enclosure of self-importance. Such a position keeps Mother perfect and filled with only "good reasons" for her actions and speech. Mother's glittering night moon could shine on Arlene when she felt "the favorite"—hence her opening story and convictions of being the favorite early in the analysis. That was the more consciously available and acceptable version of the family relations. The dark side of Mother's moon could make her disappear into a frightening and empty universe.

INTERNALIZED GENDERED FAMILY DISCOURSE

Arlene's focus on writing (in her professional world as an adult) and creativity was linked to sensitivity around her femaleness and stereotypic notions of "femininity." She was fearful of being sterile—not manly in her family—but *not fully womanly*. After all, the mother is always the gold standard of childbearing creativity, especially for a female child (Balsam 1996; 2012), and even though Arlene already had given birth twice, internally she was still wavering about the self-estimate of her own gender-role success. She feared that Lauren had retained more connection with some essence of maternal creativity (as if it were biologically inbuilt), even though, in adult life, Lauren in fact was childless. These were painful explorations for Arlene. Refusal to paint with Mother had once protected her from being swallowed up by dyadic intensity and Mother's possessiveness and insistence of "sameness." Her resistance had allowed her to make more school relationships and identify with women teachers who promised attachment with more freedom. But her refusal to have "good hands" also produced a profound uneasiness about Mother's slanted and narrow reading of her behavior, which was the *real* truth in her own estimate, that is, that she was refusing, she said, to become a "feminine" woman. The "good hands" also held more associative links to her own "bad hands" of masturbation, and a body exploration that she was sure Mother disapproved of and that, for Arlene, was associated with wishful fantasies of peeing like a boy with naughty "bad hands." (Perhaps Mother did disapprove, perhaps not. No one will ever know.) Arlene became convinced that Mother was dead set against her body's female procreativity (for example, Mayer 1985). But Arlene's own ambivalence about owning fully this same female body became greatly intensified in adolescence by her graphic fears of carrying a child and experiencing childbirth, fears that accompanied her mother's giving birth to Lauren when Arlene was ten and prepubertal.

The analytic listener can appreciate how much more texture can keep unfolding in such a deepening analytic process. The role of the father has not been included here but was complex.

Arlene's early attempt to free herself from her mother by denying her sameness and loudly insisting on her otherness was a gendered constellation. She tried mightily to enlist her father, and tried to tie herself tightly to him instead, to escape from Mother's "handcrafting" ambiance. (I have found that the mother-to-daughter's comparisons of hands carries special significance for the tone of their comfort or discomfort in the inevitable blending and separating rhythms that proceed between them, as the daughter grows by comparison to each feature of the mother's body [Balsam 2001; 2012].) The accusation of Arlene's "bad hands" had a special hurt. The mother's hands are the enablers of the child's welfare, and the child is deeply familiar with their touch. This insult represented the mother damning her daughter's capacities to be like her, as she had known intimate caretaking . . . also the basis for sensuality and lovemaking. The girl of course partially welcomed this, as it meant freedom to her—freedom to try to be close to Father as her preferred parent, and to be like him. Arlene was attracted by the freedom that boys had, as she thought, and was more of a "tomgirl" than Lauren. In Arlene's view, then, Lauren stayed close to her mother as "the girly baby," while Arlene was pushed out of any semblance of babyhood by the birth of Lauren. Juliet Mitchell (2003) would see clearly here Arlene's rage and loss of identity as "the unique baby." If we consider that she was ten years old at the time, I will add Arlene's burgeoning acute teenage gender trouble, which becomes easy to imagine. I also think that her "unique baby" identity as the solo child was blended with her repudiated female body identity. This was one route to become stirred up with the birth of Lauren. After all, she had tried to reject Mother early from her inner pantheon. The tomgirl with "bad hands" became good at sports and tried to get Father to take her to games. Of course, there was a heterosexual oedipal thread in these dynamics, too. One can appreciate gradually the weaving together in Arlene's growth, the vertical and the lateral dynamic dimensions of parental and sibling relationships.

The mother grew large and pregnant before Arlene's eyes, and suddenly, it seemed, in a triumph of her oedipal competition for her father, and in awe and admiration of Mother's "creativity," Arlene allowed herself to become envious of her mother's new splendor. The pregnancy newly enhanced the vision of her previously rejected Mother. (This does not at all always happen to a young preteen when her mother becomes pregnant!) Such are the surprising paths and vicissitudes of development. At the juncture when Lauren was born, Mother reciprocally started to appreciate Arlene, and thus the path to maternal child caretaking (and also angry overcontrol) of Lauren began for Arlene, with Mother's blessing and accolade, "You'll be a wonderful mother some day!" The latter praise too became a pleasurable voice in her mind, and a thread to the actuality of her enjoyment and pride in the mothering of her own two children.

But the interfemale matrix of interaction among Mother, Arlene, and Lauren also became fraught here with ambitious strivings, jealousies, envies, and with renewed anger for Arlene, this time complicated by her displacement by the baby Lauren, now perceived as Mother's favorite. Mitchell's view of this complicated love and hate is: "I suggest loving one's sibling like oneself is neither exactly narcissism nor object-love. It is narcissism transmuted by a hatred that has been overcome" (2003, pp. 35–36). Young Lauren meanwhile grew up liking her mother more than did Arlene. She had her own jealousy of Arlene's sports and relative closeness with her father. But she eagerly compensated for this and shared her "good hands" with Mother's artistic gifts.

In the tussles that I described above, how could Juliet Mitchell's "Law of the Mother" help us understand and sort out some of these dynamics? Theoretically, Mother should have been able to help Arlene feel secure as "herself," safe with her own offerings within the family to be the older sister. She should theoretically have been able to see Lauren as separate, with her own distinct personality. That would be the task of facilitating seriality and effecting the "Law of the Mother." However, the complication here was that Mother herself was not skilled in triadic dynamics. She herself was fixated in a dyadic state, which tends to exaggerate all competition to ferocious heights and insists on "sameness" at the same time as rebelling, because it is too voracious a position for comfort. She thus pulled in Arlene, cast out Lauren, or alternately pulled in Lauren and locked out Arlene emotionally. That was her version of seriality . . . but not the position of an individuated mother. As I often say in transferential comments to patients like Arlene, concerning their dubiety about this tenuous state of object connectedness, "You believe that I have no room in my heart for more than one person."

During the course of a successful analysis of this kind of sibling bond, the siblings as adults often begin to newly discover one another. A shared critical perspective develops on their joint experience with a mother for whom each seemed able to secure more psychological separateness, and results in their healing interactions as adults. These sisters eventually shared their fears of being accused individually of failing to glorify sufficiently Mother's capabilities by her mirroring of same-gendered "virtues"—in Arlene's case, her pained inability to paint, and in Lauren's case, her pained inability to have a successful marriage and the pain of remaining childless.

Working with Regression in the Analytic Situation

Neubauer (1982) had noted that when adult patients give accounts of reuniting with their families, it often seems that the original sibling hierarchies quickly become reestablished, as if sibling interactions can have a tendency to remain "static"—"even though the vicissitudes of life may substantially have altered the circumstances of individuals." He wonders if "the inability . . . to change the relationship to siblings and to find new ways of coexistence is an indication of partly unresolved preoedipal and oedipal conflicts" (p. 127). Neubauer was here implying a preoedipal and oedipal scenario that includes the "early role of multiple objects and their relationship to each other" (p. 122). (He questions an exclusive emphasis on the mother as the sole important figure who achieves eminence in the child's inner world.) A phenomenon he calls the "static sibling" may be observed in ongoing analytic work. "Examining sibling experience and rivalry, we become increasingly aware of the additional role of objects other than the mother in early life" (p. 130). These will later naturally be reflected in multiple transferences to an analyst during adult treatment. Thus by sheer logic, Neubauer demonstrates his 1982 struggles away from the exclusive oedipal paradigm that Mitchell, Agger, and others have noticed as restrictive, working out that siblings created separate transferences.

Eloise Agger (1988) offered the following clinical help about working in the dramatis personae of the family stage: "Attention to sibling issues within the therapeutic relationship will often forge new pathways to unconscious material. The therapist must speed up his or her reaction time in perceiving how rapidly his or her transference meaning for the patient is shifting. At times, an hour might seem like a slide show with lights and sound effects. The slides are projected one after another in wild succession; now the therapist is seen as mother, now father, now sibling, now subject, now the whole crowd, and so forth. *It's like a night back at the family dinner table.* Or the aftermath of a family crisis" (p. 27; italics mine). The "Law of the Mother" can thus also become restored to "the night back at the family dinner table" in the course of some analyses, through the vicissitudes and the "good enough" working-through of the transference. Arlene became "creative" again in this treatment and once more began to write. And this may have suggested the resolution put forth in Mitchell's overarching theory, that acceptance of seriality by the child (who is also obeying the vertical maternal prohibition of that child's lost ambitions to have competed with Mother's generation of procreation) will play a role in her mind developing freely, and hence her creativity.

BIBLIOGRAPHY

AGGER, E. (1988). Psychoanalytic perspectives on sibling relationships. *Psychoanalytic Inquiry* 8:3–30.

AINSLIE, R. C. (1999). Twinship and twinning reactions in siblings. In *Brothers and Sisters: Developmental, Dynamic, and Technical Aspects of the Sibling Relationship*, ed. S. Akhtar and S. Kramer, pp. 25–53. Northvale, NJ: Jason Aronson.

AKHTAR, S., AND S. KRAMER (1999). Beyond the parental orbit: Brothers, sisters and others. In *Brothers and Sisters: Developmental, Dynamic, and Technical Aspects of the Sibling Relationship*, ed. S. Akhtar and S. Kramer, pp. 1–24. Northvale, NJ: Jason Aronson..

BALSAM, R. H. (1996). The pregnant mother and the body image of the daughter. *Journal of American Psychoanalytic Association* 44S:401–27.

———— (1997). Active neutrality and Loewald's metaphor of theater. *Psychoanalytic Study of the Child* 52:3–16.

———— (2001). Integrating male and female elements in a woman's gender identity. *Journal of American Psychoanalytic Association* 49 (4): 1335–60.

———— (2012). *Women's Bodies in Psychoanalysis*. London: Routledge.

BANK, S., AND M. KAHN (1983). *The Sibling Bond.* New York: Basic Books.

BENJAMIN, J. (1988). *The Bonds of Love.* New York: Pantheon.

BERMAN, L. (1978). Sibling loss as an organizer of unconscious guilt: A case study. *Psychoanalytic Quarterly* 47:568–87.

BURLINGHAM, D. (1952). *Twins: A Study of Three Pairs of Identical Twins.* Madison, CT: International Universities Press.

COLES, P. (2003). *The Importance of Sibling Relationships in Psychoanalysis*. London: Karnac Books.
COLONNA, A. B., AND L. M. NEWMAN (1983). The psychoanalytic literature on siblings. *Psychoanalytic Study of the Child* 38:285–309.
DENT, V. (2009a). The bright forms shining in the dark: Juliet Mitchell's theory of sibling dynamics as illuminated in A. S. Byatt's "The Chinese Lobster." *Psychoanalytic Dialogues* 19:155–68.
——— (2009b). Reply to commentary by Juliet Mitchell: Siblings in clinical work. *Psychoanalytic Dialogues* 19:171–74.
EDWARD, J. (2011). *The Sibling Relationship: A Force for Growth and Conflict*. New York: Jason Aronson.
ELLMAN, S. (2010). *When Theories Touch: A Historical and Theoretical Integration of Psychoanalytic Thought*. CIPS Series on the Boundaries of Psychoanalysis. London: Karnac.
FREUD, S. (1910). Five lectures on psychoanalysis. In *Standard Edition*, vol. 11, pp. 7–55.
——— (1920). Beyond the pleasure principle. In *Standard Edition*, vol. 18, pp. 7–64.
HERZOG, J. (2001). *Father Hunger: Explorations with Adults and Children*. London and New York: Routledge.
KENNEDY, H. (1985). Growing up with a handicapped sibling. *Psychoanalytic Study of the Child* 40:255–74.
KIEFFER, C. C. (2008). On siblings: Mutual regulation and mutual recognition. *Annual of Psychoanalysis* 36:161–73.
KRIS, M., AND S. RITVO (1983). Parents and siblings: Their mutual influence. *Psychoanalytic Study of the Child* 38:311–24.
KUBA, S. (2011). *The Role of Sisters in Women's Development*. New York: Oxford University Press.
LAMENT, C., AND I. WINEMAN (1984). A psychoanalytic study of nonidentical twins: The impact of hemophilia on the personality development of the affected child and his healthy twin. *Psychoanalytic Study of the Child* 39:331–70.
LEICHTMAN, M. (1985). The Influence of an older sibling on the separation-individuation process. *Psychoanalytic Study of the Child* 40:111–61.
LEVIN, C. (2010). *Siblings in Development: A Psychoanalytic View*. Ed. Vivienne Lewin and Belinda Sharp. London: Karnac, 2009, 184 pp. *Canadian Journal of Psychoanalysis* 18:345–51.
LICHTENBERG, J., F. LACHMANN, AND J. FOSSHAGE (2010). *Psychoanalysis and Motivational Systems: A New Look*. Vol. 33 of Psychoanalytic Inquiry Book Series. New York and London: Taylor & Francis.
LOEWALD, H. (1975/1980). Psychoanalysis as an art and the fantasy character of the psychoanalytic situation. In *Papers on Psychoanalysis*, pp. 352–71. New Haven, CT: Yale University Press.
MAYER, E. L. (1985). 'Everybody must be just like me': Observations on female castration anxiety. *International Journal of Psycho-Analysis* 66:331.
MITCHELL, J. (2000). *Mad Men and Medusas: Reclaiming Hysteria and the Effects of Sibling Rivalry on the Human Condition*. London: Hamish Hamilton / Penguin.

——— (2003). *Siblings: Sex and Violence*. Cambridge: Polity Press.
NEUBAUER, P. B. (1982). Rivalry, envy and jealousy. *Psychoanalytic Study of the Child* 37:121–42.
PROVENCE, S., AND A. J. SOLNIT (1983). Development-promoting aspects of the sibling experience. *Psychoanalytic Study of the Child* 38:337–51.
SAFER, J. (2003). *The Normal One: Life with a Difficult or Damaged Sibling*. New York: Delta.
SOLNIT, A. J. (1983). The sibling experience—Introduction. *Psychoanalytic Study of the Child* 38:281–84.
SZALITA, A. (1968). Reanalysis. *Contemporary Psychoanalysis* 4:83–102.
VIVONA, J. M. (2007). Sibling differentiation, identity development, and the lateral dimension of psychic life. *Journal of the American Psychoanalytic Association* 55:1191–1215.
——— (2010). Siblings, transference, and the lateral dimension of psychic life. *Psychoanalytic Psychology* 27:8–26.
VOLKAN V., AND G. AST (1997). *Siblings in the Unconscious and Psychopathology: Womb Fantasies, Claustrophobias, Fear of Pregnancy, Murderous Rage, Animal Symbolism*. Madison, CT: International Universities Press.
YOUNG-BRUEHL, E. (2011). The trauma of lost love in psychoanalysis. Chap. 10 in *On Freud's "Beyond the Pleasure Principle,"* pp. 250–65. IPA Contemporary Freud: Turning Points & Critical Issues, ed. Salman Akhtar, Mary Kay O'Neil. London: Karnac Books.

The Theory of Sibling Trauma and the Lateral Dimension

KAREN GILMORE, M.D.

Juliet Mitchell has made an invaluable contribution to psychoanalytic developmental theory with her elucidation of sibling trauma. She suggests that this is a universal experience of the preoedipal child who becomes aware of the world of similar others through the birth of a sibling or the dawning recognition of the ubiquitous peer group. Suddenly no longer unique, the child is in dread of displacement and confronted with the loss of the special status of "the baby." Two examples from adolescent analyses are offered to illustrate the power of the lateral dimension.

JULIET MITCHELL'S CONTRIBUTION TO PSYCHOANALYTIC DEVELOPmental theory has been hugely significant, not only due to her persistent focus on the role of siblings in mental life but also because she has taken the critical step toward theory making. In general, the problem of siblings constitutes the bread and butter of child clinicians, but it has never been acknowledged for its profound role in human development and psychopathology. In my experience as a child analyst and a teacher of development, I am repeatedly confronted with the power of the "lateral dimension," the trauma attendant on the birth of the actual sibling and the shocklike experience of the multitude of similar others, the metaphoric siblings.

Mitchell raises the crucial question: Why should such a pervasive phenomenon have been, from its inception, underappreciated in psychoanalytic thinking? And, luckily for psychoanalysis, she not only points out the problem but also offers an answer and a solution. She reminds

---

Dr. Karen Gilmore is Clinical Professor of Psychiatry at Columbia University College of Physicians and Surgeons and Senior Consultant at the Columbia University Center for Psychoanalytic Training and Research.

The Psychoanalytic Study of the Child 67, ed. Claudia Lament, Robert A. King, Samuel Abrams, A. Scott Dowling, and Paul M. Brinich (Yale University Press, copyright © 2013 by Claudia Lament, Robert A. King, Samuel Abrams, A. Scott Dowling, and Paul M. Brinich).

us that observations without theory to crystallize them remain relevant but unintegrated. Her assertion that, like the experience of parents, the sibling experience is both infinitely variable but also invariable, and her subsequent explication of its meaning have been revolutionary despite her protestations to the contrary. Psychoanalytic theory today is not unitary, but there are no schools of thought that differ on this point; none, until Mitchell, has developed a theory of sibling trauma.

Stimulated by her ideas, I too have pondered the dearth of sibling theory, which is noteworthy even in the developmental literature. In 1988, Ian Graham observed that psychoanalysis has treated siblings with the "contempt of familiarity" (p. 88). Clearly, such dismissal serves a defensive purpose, since the "fraternal complex" has been a powerful, divisive force within our field over the course of our history and the world is, tragically, full of examples of tribal conflict where the "siblings" are split into good and bad, unleashing massive destructive aggression. Moreover, the presence of the fraternal complex in all aspects of our daily work is both undeniable and unacknowledged and so suggests that there is powerful unconscious motivation in our inattention. Perhaps one reason why, beyond the rationalization of variability of the sibling experience, is that the painful and powerful affects associated with siblings may be more difficult for us to manage than our preferred formulations in our professional institutions and in our consulting rooms. It is more comfortable, as Mitchell suggests, to retreat behind the vertical formulation, where the power hierarchy and incest taboo feel secure. Indeed, the intensity of impulses directed toward siblings and triggered in the context of sibling transference and countertransference is (1) less modulated by dependency and ambivalence; (2) less subject to the incest taboo; (3) less dampened by the power differential, the original status hierarchy, and the typical anxieties of childhood; and (4) therefore, more brutal and violent than the vertical dimension. The lateral dimension is of course inevitably woven into the vertical one, and the number of triangular dynamics is infinite. To again quote Graham:

> The sibling is both a developmental companion and a transferential shaper. This shifts the model of the patient's internal psychic organization from a single planetary one that has the primary parental objects at the center and the sibling objects in orbit around them to that of a miniature universe of great complexity. To Winnicott's aphorism that there is no infant, but only a mother/infant dyad, I would add that there is usually no mother/child dyad in a multisib family, but, rather, environmental and orbiting triads impacting from the earliest mother/infant symbiosis to the epigenesis of the adult neurosis. (1988, p. 91)

To this, Mitchell has added two crucial dimensions: The child need not have siblings to have the sibling experience, and this is one of the central and inevitable traumas of childhood.

Mitchell insists that the sibling trauma, the trauma of the lateral dimension, is a universal experience that is responsible for much of the neurotic psychopathology of early childhood. Most of my own practice illuminates the intensity of the sibling dynamic, including my patients without siblings. The latter often see all or selected other children as rivals and enact the sibling struggle there. Unfortunately, the tendency to link pathogenic sibling relationships to problems both within the parental relationship and in the parent-child relationship is still ubiquitous. And while disturbances in these relationships, as experienced by the children, no doubt have far-reaching impact on their conflicts and development, including their notions about adult relationships and their place within them, I agree with Mitchell's idea that sibling trauma and its repercussions are a *separate complex system*. Of course, this system interfaces with the vertical one but also interfaces with all other aspects of personality development and must be recognized as both a universal trauma of childhood and an ongoing influence on personality development. Indeed Mitchell's emphasis on this issue of sibling trauma supports ideas that emerge in all discussions of childhood development, but without a convincing theoretical frame.

In terms of the developmental sequence, Mitchell suggests that the lateral dimension explodes on the mental scene of the late toddler preceding the Oedipus. The toddler is sufficiently separated from the maternal orbit to take in the reality of the other: He may be directly experiencing the birth of a sibling, surrounded in various settings by pregnant women, becoming cognizant of his own interest in babies, awakening to intrusions of various types into his own dyadic unit, or beginning to pursue sexual researches about the mysteries of parental activity and how babies are made. Moreover, the toddler is facing a new demand to self-regulate in regard to his aggression; indeed, "no" is the repeating refrain of parental communication to the two-to-three-year-old child. The shock of displacement, without the cushioning of verticality, is a trauma beyond imagining for the young child, and in my experience it is linked inevitably to recognition of the world of similar others, the arrival of babies, and their dreaded appearance in his own dyadic paradise (whether or not it materializes). This is nowhere better immortalized than in the early life of Peter Pan, when he tries to go back to his mother after his infant flight to Kensington Gardens and habitation among the fairies:

> He went in a hurry . . . because he had dreamt that his mother was crying, and he knew what was the great thing she cried for, and that a hug from her splendid Peter would quickly make her to smile. Oh, he felt sure of it, and so eager was he to be nestling in her arms that this time he flew straight to the window, which was always to be open for him. But the window was closed and there were iron bars on it, and peering inside he saw his mother sleeping peacefully with her arm round another little boy. (Barrie 1906, pp. 75–76)

This passage also underscores a profoundly underappreciated aspect of the birth of a sibling; even before the child turns his attention fully to oedipal matters, he is unrelentingly exposed to a different and perhaps more personally galling primal scene, that of mother and baby in passionate intimate connection, a connection from which he has only recently been ousted and whose pleasures he understands completely. The stimulus for aggression and the narcissistic mortification of exclusion is not softened by promises for compensation in the very distant future, but rather poignantly highlights the permanent loss of the very recent past. Being the beloved and pampered little one is now gone forever, even though the toddler remains painfully little in all other ways. Mitchell's discussion of the loss of identity that the sibling entails incorporates this mortification; the adorable baby is now big brother or big sister, an identity that holds few gratifications and multiplies the demand for self-control. Becoming a grown-up is an interminable wait, with dimly perceived pleasures about which the toddler vaguely imagines but has no experience, but at least there are promises of future pleasure. What compensates a child for the birth of a sibling? Most children consider the event to be, conclusively, a permanent and irrevocable loss of the splendid baby-place in their mother's arms. Peter's answer is a familiar one to all of us who treat children: "I won't grow up!"

The developmental juxtaposition of this crushing trauma of displacement with the oedipal drama is, of course, nowhere more in evidence than in the story of Peter Pan and his subsequent withdrawal into Neverland, where his rage is absorbed by the vertical dimension, as he is compelled to join forces with similar others to combat the oedipal threat, Captain Hook. Mitchell makes a point of placing the sibling trauma prior to the Oedipus and fully evolved mental representation. This resonates with an observation in one of the handful of useful papers about siblings in our literature: *Oedipal Sibling Triangles* by Sharpe and Rosenblatt (1994). In it, they differentiate oedipal and preoedipal sibling triangles, but Mitchell takes this a step further, saying that the actual moment of the sibling trauma is always preoedipal. Sharpe and Rosenblatt's idea of the preoedipal sibling configuration, corresponding to Mitchell's idea of the universal sibling trauma, has the qualities of unmodulated aggression, primitive splitting of mental representations impervious to subsequent integrative mental capacity, and overall rigidity typical of traumatic experiences. They suggest an alternative configuration, the "twinning reaction," which in my experience, even with twins, is a massive defensive denial of difference and an attempt to annihilate by merger. I'll come back to this reaction a little later.

The other juxtaposition of this particular trauma and ongoing development that Mitchell points out is that it occurs simultaneous with the first flowering of semiotic capacity and imagination. The third year of life is momentous because it marks the explosion of the child's capacity to symbolically represent and to pretend. The introduction to make-believe begins much earlier in infancy, when the mother uses marked affect to introduce play and pretending. Miraculously, a child as young as six months old knows when her mother is pretending to be sad or surprised, and she is able to demonstrate his awareness by her playful response. This is a very different picture when the mother is really experiencing difficult emotions, a circumstance that elicits distress in her preverbal offspring. Of course, this early form of make-believe requires the active participation of the parent to carry the child over the threshold into play. The child's own capacity to initiate make-believe occurs later, and the full flowering of her imaginative world is just taking off in the late toddler.

I believe the capacity to pretend is crucial for subsequent development but, for the late toddler, not yet fully secure; psychic equivalence, that is, the tendency to confuse mental contents with reality, is still prominent until three or four years old. In Mitchell's timeline, the early efforts to manage the nature of thought and reality through the pretend mode are thus inevitably intruded upon by the trauma of the sibling. Perhaps the appropriation of pretending by the child is accelerated by the need to cope with the trauma of displacement and the threatened eruption of overwhelming aggression from within, which take on a concreteness consistent with psychic equivalence. The pretend mode, as elaborated in the series of papers by Fonagy and Target (1996; 1998; 2000; Target and Fonagy 1996), offers the child a clearly delineated arena to differentiate thought from reality, even while this differentiation is not fully established. Thought is still in grave danger of being confused with reality, and the parameters of pretending must be underscored by the oft-repeated statement "Let's pretend. . . ."

As mentioned earlier, Mitchell describes the role of the sibling trauma in the evolution of sense of self, a very thought-provoking idea that resonates with my clinical experience. It is the baby-self that is now appropriated by the newborn; the toddler's regression is an identification with this usurper baby as well as a struggle to recapture that coveted identity. The toddler, formerly the beloved baby, is now just an ordinary child, who is still littler and less capable than everybody else and yet expected to do all kinds of ungratifying things, like be nice to the new baby and control his own body and emotions. This is particularly problematic vis-à-vis aggression, because the toddler's aggression is powerfully stimulated by the littleness, helplessness, and intrusiveness of the new baby. The sequence of triggers for aggression, described so well by Mayes and Cohen (1993), describes the earliest form as aggression in regard to possession; the sibling is a profound challenge to the child's possession of place (the baby role), person (the mother), and eventually objects (toys). The second wave of aggression will be discussed a little later.

Mitchell notes that it is the gendered self that bursts on the scene with the arrival of the gendered sibling, thereby dispelling the presumption of omnipotentiality. Her idea is that for the child, gender is not personally meaningful until the sibling trauma, when the "similar other," who is strongly identified as having a gender, intrudes and the child is forced into a comparison. A correlation from a different vantage point is provided by de Marneffe (1997), whose study of toddlers' understanding of gender and its chronology is consistent with Mitchell's position. Using clinical play interviews, de Marneffe presented very young children with anatomically correct dolls, also bearing other conventions of gender difference, such as hair length, and asked the toddlers to explain which one was like themselves. Those under thirty-six months chose the doll with superficial features that placed them in a girl or boy category—like hairstyle and clothing. It was only at thirty-six months that they made the link to a fixed body part, the genital. While I believe that toddlers know that they are boys and girls before thirty-six months, they do not understand the relationship of that fact to their bodies, they do not see the connection between gender and genital, and, in fact, they struggle to accept the fixity of gender up until latency (Senet 2004). The toddler, with ample opportunity to observe genital difference or sameness in a similar person, is faced with the birth of a sibling or is anticipating such a displacement. He is now neither baby nor grown-up, but, according to everyone, definitely boy or girl. Moreover, he is burdened by an exquisite sense of deficiency, of not being sufficient or the best, due to his growing awareness of other children and the looming potential for displacement that is the dark cloud of his childhood. He is permanently gendered, without any say in the matter, and has the impossible task of protecting his fragile ego from assaults of various types, from various places, including his own beloved parents, because he is little. This constitutes the second key trigger for aggression in the older child: Narcissistic injury takes ascendance over the struggle for possession in the course of early childhood (Mayes and Cohen 1993). The child loses his bearings and is now neither "his majesty the baby" nor the partner of his desired parent; everyone is cuter and more babied or smarter, bigger, and more capable.

I would like to describe some clinical material to further illustrate the reverberations of the sibling trauma and its interactions with subsequent developmental challenges, especially in regard to adolescence. It seems to me that puberty and adolescence are especially primed to reawaken this traumatic constellation, because one central task of adolescence is the integration of all childhood trauma (Blos 1968) and especially because this developmental period puts pressure on the very same fault lines: separation, identity, impulse control—both sexual and aggressive—gender, and a heightened requirement to compete and distinguish oneself from similar others (Vivona 2007). In fact, the hugely increased importance of the peer group in adolescence and the dual demands of fitting in and standing out (for example, as an excellent student, the popular girl, the star athlete) make this a time fraught with sibling-related conflict. In addition, adolescents must rework the relationship to the parents and embrace a new level of autonomy. These changes are powerfully affected by the unmistakable physical transformation, as the child becomes even more gendered, so to speak, and becomes a young man or woman with sexual desires that require further distancing from the oedipal objects. Suddenly (to paraphrase one of the patients I will describe, who frequently experienced transformations as explosions), there is the real possibility of creating children themselves and of repeating their own sibling trauma. This last point refers to another sibling issue that is frequently observed but never raised to the level of theory: Parents regularly experience a reedition of their childhood sibling experience with their own children, identifying with one offspring and seeing another as an important loved or hated sibling. Thus, the next generation is burdened with their traumatic legacy.

CLINICAL EXAMPLES

My clinical vignettes, which on the surface bear very little resemblance to each other, are distinguished by the struggle of each patient to manage the impact of the sibling trauma on the sense of self during its most crucial unfolding through adolescence. The first is Sonia, a girl of eleven, whose parents never married over many years of cohabitation and were in the midst of a painful but nonetheless relatively amicable separation. Her father, a charismatic figure in a glamorous industry, was also father to a much older child from a prior relationship, and already had moved on to a third partner. Sonia presented as an odd girl, with poor eye contact, impulsivity, and dysregulated affect. She was whiny, rambunctious, rude, and imperious. Raised bilingual, she was idiosyncratic in her syntax, often using phrases in a way that suggested she didn't understand the meaning of the words but treated them like objects to be hurled. For example, she often said to me, "You're spoiled!" in a singsong way that made no sense in the given moment and seemed like a parental admonition (which, incidentally, both parents denied using). Her behavior at school was described as peculiar and even bizarre at times; she seemed to be in her own world, talking to herself and unengaged in learning. Her relationships were typically threesomes formed with younger boys, in which someone was routinely hurt and excluded. After about six months of treatment, noteworthy for regressed behavior and childish play in sessions but overall improvement elsewhere, her father informed me that his new girlfriend was pregnant, and he asked for guidance as to how to address this with Sonia. Sonia's relationship to her father was already problematic; she was especially immature and provocative with him, frequently stating baldly, "I don't like him." She maintained this unmodulated stance despite her repeating play stories, enacted with a range of figurative toys, that focused on a paternal figure with longing, idealization, and anger. Her father's conversation with her about the expected baby was met by an unanticipated eruption. Sonia refused to go away on a planned trip with her father, his new partner, and her older half sibling. She was violently angry, refused to see the father's girlfriend, referred to her contemptuously as Monkeyface, and called the expected baby "the thing." What is interesting about this case in regard to our discussion is the dramatic impact of the mental representation of the baby, well in advance of its appearance. Mitchell's ideas shed new light on Sonia's repetition of exclusionary triangles, suggesting that sibling trauma may have been operating throughout this girl's development. I had addressed her need to triangulate and exclude as an enactment of her experience of her parents' former intense intimacy and her attempts to rupture it or intrude upon it. There is certainly evidence for the oedipal layer; Sonia slept in her parents' bed until at least age five. She utterly ignored and excluded her father by speaking in her mother's mother tongue, which he did not speak nor understand. In general, the layering of oedipal and sibling trauma is quite difficult to sort out when observed in older children and in adults, since development progresses and reorganizes prior experience. Interestingly, Sonia vigorously disavowed her oedipal wishes but was highly vocal in her rage about the father's imminent newborn. Sonia's lack of modulation allowed her to express directly what Mitchell describes. She said with grief, "I want to be the littlest one. Now he will never take care of me." This, of course, also confirms the unmentionable intensity of the oedipal layer.

The juxtaposition of these events with Sonia's pubescence is particularly interesting in regard to the interplay between sibling and oedipal dynamics. Sonia was decidedly unfeminine and even slightly disheveled when I met her, but she was already beginning to develop. Her resistance to her adolescent transformation was pervasive. Her attitude toward becoming a teenager—a stage that is frequently the source of excitement and dread for children—was colored by fear and denial; indeed, she continued to deny that the time had arrived even after menarche, pointing out that there was no "teen" in age twelve. The full throttle rage about the new sibling no doubt heavily recruited her sibling trauma from toddlerhood but also served to defend against her interest, excitement, and fear about her own imminent womanhood and capacity to make babies.

Another case where the sibling trauma persisted well into adolescence is a girl I treated for several years from puberty into late adolescence. This girl, whom I will call Becca, had a younger brother, Nick, four years her junior, and was acutely aware of her mother's obstetrical history, including miscarriages and a subsequent hysterectomy that occurred when Becca first began treatment. Becca was highly symptomatic when we first met; she was very anxious, irritable, and enmeshed in a hostile dependent relationship with her mother, whom she both idolized and rejected. Her own immediate concern was a rupture in her relationship with an idealized classmate, the quintessential "popular girl," who ended their friendship because (I inferred from the evidence) Becca was too possessive. Becca's separation anxiety came into full flower in the early phase of the analysis, triggered by a failed attempt to attend sleepaway camp, the very one her mother had attended for almost a decade. From the outset, Becca was insomniac, clingy, and (she later disclosed) determined to suffer even when she began to feel a little better. Thereafter, separation anxiety became a constant feature of her life and our extratransferential work; within our relationship, she steadfastly maintained an unwillingness to "have feelings" about me. She needed to be in control, and she was not going to think about my life, my family, or my other patients.

Becca was very focused on her brother, Nick, whose birth was associated with two "sudden" disappearances by her mother: the first for the actual birth, when Becca awoke to find her parents gone and herself in the care of her grandmother, and the second, about two weeks later, when the mother was admitted to hospital once again in the middle of the night for obstetrical complications. In this case, a neighbor stepped in to "suddenly" stand in for her parents. Nick was an especially troubling sibling early in his life, since he was discovered to have life-threatening allergies, which completely absorbed their mother's anxious attention. Moreover, he was an outgoing and attention-seeking child with noteworthy athletic talent.

Through many years of analytic work, it became clear that Becca recreated her family experience by positioning herself as a self-determined outsider, either explicitly or implicitly in conflict with the popular crowd or other iterations of threatening peers. Her relationship to competition was all-consuming but entirely disavowed; she held herself above others, for example becoming the leader of the "unpops" (the unpopular girls) in middle school and declining every opportunity to reconcile with her popular former friend. Becca was very close to a next-door neighbor, Sally, almost exactly her age, who appeared to be the model for the idealized peer. This was heightened by the fact that Sally's father is a local celebrity. The two girls were raised together, with Becca rigidly claiming seniority by virtue of six weeks, while simultaneously exalting Sally and their bond in a way intended to make everyone feel left out, including both mothers. Their favorite movie, which they reenacted regularly, was *The Parent Trap*, in which one young actress plays a set of twins who try to reconcile their estranged parents. Sally was Becca's ultimate secret weapon in her battle with other girls, and the two also established a pattern of twinning, whereby Becca sought out a "soul mate" and, often intrusively and possessively, demanded an exclusive relationship. The other side of this coin was also established early, when the two girls excitedly excluded other girls of the same age, particularly those drawn to the celebrity of Sally's family. Becca went on to recreate this as she allowed girls she considered needy and "annoying" to become dependent on her and then brutally ditched them.

Becca entered adolescence with enormous anxiety. Despite her bravado and sophistication she was frightened of any kind of loss of control, including sex and openly competitive aggression. She was effortlessly capable academically, but only rarely did she really push herself. When she entered a large and rigorous high school, these traits emerged in sharp relief. She did brilliantly but did not really strive to take the most challenging curriculum. She was disdainful of other girls who were focused on college early on, as was typical for that environment. She managed to mentally obliterate the popular girls and all the boys, because of the various threats they represented. The way she managed boys is especially of interest because, despite her full control of Nick at home by relentless provocation and overstimulation, she was unable to form friendly or even friendly/fighting (that is, sadomasochistic) relationships with boys. They rarely came up in her thoughts with me and when they did, she spoke of them in one of three ways: first, fondly supercilious—an attitude she developed briefly toward some younger boys who were in a class with her; second, intensely and coldly competitive; or third, and most commonly, as objects to be gotten and used to outdo other girls. She was desperate to "keep up" with the girls who were having adolescent experiences, like hooking up and experimenting with alcohol, and to not let anyone "get ahead." However, it became clear that her anxiety and inhibitions were so great and her conflicts so intense that she could not engage with boys in a way that might lead to an actual relationship. Invariably, in typical adolescent settings where she might engage with boys (or for that matter other girls), she would complain of feeling "bored and left out," which became the catchphrase for her quasi-dissociated state of mind when surrounded by the horde of similar others interacting in exciting but terrifying ways.

At heart, she preferred, like Peter Pan, to declare, "I won't grow up," and she tried to hold back any others who would move forward. She even suggested that she was preventing her own physical development because of her deep discomfort with her sexuality. At home, up to the moment of her admission to a prestigious college, she was querulous and childish, continuing to burst into tears over separations and arguments.

Here we have all the earmarks of a sibling trauma, with impact on separation anxiety, competition, gender and sexuality, and management of aggression. Becca's analysis can be discussed from many angles, and certainly the vertical dimension is hugely important, but the lateral lens illuminates a pervasive aspect of her psychopathology and addresses a core defect in her sense of her own identity and her discrete existence. One especially poignant manifestation of this is her difficulty valuing her own life and experience and her preoccupation with the possibility that something more exciting is happening elsewhere, especially among others in her family. It is as if she is constantly reliving the experience of waking up and discovering that her mother has disappeared into the embrace a new baby and she is locked out. Another manifestation is the recurrent theme in her dream life of "suddenly" discovering that she has an additional sibling, the product of a past liaison of her mother, who has been kept secret from her. Even as she considered the possibility of attending the accepted students' weekend event at the terrific college where she will likely go, she worried about the overnight separation from home and the fact that it required that she not attend the wedding of a distant paternal cousin with whom she had no significant relationship: "I am afraid," she said, "that I'll miss out on something." Her own experience and her own opportunities for stimulation, excitement, and intimacy pale in comparison to what "the others" are doing.

These are fragments of very full and complex adolescent treatments that have many other important facets and thematic conflicts. Especially in the latter case of Becca, when the clinical picture is unfolding far from the original sibling trauma, the complexity of subsequent development is of course a confounding distortion of that early event. However, I choose these cases to show how the sibling trauma lives on in the unconscious (and indeed, the conscious) mind and shapes experience throughout life. Mitchell has done our field a huge service by pointing out the reality that siblings are a force to be reckoned with in mental life, and that the trauma of the sibling is a mental experience of early childhood that does not require the birth of a sibling. It is the dawning awareness of the world of similar others that deals a crushing blow to infantile narcissism at a very young age, even before the child has ready access to pretending, which helps to soften the disappointments of the oedipal period (Gilmore 2011).

REFERENCES

BARRIE J. M. (1906). *Peter Pan in Kensington Gardens.* New York: Scribner's Sons.
BLOS, P. (1968). Character formation in adolescence. *Psychoanalytic Study of the Child* 23:245–63.
DE MARNEFFE, D. (1997). Bodies and words: A study of young children's genital and gender knowledge. *Gender & Psychoanalysis* 2:3–33.
FONAGY, P., AND M. TARGET (1996). Playing with reality: I. Theory of mind and the normal development of psychic reality. *International Journal of Psychoanalysis* 77:217–33.
——— (1998). Mentalization and the changing aims of child psychoanalysis. *Psychoanalytic Dialogues* 8:87–114.
——— (2000). Playing with reality: III. The persistence of dual psychic reality in borderline patients. *International Journal of Psychoanalysis* 81:853–73.
GILMORE, K. (2011). Pretend play and development in early childhood (with implications for the oedipal phase). *Journal of the American Psychoanalytic Association* 59 (6): 1157–82.
GRAHAM, I. (1988). The sibling object and its transferences: Alternate organizer of the middle field. *Psychoanalytic Inquiry* 8:88–107.

Mayes, L., and D. Cohen (1993). The social matrix of aggression: Enactments and representations of loving and hating in the first years of life. *Psychoanalytic Study of the Child* 48:145–69.

Senet, N. V. (2004). A study of preschool children's linking of genitals and gender. *Psychoanalytic Quarterly* 73:291–334.

Sharpe, S., and A. Rosenblatt (1994). Oedipal sibling triangles. *Journal of the American Psychoanalytic Association* 42:491–523.

Target, M., and P. Fonagy (1996). Playing with reality: II. The development of psychic reality from a theoretical perspective. *International Journal of Psychoanalysis* 77:459–79.

Vivona, J. (2007). Sibling differentiation, identity development, and the lateral dimension of psychic life. *Journal of the American Psychoanalytic Association* 55:1191–1215.

Sibling Recognition and the Development of Identity

Intersubjective Consequences of Sibling Differentiation in the Sister Relationship

JEANINE M. VIVONA, Ph.D.

Identity is, among other things, a means to adapt to the others around whom one must fit. Psychoanalytic theory has highlighted ways in which the child fits in by emulating important others, especially through identification. Alternately, the child may fit into the family and around important others through differentiation, an unconscious process that involves developing or accentuating qualities and desires in oneself that are expressly different from the perceived qualities of another person and simultaneously suppressing qualities and desires that are perceived as similar. With two clinical vignettes centered on the sister relationship, the author demonstrates that recognition of identity differences that result from sibling differentiation carries special significance in the sibling relationship and simultaneously poses particular intersubjective challenges. To the extent that the spotlight of sibling recognition delimits the lateral space one may occupy, repeatedly frustrated desires for sibling recognition may have enduring consequences for one's sense of self-worth and expectations of relationships with peers and partners.

Jeanine M. Vivona is Professor of Psychology, The College of New Jersey, Ewing, N.J., and adjunct clinical faculty, Department of Psychiatry, Pennsylvania Hospital, Philadelphia.

The author is indebted to the patients who generously gave permission for use of their stories in this paper, a version of which was presented at the Winter Meeting of the American Psychoanalytic Association, January 2012.

The Psychoanalytic Study of the Child 67, ed. Claudia Lament, Robert A. King, Samuel Abrams, A. Scott Dowling, and Paul M. Brinich (Yale University Press, copyright © 2013 by Claudia Lament, Robert A. King, Samuel Abrams, A. Scott Dowling, and Paul M. Brinich).

WE HAVE NOT HAD A PLACE WITHIN PSYCHOANALYTIC THEORY TO house our knowledge of sibling relationships and dynamics. Lacking a home for our observations, we have tried to fit them into a theory that privileges the parent-child relationship, yielding our various useful but incomplete understandings of siblings as parental substitutes and displacements. With her theory of the lateral dimension of psychic life and the sibling trauma from which it is born, Juliet Mitchell has given us a place from which to develop our understanding of sibling relationships and dynamics. Once disparate, misrecognized, and fleeting, our insights about siblings can now be more effectively integrated, expanded, and used.

My interest is in using Mitchell's framework of intersecting lateral and vertical dimensions of psychic life for conceptualizing the entwined yet distinct roles of siblings and parents in the inner world of the individual and for understanding unique sibling influences on identity development. Previously, I have explored ways in which children position themselves within the family constellation via their identities, specifically their identifications with and differentiations from both parents and siblings (Vivona 2007; 2010). Here I focus on the interpersonal and intersubjective reverberations of such positioning, bringing together Mitchell's theory of the *lateral dimension of psychic life* and Jessica Benjamin's theory of *mutual recognition* to consider the importance of mutual recognition of identity differences within sibling relationships.

The Lateral Dimension and the Sibling Trauma

According to Mitchell (2000; 2003; this volume), all children experience themselves initially as the only child of their parents and thus at the center of the familial universe. Eventually, however, children realize the presence of their siblings, who threaten the assumed precious position at the familial center. When the child realizes she has siblings, she experiences a shocking sense of displacement, which Mitchell terms the *sibling trauma* (formerly, the crisis of nonuniqueness). The child now understands: I am *not* my parents' one and only; I am not at the center; my position in the family is not unique. This experience of dethronement, often noted in the experience of the firstborn child on the birth of the second child (for example, Adler 1927; Kris and Ritvo 1983; Sharpe and Rosenblatt 1994), is not specific to elder children but is universal. That is, because the sibling trauma is precipitated by the *awareness* or the *possibility* of siblings, not only by actual sibling birth, it is experienced by all children, regardless of birth order.

Although the sibling trauma is universal, it is shaped by the particulars of the family to which the siblings belong. Mitchell ("Siblings," in this volume) has elaborated the sibling trauma through the experience of the prototypical toddler who is displaced by the new baby, describing the trauma as involving "the arrival of . . . the one who is different but who should have been the 'same'" (see the section "The Case For . . ."). From this point on, the child must contend with difference as well as otherness, particularly the "minimal difference" of the baby, who is as the toddler was but no longer is. For the baby, on the other hand, the trauma of displacement may occur insidiously, as the baby comes to realize the presence of siblings who were undeniably already there. Whether the baby expects the older sibling to be the same or different, we do not know.

The sibling trauma compels the child to attempt to reclaim a unique position in the family and simultaneously to avert recurrence of the original catastrophe by fending off potential rivals. This struggle to regain a position of uniqueness and worth in the family propels development along the lateral dimension of psychic life. For Mitchell, the developmental challenge is to master the sibling trauma by finding a position or place of worth among the similar others of the world. For example, she has elaborated the ways in which familial trauma and autism may deny a sense of lateral place to the child (2000). Her concern is primarily an existential one, with a focus on how the child deals with and defends against the sense of annihilation that is wrought by the presence of the sibling who occludes the mother's view, thus hindering the mother's full recognition of the child.

Barring such atypical situations as trauma and autism, and departing from Mitchell (2000) on this point, I believe many children do find a place in their families and among their siblings. For such children, the predominant developmental challenge of the lateral dimension is not primarily existential but centers instead on identity: Who does my position among my siblings allow me to be? What is the shape of my place in the family and in the world? What is the value of my place?

Identity, in this sense, is the psychological manifestation of position, a way to know where you are in relation to someone else. Indeed, we can and do position ourselves with respect to others with and through our identities: You are the smart one, so I will be the funny one. Identity then records the child's attempts to resolve the sibling trauma, to regain a unique, valued place in the world, and perhaps to minimize harm to the sibling. In this way, the original sibling trauma leaves its mark on identity. Thus, identity comprises compromises, which imbue lateral relationships throughout life, including, at least potentially, the transference.

SIBLING DIFFERENTIATION

Identity is, among other things, a means to adapt to the others around whom one must fit. Psychoanalytic theory has highlighted ways in which the child fits in by emulating important others, especially through identification. With respect to the lateral dimension, for instance, the child can reclaim a sense of place in the family by identifying with a parent (Mitchell 2000). I have proposed that the child may also fit into the family and around important others through a process of differentiation (Vivona 2007). Differentiation is an unconscious process that involves developing or accentuating qualities and desires in oneself that are expressly different from the perceived qualities of another person and simultaneously suppressing qualities and desires that are perceived as similar.

I believe differentiation is a common strategy for managing the demands of development along the lateral dimension and its inherent conflicts over sibling rivalry. That is, because the child both loves and hates her siblings, she both does and does not want to defeat them in the battle for a favored position in the family. Differentiation enables the child to obviate the sibling rivalry by amplifying aspects of self that are perceived as different from those of the sibling and disowning aspects of self that are perceived as similar, effectively carving out a unique territory for oneself while eliminating or minimizing the common grounds for sibling competition. As a consequence of differentiation, siblings may appear to be quite different from one another because their similarities have been suppressed or denied by one or both. Such a strategy may be particularly likely when a child perceives a sibling to be too strong or too weak to fight, or when a familial climate is intolerant of overt sibling competition. Parenthetically, differentiation may also operate with respect to parents, for instance, toward the parent of the other sex during oedipal development; however, because such differentiation is complementary to the identification with the same-sex parent, it often goes unrecognized (see Vivona 2010).

Differentiation, like identification, is an internal process with relational consequences. The perceived and actual responses of others to the qualities one puts forth in the world, to the place one claims as one's own, inform one's expectations and experiences of lateral relationships. The child looks to others for validation of the place she wishes to take among them, a place characterized by difference as well as similarities, which the siblings must recognize (Mitchell 2003). Through mutual recognition, siblings mark the position that each may occupy; the spotlight of sibling recognition delimits the space within which the child may be or, perhaps, must be.

Mutual Recognition of Sameness and Difference

The profound importance and inherent difficulty of mutual recognition has been most fully articulated, I believe, by Jessica Benjamin. Benjamin (1988; 1998) describes recognition as the accurate perception and acceptance of the other as a subject who exists independently of the self, outside its fantasies and projections. Development of both subjectivity and intersubjectivity depends on recognition.

Benjamin's concept of recognition is an intersubjective extension of Winnicott's (1969) insight about the importance of the mother's survival of the infant's aggression. Both Benjamin's recognition and Winnicott's survival require that the other validate one's actual self, one's desires, feelings, or qualities, without either denying or repudiating them. In Winnicott's view, once the infant finds that the mother survives his aggression, the child can experience a world beyond his control, a world inhabited by separate others to whom he can then relate. In Benjamin's intersubjective extension, the child also recognizes that the mother, like the self, is a separate subject with her own desires and autonomy. Like Winnicott, Benjamin believes that a genuine interpersonal connection requires this kind of separation; by contrast, when one relates to the other as if part of the self, complementarity rather than true relatedness is the result. In this type of relatedness, the other is seen as the complement to the self in a zero-sum game between an aggressor and a victim, a doer or a done to.

It turns out to be surprisingly difficult for mother and child to recognize one another as autonomous desiring subjects, especially if the child is a girl. One obstacle to mutual recognition is the infant's ardent fantasy of an all-giving selfless mother, a mother who is an object and not a subject. This fantasy both undermines the infant's ability to appreciate the autonomous subjectivity of the mother and, because it imbues cultural ideals of mothering, complicates the mother's acknowledgment of her own desires as well as the desires of her daughters (see also Chodorow 1978). Benjamin (1995) notes that because the father is outside both the relational tangle of the mother-infant dyad and the cultural sanctions against maternal desire, he can more simply serve as the parent who recognizes the child's desiring self. In the case Benjamin (1995) uses to illustrate this point, the adult brother is a crucial source of recognition.

Benjamin's original focus was on the mutual recognition of desire and autonomy, qualities shared by mother and infant, indeed shared by all. More recently, she has elaborated the importance of negotiation of difference, in particular the challenge of clashing subjectivities, which occurs when the needs or wishes of the one are different from those of the other (Benjamin 2004; 2006). Because such clashes are unavoidable in a relationship between two separate, different people, mutual recognition inevitably breaks down. At such times, the maintenance of a relationship that fully comprises both selves requires that such failures in recognition can themselves be recognized so that they can be repaired or mourned. Such moments challenge the one (the parent, sibling, or analyst) to *surrender* to the other's way or desire or experience, to enter into it without relinquishing one's own way, such as with a feeling that one's own way is wrong, and without submitting, such as out of a sense of duty or a need to comply. This surrender requires more than tolerance of the other; it requires participation that implies acceptance of a legitimate, if different, way of doing or being. Such surrender is difficult indeed, yet it creates the potential for mutual participation in something new, something that is not *your way* or *my way* but *our way*; Benjamin calls this the "shared third" (2006) or the "one in the third" (2004).

Recognition, then, must be specific; it matters who the other is and what the other does and does not recognize. Recognition as a desiring subject by the father does not meet the need for recognition by the mother (Benjamin 1995). Recognition of sameness does not obviate the need for recognition of difference. Indeed, because identity is not unitary but comprises multiple qualities or aspects, any of which may be expressed or hidden depending on particular relational contexts (Benjamin 1998), it seems likely that recognition by the other of specific qualities, differences as well as similarities, is necessary for one to feel accepted and whole within relationships. It seems likely, too, that recognition may bolster one's ability to tolerate multiplicity within the self, a goal of development and treatment; that is, recognition potentiates the ability to own the aspects, qualities, desires, and feelings that constitute one's identity while also allowing that no single aspect, quality, or desire is ever the whole story. Recognition by the other facilitates the process of knowing and owning one's self.

SIBLING RECOGNITION OF DIFFERENTIATED IDENTITY

Weaving together Mitchell's insights about the lateral dimension, Benjamin's about recognition, and my own about differentiation, I can now make the argument that sibling recognition of differences, particularly differentiated aspects of identity, plays an important role in the development of both identity and the capacity for lateral relatedness.

Difference, I believe, may become the particular testing ground for recognition of identity. That is, when the child wants to know whether she is loved for who she *really* is, she may pose the challenge in terms of difference between self and other. By contrast, recognition of sameness of self and other can be construed as a reflection of the other's self-love (that is, she loves me because or when I am like her) and, if so, does not satisfy the desire for recognition and validation of one's own unique self. Consequently, more than the other's otherness, it is her difference from oneself that makes her recognition important in the identity development process. Yet Benjamin (2004; 2006) implies that recognition of difference may be an even greater intersubjective challenge than recognition of sameness. Moreover, if Mitchell (this volume) is correct that the toddler expects the new baby to be similar to the self, the older sibling's willingness to recognize differences in the younger may be further attenuated.

Recognition of differences that result from sibling differentiation carries special significance in the sibling relationship and simultaneously poses particular intersubjective challenges. The child undertakes the differentiation from the sibling with an unconscious hope to quell contentious rivalry and facilitate a more harmonious sibling relationship. The very differences the child has foregrounded in order to protect the relationship with the sibling, differences that are experienced as profound or even necessary, are those the child wishes and perhaps even needs the sibling to recognize in order to feel known and loved. Yet when differences are amplified and similarities suppressed, when one's identity is defined in opposition to the other, intersubjective clashes may be frequent; failures of mutual recognition are inevitable.

Sibling recognition serves a different developmental purpose than parental recognition and therefore leaves a different mark on subsequent relationships. Recognition by the one who is beside, whose differences from oneself are "minimal" yet consequential, who is a rival for the treasured place at the center of the family, acknowledges the shape of the position one has attempted to forge. Because that position is relative to the others who are beside and is meant to accommodate or to displace them, the validation of those accommodated or displaced others will secure that place, for good or for ill, and the invalidation of those same others will unsettle it.

Two Clinical Vignettes

Each of the two cases that follow illustrates a woman's yearning for the recognition of her elder sister. Although different in many respects, each woman articulated a persistently painful sense of being different from and thus unacceptable to her sister. Aspects of each woman's identity and sense of self-worth were organized around the sister. Moreover, each woman's poignant childhood longing for her sister's acceptance and validation reverberated into adulthood and through the transference. In the presentations that follow, I focus on each woman's relationship with her sister, particularly frustrated wishes for recognition from her sister and the implications for developing identity and lateral relationships. To preserve anonymity, I have omitted most of the biographical details.

ANN

Ann's entry into psychotherapy was prompted by concerns about changes in her responsibilities at work, which she knew would require her to be more interpersonally and emotionally available to others. This activated Ann's anxieties over interpersonal intimacy, particularly those prompted by interactions that required her to reveal aspects of her self. Her three siblings, and especially her only sister, Nancy, figured prominently from the start, as did an acutely mixed experience of the relationship with me, which she described early on as akin to "the anguish of being in love." Ann's guarded hopes that I would value the differences between us were often expressed in the context of thoughts about her relationship with Nancy.

Ann was the third of four children born to devout religious parents; the church played a central role in the life of her extended family, which included many missionaries. Nancy was the eldest and four years older than Ann. Ann also had two brothers, one older and one younger; all of the children were about two years apart in age.

In Ann's recollections of childhood, Nancy was the paragon of perfection. She was an outstanding student and deeply religious, an organized and orderly child who regularly exceeded the expectations of their parents. Ann both idealized Nancy and saw Nancy as fundamentally different from herself. Nancy was the personification of an unreachable ideal, the kind of person Ann felt she should be but never would. Their similarities, for instance the athletic skill that made both of them star athletes, did not preoccupy her in the ways that their differences did. Ann's longing to feel accepted and loved by Nancy was palpable into adulthood; the disappointment of that longing was a recurrent pain.

Toward the beginning of our work, Ann recounted a childhood incident that represented her present struggles with Nancy and foretold the transference. During childhood, Ann and Nancy shared a bedroom. Their differences made the sharing difficult. Ann was "very messy," with belongings cascading from drawers and strewn about the room; by contrast, Nancy was neat and tidy, keeping everything in its place. Nancy prodded Ann to be neater, more like her. On one memorable occasion, Nancy offered Ann a "surprise" if she could keep her dresser drawers closed for a full week. With considerable effort, Ann succeeded; it was difficult for her to acquiesce to her sister's way and to forego her own, but the promised prize made the sacrifice seem worth the trouble. At the end of the week, with pleasure and fanfare, Nancy presented the surprise reward: a "popcorn party."

But Ann hated popcorn and thought Nancy must know this about her. Ann was stunned, disappointed, and hurt. The ill-chosen prize confirmed Ann's sense that Nancy did not deem worthy the ways in which Ann differed from her, that she recognized and validated only sameness. Indeed, both the challenge to keep her drawers closed and the popcorn reward were designed to change Ann, to make her more like Nancy, rather than designed *for* her as she was. In the tension of difference that infused their shared room, it seemed to Ann that Nancy would accept and love her if Ann were similar to her, and would ignore, reject, or try to change her if she were different. Yet Ann longed for Nancy to recognize her as unique, not as a replica of someone else.

The context for recounting the memory of the popcorn party was Ann's upcoming trip to visit Nancy. Although Ann longed to renew her connection with Nancy, which had been relatively dormant for a few years, she dreaded the visit. She felt caught in an impossible bind: If she played it safe and kept things superficial with Nancy, she would regret the lost opportunity to reconnect with the sister she loved; yet if she talked with Nancy about the important things in her life, she would once again evoke Nancy's refusal to accept her for who she was, aspects of which Nancy viewed as sinful. Nancy's religion instructed her to change the sin while loving the sinner, both of which Nancy strived to do. Ann felt as though Nancy had always seen her as the sinner she must love, even while she prayed that Ann would eventually choose goodness over sin, neatness over messiness, compliance over uniqueness, even while she prayed that Ann would keep her drawers closed. Despite Ann's efforts and Nancy's obvious love of her younger sister, Nancy did not recognize the legitimacy of fundamental aspects of Ann's identity.

Ann's concern with Nancy's acceptance was striking, as was her sadness and longing. What made this elder sister so important to the younger's sense of self and self-worth? It is tempting to answer this question in terms of parental displacement: Ann's conflicts in relation to her mother had been displaced onto Nancy. Indeed, Ann depicted Nancy as like their mother, only more so; compared to their mother, Nancy was more perfectionistic, more devoutly religious, more self-critical and self-denying, and, in adulthood, more openly rejecting of some aspects of Ann's identity. In contrast to Nancy's explicit condemnation, Ann's mother expressed concern and confusion about Ann, but not rejection. Nonetheless, Ann also saw herself as very different from her mother and wished for greater closeness with her; by contrast, she felt closer to her father and more comfortably similar to him in ways she cherished. Perhaps, given this particular set of familial dynamics, the sister provided a clearer standard of acceptability, whereas the mother was more inscrutable. Perhaps this sister, as caretaker of her younger siblings, was the omnipresent version of a mother who sometimes disappeared into bouts of depression and self-doubt.

I believe these maternal dynamics did infuse Ann's inner relation to Nancy to an important degree, that the internalized sister was in some sense a version of the mother. Yet that was not all. There was also a longing to be loved and known as both unique and equal, which was associated particularly with the sister alongside her, with the lateral dimension. Even Ann's closest friendships tended to be unsettled by her striving for such recognition and, alongside, the expectation that she would not receive it. This was for her the "anguish of being in love," the painful simultaneous activation of specific desire, fragile hope, and palpable fear.

In the therapy, we experienced the sisterly struggles. Ann often noticed our differences, and there were many: She would never dress as I did, use a pink phone, or write an academic paper. She saw me as a decidedly different kind of girl than she was. She remarked lightly on these differences, but I had a sense she was weighing their importance. Could someone like me understand and accept her? By contrast, Ann enjoyed the ways we were similar, for instance, the similar aspects of our work.

An early interaction was emblematic of the negotiation of difference in our relationship. Ann decided she did not want to call me "Doctor," this being too formal and distancing, she said, yet she was uncomfortable using my first name. So she gave me a nickname, as she often did with those she liked, which had a similar sound to her own name. She knew this was a bold move and outside the rules; she carefully watched my reactions while declining my invitations to discuss it. I understood Ann's naming me in this way as reflecting her desire to forge a connection with me that felt intimate and unique rather than compliant and rule-bound; following others' rules and going "by the book" (which for her conjured thoughts of the Bible) did not tell her what she felt she needed to know about how I "really" felt about her or about the kind of connection I would allow her to have with me. More specifically, through this nickname, she positioned me in a particular lateral way with respect to herself: similar and different yet close.

Then she watched me to see if I would allow her to have this kind of connection to me, if I would accept her recognition of me as someone close and important to her and also unlike her in crucial ways, if I would tolerate a name and thus a connection that was uniquely ours. She was relieved that I did not reject the nickname, but the real joy came, she told me, when I started to refer to myself by the name she gave me. This acceptance through participation requires the kind of surrender to the other that is intrinsic to mutual recognition. I had a feeling of giving something up in doing this, relinquishing a bit of my comfortable authority, allowing little sister to have a say in how we would do things in our shared room.

BETHANY

Bethany, like Ann, was born when her sister was four years old. From the start of her psychotherapy with me, Bethany described a powerful sense that her true self was invisible to the world, a sense that was, particularly in our early days, associated with memories of her sister, Julie. Bethany felt that Julie had resented her birth and viewed her primarily as an unwelcome and unnecessary intruder onto the family scene. In Bethany's eyes, Julie was the prototypical firstborn who refused to be interested in the baby, and Bethany was the adoring younger sister, repeatedly rebuffed.

Bethany described Julie as a child who was easily upset and quick to anger and who required considerable attention and support from their parents. Thus, Julie took up a large space in the family, and Bethany saw no choice but to fit into the small space left for her. Consequently,

Sibling Recognition and Development of Identity 77

Bethany became "the easy one," who was responsible, did well in school, and did not make or cause a fuss for anyone, including Julie.

But Bethany sensed that her ease and accomplishments, and the parental praise she received for them, did tend to upset Julie. Indeed, Julie seemed to bristle at the role Bethany had adopted in differentiation from her. For instance, Julie protested when Bethany received "special treatment" from their parents, as seemed to happen frequently; even in adulthood, Julie sometimes referred to Bethany as "the princess in the ivory tower," who seemed to get whatever she wanted, although as an adult Bethany felt the love and humor in this characterization of her more than the criticism and resentment she felt as a child. In childhood, Bethany recalled that when she looked to Julie for validation of her accomplishments, for instance when she began to read, Julie tended to respond with a roll of her eyes and a sarcastic "Nice." Julie did not share in her enjoyment of Bethany's new abilities as Bethany wished she would.

Faced with the difficult choice of upstaging and upsetting her sister or remaining in the wings, Bethany chose the latter. She tried to stay within Julie's image of her, to stay consistent with Julie's projections rather than to move outside the spotlight of her sister's recognition. This eventually became Bethany's general interpersonal strategy with her peers, which she called "the conspiracy of cooperation." She complied with her understanding of who the other wanted or needed her to be; when she experienced tension or disagreement with another person, she interpreted this to mean that she had ceased or failed to cooperate, and she expected outrage and rejection to follow.

In a strategy similar to "cooperation," Bethany followed her mother's adage "stay under the radar" as a way to get what she wanted without calling attention to herself. Bethany saw herself as like her mother in important ways, and she appreciated the power and competence her mother showed without an apparent need for fanfare or applause. Similarly, Bethany quietly went about being a strong student and a helpful daughter. But, perhaps unlike her mother, Bethany did want attention and recognition; she became tired of being overlooked and wanted the spotlight, at least some of the time.

I wondered, then, about the roles of sister and mother in motivating the strategies of "cooperation" and "under the radar." Bethany described a childhood memory that suggested she viewed her sister as an important protagonist: When the sisters and their mother would go for rides in the car, Julie insisted on taking the front seat, leaving Bethany always in the rear. Consistent with her cooperative stance, Bethany did not recall protesting this arrangement, but she did recall that her mother instituted a policy they called "a month in the front," whereby the girls would take turns in the front seat, each for a predetermined length of time. Bethany recalled the mixed feelings she had during her turns in the front, enjoying the better view and the privileged position next to her mother while feeling guilt and discomfort that her sister was in the back. Thus, although her mother advocated "staying under the radar," Bethany perceived her mother as recognizing and validating her desire to be in the privileged position, in particular to have something more than Julie had, whereas Julie always seemed to protest.

As with Ann, I was struck by the importance of this older sister to the younger's sense of self and self-worth. The sisterly influence on Bethany was particularly striking for two reasons. First, the sister dynamics did not seem to mirror the parental dynamics. Bethany felt close to both parents and was recognized in different ways by each. Her longing to be recognized was expressed specifically with respect to Julie. Second, in her relationships beyond the family, Bethany struggled to a greater degree with her acceptance and worth in lateral relationships than in hierarchical ones. For instance, she described many experiences with co-workers when she adopted a cooperative attitude and felt invisible or when she allowed herself to take the front seat by moving outside her perception of the other's image of her and subsequently anticipated and sometimes experienced painful rejection. This dilemma became particularly pronounced after she received a promotion at work, which catapulted her from the wings into the spotlight. She recounted the "month in the front" memory in the context of exploring her intense discomfort in her relationships with her co-workers following her promotion. Her relationships with her immediate supervisors were particularly fraught, marked by competitiveness, tension, and misunderstanding. By contrast, with those higher up in the organization, Bethany was concerned about measuring up and struggled to meet expectations she perceived as contradictory, inscrutable, and ever changing. In important ways, then, Bethany's sense of what her peers in particular would and would not tolerate in her bore the stamp of her struggles for her older sister's recognition.

In contrast to the world of work, Bethany's lateral struggles were more subtle than pronounced in the transference. Bethany tended to avoid challenging my authority or expertise too vigorously, assuming perhaps that I, like Julie, wished her not to encroach on my territory. At times, she would share her enthusiastic psychological insights about others, such as her co-workers, and then watch for signs that I was "rolling my eyes" at her attempts to do "my job." When she had reason to believe she had greater knowledge or skill than I had, she tended to believe instead that I was hiding my greater expertise from her, in this way denying the possibility that she had equaled or exceeded me.

DISCUSSION: WILL SHE ACCEPT ME AS I AM?

Ann and Bethany each viewed herself as fundamentally different from her only sister, each longed for her sister's recognition and acceptance of the ways that they were different, and both despaired receiving that recognition. For both Ann and Bethany, the early sister relationship was carried forward into adult peer relationships in the form of expectations that unique aspects of self would either be ignored or repudiated; that is, both expected that they would not be recognized by peers as they had not been by their sisters. Both women believed that revealing aspects of themselves threatened their peer relationships and thus felt they gained closeness with others only if they hid aspects of themselves. For both Ann and Bethany, struggles for recognition were voiced most powerfully in the context of sibling relationships and appeared to shape lateral relationships in particular, although the influences of sibling and parent relationships and lateral and vertical dimensions must certainly be entwined.

The similar longing for sisterly recognition is perhaps all the more intriguing in light of the many obvious differences between Ann and Bethany. To name a few: Bethany felt close to her mother, saw herself as similar to her mother, and often felt recognized and understood by her; by contrast, Ann felt more distant and different from her mother. Bethany felt capable of surpassing her sister, whereas Ann felt unable to match or surpass hers; consequently, acknowledging differences between self and sister tended to evoke guilt in Bethany and shame in Ann. Bethany attempted to manage her struggles for sister and peer recognition with a strategy of "cooperation" and acquiescence, as she tried to stay within the other's image of her; by contrast, Ann mobilized opposition and, in childhood, disobedience in her struggles for recognition, more openly challenging the other to accept her way.

A final difference between Ann and Bethany concerns the way they understood the positions they believed their sisters would allow them to occupy. Ann believed her sister wanted her to be similar to herself, whereas Bethany believed her sister wanted her to remain the dissimilar baby rather than to grow up and become more like her. Thus, Ann's sister is reminiscent of the prototypical older child who expects the new baby to be the same (Mitchell, this volume). Relatedly, Ann enjoyed the many qualities and interests she shared with her only younger sibling, a brother who was her closest ally in the family; their differences did not disrupt her feelings of closeness to him the way they did with her sister. By contrast, Bethany's sister is described as one who amplifies and invests in the differences between the self and the new baby, as the older child sometimes does, and expects the baby to be and to remain different. Thus, we may speculate (remembering that we are seeing each of them through her sister's eyes) that these older sisters present two ways that the older sibling attempts to contend with the new baby: amplifying sameness and amplifying difference.

Turning to identity, the clinical material suggests that one influence on the development of identity may be the perceived acceptability to siblings of one's qualities or ways of being. What place, the child seems to ask, will my sibling make for me? Who must I be to fit into that place? Some aspects of this perceived place may fit well, as did the athleticism Ann shared with her sister. Other aspects of self, those that appear to elicit sibling rejection or ridicule, may become the danger zones of identity, the aspects of self one believes peers will not accept and whose expression threatens peer relationships. For Ann, these danger zones were defined by her differences from the obedient Nancy; her tests of others' love of her were designed to determine their tolerance and even enjoyment of her playing outside the rules. For Bethany, the danger was in exceeding her sister in their similar pursuits, so that she expected her talents and accomplishments, such as her promotion at work, to be interpersonally costly.

What accounts for the similar powerful influence of the *sister* on the sense of self and self-worth of these two different women? It cannot be explained by unusual features of the sister relationship; to the contrary, these sister relationships appear quite typical, and neither Ann nor Bethany viewed her sister's behavior as particularly surprising or untoward. In fact, much of the psychoanalytic literature on siblings addresses unusual experiences, such as having a disabled sibling or surviving a sibling's death, leaving common experiences such as these relatively unexplored.

Can the influence of the sister be understood as displacement of a parental dynamic? Indeed, it may be that the importance of recognition for identity development is rooted in parental dynamics but can be expressed with respect to siblings; perhaps a deeper analytic process would have revealed the parental foundations of the manifest sisterly dynamics. Although both treatments lasted several years, the session frequency never exceeded twice weekly. Alternately, perhaps recognition by sibling and parent shapes identity development similarly, despite the fact that sisters figured prominently in these particular cases.

Yet for both women, the danger zones defined by the sister relationship did not map onto those defined by the parental relationships, suggesting that the internalized sister was not only a parental displacement. Moreover, not only do parent and sibling recognition sometimes diverge, as in these cases; they may also conflict, as when an adolescent's popularity among friends is founded on characteristics and behaviors that parents do not abide, and when parents treasure those very qualities, such as studiousness or sweetness, that provoke ridicule from siblings and peers. The latter was true for Bethany, whose parents praised the very goodness and accomplishments her sister tried to ignore and sometimes disdained. Indeed, sibling rivalry works against the possibility that sibling and parent recognition will coincide, as siblings tease each other about the very qualities their parents praise; by extension to the world of parent and sibling substitutes, we can understand the universal unpopularity of the teacher's pet.

Recognition is an acknowledgment as well as an invitation. It implies that one can move into a particular position or role, that one can be a certain kind of person. An invitation is valid only if given by one who has the authority to extend it. Parent recognition in the vertical dimension confers acceptance to a *desiring subject* because parents have authority over how much autonomous initiative one can take over one's own desires; parents delimit what can be desired and in what ways. Sibling recognition confers acceptance to an *individual* because siblings have authority over the size and shape of the space one can take up in the lateral world; siblings delimit who one can be. Of course, the desiring subject of the vertical dimension and the individual of the lateral dimension are one and the same person; identity reflects desire, and desire reflects identity. The person cannot be fully understood through a single lens, whether that be the vertical or the lateral.

It is important to note that we have examples here only of the sister relationship. Although there seems to be no theoretical reason for expecting gender differences in the importance of sibling recognition, it may be that the recognition of a same-sex sibling takes on particular importance to the extent that shared gender implies sameness, as it so often does, against which identity differences take on greater importance to a sense of personal uniqueness. Indeed, I have suggested (2007) that sibling differentiation of identity may be either more common or more apparent in same-sex sibling pairs, whereas mixed-sex sibling pairs may use gender as the axis around which both to organize their differences and to attenuate sibling rivalry. In addition, it may be that the *longing* for the sibling, the powerful feeling in these cases that ultimately revealed the desire for recognition, is more likely to be expressed by women than men, given cultural expectations about women's emotional expressiveness and close personal relationships, sister relationships in particular. Perhaps a man's longing for his brother's recognition would typically be disguised or defensively repudiated. Clearly, such questions about gender warrant further consideration.

Conclusion

The belief that there is but a single vertical axis around which all development revolves has been unshakable, despite the fact that it is supported by little more than conviction and convention. If we assume that development is organized exclusively around the vertical axis of parental relationships, then we need particularly striking evidence to convince us that there are developmental processes and dynamics that center uniquely on siblings. Instead, such processes are likely to remain unseen or misjudged as fundamentally parent-related. Alternately, if we envision the developmental terrain as mapped by two intersecting axes, even with the vertical predominating much of the time, then we have made room for considering the presence of sibling-related processes, including sibling differentiation and recognition.

Like Mitchell, I found that once I began to envision the psychic landscape as comprising two dimensions, I saw the concerns of the lateral dimension lurking everywhere, including in important aspects of identity development and ongoing peer relationships. Moreover, I began to see new aspects of the vertical dimension, in particular, the importance of difference between self and other, as distinct from otherness. Indeed, difference and differentiation are not only crucial to developments and relationships associated with the lateral dimension, and thus to some extent revealed by them, but also to those of the vertical dimension, although there we have been focused primarily on sameness and identification.

To understand identity fully, it turns out, we must consider the way one is positioned with respect to the siblings who are beside as well as to the parents who are above. We must take account of difference and similarity simultaneously. We must consider both intrapsychic mechanisms, such as differentiation, and intersubjective ones, such as recognition. Identity is not a point on the matrix but a pattern, unique for each person; the coordinates are not fixed for all, but relative to the important others in relationship to whom one finds a place of uniqueness and value in the world and at the same time shifted and shaped by the mutual recognition of that place attained with those others.

REFERENCES

ADLER, A. (1927). *Understanding Human Nature.* New York: Greenberg Press.
BENJAMIN, J. (1988). *The Bonds of Love.* New York: Pantheon.
——— (1995). Father and daughter, identification with difference: A contribution to gender heterodoxy. In *Like Subjects, Love Objects*, pp. 115–42. Cambridge, MA: Harvard University Press.
——— (1998). *Shadow of the Other: Intersubjectivity and Gender in Psychoanalysis.* New York: Routledge.
——— (2004). Beyond doer and done to: An intersubjective view of thirdness. *Psychoanalytic Quarterly* 73(1): 5–46.
——— (2006). Two-way streets: Recognition of difference and the intersubjective third. *Differences* 17(1): 116–46.
CHODOROW, N. (1978). *The Reproduction of Mothering.* Berkeley, CA: University of California Press.
KRIS, M., AND S. RITVO (1983). Parents and siblings: Their mutual influences. *Psychoanalytic Study of the Child* 38:311–24.
MITCHELL, J. (2000). *Madmen and Medusas: Reclaiming Hysteria.* New York: Basic Books.
——— (2003). *Siblings: Sex and Violence.* Oxford: Polity Press.
SHARPE, S. A., AND D. A. ROSENBLATT (1994). Oedipal sibling triangles. *Journal of the American Psychoanalytic Association* 42:491–523.
VIVONA, J. M. (2007). Sibling differentiation, identity development, and the lateral dimension of psychic life. *Journal of the American Psychoanalytic Association* 55:1191–1215.
——— (2010). Siblings, transference, and the lateral dimension of psychic life. *Psychoanalytic Psychology* 27:8–26.
WINNICOTT, D. W. (1969). The use of an object and relating through identifications. In *Playing and Reality*, pp. 86–94. London: Tavistock, 1971.

Three Contextual Frameworks for Siblingships

Nonlinear Thinking, Disposition, and Phallocentrism

CLAUDIA LAMENT, Ph.D.

This discussion of Juliet Mitchell's paper "Siblings: Thinking Theory" places her work within the context of three frameworks: nonlinear thinking, disposition, and phallocentrism. The nonlinear dimension of the developmental process demonstrates how the sibling experience is not static, but rather is subject to a natural transmogrification toward new adaptive forms and meanings that occur over the sequential progress of organizational growth. Secondly, dispositional variables tend to be overlooked in their role in how brothers and sisters engage one another, titrate closeness and separateness, and creatively live out their love, admiration, hate, envy, and rivalry with each other. Sensitivities in dispositional leanings, such as special empathic qualities, may even serve to mitigate sibling turbulence. Lastly, the phallocentricity in Western societies privileges an implicitly male perspective that envisions sibling relationships in terms of threatening competitors, as the common linguistic phrase sibling rivalry *suggests. This inflection in culture disregards more-expanding qualities*

Claudia Lament, Ph.D., is Training and Supervising Analyst at the Institute for Psychoanalytic Education, an affiliate of the Department of Psychiatry, New York University Langone Medical Center. She is Assistant Clinical Professor in the Department of Child and Adolescent Psychiatry, the Child Study Center, New York University Langone Medical Center. She is also Senior Managing Editor of *The Psychoanalytic Study of the Child*.

The Psychoanalytic Study of the Child 67, ed. Claudia Lament, Robert A. King, Samuel Abrams, A. Scott Dowling, and Paul M. Brinich (Yale University Press, copyright © 2013 by Claudia Lament, Robert A. King, Samuel Abrams, A. Scott Dowling, and Paul M. Brinich).

in object relationships and aim-giving strategies that are exchanged in sibling play.

These variables are not the sole contributors to the sibling experience, but a sampling of influences both from within and outside the child that affect that experience.

INTRODUCTION

JULIET MITCHELL'S PAPER PROVIDES A RICH STIMULANT FOR REvitalizing the psychoanalytic view of siblingships. In this discussion, I wish to place this topic within three contextual frameworks: that of nonlinear development, dispositional variations, and gender.

There is a tendency in psychoanalytic developmental theory to view growth as exclusively continuous, namely, this present is the heir to that past, and that past leads to this present. This psychogenic fallacy (Hartmann 1955; Hendrick 1942; Lampl-De Groot 1939; Westen 1989), or what might also be referred to as the "continuity fallacy," can be observed in the idea that straight through-lines can be drawn between psychological disorders and their beginnings in specific developmental periods. Other versions of such beliefs can be seen in the predilection to link findings from early childhood research and apply them directly to features of adult behavior, relationship dynamics, and transference-countertransference paradigms (Gilmore 2008). Such misconceptions oversimplify the inordinately complex network of variables in perpetual interaction that comprise forward movement. Such biases obscure those influences arising from both linear and nonlinear domains that mark developmental passage. For the purpose of this discussion, they also interfere with how we evaluate the sibling experience, as it too will be subject to the multiple discontinuous shifts that happen over the sequential progress of organizational growth.

Secondly, there is a troubling ease with which the impact of dispositional variants is dismissed in our appraisals of health and disorder. This leads to greater attention to outer stimuli, such as the overprivileging of parental caregiving styles, or the above-mentioned penchant to locate disturbance in phase-specific organizations. Freud (1913; 1933; 1937) spoke of this domain as a significant feature in the formation of pathology, such as obsessional neurosis, but also as one that was insufficiently studied as to its role in why some individuals are rooted to their disturbances.

Innate endowment will affect the rate of progress of the flowering of maturational processes—such as affect regulation, frustration tolerance, structure building, the development of symbolic thinking—and the nature of the course they follow (A. Freud 1976; Hartmann 1964). Variations in basic equipment and dispositional trends will impact the development of these processes as they follow a relatively smooth trajectory or are burdened by delays or detours (A. Freud 1965; 1974; 1978). Even the quality of phase organization is impacted by disposition, such as its overall coherency and range of integrity (Abrams 1986). Such dispositional features will be in concert throughout phase sequencing with the environment and the intersubjective exchange (A. Freud 1978; Gergely and Watson 1996; Gilmore 2005). Their effects cannot be actualized until they are brought into contact with outside forces. This state of affairs sets the stage whereby a mutually influential exchange takes shape. Indeed, disposition may be shaped and influenced by environmental forces, although some disorders show a stasis that resists influence from external sources. Gifts, talents, and dispositional advantages are also part of the package of disposition and may be harnessed to work against aberrations or anomalies in other areas of the personality (Abrams 2001). These innate givens will skew the sibling experience by tilting it in the direction of pleasure-seeking or more-aggressive engagements. Sensitivities in dispositional leanings, such as special empathic qualities, may even serve to mitigate expectable sibling turbulence.

My third contextual framework is that of gender. A phallocentric bias in psychoanalytic theory (Balsam 1991; 2008; Bassin 1996) informs the sibling experience and privileges a male-centered perspective that is especially sensitive to aggressive narratives. Consequently, the reading of the arrival of a sibling leans toward its being perceived by outside observers as an inherent assault to which the older child reacts with strategies of violence. The term *sibling rivalry* has become a tradition-bound aphorism or cliché treated as an objective fact and reified truth that takes precedence over other interpretations. Its prevalence as an embedded structure tells its own story about how culture builds meaning and inflects the narrative of family. Rangell (1965) signaled this development in what he called "falsifying trends." People intuitively associate values that are felt to belong together. Such automatic linkages abet an unfortunate cycling and recycling of belief systems that are reinforced through language and eventually result in abiding structures as in truisms. Thus, informed primarily by a male oriented lens, the term *sibling rivalry* has an unquestioned and stalwart place in our lexicon. It has the effect of valorizing what has become normative in culture and turning a blind eye to how meaning is subsequently reorganized with the advent of new hierarchical progressive developmental shifts that affect all spheres of cognitive and intrapsychic life.

Three Contextual Frameworks for Siblingships 87

SETTING THE CONTEXTS: NONLINEAR PERSPECTIVE,
DISPOSITION, AND PHALLOCENTRISM

By looking at clinical settings from different points of view, sibling interactions may also be recognized as instrumental in enriching relationships and shaping more-felicitous psychological structures—potential facilitators of the developmental progression rather than simply pathogens waiting to be realized. Mitchell too recognized this feature in her book (Mitchell 2003), wherein she remarked on the possibility of "a new form" of love when the desire to murder is resisted (p. 30). This is followed later in the close of her book by her reflections upon the hoped-for transformation of narcissism into love for others, and murderousness into an "objective hatred for what is wrong or evil in the self and other: these are the building blocks of a lateral not a vertical paradigm" (p. 225).

Inherent in Mitchell's formulation is the strand of discontinuity that, in addition to continuity, is a foundational feature of the developmental process. Freud's discoveries clarify this position. His work that resulted in a mapping of unconscious forces within the mind and an epigenetic psychosexual sequence defined what was and still is considered normative in the developmental process. It detonated an explosive reaction in the early part of the twentieth century that culminated in the psychoanalytic movement. Freud's revolutionary theory of development contained both continuous and discontinuous features. He saw that certain psychological features rooted in childhood could press forward unchanged and distort the adult's perception of her contemporary world. He also detected that the developmental process was marked by nonlinear, discontinuous features that startled the observer with the dizzying shifts in cognition and psychology that appear in succession. He was struck by the recognition (1905) that development moves in a sequential hierarchical series of reorganizations. The observer could track epigenetic growth—the remarkable transformations that occur in the child's developmental trajectory as one looks backward toward the past or forward into the future.

One need only to eavesdrop on conversations between parents on the playground, in which they exchange narratives about the seemingly miraculous changes in their children's advance steps to new psychological and cognitive levels of achievement, to acknowledge its ubiquity in the day-to-day experience of watching children grow up (Piaget 1952). Interacting features of maturational processes, brain functioning, disposition, and constitution, as well as the intersecting vectors of environment and sociocultural factors combine in unpredictable fashion to create the unique individual (A. Freud 1965; Neubauer 1996; Abrams and Solnit 1998; Mayes 2001; Mayes and Cohen 1996). The child will also create adaptive or maladaptive resolutions to the new conflicts that accompany them as she moves forward into each new organization. How she manages the fresh dilemmas of an oedipal threesome may show little resemblance to how she dealt with the same threesome as a toddler. Memory too undergoes transformative restructuring and reorganization (Tuch 1999; Weinstein 1998). This is not to throw the proverbial baby out with the bathwater, but to say that memory along with other functions are subject to continuous revision.

The study and application of this feature of development to clinical work has been largely at the edges of the psychoanalyst's viewfinder (Abrams 2001); she may see it with her peripheral vision and take for granted its theoretical validity, but it has been largely eclipsed by the linear, reductionistic perspective that took precedence in clinical practice and its translation into therapeutic action (Abrams 1977; Hartmann and Kris 1945). The dazzling import of Freud's rearward gaze rendered a new brand of semiotics to childhood fantasy: The genetic point of view had a staying power that foregrounded continuity and backgrounded the discontinuous feature of Freud's theory. Yet, both perspectives were always present; a different lens was necessary to recognize them. Why the perspective of discontinuities and nonlinearity has been marginalized may become a study in itself. Certainly, juggling the complexities of linearity and nonlinearity produces unknowns—uncertainties and conjectures that confront our field with serious challenges to the quest for "objective truths" (Spence 1980; Abrams 2011). Perhaps for some psychoanalysts, this is felt as a threat to their identities as truth seekers of histories.

Freud contended with the power of dispositional variants, or constitutional factors, throughout his writings, but in "Analysis Terminable and Interminable" (Freud 1937; Strachey 1937)) he placed particular emphasis on their place as impediments to the psychoanalytic process. Here he spoke of the strength of instincts versus a restricted ego as one set of determinants that augur poorly for a favorable analytic outcome. He also states with clarity his view that analysts were headed in the wrong direction with respect to their continued efforts in grasping how an analytic cure happens. Instead, he felt that the correct track to follow was in studying the domain of *obstacles* (italics mine) that impeded cure. For him in this paper, the impact of constitutional variables was well deserving of investigation, and their selection as a serious topic of study had been overlooked. Despite Freud's urging that analysts take this route in their future explorations, the leaning toward avoidance of systematic scrutiny of inborn traits, equipment failures, or precocities has been a perpetual ellipsis in psychoanalytic theory and clinical work. Abrams (1986) took note of this prevailing current and proffered an explanation that environmental influences wield a broad and mighty force that overshadows internally driven variables such as disposition. He suggested that disposition and endowment may be undervalued or rationalized in our field as exerting a small quota of impact upon personality formation because it seems that little can be done about them. This notion defies Freud's own opinion on the topic and admits defeat a priori. Therapeutic techniques that take into account such inborn qualities have been considered (Lament 2008; 2011; Olesker and Lament 2008; Knight 2008) and proven successful. Neubauer (1996) also remarked on the significance of inborn aspects and noted their contextual placement within the variations of each child's timetable of growth. He underscored the proclivity among analysts toward explaining a child's departures from normative expectations as rooted in environmental failures instead of weighing the influences from endowment and disposition.

This challenge was taken up most vigorously by Anna Freud (1965; 1974). In her study of childhood disturbance, she pinpointed the importance of dispositional features in their interactivity with other factors as contributing to areas of healthy engagement as well as to features of pathology. Disturbances in affect regulation, excessive states of anxiety or passivity, rigidities in managing transition and separation, porous structure formation that lacks vitality, aberrations in integration and synthesis, a propensity toward concretism, disrupted growth in symbolic processes, difficulties in how children internalize outside influences, and imbalance between hate and love are particularized aspects of disposition that often exert a continuous press upon growth. With regard to sibling interactions and relationships, dispositional variables play a part in how brothers and sisters engage one another, regulate closeness and separateness, and creatively live out their love, admiration, hate, envy, and rivalry with each other. Differences and similarities in dispositional features will also impact on how siblings assist or hinder each other's forward growth. Finally, how sibling birth is experienced by the older child, that is, whether it is experienced as a "trauma," will have much to do with dispositional traits and managing emotional separateness from internalized objects.

The context of gender role identity (Benjamin 1991; Stoller and Wagonfeld 1982; Tyson and Tyson 1990) provides another vantage point from which to view the traditional understanding of siblingships. It pivots our attention to how males and females experience themselves and the world and how they live and behave within society. The sociocultural environment is an important factor (Kramer and Prall 1978; Meissner 2005; Layton 2011) in how a child's growing perception of himself as a gendered self develops. A child's same and cross-gendered identifications with significant familial and external figures is another influence in how the growing child establishes this aspect of identity (Balsam 2001; Bassin 1996; Benjamin 1995; Chodorow 1996). Finally, from within the matrix of the child's psychobiologically propelled transformations over the course of the developmental process, the child's self and other representational structures are subject to continuous and profound shifts that include reconfigurations of gender roles. Knight's (2011) research is a vivid case in point that demonstrates that fragmentation and fluidity of such percepts are normative features of growth during the middle years.

How mothers influence the ways that a child adopts stylistic relational attitudes and behavior has been explored by researchers in early childhood (Olesker 1984; Biringen, Robinson, and Emde 1994). For example, mothers lean toward encouraging their sons to exhibit autonomous, independent behaviors, while abetting their daughters to focus on interactivity with others and the promotion of positive relating and relatedness. The false axiom that a boy has a relative lack of emotionalism compared with his female cohort is taken up by Galasinski (2004) as reported in Balsam (2008). Galasinski states that in contemporary sociogender and sociological literature studies, men's so-called emotional backwardness is put forward at the level of truth that requires no supporting evidence; it is baldly presented as de facto. Cultural mores in Western civilization overtly embrace the traditional stereotypic perception of male strength as embodying emotional suppression, as opposed to one of open expressiveness and receptivity of feelings. How these pressures stimulate certain male-oriented, sociocultural proclivities in sibling relations and the origins and maintenance of fixed views on lateral relations should be given proper weight. Mitchell's discussion of the phallocentrically based exclusion of this dimension in theory and culture has a broadening reach by its extension to common linguistic forms, most notably the epithet *rivalry* that accompanies the term *sibling*. What might be categorized as feminine-based adjectival descriptors to the word *sibling*, such as *love, attachment, concern*, or even *bond*, are nonexistent and appear to go unnoticed and uncontested. The implicitly male perspective that envisions siblings as threatening rivals also tramples on expanding object-relationships and aim-giving strategies that are exchanged in sibling play. These offer a multilayered view of siblings that would heighten the value of the emerging developmental potential.

Why Has the Lateral Axis of Siblings Eluded a Comprehensive Theory?

Mitchell's view of the sibling arrival as "traumatic" and the accompanying unconscious fantasies of incest and murder is the cornerstone of lateral relationships in her conceptualization of what must be added to the theoretical superstructure. She states that the recognition of the significance of siblings (including fantasied siblings in the case of the only child) challenges the tradition-bound privileging of the child-parent matrix. This is troubling to our sociocultural surround because both "social and individual psychology has always been understood from the side of the man" (Mitchell 2003, p. 3). Mitchell draws a parallel between psychological states of mind that are typically associated with femininity and sibling relations, such as fears of annihilation, loss of love, and an excessive narcissism, which seek validation by the positioning of the female in the object/receiver role in love relationships. She suggests that siblings and femininity have been burdened by "overlooked destinies"(2003, p. 4).

Drawing upon such gender-based connotations, I would add that particular qualities of feminine-informing features in relationships in general and in siblingships in particular have been minimized and undervalued. As previously mentioned, even the scaffolding for sibling relationships observed in the embedded linguistic aphorism *sibling rivalry* derives from phallocentric stereotypes of male styles of relating that punctuate aggressivity. Elements that incorporate more feminine informing aspects of sibling relationships are inclusive of a readiness for empathic attunement and the movement toward the pleasure of relating to persons as opposed to things or activities (Abrams and Neubauer 1976).

Cast in this light, Mitchell's notion of the sibling arrival as always "traumatic," which carries a phallocentric, aggressivized meaning, can be argued. Importantly, omitting the idea of "trauma" as inherent within the sibling experience does not dismiss the inclusion of the lateral axis within the overarching theory. As Mitchell notes, generalizability[1] to the entire population is a requisite criterion in the creation of a new

---

1. A theoretical construct must be generalizable—something we all experience—if it is to play a role in the construction of the unconscious aspect of the human psyche.

addition to the theoretical superstructure. For me, what is universal about the sibling experience is not its traumatic nature; rather, it is its existence for all children. It is the presence of the only child that has been a sticking point in this regard. But Mitchell's enlightening note that the only child has a multitude of fantasied siblings remedies the problem: That all children feel a quality of "trauma" is not required to prove the universality of the sibling experience.

In addition to these sociologically based obstacles concerning gender biases, I would postulate additional barriers that are endemic to the psychology of the sibling experience that have interfered with theory-building efforts. In that light, the following factors may have burdened this criterion.

The factor of *timing*: The parent-child vertical axis is a constant pillar in a child's familial relationships. Looking diachronically through the vertical scree of development moving in a forward direction, a child will shape her views of her parents in ever-increasingly sophisticated ways (cognition, the architecture of mental structure, memory, ego functions, and unconscious fantasy all undergo transformational or nonlinear shifts) as she passes through the progressive hierarchical organizations.

The child will do the same for her siblings, with the important difference that siblings are not ever-present for the child as are parents; they arrive on the scene at different organizational time zones on the child's developmental continuum (with the notable exception of twinships). Unconscious or conscious fantasies of incest and murder target every child in Mitchell's superstructure, but their inflections will occur on different levels of cognitive and psychological maturation. For instance, a six-year-old who experiences a new sibling may have to struggle with the tasks of mourning oedipal defeat but will transform this experience into new abiding structures. These will provide him with the necessary leverage to assist in the achievement of unheralded capacities in grasping the complexities of relationships on a triadic level. This child will have undergone radical cognitive changes, representational shifts, new ego capacities in delaying gratification, and greater affect tolerance while also moving toward the outer world of the peer group and activities beyond the home. This circumstance is in marked contrast to what she might have experienced several years previous, when the second child was born and she was three.

Thus, the matter of *birth order* and its concurrence with developmental transformations will inflect the sibling experience with those meanings and affective reactivity that attend the child's developmental organization. The experience of having older siblings versus younger siblings and *how many years* between them is not generalizable to the entire population and will result in different outcomes. For instance, Mitchell speaks of the experience of the older toddler viewing the newborn with jealousy, death wishes, and perhaps incestuous feelings. The toddler also readily identifies with both baby and mother. Such fluid identifications fit the structural features of the young child where porousness of self/object boundaries are normative. But looking at a sibling coupling from the viewpoint of the younger one, I postulate that this child may *use* the older sibling to actualize the developmental thrust forward that pulls the younger child along to a new organizational level via identificatory processes and experiential exchanges. The younger sibling is rehearsing for his debut on the new stage through play and fantasy with his older sibling. This is a decidedly positive aspect of the sibling relationship, one that comingles with developmental processes. That is, the older child provides a natural, in-house developmental assist, along with the aspects of jealousy that Mitchell describes and differentiates from envy. (Although here, I believe the younger child will also envy the elder.)

What about the child in the middle? Traditionally, this child is dubbed as "lost," sandwiched between elder and younger: The accident of birth order that holds the bookended children in place fails to provide a secure identity for the middle child. Or, do his multiple identifications provide him with a greater variety of creative solutions with regard to murder, incest, or jealousy? And, to further the phallocentric argument in this regard, a female-centric culture would honor object-seeking and engagement of others in its foundation, foregrounding these elements in favor of the masculine ones. What about the "only child" who must identify in fantasy and, as Mitchell points out, may have a far more active fantasy life than those peers who are siblinged? Perhaps the parents double in the child's mind as siblings.

Disposition and constitutional variables will also inflect sibling theory building. When considering development from the viewpoint of the unfolding of dispositional and maturational processes, as Anna Freud did with her developmental lines (1965), one sees incremental, nonlinear shifts that have transformational consequences (Neubauer 1984; Abrams 2007; Abrams 2001). This synchronic mapping may be loosely coordinated with the diachronic mapping of the newly emergent, progressive, hierarchically ordered organizations. These maturational processes, such as structure formation, self-object differentiation, cognitive processes, symbolic functioning, motoric advances, and so forth are subject to wide variations. Anna Freud theorized and demonstrated empirically that the rate at which these processes developed varied within the child; further, one typically observes disharmonies when tracking growth along these continuums. Not only the organizational component of where she is on her developmental trajectory must be considered (and how the sibling relationship may transmogrify over the course of her development), but the dispositional aspects that she brings from her biologically inspired program will play a part as well. The progressive-regressive balance may be useful to apply to this domain as well: The stronger the innate pull forward toward the next organization, the more likely the child will discover persons in her milieu to engage and advance that progressive surge. The sibling experience then, is coincidental with an organizational "set" (on the diachronic level) and the complex array of maturational processes (on the synchronic level) that the child is experiencing at any given moment. The idea that sibling arrival is "traumatic" for the older child is not a ubiquitous structure. Placing the child on a continuum of reactivity in regard to the experience of sibling birth allows more room for individual variation.

For instance, the two-year-old is moving through her own extraordinary transformations that are partially informed by disposition, constitutional variables and their interaction with the environment. Mitchell's inclusion of Winnicott's notes concerning Joan, a two-year-old with volatile and violent reactions to her sibling's birth is a pertinent illustration. What if little Joan's responses to her newborn brother are a manifestation of certain dispositional vulnerabilities—despite Winnicott's observation that attests to her overall health and love-ability? Can we fairly attribute her extreme reactivity and "violent reactions" to the birth of the sibling alone? Anna Freud might conjecture that Joan brings to the experience of her brother's birth a whole set of interacting systems and subsystems: fragilities, precocities, and disharmonies among newly emergent capacities within her. In turn, how do these systems respond to environmental factors in the world outside her?

Environmental Considerations

The familial and larger societal-cultural environments are significant shaping systems that affect the features mentioned above: timing of the sibling's birth in terms of the older child's psychological and cognitive organization, the baby's arrival with respect to birth order, and the child's dispositional features. When a baby arrives to the family surround, whether and how the adults in the household are sensitive to the older child's reactions can be critical to the freshness of experiencing this new being. The adults may either assist or hinder the child's hurt, anger, or pleas to welcome the new infant into the fold.

Three Contextual Frameworks for Siblingships 95

The child's dispositional strengths and vulnerabilities may be ignored or accurately understood or intuited by the parents and extended family members. A critical factor to consider is how these features of the child can be enlisted or mitigated by an adult's timely and thoughtful interventions to help in the expression of feeling. A fearful or shaming reaction from a beloved adult can intensify a young child's embarrassment about the natural and expectable feelings of anger or hurt. Or the young child's excitement "to help" may be overlooked by the hubbub of activity and visitors that threaten to shut out the wide-eyed expectancy to be a part of the new family configuration. A three-year-old whose capacity for affect tolerance is immature may be especially upset by such responses. Or, a five-year-old with speech and language delays may require additional assistance in finding ways to express her reactions. A child whose sense of agency seemed lacking might be spurred to stretch this aspect of ownership of self and identity by the very presence of another being who is closer in age than the adults in the family.

A parent may overemphasize a loving attitude toward the baby or may dismiss the possibility that the child's demandingness or tantrums can be soothed by finding a way to include her in the family's newly emerging structure and dynamics: She can now be cast as a "big sister" whose position is unique and valued.

The wider social and cultural surround can emit a generative response to the family's new addition. Teachers, parents of a child's friends, grandparents, and neighbors can provide a needed respite from the cascade of feelings that the arrival of the newborn may engender in the older child. She may locate new ways of refinding what might be felt as her "lost self" prior to the baby's entry on the scene. As well, the child may learn from her playmates' strategies of interacting with siblings. A sibling can be helpful or fun or a nuisance. Now, her playmates may function as identificatory models for discovering the world of siblings.

The sibling experience may be understood as inclusive of a catalogue of interweaving considerations: the age of the child when the sibling arrives, birth order, how many other siblings has the child experienced and at what organizational level, dispositional features and how these react to forces within the child's local environment and larger sociocultural context. How will these inform and shape fantasy formation for later sibling arrivals, for better or worse?

Summary

Mitchell has provided us with a rich legacy in her groundbreaking position: the universality of lateral relationships and their formidable imprint in psychic life. What I attempted to demonstrate in this paper are three perspectives through which to view siblingships: first, the non-linear point of view, by which the sibling experience undergoes a natural transmogrification toward new adaptive forms throughout the developmental process; second, the dispositional aspect of a child's character formation and its interaction with environmental features that will influence the sibling relationship; and, last, the propensity of socioculturally influenced maxims to recruit phallocentric biases that distort the nature of the sibling experience and its unfolding process. These perspectives locate the sibling experience in narrative forms that are multicontextual and that obviate the need to structure it as traumatic. That it is a universal feature of the human experience can be proved for the only child who populates his fantasy life with imaginary brothers and sisters.

These variables are not the sole contributors to the sibling experience but are a sampling of influences that affect the child both from within and outside. The mutual interactivity of these and other factors combine and recombine to produce expressions of siblingships that change not only over the developmental sequences but will also persist over the course of adult life. It is only when there are *failures* of progressive, discontinuous shifts that one may observe in pure culture the starkness of aggressivity and murderousness that exist in fantasies about the sibling. These may arise from dispositional variants, environmental forces within and outside the family milieu—and, as highlighted in this paper, abiding male-oriented proclivities in Western societal structures. The latter have privileged the moment of sibling birth in an aggressivized and threatening contextual narrative that has been transmitted and re-cycled through the generations. Such a bias is overturned by the underlying dynamism that is continuously operating in human growth and that informs the sibling experience, even at its inception. This ever-present synergy is a necessary reminder of the place of uncertainty as we consider the mercurial nature of unconscious fantasy and its impact upon the child's unfolding narrative of her life.

REFERENCES

ABRAMS, S. (1977). The genetic point of view: Antecedents and transformations. *Journal of the American Psychoanalytic Association* 25:417–25.

——— (1986). Disposition and the environment. *Psychoanalytic Study of the Child* 41:41–60.

——— (2001). Summation—unrealized possibilities: Comments on Anna Freud's *Normality and Pathology in Childhood*. *Psychoanalytic Study of the Child* 56:105–19.

—— (2007). A forward view: Celebrating the 150th birthday of the founder of psychoanalysis. *Psychoanalytic Study of the Child* 62:3–17.
—— (2011). Historiography 101 for psychoanalysts. *Psychoanalytic Study of the Child* 65:103–28.
ABRAMS, S., AND P. B. NEUBAUER (1976). Object orientedness: The person or the thing. *Psychoanalytic Quarterly* 45:73–99.
ABRAMS, S., AND A. SOLNIT (1998). Coordinating developmental and psychoanalytic processes. *Journal of the American Psychoanalytic Association* 46:85–104.
ARAGNO, A. (2008). The language of empathy. *Journal of the American Psychoanalytic Association* 56:713–40.
BALSAM, R. (1991). Review of *Thinking Fragments: Psychoanalysis, Feminism, and Postmodernism in the Contemporary West*, by Jane Flax (Berkeley: University of California Press, 1990). *International Review of Psycho-Analysis* 18:128–30.
—— (2001). Integrating male and female elements in a woman's gender identity. *Journal of the American Psychoanalytic Association* 49:1335–60.
—— (2008). Fathers and the bodily care of their infant daughters. *Psychoanalytic Inquiry* 28:60–75.
BASSIN, D. (1996). Beyond the he and the she: Toward the reconciliation of masculinity and femininity in the postoedipal female mind. *Journal of the American Psychoanalytic Association* 44S:157–90.
BENJAMIN, J. (1991). Father and daughter: Identification with difference—a contribution to gender heterodoxy. *Psychoanalytic Dialogues* 1:277–99.
—— (1995). Sameness and difference: Toward an "overinclusive" model of gender development. *Psychoanalytic Inquiry* 15:125–42.
BIRINGEN, Z., J. L. ROBINSON, AND R. N. EMDE (1994). Mother's style of sensitivitiy during late infancy: The role of child's gender. *American Journal of Orthopsychiatry* 64:78–90.
CHODOROW, N. (1996). Theoretical gender and clinical gender: Epistemological reflections of the psychology of women. *Journal of the American Psychoanalytic Association* 44S:215–38.
—— (2000). Reflections on the reproduction of mothering—twenty years later. *Studies in Gender and Sexuality* 1:237–48.
FONAGY, P., AND M. TARGET (2007). Playing with reality: IV. A theory of external reality rooted in intersubjectivity. *International Journal of Psychoanalysis* 81:917–37.
FREUD, A. (1965). Normality and pathology in childhood: Assessments of development. Vol. 6 of *The Writings of Anna Freud*. New York: International Universities Press.
—— (1974). A psychoanalytic view of developmental psychopathology. In *The Writings of Anna Freud*, 8:57–74.
—— (1976). Psychopathology seen against the background of normal development. In *The Writings of Anna Freud*, 8:82–95
—— (1978). The principal task of child analysis. In *The Writings of Anna Freud*, 8:96–109.
FREUD, S. (1905). Three essays on the theory of sexuality. In *Standard Edition of the Complete Psychological Work of Sigmund Freud*, ed. James Strachey, vol. 7,

A Case of Hysteria, Three Essays on Sexuality and Other Works, pp.130–243. New York: W. W. Norton.

——— (1913). The disposition to obsessional neurosis. In *Standard Edition* vol. 12 (1911–13), *The Case of Schreber, Papers on Technique and Other Works*, pp. 317–26. New York: W. W. Norton.

——— (1933). Lecture 34: Explanations, applications and orientations. In *Standard Edition*, vol. 22 (1932–36), *New Introductory Lectures on Psycho-Analysis and Other Works*, pp. 136–57. New York: W. W. Norton..

——— (1937). Analysis terminable and interminable. In *Standard Edition*, vol. 23 (1937–39), *Moses and Monotheism, An Outline of Psycho-Analysis and Other Works*, pp. 216–53. New York: W. W. Norton.

GALASINSKI, D. (2004). *Men and the Language of Emotions*. Palgrave, UK: Macmillan.

GERGELY, G., AND J. WATSON (1996). The social biofeedback model of parental affect-mirroring. *International Journal of Psychoanalysis* 77:1181–1212.

GILMORE, K. (2005). Play in the psychoanalytic setting: Ego capacity, ego state, and vehicle for intersubjective exchange. *Psychoanalytic Study of the Child* 60:213–38.

——— (2008). Psychoanalytic developmental theory: A contemporary reconsideration. *Journal of the American Psychoanalytic Association* 56:885–907.

HARTMANN, H. (1955). Notes on the theory of sublimation. *Psychoanalytic Study of the Child* 10:9–29.

——— (1964). *Essays on Ego Psychology*. New York: International Universities Press.

HARTMANN, H., AND E. KRIS (1945). The genetic approach to psychoanalysis. *Psychoanalytic Study of the Child* 1:11–30.

HENDRICK, I. (1942). Instinct and the ego during infancy. *Psychoanalytic Quarterly* 11:33–58.

KRAMER, S., AND R. C. PRALL (1978). The role of the father in the preoedipal years. *Journal of the American Psychoanalytic Association* 26:143–61.

KNIGHT, R. (2008). Blood, sweat, and tears: The effort of narrative change in psychoanalysis. *Psychoanalytic Study of the Child* 63:292–311.

——— (2011). Fragmentation, fluidity, and transformation: Nonlinear development in middle childhood. *Psychoanalytic Study of the Child* 65:19–47.

LAMENT, C. (2008). Transformation into adolescence. *Psychoanalytic Study of the Child* 63:280–91.

——— (2011). Transformational processes and therapeutic action: What David knew. *Psychoanalytic Study of the Child* 65:5–18.

LAMPL-DE GROOT, J. (1939). Considerations of methodology to the psychology of small children. *International Journal of Psycho-Analysis* 20:408–17.

LAYTON, L. (2011). On the irreconcilable in psychic life: The role of culture in the drive to become both sexes. *Psychoanalytic Quarterly* 80:461–74.

MAYES, L. (2001). The twin poles of order and chaos. *Psychoanalytic Study of the Child* 56:137–70.

MAYES, L., AND D. COHEN (1996). Anna Freud and developmental psychoanalytic psychology. *Psychoanalytic Study of the Child* 51:117–41.

MEISSNER, W. W. (2005). Gender and the self: II. Femininity, homosexuality, and the theory of the self. *Psychoanalytic Review* 92:29–66.
MITCHELL, J. (2003). *Siblings*. Cambridge: Polity Press.
NEUBAUER, P. (1984). Anna Freud's concept of developmental lines. *Psychoanalytic Study of the Child* 39:15–27.
——— (1996). Current issues in psychoanalytic child development. *Psychoanalytic Study of the Child* 51:35–45.
OLESKER, W. (1984). Sex differences in 2- and 3-year-olds: Mother-child relations, peer relations, and peer play. *Psychoanalytic Psychology* 1:269–88.
OLESKER, W., AND C. LAMENT (2008). Conceptualizing transformations in child and adult analysis. *Psychoanalytic Study of the Child* 63:273–79.
PIAGET, J. (1952). *The Origins of Intelligence in Children*. New York: International Universities Press.
RANGELL, L. (1965). The scope of Heinz Hartmann—Some selected comments on his *Essays on Ego Psychology* an appreciative survey on the occasion of his 70th birthday. *International Journal of Psycho-Analysis* 46:5–30.
SPENCE, D. P. (1980). *Narrative Truth and Historical Truth: Meaning and Interpretation in Psychoanalysis*. New York: W. W. Norton.
STOLLOR, R. J., AND S. WAGONFELD (1982). Gender and gender role. *Journal of the American Psychoanalytic Association* 30:185–96.
STRACHEY, J. (1937). Editor's note to Analysis terminable and interminable. In *The Standard Edition of the Complete Psychological Work of Sigmund Freud*. Vol. 23 (1937–39): *Moses and Monotheism, An Outline of Psycho-Analysis and Other Works*, pp. 211–15. New York: W. W. Norton.
TUCH, R. (1999). The construction, reconstruction, and deconstruction of memory in the light of social cognition. *Journal of the American Psychoanalytic Association* 47:153–86.
TYSON, P., AND R. TYSON (1990). *Psychoanalytic Theories of Development: An Integration*. New Haven, CT, and London: Yale University Press.
WEINSTEIN, L. (1998). Lissa Weinstein. *Journal of the American Psychoanalytic Association* 46:67–74.
WESTEN, D. (1989). Are "primitive" object relations really primitive? *American Journal of Orthopsychiatry* 59:331–45.

WORK WITH PARENTS

Concurrent Work with Parents of Adolescent Patients

KERRY KELLY NOVICK AND JACK NOVICK, Ph.D.

Over the last ten years we have seen an increasing acceptance of the general idea of working with parents of child patients. What remains, however, as an area of controversy, conflict, and resistance, is the question of whether and how much therapists should or can work with the parents of adolescent patients. Questions cluster around how to maintain confidentiality and lead to the even larger issue of conceptualizing the developmental goals of the phase of adolescence.

We see the major developmental tasks for both parents and adolescents as involving transformation of the self and the relationship, in the context of separateness rather than separation. If adolescent therapists work from the assumption that the goal of adolescence is transformation, concurrent work with parents and adolescents will move them all into a new level of relationship. Without concomitant change in parents, it is doubly hard for adolescents to progress into adulthood.

In this paper we offer clinical material from five older adolescents and their parents to illustrate the techniques that follow from our model of dynamic concurrent parent work throughout the phases of treatment.

Jack Novick is a Training Analyst of the International Psychoanalytic Association and on the faculties of numerous institutes. Formerly Clinical Associate Professor of Psychology, Departments of Psychiatry at the University of Michigan and Wayne State University, he also chaired the Child Psychoanalysis Training at the Michigan Psychoanalytic Institute.

Kerry Kelly Novick is a Training Analyst of the International Psychoanalytic Association. Also on the faculties of numerous institutes, she was formerly Lecturer in Psychoanalysis, University of Michigan Department of Psychiatry, President of the Association for Child Psychoanalysis, and a founder of Allen Creek Preschool.

The Psychoanalytic Study of the Child 67, ed. Claudia Lament, Robert A. King, Samuel Abrams, A. Scott Dowling, and Paul M. Brinich (Yale University Press, copyright © 2013 by Claudia Lament, Robert A. King, Samuel Abrams, A. Scott Dowling, and Paul M. Brinich).

Using the tasks of the therapeutic alliance as a conceptual framework, we describe working toward the dual goals of restoration to the path of progressive development and restoration of the parent-child relationship. We pay particular attention to the unfolding of conflicts between closed-system omnipotent functioning and open-system reality mastery, and the role of fathers in late-adolescent development.

A 2011 VOLUME OF THE *JOURNAL OF THE AMERICAN ACADEMY OF Child and Adolescent Psychiatry* contained an editorial by David Reiss, who cited important studies demonstrating the interrelationship of child and parental pathologies. On the basis of the research he summarized, he called for "better integration of child and adult mental health services. Under ideal auspices, we may consider two levels of integration. First is to make the parent-child dyad the *unit of assessment*. . . . A second and more complex integration of care is where the parent and child become the *unit of treatment*" (pp. 432, 433).

One hundred years earlier, in 1911, Freud said that development in a child can only take place "provided one includes the care it receives from its mother" (p. 220). Many years later Winnicott (1965) said that there is no such thing as a baby, there is only a mother and a baby. Between those two psychoanalytic comments and in subsequent years there has been a neglect of the role of parent work in the dynamic treatment of children and adolescents. In a review of our 2005 book *Working with Parents Makes Therapy Work*, Yanof described this as "a subject that is almost never written about in psychoanalysis, even though . . . [it] is one of the most commonly encountered aspects of treating child patients" (2006, p. 54).

We have talked since 1990 about an evolving model of parent work and summarized our views in a book (K. Novick and J. Novick 2005) and in papers published and presented subsequently (J. Novick and K. Novick 2008; 2011; K. Novick and J. Novick 2008). The model asserts that parent work is substantive and legitimate and makes use of the full repertoire of psychoanalytic interventions. Progression through the phases of the child's treatment affects and is dynamically affected by interaction with the parent work. Parental consolidation in the phase of parenthood may also be profoundly impacted by the child's forward developmental movement.

WHY WORK WITH PARENTS OF CHILDREN AND ADOLESCENTS?

The main reason for working with parents is pragmatic, since we can demonstrate that it helps people enter treatment, stay and do the neces-

sary work, and leave in a timely fashion, maintaining the benefits of the work (K. Novick and J. Novick 2005, see especially p. 167).
Additional reasons are:

- Children continue to live in and will return to their family and environment; treatment gains are more likely to be retained if the family has changed, too.
- Parenthood is a phase of development; adaptive growth in parents supports child change; parental pathology destroys child treatment gains.
- Parents are a big part of the child's world, sometimes the best part (Furman 1995). They are also part of the child's troubles, either primarily as part of the cause or secondarily as affected by the impact of disturbance.
- Parents have anxieties specific to each phase of treatment, which can affect maintenance of the treatment and termination.

Over the last ten years we have seen an increasing acceptance of the general idea of working with parents of child patients. The real change seems to be that child analysts now feel free to talk about what many have always done. Child analysts, with the exception of orthodox Kleinians, have always seen the parents of their child patients in one way or another. Current accounts of child cases increasingly include description of parent work (see, for instance, Todd 2012; J. Novick and K. Novick 2012). Whatever the techniques described, there is much greater comfort in discussing work with parents of infants, preschoolers, and schoolchildren.

What remains, however, as an area of controversy, conflict, and resistance is the question of whether and how much therapists should work with the parents of adolescent patients. Questions cluster around how to maintain confidentiality and lead to the even larger issue of conceptualizing the developmental goals of the phase of adolescence. We have noted the traditional psychoanalytic description of adolescents as unanalyzable, the high rate of premature terminations in adolescent treatments, and the high turnover of professionals in inpatient and outpatient facilities that deal with teenagers (J. Novick and K. Novick 2008). We have said, "If we expand the domain and include substantive concurrent work with parents as integral to the treatment of adolescents then we can increase the rate of success and increase retention of adolescent workers" (ibid., p. 147).

What are the assumptions underlying our model of parent work?

- Parenthood is a normal adult developmental phase, with subphases that are affected by dynamic interactions with their children (Benedek 1959).
- Parents and children are involved in a lifelong complex interaction.

- Growth consists of a series of transformations in children, parents, and the relationship between them.
- Development involves epigenetic interactions at all levels of complexity, but foremost in this context are the interactions between child and parents throughout life.
- The "growth of self-regulation is a cornerstone of early childhood development that cuts across all domains of behavior." (National Research Council 2000, p. 3)
- The mode of self-regulation can be characterized in terms of two systems of functioning, which we have called "open" and "closed."
- Treatment of children has dual goals.
  - *Restoration of the child to the path of progressive development* (A. Freud 1970)
  - *Restoration of the parent-child relationship to a lifelong positive resource for both*
- The therapeutic alliance is a conceptual framework for ongoing parent work. It operationalizes the open system of self-regulation.
- Accomplishment of therapeutic alliance tasks promotes attunement.

All of these assumptions apply equally, in our view, to work with adolescent patients and their parents. We have noted (DeVito, Novick, and Novick 2000 [1994]) that most psychoanalytic adolescent therapists and theorists have held definitive views that the goal of adolescence is separation; that normal adolescents need to keep thoughts, wishes, and activities secret from parents as part of the separation process; and that adolescents need allies in the inevitable clash of generations, because of a "normal" need to rebel against all authorities. Each of these views has been axiomatic both in child analytic education and indeed in the cultural view of adolescence, and each has influenced technical choices in how adolescent treatments are designed. With this standard concept of adolescent development, parental intrusion and/or the young person's inability to separate are seen as the major obstacles to adolescent treatment and growth. Many analysts who work with adolescents therefore regularly refer parents to another clinician.

Our view of adolescence is different. We see the major developmental tasks for both parents and children as involving transformation of the self and the relationship, in the context of separateness rather than separation, particularly physical separation (K. Novick and J. Novick 2005; J. Novick and K. Novick 2008; 2011). Adolescence is a multidimensional challenge to young people and the adults who care for them. If adolescent therapists work from the assumption that the goal of adolescence is transformation, concurrent work with parents and adolescent will move them all into a new level of relationship. Without concomitant change in parents, it is doubly hard for adolescents to progress into adulthood.

The editors asked us to write a "position paper" on parent work as it applies to adolescent treatment. The general model can be found in our 2005 book and numerous papers. Here, we will illustrate particularly the techniques that follow from our model of dynamic concurrent parent work with material from adolescent patients and their parents throughout the phases of treatment.

We want to emphasize that we are assuming that the center of the treatment plan is the therapeutic work with the individual adolescent. Whatever one's theoretical orientation or theory of technique, the individual treatment is where the young person grows and changes. Concurrent parent work supports and facilitates that effort and does not substitute for it. Here we would like to tell the stories of five late adolescents, four young men and one young woman, as they and their parents negotiated the passage from late adolescence into young adulthood, with a focus on the interaction between the parent work and the individual treatments.

Not every treatment can or should be the same; this is not a prescriptive model or an effort to establish rules for doing analysis. Some young people refuse to let their parents be seen; some parents are disengaged; some parents micromanage their children's lives; sometimes adolescents and their parents live at great distances, with college attendance far away from home, work or military commitments necessitating absence; contentious divorce or pathology can make teamwork difficult; death or illness can make a parent inaccessible.

What we deem central, however, beyond the practicalities of particular treatment plans, is that analysts keep the parents in mind, hold the parent-child relationship in the world of the treatment. In this paper we suggest that much more can be accomplished in adolescent treatment, more quickly and deeply, when the analyst includes this dimension in all aspects of the therapeutic endeavor. Psychoanalysis is the only general psychology that encompasses the complexity of individuals and their families. As such, it generates multimodal techniques. Our goal in exploring concurrent parent work is to expand therapists' repertoire, just as treatment aims to expand the individual's adaptive capacities.

We have realized that people often find it helpful to see ideas set out in a visual summary. Included here, therefore, is a table entitled "Dynamic Concurrent Parent Work through the Phases of Adolescent Treatment," where we list the alliance tasks and challenges for parents, their feelings and anxieties around those tasks, the defenses and

Dynamic Concurrent Parent Work through the Phases of Adolescent Treatment

	EVALUATION	BEGINNING	MIDDLE	PRETERMINATION	TERMINATION
Alliance tasks for parents	Engage in transformations.	Allow child to be with another person.	Allow psychological separateness, individuation, autonomy.	Enjoy and validate progression.	Allow child to mourn. Internalize relationship with analyst.
Parental affects/ anxieties	Guilt, helplessness Failure/unimportance Hatred of child Fear of hostility Fear of exclusion	Loss of child Loss of love Guilt over lack of authentic love	Abandonment Loneliness Loss of love Fear of child's assault on parents' personalities	Fear of abandonment Sense of uselessness Transference fear of being discarded by analyst	Fear of sadness, love, and loss Fear of reliving core conflicts
Parental resistances/ defenses	Blaming the adolescent or external factors Pushing for immediate relief Abdication of parental role	Uninvolved / too involved Externalizations	Reactive hostility Withdrawal from child Protection of character defenses and superego Protection of dysfunctional marriage Resistance to revival and potential revision of past	Revival of past patterns Preemptive, premature termination—passive to active	Avoidance Premature leaving or withdrawal

Therapist's techniques, interventions, and goals	Emphasize continuing importance of parents. Present dual goals. Access primary parental love. Clarify contract. Differentiate privacy and secrecy. Resist urgency. Articulate learning, strength-building model (emotional muscle).	Help parents see adolescent as unique. Provide psycho-education re: adolescent development. Link parental past to present. Interpret sadomasochistic relationships. Generate alternatives.	Consolidate parental strengths. Interpret past roots of equating loss or death with separateness. Reinforce idea that growth is not loss. Support reality testing leading to reparation. Engage with parental hostility as resistance to change.	Interpret repetition. Do not rationalize a bad good-bye as normal development. Address need to learn about parting. Support transformation.	Acknowledge deep bond between parents and therapist. Work until end.
Parenthood-phase components	Integration and ownership of parental role	Security in primacy as parent despite physical separation	Continuity of parent-child relationship in context of psychological separateness	Capacity to transform the parent-child relationship through development	Maintainance of love and connection despite physical and psychological separateness

resistances they may mobilize in response, and the therapist's interventions to address those.

In an effort to initiate more general discussion on this important topic for theory and practice, the editors will engage at the end of the paper in a dialogue, interviewing us about salient aspects of the paper and the model.

From the Evaluation and Recommendation to the Beginning of Treatment—Kevin

To us, evaluation is a crucial phase of work with a family. There is the effort to encompass the world of the potential patient and his parents; the analyst works to initiate various psychological transformations in the service of assessing capacity for change, discerning areas of strength, as well as resistance or pathology, and creating a therapeutic alliance; the road map and working conditions for a possible treatment are laid down. All this takes time—varying amounts for different families.

Kevin's mother called me to arrange a meeting with her nineteen-year-old son. She said he wasn't interested in therapy, since he thought the problem was all his dad and that his dad should go into therapy. She too thought her husband was troubled, but Kevin was really struggling with serious problems. He was on academic probation and was very depressed. The two antidepressant medications that had been prescribed did not seem to be working. Kevin had not spoken with his father in a whole year.

She was in town from a distant city, helping Kevin move to new lodgings, since he had left (or been asked to leave?) his fraternity. Could she have her son call me if he would accept her idea? She thought that he would refuse. I suggested that first we could meet, since she was here now. In that interview she recounted some history of both parents' families and offered her hypothesis that Kevin's troubles stemmed from the father's job loss when Kevin was a young adolescent. As she described the upheaval and disputation in the family business around Father's role, it became clear that everyone was still reverberating. Mother was dealing with tremendous sadness and frustration. I then defined it as a family trauma, which suggested a way to talk with Kevin about coming in.

Rather than telling Kevin he needed therapy, I suggested that she say that she had talked to me about the job loss, the father's subsequent anger and withdrawal, and its impact on everyone. She could say that I had called it a trauma that everyone in the family needed to talk about. It had helped her to talk to me about it, and it might help Kevin too.

Kevin called that afternoon, and I saw him several times over the next few days. He first vented about his father being controlling, demeaning, and blaming. He felt no respect for his father anymore and didn't want to talk with him. I said I could see from what he and his mother had told me why he felt so disappointed and angry. Then I wondered why Kevin was having so much trouble in school and with friends if the problem was all his father. He told me it was his father's fault, since he had never felt bad before, the way he did at the present time. He talked about his academic difficulties and the isolation and alienation he felt from other kids. He worried that they found him weird, even gross.

It sounded as if he were damaging himself in order to get back at his father. Building on Kevin's interest in Middle East politics, I remarked that he was being like a suicide bomber, attacking the enemy by destroying himself. Kevin was very taken with this metaphor. I noted that suicide bombing is a weapon of people who feel helpless. Did Kevin feel so helpless? Was he interested in finding some other way to feel effective?

Over the next week, we continued to meet and talked about finding the strength to explore more adaptive solutions and do without medication. I introduced the idea of emotional muscle, and Kevin found this so intriguing that he called his mother to tell her how useful he was finding the metaphors we were coming up with. She called me to say how encouraged she felt by Kevin's involvement; she hadn't heard him this positive in years. This allowed me to say that Kevin and I had discussed stopping his medication.

Kevin's mother began to talk about therapy, and I agreed that this now seemed a realistic possibility. I said I would talk with Kevin about this. But a treatment plan could not be finalized until I had spoken with her and her husband about the dual goals of treatment and the working arrangements for our collaborative effort. I explained that treatment would aim to restore Kevin's capacity to choose progressive solutions and equally include work to strengthen the parent-child relationship. I asked her to convey this to her husband and said I would like to speak with him soon.

When Kevin and I discussed embarking on a regular analysis, meeting four times a week with the specific goal of finding his strengths, building on them, and transforming his relationship with his parents, I told him that any treatment with him would have to involve his parents as well. He had no objection; Kevin wanted me to talk with his father, since he still believed his father was the source of all his troubles. Kevin wanted treatment for himself, and he retained the wish that I would also treat his father and change him.

Although Kevin expressed no concern about confidentiality, I raised it, emphasizing the distinction between secrecy and privacy. I said that the details of his own story, which we would learn together in various ways, would be kept absolutely private. Thoughts and feelings are private to him, and he would be making the choice whether to share them with me or anyone else. Actions are public; dangerous or potentially dangerous actions don't come into the realm of privacy, and we would work out together what to do in such an instance.

With the goal of transforming his relationship with his parents in mind, I said to Kevin I would share with him things that came up in my conversations with his parents. Ultimately, he and his parents would have freer communication and pleasure in sharing their experiences with each other.

We have written in a number of places about the crucial distinction between privacy and secrecy, which corresponds with the distinction between reality-based open-system functioning and closed-system power relationships, where secrets are a source of dominance (K. Novick and J. Novick 2005; J. Novick and K. Novick 2008; 2011). Nevertheless, the issue of confidentiality is always the main stumbling block in therapists' minds to doing parent work in adolescent treatments. So we have to devise techniques that reassure therapists that they can protect the patient's privacy, help parents tolerate the frustration of not knowing everything, foster greater communication and sharing between parents and adolescent, and redefine separateness and separation from them.

> We talk with parents and adolescents from the beginning about the difference between privacy and secrecy. Privacy is a given of mental life and a right related to mutual respect between separate individuals. Secrecy is motivated withholding that is often hostile and can carry a connotation of knowledge used to feel powerful in relation to excluded others. Differentiating between privacy and secrecy gives the therapist a needed vocabulary to explore family secrets, parents' secrets, the adolescent's secrets. Failure to make the distinction leaves the analyst vulnerable to a "silent countertransference," an internal resistance to engaging with areas of the patient's privacy, which then can have the destructive impact of turning private matters into powerful secrets. (J. Novick and K. Novick 2008, p. 148)

Kevin responded to the discussion of privacy and secrecy by phoning his father, speaking to him for the first time in over a year. All of my contacts to this point had been with the mother, but, following Kevin's phone call, the father joined our next parent meeting. As we talked, the father expressed his gratitude for the change and was impressed that Kevin had taken the initiative to stop his medication. Mother agreed enthusiastically with working arrangements for an analysis, including regular parent phone sessions and occasional meetings when they came to town. Father, although grateful, was still ambivalent and wanted us to work month-to-month. He also had various controlling strictures about fees, payment, and billing statements. These would become issues later but gave me a current reality confirmation of Kevin's description of his father's style.

In our joint phone sessions, both parents talked more about Kevin's history and gave me a vivid picture of what he was like when he was little. I began to hear how much Kevin had looked up to and idealized his father before the family trauma. I could take up with the parents and with Kevin how important their mutual love had been to them all and what a loss they had all experienced. Despite the father's prickly stance, it was clear that he loved his son. This primary parental love was essential knowledge for me in withstanding the times when the father reverted to his bullying style. I was able to stand firm that a month-to-month arrangement would undermine the treatment; on the basis of his underlying wish to do the best for his son, the father could allow me to be in charge of knowing how best to conduct Kevin's treatment.

I encouraged both parents to call or e-mail any time they had questions or concerns. During the first few weeks of analysis, Kevin's mother called numerous times with worries about Kevin's moods, wondering if he needed her to come. These talks with her helped me discern immediately a dynamic pattern that had not yet appeared in the early sessions with Kevin. I told him each time his mother called and wondered if he was aware that his distress always mobilized her anxiety and made her wish to fly in and rescue him. Fairly soon we established a shorthand vocabulary for such interactions and could spot them as they arose.

As he began to control his need to worry his mother, he brought this dynamic into the treatment relationship. His mastery of alternative ways to connect with his mother showed in Kevin's humor when we both picked up his whining or being pathetic, and he joked that he had better call his mother, so she would fly in. After six weeks of analysis, when he went home for Thanksgiving, the whole family noted Kevin's changes. They were thrilled to see his increased lightness and engagement. Kevin, however, reported to me that he felt weird, not knowing what to say or how to relate.

This dynamic sequence illustrates the complexity and immediacy of concurrent individual and parent work. Mother first brought the "connection through pain" (J. Novick and K. Novick 2007 [1996]) in her distress. I took this up with Kevin, who then became more aware that this was his way to stay close and have a unique relationship to his mother. Kevin and I worked on this, and I simultaneously talked with both parents about their side of the dynamic. My established good relationship with the mother allowed me to suggest and reinforce other ways of responding to Kevin, but the father became an unexpected ally, as he said he had always worried about her coddling Kevin.

Kevin's experience of emptiness over the November long weekend break pointed the direction for continued work in his analysis on the role pain played in his overall personality and history. We could see that there would be a struggle to set aside this closed-system functioning and discover alternative ways to relate to himself and others. Kevin's analysis was by now well established in the beginning phase. We could of course anticipate intense resistance arising from various sources in Kevin, his mother, and his father at different times.

These early months of Kevin's treatment brought various changes. His parents began to engage in a number of transformations, reworking aspects of their relationship with each other, Kevin and his siblings, and with the events of their shared histories. They no longer felt helpless nor needed therefore to externalize responsibility. Their importance as parents of an adolescent was established, and they embraced the dual goals of treatment. They did not feel excluded but respected the privacy of Kevin's analysis.

Kevin moved from a position of holding an unrelenting grudge, from psychic stasis, to beginning a dynamic reworking of his personality structure. He could allow himself to be with his analyst, beginning to engage in joint work. Moving out of a fixed, sadomasochistic stance with each of his parents, Kevin began to relate to them as separate individuals. He began to experience his conflicts inside. All of these gains were enriched and accelerated by the concurrent parent work.

From the Beginning to the Middle of Treatment—Melinda

Melinda's mother called because her eighteen-year-old daughter, a first-year student at university, was having panic attacks. Melinda had been seen by a therapist and treated with Cognitive Behavioral Therapy to little effect. The mother wanted to know if I use CBT. I responded that I use a multimodal technique that is responsive to particular individuals' needs and where they are in their development. I said that if Melinda and I decide to work together, I would also want to include her parents; the only technique I don't use is to prescribe medication. In that context the mother told me that she herself had been anxious for many years and had tried many therapeutic modalities. She and all the rest of the family members were currently on medication, and she wondered if this could help Melinda, who had not wanted medication.

I met Melinda the next week; after an evaluation period, we started twice-weekly sessions for a period of "exploratory work," to find out together what the dimensions of her situation were and how much she wanted to and could engage with benefit in this kind of treatment. I spoke to Melinda's mother once a month on the phone. Melinda felt comfortable that this was part of our work together.

Melinda's panic attacks quickly subsided as she settled into therapy. Her sessions were filled with intense feelings and stories about her long-standing boyfriend. She began to see how much she relied on him to manage her feelings. Despite a wish to break up with him, she feared that she would be unable to deal on her own. Much of the early work centered on her strengths and the idea of her developing her own voice. A crucial early interpretation was how she had made him into a mother figure, and in turn seemed to feel she had to function as his mother, too.

At the start of her sophomore year, Melinda decided that she should leave her boyfriend, as she realized that she was holding herself back from having the experiences and challenges offered by college. At first she handled the separation very well. It was her parents who seemed heartbroken by the ending of the relationship. They kept hoping the young people would get back together and kept referring to the breakup as temporary. This created enormous pressure for Melinda.

I sympathized with Mother's sadness around the young man, who had been very involved in the family for several years. The parent work offered the chance to address the parental concern that I was responsible for the breakup. The mother said that she and her husband had "joked" that "the shrink didn't like the young man." It clearly was not a joke. Without parent work, this probably would have led to a premature ending, with a young person who was still very compliant to parental wishes. Instead, after saying that my goal at this point in the treatment was to help Melinda find her own wishes and desires, we could look at the mother's overinvolvement with Melinda's life. At the same time, Melinda became more capable of standing up for herself; she assertively confronted her parents and other siblings, telling them they weren't respecting her choice and allowing her space to live her life.

Melinda then became involved with a new young man. This relationship was much more mature. Melinda worked hard to keep her anxiety to herself, avoiding turning him into another mother. However, the combination of the new boyfriend leaving to do an internship in another city, her mother reminding her of the old boyfriend, and a tenacious flu overwhelmed Melinda. Panic attacks recurred. In conversations with both Melinda and her mother, I suggested that she needed more intensive work, and we began meeting four times per week, while continuing phone work with her mother.

Once Melinda was in analysis, we could see in more detail the longstanding pattern of exclusive closeness with her mother around their shared propensity for panic. Melinda began to associate to memories of childhood, for instance, when she was excited in anticipation of being in the school play. She told her mother that she "couldn't wait," and her mother said, "Oh, you're anxious." Every time Melinda felt enthusiastic or eager or appropriately "pumped" for a performance or school test, her mother characterized the feelings as anxiety. Mother stressed her understanding as based on their similarity to each other and offered Melinda all her own tricks for distracting herself and getting rid of the feelings.

Melinda brought this dynamic into the transference with her organizing belief that the only way to keep me with her was to be a helpless, anxious child. She had worked to connect with her new boyfriend in a different way, and he had still left. What would happen in the analysis if she didn't come with anxiety? Would I still want to see her? Would I still be interested in her? She came in one day, saying, "I am so pleased at the change! I realized as I was coming here that I wasn't anxious, and I still knew that you would want to see me and want to hear about my non-anxious day." This was followed by a wave of sadness, as she associated to the fact that she hadn't spoken to her mother in a few days, whereas she used to call her multiple times daily for comfort and advice on how to deal with whatever anxiety she was currently feeling.

During this period, work went on with her mother around their exclusive bonding through anxiety. Her mother took this to heart and made a conscious effort to stop interacting the old way. But she too felt a bit lost. With my support she was able to step back from her automatic responsiveness to Melinda's anxiety. On the phone she would ask Melinda to tell her about other aspects of her day and would suggest that Melinda bring her anxiety to her treatment.

This work made space for Melinda to move beyond the understanding of the anxiety as a mode of attachment to consider its other functions. We began to examine the defensive role of her constant worrying. She said, "What am I hiding with my anxiety?" Legitimate, age-appropriate, realistic questions about herself began to emerge, as she grappled with genuine uncertainty about the career ambitions her parents had always encouraged and the nature of her relationships.

She realized that she had always omnipotently believed that asserting her own ideas and feelings was hostile and that her family would not be able to handle them.

The transformation of the exclusive anxious tie between Melinda and her mother to richer relationship between two separate people created new space for both of them to truly include others, especially Melinda's father. He had always supported Melinda's treatment but never participated in the parent sessions. Melinda said she had always felt he really didn't understand her. My impression was that he had been squeezed out.

One weekend during this period, Melinda's father called her and had a relaxed conversation about what she'd been doing, in contrast to his earlier awkward style of questioning her like a younger child. Melinda was very moved and happy, feeling like she really had a dad. I had my first conversation with him soon after. The parent work and Melinda's treatment and growth were something he could now feel part of.

The Middle of Treatment—Frank

Frank's parents called seeking treatment with medication and CBT, as he had received a diagnosis of severe obsessive-compulsive disorder. Both parents were in long-term therapy, and Frank's mother was on medication, following her hospitalization for a breakdown when Frank was a preteen. I suggested doing an evaluation to see what would actually prove most useful for Frank, who was a first-year student in a challenging university program.

Frank did indeed suffer from severe OCD, and the first eighteen months of his analysis saw mighty struggles and great progress. I had, as usual, described the dual goals of treatment, to which Frank responded with relief that his parents would have someone to help them. His parents were equally glad to have the chance to be part of the process and improve the possibility of transforming their relationship with Frank, which had been burdened all his life by their concern for his level of anxiety. They felt great guilt around the possible impact of their psychological difficulties on his development.

The first transformation in the beginning phase involved Frank's parents' understanding that his struggles and his OCD were not due to bad genes or a brain disorder, but rather represented a solution that he had found around conflicts that made perfect sense to them. With Frank's permission, I had shared with the parents his conflicts over feeling responsible for his mother's breakdown and his father's rages.

His father exclaimed, "Oh, my god, that's just like me, and it's what I'm working on in my therapy."

These parents were very loving and supportive, but they were estranged from Frank, perceiving him as somehow alien to them, incomprehensible and inaccessible. This distance was yielding when they called me in a panic. Frank had spoken to them on the phone about being angry with a professor. His mother was concerned that he was losing control and thought he should get medication; his father seemed to have no idea of how to respond to either Frank's feelings or the mother's anxiety.

I pointed out to them that much of the recent work in the second year of Frank's analysis focused on his trusting himself and his feelings, using them as signals, rather than something to be squashed and subdued by obsessional thoughts. Frank was becoming more spontaneous, more joyful, and more expressive. What an achievement it represented for him to know he was mad at his teacher, to be able to tell his parents about it as a point of information, and to move on from that experience! His father responded with the idea that this was worthy of celebration, not worry. He then said that he realized that they had never, ever heard Frank say he was angry. This was a watershed moment.

When I told Frank about my talk with his parents, he said that he hadn't realized he had upset them; should he call and apologize? We were then able to analyze his old omnipotent idea that his feelings were so dangerous that they had sent his mother to the hospital or his father into uncontrolled rage. He and his parents were all working hard to change the functions these beliefs had served in their personalities.

This vignette captures the work of the middle phase. For Frank, the focus was continuing work on how and why he held on to omnipotent beliefs in the destructive power of his feelings, with the OCD symptoms as a closed-system solution to the helplessness he felt throughout childhood. For his parents, there was a lot of work to transform the old patterns of relating to Frank as an externalized reflection of their own troubles managing affect. The concurrent parent work allowed these changes to take place in parallel, so that Frank and his parents could help each other grow.

The Middle to the Pre-termination Phase of Treatment — Basil

Basil was in crisis at the end of his first year of university; he was failing in his studies, had no friends, and felt suicidal. He felt virtually unable to function without stimulant medication, but he also sedated himself with constant marijuana, prescription drugs, and alcohol. He spent a lot of time on his computer frequenting pornographic sites. He had grandiose, "Darwinian," almost delusional ideas about his vast superiority to everyone else, especially women. He hated his father and was enmeshed in an intensely ambivalent, clinging relationship with his mother.

Throughout the early period of evaluation and the beginning of analysis, Basil's parents were in frequent touch with me by phone, as well as in several meetings with both of them. They came across as polar opposites in style and in their parenting approaches. His father was truculent and aggressive, impatient with both Basil and his wife, whose extreme anxiety led him to outbursts of impotent rage. The mother, who had suffered multiple losses in her family of origin, as well as many miscarriages, seemed unable to ever be calm and secure. An initial technique was to address both the rage and the anxiety directly, suggesting to the parents that they should call me with those feelings rather than share them with Basil. Their conversations with Basil would be better spent developing habits of more grown-up discussions, transforming their interactions from crisis management to sharing interests, of which this family had many.

College students usually leave town when the school year is done. This disrupts analysis and the therapeutic effort, and yet it is often not realistic to expect them to stay only for the purposes of treatment rather than go to jobs, internships, and needed developmental time with family. In these cases, we assume that the work of treatment will be continued by regular phone or Skype sessions. Young people nowadays take this in stride. Parents are sometimes surprised at the idea at first but usually seem grateful that the work will continue. This also provides live material from the late adolescent and the parents about ongoing parent-child interactions. It creates a laboratory for both parents and adolescent to practice new ways of interacting.

With this immediacy we can more easily take up the adolescent's responsibility, or defensive avoidance, to address issues directly with parents and see their own part in maintaining pathological interactions. For instance, Basil described driving his mother to the store. She freaked out, terrified that he would crash the car and kill them. When I heard about this in Basil's session, he admitted that he was driving more recklessly than usual. This allowed us to examine the dynamic interplay between her disproportionate anxieties and his provocation to create a heightened atmosphere between them, reproducing intense childhood excitement.

A year later, when Basil again was driving the car too fast, his mother was able to address it directly, asking him why he was doing it. He moderated his speed without a fight and told her he thought there was a part of him that still wanted her to be his hovering, clinging, frantic mom. They each described this incident with pride and pleasure in how much they had changed.

Two years into Basil's analysis, he had a stellar academic record, was totally off both marijuana and prescription drugs, had no suicidal thoughts, and was making realistic future career plans. When he occasionally retreated to closed-system solutions like watching porn, he brought the incidents to his session, taking the initiative to examine what he was trying to deal with in the old way. Almost always, the trigger was an experience of success or growth. This allowed us to move into more explicit analytic work on the conflicts and confusions in his relationship to his father and his masculine identifications.

Basil's parents continued to struggle with their opposite styles, but they saw this as an ongoing task for them to deal with. They were able to make good use of a somewhat reduced frequency of parent phone sessions, as Basil was shouldering so much of the responsibility for transforming their relationships with him. In a session with all three, when Basil's parents were visiting to help him move into a new apartment in a multistory building, Basil's father was enthusiastic, but his mother seemed hesitant. Basil put his arm around her, smiled, and said, "Don't worry, Mom. I won't jump; I'm too much in love with life now to do that."

As Basil approached the end of his third year, he wondered what we had left to work on. The notion of "having covered everything" had come up several times earlier as a resistance to making the next developmental step, and we had worked on it as such. This time, we again canvassed whether there was something being avoided, but we both then felt that the issues we were now working on were the crucial ones remaining. I spoke to Basil about the work of an ending time and the importance of taking some time beforehand—a "pretermination" phase—to make sure we were both ready to do the hard work of finishing (J. Novick and K. Novick 2006).

The major remaining issue was Basil's confusion between assertion and aggression. This confusion is rife in our culture, but it was lived out by his father, who ascribed all his personal and professional success to his "mano a mano" style of destroying the opposition. Basil's father felt that aggression is the sine qua non of masculinity. At various points in Basil's life, when he felt Basil fell short of this ideal, he called him feminine, weak, babyish, or "faggy." Basil had started analysis hating his father, yet completely identified with these attitudes, struggling with intense self-loathing as well as self-righteous rage. His suicidality and his grandiosity represented in part his terrible conflict.

As we began to discuss pretermination, Basil was actively grappling with the consequences of his identification with his father's beliefs. He experienced a different kind of conflict, one we have written about as between open- and closed-system solutions, as he now had an alternative world view in which aggression functioned as an important emotional signal but constituted an interference and retreat from reality if used as an emotional weapon to bully others (K. Novick and J. Novick 2002b). By this time Basil was active and assertive; he took great pleasure in the exercise of his "emotional muscles" of persistence, work, and satisfaction from process (K. Novick and J. Novick 2010; 2011). This brought him into internal and external clashes with his father's values. Basil suggested, and I agreed, that perhaps it was time to resume more frequent meetings with his parents.

Basil had told his parents that we were in a "pretermination phase." This didn't mean we were ending, but that we were thinking about how to get ready for that. His mother worried that I meant to stop the analysis immediately, and his father was concerned that Basil wasn't ready, since he still "withdrew from challenges." He thought Basil would continue to avoid a fight even if he went into a competitive field, as he was considering, and then would fail for lack of adequate aggression.

My work with Basil's mother was fairly straightforward but crucial. I spoke with the parents separately during this time, as they each had different issues. I explained that a pretermination phase was expressly designed to avoid precipitate action by anyone. There is no time limit, all issues can be discussed, and we all want to make sure that Basil is ready to do the important work of ending and beyond. I assured her that we would work together and stay in touch around this task. This exchange also gave us another opportunity to talk about her ongoing anxiety, to applaud her continuing efforts to keep it out of her interactions with her son, and to discuss how she felt she needed constant reinforcement from Basil and me to do so. She always kept her anxiety away from her husband since it made him so angry. Her fear of her husband's rage offered a useful opening for a long period of work with Basil's father in relation to his conviction that it is only his anger that has made him successful, in contrast to the passive wimp he felt his own father had been.

Basil's individual work paralleled the parent work with his father. With both we were exploring the fixed belief that masculinity equates with aggression, which produces success. For Basil, this represented an identification with his father, a sense that this was the only way to maintain his tie; for his father, it was a negative identification with his own father, supported by an ongoing therapy in which he was encouraged to let go of any guilt about aggression. At times I felt discouraged about getting anywhere with Basil's father, who had told me at the beginning of the treatment how he would get ready for an important sale. He said, "I pump myself up by thinking that the customer is taking the food out of my family's mouths. I get so furious that there is no stopping me and I grab the deal."

But I was not alone in my efforts, as Basil was an ally in the work. He felt his father was beginning to register Basil's successes as a result of assertive activity. He said his father seemed really surprised by how much pleasure Basil was getting from working, trying, and persisting.

Basil said to me, "I enjoy getting an A, but that's the cherry on top. It's using my mind, the same way it feels good using my body when I'm running." I asked Basil's permission to share this in my next talk with his dad. When I did so, his father remarked that he was indeed surprised and impressed that Basil now seemed to be enjoying intellectual challenges rather than retreating from them. "At the end of the day," he said, "he doesn't seem as exhausted as I am when I finish work. You both may have something there after all. He's beginning to look like a pretty successful guy, so maybe he doesn't have to go out and beat everyone down." This work extended over many months, as Basil and his father each wrestled with the idea that there were alternative, joyful ways to achieve success and be a man. We all finally seemed ready to pick a date and start a three-month termination phase.

Termination of Treatment and Beyond—Luke

In our book on parent work (K. Novick and J. Novick 2005) we trace the six-year analysis of Luke, who had nearly died following a suicide attempt at sixteen. Any positive change in Luke usually brought dramatic and often tempestuous reactions from his two emotionally challenged parents. At one point, as the history of Mother's childhood physical abuse came to light, she decided to stop parent work. There was, however, a strong enough alliance with Luke's father that he continued regular sessions. The details of the concurrent work with Luke and his parents from the beginning to termination may be found in our book, with both general points and issues specific to this case described. Here we summarize some of those points.

The termination phase in the treatment of late adolescents is a topic notable for the absence of discussion. As we have pointed out, most adolescents end treatment prematurely (Novick 1990; J. Novick and K. Novick 2006). The high incidence of premature termination in our own work and that of students and colleagues was one element that first turned our attention to considering what role parent work could play in helping treatments begin well, continue, and terminate well at the appropriate time.

Since we have begun practicing and teaching concepts and techniques of concurrent parent work, we have found greater success for ourselves and others using these ideas. We are finding increasingly that even adolescents can accomplish a full treatment and end in a mutually enhancing and growth-promoting way, despite the traditional psychoanalytic pessimism about analysis of adolescents (J. Novick and K. Novick 2008; 2011).

In the field in general, there is again a wave of recognition that termination matters (Schlesinger 2005; Salberg 2010; J. Novick and K. Novick 2006). Child-and-adolescent analysts are beginning to see that the end of a treatment is not only significant for the patient but makes specific demands of parents, with corresponding vulnerabilities, challenges, and dangers.

In *Working with Parents Makes Therapy Work* we wrote that "termination work with parents is crucial to helping them to support their child's adaptive use of the termination work; to meet the child's legitimate need for a supportive, validating person when the analyst is no longer available; and to foster their own autonomous capacity to use the positive parenting skills they have developed" (K. Novick and J. Novick 2005, pp.141–42). We went on to point out that "these are significant demands on parents, which can give rise to fears of sadness, love, and loss, and to fears of reliving core experiences of grief and conflict around good-byes. Parents may try to deal with these anxieties by avoidance or premature withdrawal from the parent work, or they may use parent work as an opportunity to learn a new way of saying good-bye" (ibid., p.142).

One of Luke's father's responses to imminent termination was to withdraw and consider stopping his parent sessions. He said that he would support Luke's work, but that he himself is happy with his relationship with his son and thought this was a good time to stop the parent work. I focused on the changes in him, especially his capacity to access a wider range of feelings, but wondered if he might now be retreating a bit. I said that Luke was using his sessions to practice listening to his feelings and consolidate confidence in his ability to manage his emotions and use them adaptively. I suggested that tensions can arise when people have very different modes of handling feelings, leading to greater distancing from each other. As we talked, Luke's father associated to his family's military tradition of suppressing feelings and how he had been called a "brave little soldier" for not crying when his father went away and was killed at war when he was four years old.

Luke's father continued concurrent parent work throughout Luke's termination phase. He consolidated his own growth as a parent, including his capacity to become more conscious of and find more adaptive ways to cope with his very fragile wife. He was supportive of Luke's mourning for the analysis and the analyst. At the end both father and Luke were able to

> come to terms with their feelings about the fact that what we have termed "closed-system sadomasochistic functioning" was still present and available. It had not been eradicated, only decreased in intensity and contained by alternative open-system possibilities. They would both have to continue working after analysis to address conflicts between these alternative ways to regulate themselves and resolve conflicts. But they were equipped with the capacities gained in the course of mastering the therapeutic alliance tasks during each phase of treatment. Father and Luke could then imagine the postanalytic phase realistically, sensitive to signs of reverting to closed-system functioning and aware of being equipped to deal with these conflicts. This included the knowledge they could contact the analyst at any time if they needed or wanted to. (ibid., p. 147)

Difficulties in Concurrent Parent Work

The five vignettes above describe successful passage through some of the many shoals that can make treatments founder and end suddenly or prematurely. But they may not adequately convey either the detailed difficulties of parent work or the impact of parental pathology on the process. Even as we seek to engage the best parts of parents in the endeavor, we have to stay mindful of the darker dimensions of parental hate and destructiveness to children, both individual and cultural (Young-Bruehl 2011), and the potential for parents to sacrifice their children for their own psychic needs or the survival of the marriage.

PARENTAL DEFENSES

Kevin's father, for instance, idealized the harsh treatment he had received from his own father. He often declared to Kevin, "My father was tough on me and he always told me I'd appreciate it when I was older. And I do! So I expect you will be glad of my tough love someday." But what Kevin's dad called "tough love" was actually unrelenting lifelong disparagement, criticism, and invidious comparisons of everything Kevin did with others, including himself. Father's florid negativity made it easy for Kevin to keep the issue externalized. It took a long time to reach the insight that he had internalized the attacks and created a bond with his father based on a closed-system sadistic superego (J. Novick and K. Novick 2004).

It was hard for Kevin's father to begin to question his own idealization of his own father's abusive behavior. Only when this dynamic process was set in motion in the parent work could he abate his relentless criticism of Kevin, which in turn created space for Kevin to take responsibility for his self-destructiveness.

REVISITING FAMILY HISTORY

There was a repeated pattern in Frank's material of misery and intensification of his obsessional symptoms every time he felt good or had a success. This was even more marked around separations. I asked his mother about the family's history of losses and separations. She denied that there was anything significant.

But, in fact, Frank's family had moved back to his mother's country of origin to be near extended family after his birth. His mother described Frank flourishing in the warmth of the family, toddler teachers, and their community. The original plan for father's continuing career there failed, and they had returned when Frank was two years old. His mother thought Frank was too young to have any reactions to the move. I noted that even very small children register big changes and that they can reverberate later. His mother then said that she had fallen into a serious depression after the move.

Difficult or painful events in family histories, like family secrets, can all too easily become a toxic inhibition of forward movement in a treatment. If they go unaddressed, there can be a validation of omnipotent belief that thoughts and feelings are really dangerous. This creates a destructive fault line in the treatment.

Frank's mother missed the next parent session because she forgot. When we spoke again, she said she had been very upset since we opened up this topic. She found it painful and she felt guilty. She kept thinking about the idea that Frank had lost his first home and his mother at the same time. Drawing on the strength of our established alliance, I could acknowledge her pain and her wish to run away from our work and these difficult feelings. But I also could speak to her powerful primary love for Frank. For the sake of that love, she could face anything. She then went on to fill in the details that allowed us to reconstruct how this bright little boy had put together the theory that his own pleasure in being the center of loving attention, his excitement, and his progressive development led directly to loss and loneliness.

With this material, Frank's construction of obsessional symptoms and his use of them to regulate any dangerous feelings, including anger, became much more available in his treatment. It also enabled his parents to share and talk about feelings more freely in general, something that had been markedly inhibited in this family.

PATHOLOGICAL PARENTAL INTERACTIONS

Divorced parents are a challenge to all child-and-adolescent therapists. One way this manifests is in one or both parents disclaiming any interest in participating in parent work: "I don't need treatment" or "Just deal with my kid" or "I don't want to be in the same room with her/him." This stance alerts us to the probability that externalization is a major mode of functioning in the family. In our 2005 book and in our 2008 paper, we discuss externalization more extensively. Here we can note that this parental pathology can scuttle an adolescent's treatment either when the child is loaded with all the blame for family problems or the ex-spouses are so invested in continuing to fight their old battles that they are willing to sacrifice their child for it. There is also the externalization of responsibility by dumping the child on the analyst, with parents abdicating their role in further development by refusing to engage in any parent work.

Divorced parents highlight general obstacles to concurrent parent work, such as externalization, refusal to engage, refusal to take responsibility, the use of the therapy to maintain their pathological equilibrium, the use of the child for their own needs, and so forth. All of these may be characterized as a negative therapeutic motivation (J. Novick and K. Novick 2007 [1996]), in which parents bring a child to treatment in order to make it fail. There are also situations where the level of hatred and bitterness is so great that there is no remedy and treatment cannot get started or be maintained.

However, even when the level of acrimony is quite high, we have found ways to implement our model of concurrent parent work. There may have to be an extra effort to point out that parents have not divorced themselves from their important parenting function by maintaining conviction about the dual goals. The task of transforming relationships with two adversarial parents is greater for the young person, especially when parents promote loyalty conflicts. Our model gives therapists room to be creative in structuring the work. One can work with both parents together, with them in separate alternating sessions, by phone, e-mail, or Skype, including the patient or not, and so forth. Flexibility and willingness to meet each family's configuration are crucial.

For example, in our parent-work book, we describe Christina, whose parents had a high-conflict divorce when she was a toddler. She was in analysis from four to seven years of age. In the concurrent parent work during her childhood treatment, her parents and stepparents became able to function together as parents, able to prioritize the child's needs over their own narcissistic wishes.

Christina's developmental transitions seemed to stress the parents' phase dominance. Old defensive patterns of relating with each other and with Christina flared up and interfered with Christina's progressive development each time she was poised to enter a new phase. During college in her late adolescence, when it came time to choose a major field of study, Christina found her parents impossibly demanding and rigid, and the parents were at loggerheads. Christina asked to see me.

After two sessions with Christina, it was clear that she was actually doing well but felt threatened by her parents' pathologies. We met jointly with all four parents to talk through the issues that they were having such trouble about. Although the session focused on the concrete problem of supporting Christina in choosing her field, the process and my presence seemed to reestablish the parents in the phase of parenthood they had achieved earlier. This unconventional grouping of two divorced parents, two stepparents, and a late adolescent together in the room met this family's complex needs effectively.

CONCLUSIONS

THE DEVELOPMENTAL POINT OF VIEW

We locate the work described in this paper in both the century-old psychoanalytic tradition and in the capacity of psychoanalysis continually to expand and absorb new findings. Many years ago, Freud (1916) confronted the age-old nature-versus-nurture debate by suggesting a complemental series, where the two are in constant interaction. Erikson elaborated this to formulate an epigenetic series in which development occurs from complex interactions that continue across the life span (1950). The most recent neuroscientific work takes the same position. The Harvard neurobiologist Steven Hyman states, "The old 'nature vs. nurture' debate has long receded into scientific irrelevance. Instead the frontier lies in understanding the mechanisms by which environmental factors . . . interact with the genome to influence brain development and produce diverse forms of neuroplasticity over the life time" (2009, p. 241).

Psychoanalysts from Freud on have articulated the process by which behavior is not predetermined by brain functions or genomes alone, but intersects at crucial developmental moments to express innate factors and then interact with subsequent environmental input to produce the variety of behavior we see in humans of all ages. Neuroscientists now say, "In neuroimaging, as in life, it is more about the journey than the destination" (Giedd et al. 2009, p. 469). This should be a familiar idea for psychoanalysts, and a developmental approach to all behavior is where we start. All this is to state that it may take cutting-edge neuroscience research to remind psychoanalysts that the unique contribution of psychoanalysis lies in its developmental perspective.

Each discipline works with a set of assumptions and an epistemological strategy. As psychoanalysts we assume the following:

- The developmental approach is a crucial metapsychological dimension of understanding personality functioning.
- The developmental approach is what differentiates psychoanalysis from many other psychological theories.
- A developmental approach assumes that all behavior has meaning and a history.
- Development can only take place in the context of relationships.
- A child's history encompasses generations, at the very least the parents and the beliefs and fantasies they bring to rearing the particular child. Cultural influences are transmitted through parents and other relationships and experiences in the child's life.
- The first determinant of any current behavior is likely to be found in the parent-child relationship, especially, as we have emphasized, in the pleasure/pain economy of that relationship.
- Behavior evolves through phases in which current levels of psychological and biological functioning influence and are influenced by previous phases.
- Transformation is the main characteristic of this epigenetic evolution.
- No one phase has more importance than any other, and developmental transformations continue throughout the life span.
- Each phase brings something unique to the mix, which may compensate for earlier difficulties or raise prior dormant issues to problematic intensity (*Nachträglichkeit*, or "deferred action") (J. Novick and K. Novick 2001a).

These assumptions inform our model of parent work in general, as parents constitute a major, primary environmental influence in ongoing ways throughout the child's life. In the specific context of our current discussion of late adolescence, we note the continuing plasticity of the adolescent brain, the opportunity for adaptive identifications, and the particular transformation tasks of late adolescence, with the challenge to young people and their parents to opt for progressive, open-system solutions and set aside old patterns of omnipotent, closed-system functioning.

THE ROLE OF FATHERS

When we contemplate the developmental tasks of late adolescence, there is a convergence among transformation of relationships to self and others, realignment of the relationship between the pleasure and reality principles, and the consolidation of identity. We have noticed that many who now accept the importance of parent work in general nevertheless work predominantly with mothers. Various theoretical approaches have also tended to give more weight to the maternal than paternal relationship, but that can lead to rationalized explanations for tolerating father avoidance. Often practical difficulties in father participation are cited, and those have to be given due weight, but we think there may be other, less-conscious factors involving fears and fantasies of paternal power and retaliation (K. Novick and J. Novick, 2005; J. Novick and K. Novick 2012). Both male and female therapists may be subject to such worries.

As we were writing this paper and thinking about the group of cases described above, as well as others, we realized that progress in each family depended eventually on the participation of the fathers. Whether or not they were initially involved, sooner or later their active involvement created turning points in the work with each patient. This preliminary finding has technical implications, in addition to the affirmation of the importance of the developmental dimensions referred to above. The role of fathers as a bridge to reality and the outside world is well established (Pruett 1992). In our experience, transformation of the relationship to both mothers and fathers is critical for open-system identity formation in young men and young women alike.

Technically this impacts the structure of the treatment and the network of therapeutic alliances. When fathers don't engage right away, it is useful for therapists to stay flexible about their participation. Probably even more important is to keep an open mind and hold the father present in our mental map of the patient and family's representational landscape. Then we will be ready to enlist fathers whenever they feel able to join the work.

THE IMPORTANCE OF THE THERAPEUTIC ALLIANCE

Accomplishment of therapeutic alliance tasks promotes attunement in relationships. Current neuroscience supports the importance of attachment and communication in maintaining brain plasticity and growth (Schore 2000; 2002). It seems to us that there is again convergence between important factors in this late-adolescent work. The therapeutic alliance with parents has been empirically shown to have significant correlation with treatment outcome (Kazdin, Whitley, and Marciano 2006; Garcia and Weisz 2002; McCleod and Weisz 2005; Novick, Benson, and Rembar 1981). Since the therapeutic alliance tasks correspond with open-system functioning, and one way we conceptualize treatment is in terms of movement from predominantly closed-system to greater open-system self-regulation, it follows then that concurrent parent work, whatever the age of the patient, will contribute to greater therapeutic success (K. Novick and J. Novick 1998; J. Novick and K. Novick 2000; 2002b).

In our 2005 book we describe various sources of resistance to substantive work with parents, discussing social-historical, theoretical, dynamic, and political factors. Here we would add another historical aspect, which stems from the fact that many early child analyses were conducted within a very small group of colleagues. For instance, Melanie Klein analyzed her own children; Anna Freud analyzed several of the children of her best friend and colleague, plus others of their classmates. Under such circumstances, no parent work was possible; no therapeutic alliance with parents could be formed, and no dynamic changes in parents could be initiated and worked through systematically.

The field of child-and-adolescent analysis has moved on, and we think it is now ready to accept the utility and impact of concurrent parent work for all ages, including adolescents. It is still an evolving model with many questions of technique to solve. But our experience of the past twenty years of experimentation allows us to share the following technical recommendations.

TECHNICAL RECOMMENDATIONS

Make use of the full repertoire of psychoanalytic interventions.

Developmental interference in parenting can be understood as pathology amenable to therapeutic work. It follows then that we consider it necessary and appropriate to use the full conceptual and technical repertoire from individual work with children and adults in the context of parent work. We do not define parent work negatively, that is, in terms of what it is not, or what the restrictions may be. Rather, we see it as substantive, significant, and legitimate in its own right. Parent work therefore includes interventions traditionally labeled as "therapeutic," for example, analysis of defenses, verbalization, insight, reconstruction, interpretation, and the use of transference and countertransference for understanding and technique.

In addition to the traditional use of education, support, validation, modeling, facilitating, and so forth that have been staples of parent guidance, we can illustrate the relevance and utility of using the full range of techniques both by the difficulties that arise when the therapist pulls back from using these skills and, in the positive sense, when *interpretation* and *working through* are crucial to the success of both of the dual goals of treatment.

In our experience, use of the full range of therapeutic techniques in parent work does not compete or interfere with individual therapy for parents. Indeed, parent work may lead to acceptance of a referral for individual treatment while maintaining the relationship with the child analyst for work on parenting issues. Parent work focuses on the parent-child relationship; other issues in the parents' lives are engaged with only as they have relevance to their relationship with their child. Thus we may use the full range of our skills without inhibition in the very limited and focused area of parenting.

Successful parent work demands internal conviction and explicit presentation of the dual goals of treatment.

Anna Freud defined the goal of child analysis as restoration of the child to the path of progressive development (1970). We have extended this idea to include a second goal: helping parents achieve the developmental phase of parenthood, that is, restoring parents to the path of progressive adult development, in which parenthood is one phase.

Our view of the parent-child relationship provides a framework for evolving a technique of parent work that encompasses both the resistances and the developmental aids to therapy. The aim of child-and-adolescent analysis can be recast as not only the restoration of the child's progressive development but also as the restoration of the parent-child relationship that has been disrupted by pathology to its potential as a lifelong positive resource for both. Thus we are mindful throughout child or adolescent treatment of these dual goals of the work.

This idea is not only an implicit assumption but also an active and explicit assertion. We tell parents early in the evaluation that we have these two goals for our endeavors together. We work with this idea until it becomes an intrinsic motivation for continued treatment.

It is not only an intrinsic motivation for parents; it also has to be a sincere conviction for the analyst. Parents assess the authenticity and competence of therapists to whom they consider entrusting their child, even their almost grown-up child. In the current cultural climate that glorifies quick fixes, psychoanalysts feel terribly vulnerable and often not very confident in making recommendations for a long and intensive treatment. Each of the five patients we described came with his or her own treatment plan, as did the parents. Four were either on medication or being pressured by family and friends to obtain it. The fifth was self-medicating through substance abuse. It takes confidence and support to hold out for the evidence-based efficacy of analysis, especially analysis with concurrent parent work.

It is beyond the scope of this paper to detail the many ways that younger therapists can surmount these obstacles, but it is an important topic to discuss. One approach may be a focus on building emotional muscle in therapists, so that they will feel confident that they can tolerate uncertainty and frustration, withstand hostility, and know that they can live through hard times with patients and their parents (K. Novick and J. Novick 2010; 2011).

Differentiating privacy and secrecy is central.

When we differentiate privacy and secrecy it helps us define confidentiality more precisely. We talk with parents and adolescents about the intrinsic privacy of thoughts and feelings but state that actions are public. Safety is the paramount clinical requirement, and it will be destructive of the treatment, and perhaps dangerous to the adolescent, if unsafe actions are concealed. Confidentiality should be maintained in support of privacy, but not as a reflexive collusion with secrecy. Our clinical goal is to make secrecy an object of therapeutic exploration and insight, so that adolescents and their parents can begin to take pleasure in fruitful sharing and communication.

This is one of the most sensitive and difficult aspects of treating adolescents. Concerns about confidentiality have always been one of the major reasons that adolescent therapists have avoided concurrent parent work (J. Novick and K. Novick 2008). As we noted in our parent-work book:

> There is a hierarchy of clinical values that we apply to treatments of patients of all ages. The establishment of safety—for the patient, the parents, the therapist—is paramount. It is in the best interests of the child

[or adolescent] that he be kept safe from harm. These are the priorities of the therapeutic setting for the therapist. Trust and security are crucial ingredients of the sense of safety; knowing that thoughts and feelings will be respected as belonging to one's private mental life allows for gradual relaxation into sharing them with the analyst. Progress along the developmental line of the sense of self includes increasing reliance on the privacy of one's mind. Knowing that dangerous actions toward others or the self will be addressed definitively also provides a sense of security to the child [and adolescent] who fears his own loss of control; he then feels that his impulses will be checked with the help of another. (K. Novick and J. Novick 2005, p. 53)

Concurrent parent work confirms the centrality and importance of parents and their primary parental love for their child.

We talk with parents from the beginning about establishing a partnership (therapeutic alliance) to support their ongoing important role with their adolescent child. Much of the work addresses the externalization of responsibility for staying engaged in transformations. Externalizations can have many different sources, ranging from characteristic defense styles to fatigue and helplessness in the face of adolescent pathology. We work hard in the initial phases of treatment to place parents in their rightful position in the mental life of the adolescent, and the adolescent in the center of the parents' consolidation in the phase of parenthood.

Most parents come for consultation at a time when they feel angry and helpless and very often terribly guilty and ashamed that they can no longer find their love for their child. But without that love, no treatment and no change can take place. Part of the analyst's task is to believe that some love is there, and then focus on helping parents access it, recover it, and enhance it. Unless analysts can sincerely work in this realm, they will be unable to respect and care for the parents; without that regard, the treatment will founder, as parents will feel criticized and rejected.

We have found that our model of dynamic concurrent parent work, with its emphasis on developing an alliance with parents that is based on mutual respect and trust, work that taps into the potential for primary parental love, is effective not only with children but also with adolescents.

REFERENCES

BENEDEK, T. (1959). Parenthood as a developmental phase: A contribution to the libido theory. *Journal of the American Psychoanalytic Association* 7:389–417.

DeVito, E., J. Novick, and K. K. Novick (2000 [1994]). Cultural interferences with listening to adolescents. *Journal of Infant, Child, and Adolescent Psychotherapy* 1:77–95.

Erikson, E. (1950). *Childhood and Society*. New York: Norton.

Freud, A. (1958). Adolescence. In *The Writings of Anna Freud* 5:136–66. New York: International Universities Press.

——— (1970). Problems of termination in child analysis. In *The Writings of Anna Freud* 7:3–21.

Freud, S. (1911). Formulations on the two principles of mental functioning. In *Standard Edition of the Complete Psychological Works of Sigmund Freud*, ed. James Strachey, vol. 12, pp. 213–26. London: Hogarth Press.

——— (1916). Introductory lectures on psycho-analysis. In *Standard Edition*, vol. 16, pp. 346–47.

Furman, E. (1995). Working with and through the parents. *Child Analysis* 6:21–42.

——— (1999). The impact of parental interventions. *International Journal of Psychoanalysis* 80:172.

Garcia, J., and J. Weisz (2002). When youth mental health care stops: Therapeutic relationship problems and other reasons for ending youth outpatient treatment. *Journal of Consulting and Clinical Psychology* 70:439–43.

Giedd, J., F. Lalonde, M. Celano, S. White, G. Wallace, N. Lee, and R. Lenroot (2009). Anatomical brain magnetic resonance imaging of typically developing children and adolescents. *Journal of the American Academy of Child & Adolescent Psychiatry* 48 (5): 465–70.

Glenn, J., L. Sabot, and J. Bernstein (1978). The role of the parents in child analysis. In *Child Analysis and Therapy*, ed. J. Glenn. New York: Jason Aronson.

Hyman, S. (2009). How adversity gets under the skin. *Nature Neuroscience* 12 (3): 241–43.

Kazdin, A . E., M. Whitley, and P. Marciano (2006). Child-therapist and parent-therapist alliance and therapeutic change in the treatment of children referred for oppositional, aggressive, and antisocial behavior. *Journal of Child Psychology and Psychiatry* 47:436–45.

McCleod, B., and J. Weisz (2005). The therapy process observational coding system-alliance scale: Measure characteristics and prediction of outcome in usual clinical practice. *Journal of Consulting and Clinical Psychology* 73: 323–33.

National Research Council and Institute of Medicine (2000). *From Neurons to Neighborhoods: The Science of Early Development*. Ed. Jack P. Shonkoff and Deborah A. Phillips. Washington, DC: National Academy Press.

Novick, J. (1990). Comments on termination in child, adolescent, and adult analysis. *Psychoanalytic Study of the Child* 45:419–36.

Novick, J., R. Benson, and J. Rembar (1981). Patterns of termination in an outpatient clinic for children and adolescents. *Journal of the American Academy of Child Psychiatry* 20:834–44.

Novick, J., and K. K. Novick (2000). Love in the therapeutic alliance. *Journal of the American Psychoanalytic Association* 48:189–218.

―――― (2001a). Trauma and deferred action in the reality of adolescence. *American Journal of Psychoanalysis* 61:43–61.

―――― (2001b). Parent work in analysis: Children, adolescents and adults. Part 1: The evaluation phase. *Journal of Infant, Child, and Adolescent Psychotherapy* 1:55–77.

―――― (2002a). Parent work in analysis: Children, adolescents and adults. Part 3: Middle and pretermination phases of treatment. *Journal of Infant, Child, and Adolescent Psychotherapy* 2:17–41.

―――― (2002b). Two systems of self-regulation. *Psychoanalytic Approaches to the Treatment of Children and Adolescents*. Special issue, *Journal of Psychoanalytic Social Work* 8:95–122.

―――― (2004). The superego and the two-systems model. *Psychoanalytic Inquiry* 24:232–56.

―――― (2006). *Good Goodbyes: Knowing How to End in Psychotherapy and Psychoanalysis.* Lanham, MD: Jason Aronson / Rowman & Littlefield.

―――― (2007 [1996]). *Fearful Symmetry: The Development and Treatment of Sadomasochism.* Lanham, MD: Jason Aronson / Rowman & Littlefield.

―――― (2008). Expanding the domain: Privacy, secrecy, and confidentiality. *Annual of Psychoanalysis* 36:145–60.

―――― (2011). Mastery or trauma: The adolescent choice. Presented at the Conference of the International Society for Adolescent Psychiatry and Psychology, Berlin, September.

―――― (2012). Discussion of Victoria Todd's Paper "Saving the treatment: affect intolerance in a boy, his parents, the mental health community, and his analyst." *Psychoanalytic Study of the Child* 66:28–32.

NOVICK, K. K. AND J. NOVICK (1998). An application of the concept of the therapeutic alliance to sadomasochistic pathology. *Journal of the American Psychoanalytic Association* 46:813–46.

―――― (2002a). Parent work in analysis: Children, adolescents and adults. Part 2: Recommendation, beginning, and middle phases of treatment. *Journal of Infant, Child, and Adolescent Psychotherapy* 2:1–27.

―――― (2002b). Parent work in analysis: Children, adolescents and adults. Part 4: Termination and post-termination phases of treatment. *Journal of Infant, Child, and Adolescent Psychotherapy* 2:43–55.

―――― (2005). *Working with Parents Makes Therapy Work.* Lanham, MD: Jason Aronson / Rowman & Littlefield.

―――― (2008). The dynamic interaction of transformations of parental and adolescent defenses: The importance of parent work concurrent with adolescent analysis. Workshop presented at the Annual Meeting of the Association for Child Psychoanalysis, St. Louis, May.

―――― (2010). *Emotional Muscle: Strong Parents, Strong Children.* Bloomington, IN: Xlibris.

―――― (2011). Building emotional muscle in children and parents. *Psychoanalytic Study of the Child* 65:131–51.

PRUETT, K. (1992). Latency development in children of primary nurturing fathers—Eight-year follow-up. *Psychoanalytic Study of the Child* 47:85–101.

REISS, D. (2011). Parents and children: Linked by psychopathology, but not by clinical care. *Journal of the American Academy of Child & Adolescent Psychiatry* 50 (5): 431–34.

SALBERG, J. (2010). *Good Enough Endings: Breaks, Interruptions, and Terminations from Contemporary Relational Perspectives*. New York and London: Routledge.

SCHLESINGER, H. (2005). *Endings and Beginnings: On the Technique of Terminating Psychotherapy and Psychoanalysis*. New York and London: Routledge.

SCHORE, A. N. (2000). Attachment, the right brain, and empathic processes within the therapeutic alliance. *Psychologist Psychoanalyst* 20:8–11.

——— (2002). Advances in neuropsychoanalysis, attachment theory, and trauma research: Implications for self psychology. *Psychoanalytic Inquiry* 22:433–84.

TODD, V. (2012). Saving the treatment: Affect intolerance in a boy, his parents, the mental health community, and his analyst. *Psychoanalytic Study of the Child* 66:3–27.

WINNICOTT, D. W. (1965). The theory of the parent-infant relationship. In *The Maturational Processes and the Facilitating Environment*, pp. 37–55. New York: International Universities Press.

YANOF, J. (2006). Review of *Working with Parents Makes Therapy Work*. *Journal of the American Psychoanalytic Association* 54:1437–41.

YOUNG-BRUEHL, E. (2011). *Childism: Confronting Prejudice against Children*. New Haven, CT: Yale University Press.

Dialogue with the Novicks

SCOTT DOWLING, M.D., AND CLAUDIA LAMENT, PH.D., EDS., WITH KERRY KELLY NOVICK AND JACK NOVICK, PH.D.

Two of the editors of The Psychoanalytic Study of the Child *converse with authors Kerry Kelly Novick and Jack Novick, Ph.D., about their paper "Concurrent Work with Parents of Adolescent Patients." Highlights include the authors' stated goal of restoring a positive relationship to the teen-parent bond, a new extension of the work of analysis with adolescents, the transference-countertransference complexities when the same analyst works with both adolescent and parents, and the uses of the term transformation—its traditional meaning in the developmental process of the individual and the authors' conceptualization of the term in their adolescent-parent treatment paradigm.*

WE, KERRY AND JACK NOVICK, ARE GRATEFUL TO THE EDITORS FOR the thoughtful questions that follow. Each could actually evoke detailed and lengthy responses, indeed a whole paper, to elaborate the thoughts. Here, however, we will try to respond briefly to clarify, emphasize, or extend particular points.

1. We know you've thought a great deal about the therapeutic value of working with parents in the course of analysis with children of all ages. You describe two

---

Scott Dowling is Training and Supervising Analyst, Cleveland Psychoanalytic Center, Cleveland, Ohio; Associate Clinical Professor of Child and Adolescent Psychiatry, Department of Psychiatry, Case Western Reserve University, Cleveland, Ohio; and Editor of *The Psychoanalytic Study of the Child*.

Claudia Lament, Ph.D., is Training and Supervising Analyst at the Institute for Psychoanalytic Education, an affiliate of the Department of Psychiatry, New York University Langone Medical Center. She is Assistant Clinical Professor in the Department of Child and Adolescent Psychiatry, the Child Study Center, New York University Langone Medical Center. She is also Senior Managing Editor of *The Psychoanalytic Study of the Child*.

The Psychoanalytic Study of the Child 67, ed. Claudia Lament, Robert A. King, Samuel Abrams, A. Scott Dowling, and Paul M. Brinich (Yale University Press, copyright © 2013 by Claudia Lament, Robert A. King, Samuel Abrams, A. Scott Dowling, and Paul M. Brinich).

goals of this work. The first is pragmatic: "Working with parents . . . helps people [individual children] enter treatment, stay and do the necessary work, and leave in a timely fashion." *The other goal is an interesting, totally new extension of the usual reason for child analysis:* "Restoration of the parent-child relationship to a lifelong positive resource for both." *This is a social, multiperson, long-term goal, usually thought of as a possible result rather than as a goal of psychoanalysis. Tell us more about your focus on the relationship itself and how this alters your view of psychoanalysis.*

We feel that the importance of the parent-child relationship as the context for development and the delivery system of the environment's impact on a child's development is already established, both in our work and in all modern developmental research. In the paper in this volume we describe the pragmatic impact of actualizing that conceptual assumption for making treatments of late adolescents work.

If we restrict the idea of child analysis only to the individual child, then we would be denying the knowledge that psychoanalysis is about the complexity of development and the relationships that foster both health and pathology. If we focus only on a child's symptoms, that is not a psychoanalytic approach. From the beginning of an evaluation, we assume and communicate to child and parents that the child's troubles are part of a larger parent-child history. For full understanding and therapeutic change, we say that both individual and family aspects will need attention. We note in the paper that it's central for the analyst to keep the parent-child relationship in mind, no matter what the treatment structure happens to be.

This question also gives us a chance to revise any potential misunderstanding of the notion of the parent-child relationship as a "lifelong *positive* resource for both." Perhaps it would be clearer to speak instead of a *"realistic"* resource. Most parents and most children and adolescents welcome the idea of an improved and closer relationship with hope and relief, and the outcome is usually eventually positive.

But there are some situations in which there are irreparably toxic elements and the reality is not positive. Then the hierarchy of clinical values that mandates physical and emotional safety as the highest priority takes precedence. The realistic outcome of parent work under such circumstances is to help the adolescent and/or the parent come to a place where they can take what they need from the relationship for their own good. That might, for instance, involve not having contact with the toxic parent or meeting only under supervision.

A basic thrust of all our work has been the effort to reclaim the metapsychological complexity of human development and functioning.

These ideas come into our answers to the other questions below and are detailed in our 2002 paper. Rather than seeing our formulations in this paper as a new paradigm, we tend to think of them as a return to the original richness of psychoanalysis.

In a recent description of parent work we say that psychoanalysis is not only directed at dealing with pathology but is equally a strength-building learning experience. It leads to the development of mastery, competence, joy, and emotional muscle. Psychoanalytic theory and knowledge attempts to encompass the full complexity of individuals and their families. It follows then that any techniques based in analytic thought must be multimodal, flexible, creative, and individualized (K. Novick and J. Novick 2013).

2. In your paradigm, the therapist's agenda is to strengthen the ties between child and parent. Are there instances in which this goal may be at loggerheads with the adolescent's developmental aim of separateness from her parents, as you define it? For some, this may call for periods of time when the parents are persona non grata. What is your thinking about this, and how do you deal with it in the clinical situation?

We think that making one's parent persona non grata is usually the adolescent's pathological solution to the healthy, realistic challenge of establishing psychological separateness and identity and represents an avoidance of that task. Physical separation may also be used as a pathological response to that normal phase challenge.

Even in worst-case situations, for instance parental sexual abuse of an adolescent or endangerment through drunk driving, the adolescent has to come to a realistic perception of her parent, accepting both limits and opportunities for parental change and the eventual nature of the relationship.

The original adolescent stance of dismissal costs too much for his or her development because it preserves closed-system solutions and may perpetuate or consolidate a pathological tie. Transformation of the relationship may involve a loosening of a pathologically intense tie.

We don't think of this as the "therapist's agenda." Rather this is an explicit, shared treatment goal. In the example of Kevin in the paper in this volume, his solution for his depression, colluded with by his family, was to go far away for college and not to speak to his father at all for more than a year. This solution, combined with heavy-duty medication, was destructive. One of his symptoms was severe passivity, with an inability to make even the simplest of decisions. Once he began to do some of the work of transforming his relationship with his father, he became more active in other areas of his life. In this case, it was only when he could give up the solution of making his father persona non grata and reengage with the complexities of their interactions that ego capacity was freed up to engage with other tasks of development, like finding a girlfriend and working effectively in school.

3. At a number of points in the paper in this volume you write about "transformations" of parents who are reworking aspects of their relationship with each other or with their adolescent, as well as "transformations" of your patients themselves. Help us to understand more explicitly what you mean by a "transformation." Freud and others have used the term to define the biologically inspired organizational progression in the developmental trajectory. Does "transformation" in your approach refer to the adolescent's step into a new hierarchical organization, or does it imply a behavioral change in the relationships between individuals?

Freud talked in 1915 about the transformations of puberty under the impetus of biological changes. But his position was more complex and modern than is usually understood. Many years ago, Freud confronted the age-old nature-versus-nurture debate by suggesting a complemental series, where the two are in constant interaction. Erikson expanded this to formulate an epigenetic series where development occurs from complex interactions that continue across the life span. Psychoanalysts from Freud on have articulated the process by which behavior is not predetermined by brain functions or genomes alone but intersects at crucial developmental moments to express innate factors and then interact with subsequent environmental input to produce the variety of behavior we see in humans of all ages. Recent neuroscientific work has arrived at the same position. Most modern neurobiologists agree that the old nature-versus-nurture distinction is obsolete.

It is in the spirit of these formulations that embrace the complexity of interaction that we think about developmental transformations. At the psychological and behavioral level, we posit:

- The first determinant of any current behavior is likely to be found in the parent-child relationship, especially, as we have emphasized, in the pleasure/pain economy of that relationship.
- Behavior evolves through phases in which current levels of psychological and biological functioning influence and are influenced by previous phases.
- Transformation is the main characteristic of this epigenetic evolution.
- No one phase has more importance than any other, and developmental transformations continue throughout the life span.
- Each phase brings something unique to the mix, which may compensate for earlier difficulties or raise prior dormant issues to problematic intensity (*Nachträglichkeit*, or "deferred action").

The adolescent has to go through this whole process to transform his relationship to his body, his mind, his self, the realities of the world, social and cultural expectations, and other people. At the same time, parents are also moving through their own developmental phases, adapting to changes in their bodies and capacities, taking on new responsibilities and so forth. In the culture, and particularly in our clinical population, we find that one area of transformation that is ignored or scotomized is the parent-child relationship.

All these transformations manifest in behavioral changes, but they represent psychic change at all levels of the body and mind in all the relationship configurations. Psychic change in the individual patient may bring about behavioral change in parents, which can then be invoked by the therapist in parent work to help parents change internally. Simultaneously, change in parents can create an opportunity for the therapist to work with the adolescent patient on retention of old patterns. It's always hard to change sadomasochistic relationships, but if a parent can be helped to not respond in their usual sadistic ways to adolescent provocation, it creates space for the individual work with the adolescent on deeper levels of his need to be a perpetrator or victim.

This is not a simple picture; we are describing multifaceted problems, conflicts, personality organizations, and resolutions. Such complexity challenges analysts to respond with equal sophistication and engagement with the vagaries of each clinical situation. What this means is there is constant dynamic interaction of the multimodal, multilevel work of transformation proceeding with all parties.

4. Traditionally, the parents of adolescents have been treated by a separate therapist in order to free the adolescent therapist from being overburdened by the inordinate complexities of individual, parental, and familial subsystems. In your method, in which the same therapist works with both parents and teenager, the inevitable infiltration of unconscious determinants—running bidirectionally—must influence the open dialogue among all four participants. How does the therapist monitor and track the multilayered and unconscious features of transference, countertransference, resistance, and other structural domains of the therapeutic situation? Here are some examples of what we mean:

> *A. In the cases you describe, the parents have an impressive capacity to trust in your selection of treatment details to expose to the adolescent; in like manner, the adolescent must trust in your promise concerning the specific nature of the communications that you transmit to the parents. The patients you discuss don't appear to object to your format, but have you encountered situations where unconscious mistrust in your model's approach is an unspoken obstacle to the treatment?*

> B. The therapist's impressions of the parents would have a subtle impact on the way the therapist listens to the adolescent's perception of the parents. Does this affect the adolescent's evolving perceptions and discoveries concerning them?
> C. You report conveying discoveries from the adolescent's treatment to the parents. Does this have an impact on the adolescent's own agency (or fears and defenses against it) in her allowing the therapist to take this role?

This question gets to the heart of the concerns and confusions surrounding parent work in general and parent work in relation to adolescents in particular. In this paper and in our 2005 book, we address some of the historical, theoretical, and technical objections to the very idea of parent work. Here, in addition, Dowling and Lament give us the opportunity to address the issues that arise from the side of the therapist grappling with a complex situation.

A. It has been surprising to us that parents and adolescents experience enormous relief when the dual goals are articulated. The fact that adolescent patients usually welcome our parent work belies the theory of "normal" adversarial adolescence, which derives from an Anglo-American cultural tradition that predates psychoanalysis and was unfortunately incorporated in the classical model of adolescent turmoil and rebellion (DeVito, Novick, and Novick 2000).

This reaction from patients and parents validates the position we state in the paper that the standard psychoanalytic model of adolescent development is flawed. It follows then that the conventional practice of farming out the parent work may be based on false premises and compounds difficulties by making the transferences and countertransferences even more complicated. Then there is the possibility that far too much is left unconscious and therefore not dealt with. We have also often found that conscious or unconscious rivalry between the adolescent's therapist and the parent worker can lead to treatment failure.

Parents come in carrying this standard conception of adolescent development. They expect us to confirm it and support their children in moving away; clearly this contributes to parental fears and ambivalence about treatment. It is often diagnostic when parents are conversely all too willing to hand the adolescent over to the therapist and have nothing to do with the treatment. This may constitute a passive-to-active preemptive rejection of their child.

Adolescents come in thinking that they should hate their parents and be rebelling. They assume we expect them to do so, and there is often a preconscious or unacknowledged anxiety that we will see them as failures because of their continued attachment to their parents. They are often ashamed of having *any* attachment.

The relief that parents and patients experience around the dual goals seems to inspire realistic trust in the analyst and the treatment method. We think this basic trust is fundamental to the therapeutic alliance and then allows for mutual exploration of inevitable eruptions of distrust. Moments of distrust are markers of transference manifestations against the backdrop of realistically established trust.

For instance, Melinda welcomed the analyst taking some of the pressure off her by talking with her mother about accurately labeling feelings. But after she broke up with the boyfriend her parents were so invested in, she was suddenly worried that the analyst would talk with them about her sexual activities. Given the established experience of secure communications with her parents, this could be taken up right away as a sign that something else was going on. Eventually what emerged was that this young woman who had been speaking with her mother multiple times a day on the phone had been carrying on a secret sexual life since early adolescence. So the disruption of realistic trust marked an important opening for a shared exploration of an important area of pathology.

We have of course also encountered situations in which the adolescent actively resists or forbids any contact between therapist and parents, sometimes making this a condition of treatment. A standard model might present this as an exaggerated normal reaction. Our model allows us to take this as a symptom of a very troubled parent-child relationship, which needs ongoing work. In our book on working with parents, there is an example of such a case, in which the young woman was afraid that her mother would intimidate the analyst. The only contact for some time was when the mother would telephone to harangue the analyst about the iniquities of the girl. But these "conversations" allowed some opportunity for realistic empathy with the patient's experience of her mother, and for some beginning contact that bore fruit in the mother's gradual change in attitude.

B. Psychoanalysis has taught us that people do various things with their perceptions of difficult realities. Difficult internal realities are dealt with by repression; difficult external realities are dealt with by denial. Freud started psychoanalysis by describing the operation of defense, which differentiated the new field from contemporary neurological ideas of mental functioning. But theoretical excitement soon shifted to unconscious content and its derivatives. The field was moving only in that direction until Anna Freud enriched the discourse by pointing our attention to the operation of defenses and their analysis as the gateway to understanding and change. Since the death of Anna Freud in 1982 and the rise of Kleinian-derived and relational theories, the concept of "defense" has been eclipsed, with focus returning to unconscious content, especially early infantile relationships.

If we use the lens of defenses to look at treatment and treatment material, we may say that repression is directed against unconscious content, whereas denial is directed at painful, traumatic reality. Ongoing contact with parents puts the therapist in a position to see denied, traumatogenic factors both in adolescents and their parents.

We find that actual ongoing contact with parents creates a realistic basis for the therapist to assess positive and negative aspects of the relationship between the parents and with the adolescent. The fact that we have met with and talked with the parents, and that we have shared some ideas about the parent-child relationship with the patient, helps patients feel that we know what they are talking about. We actively bring these real issues into the discourse with the patient when the material warrants it.

Nancy, a beautiful middle adolescent, came to treatment because of school failure, but she was actually struggling in every area of functioning. The analyst met with the parents from the beginning, but most of the work centered on Nancy's self-destructiveness. As Nancy stabilized, her conflicts about doing well emerged. A major determinant was her fear of her mother's envy. This could have been discovered without parent work and standard interpretations could have been made.

But the analyst knew this mother and had seen that she was grossly obese, highly competitive, and sadistically derogatory of Nancy. On the basis of this reality perception, Nancy's denial of her mother's physical and psychological characteristics could be interpreted with confidence. The analyst couldn't collude with Nancy's ego-distorting defensive protection of her mother, and therefore was in a position to address the conflict. Nancy's conflict between knowing and not letting herself know came alive.

C. The dual goals include improved communication between parents and children. From the very beginning we differentiate privacy and secrecy with all parties. So it's a deliberate decision made with the patient when we choose to convey something specific about the adolescent or from the adolescent's treatment to the parents. Similarly, we talk with parents about the usefulness or importance of something they have talked about being shared with the adolescent.

In the early stages, when the therapist is often the person opening up the communication, we remind everyone explicitly of the goal of eventual open discourse between parents and children. But in the initial phases, many factors can make it hard or apparently impossible for direct conversation between them.

For example, Sarah, a late-adolescent child of divorced parents, lived with her very disturbed mother. She had taken on parenting responsibilities far too early. She started treatment in the midst of an ongoing family crisis. She thought it was her job to solve the crisis; this interfered with her actual responsibilities to her schoolwork and her self-care. Her therapist pointed this out, and Sarah tearfully said that she had been doing this all her life and felt too guilty to think of or do anything about it. Identifying this together as a major area needing work, the therapist also offered to speak to both her parents about her need for them to stop loading their emotional burdens on her. There was an immediate improvement on all fronts, and Sarah could then settle into her analysis, which included work on the gratification afforded her by becoming the mother in the family from an early age.

We assume and work toward change over time in adolescents taking responsibility for keeping their parents in touch with treatment issues and discoveries. A year later, when someone in the extended family died suddenly, Sarah and her parents talked together constructively about her role and its limits, and her parents also consulted the analyst to good end. Sarah herself said that she felt more confident that she could do what was best for her, since she couldn't be responsible for everyone else's feelings and reactions.

REFERENCES

DeVito, E., J. Novick, and K. K. Novick (2000 [1994]). Cultural interferences with listening to adolescents. *Journal of Infant, Child, and Adolescent Psychotherapy* 1:77–95.

Novick, K. K. and J. Novick (2002). Reclaiming the land. *Psychoanalytic Psychology* 19 (2): 348–77.

——— (2005). *Working with Parents Makes Therapy Work*. Lanham, MD: Jason Aronson / Rowman & Littlefield.

——— (2013). A new model of techniques for concurrent psychodynamic work with parents of child and adolescent psychotherapy patients. *Child and Adolescent Psychiatric Clinics of North America* 22 (2), April.

CHILD PSYCHOANALYSIS

Weaving Child Psychoanalysis

Past, Present, and Future

PAUL M. BRINICH, PH.D.

Using the metaphor of a fabric woven from many threads, this paper describes nine of the many conceptual strands that have contributed to the development of child psychoanalysis over its first century. It notes the unfortunate isolation (sometimes self-imposed) of child analysis from related fields (including adult analysis) and argues that we must recognize both the strengths and weaknesses of our psychoanalytic tools if we are to collaborate with and profit from the work of nonanalytic colleagues. It closes with the suggestion that the continued weaving of child analysis will require the creation of new looms, structures that are able to support a new generation of child analysts and the continued elaboration of the field.

INTRODUCTION

I WAS TRULY DELIGHTED—AND HONORED—BY THE INVITATION TO deliver this thirty-first annual Marianne Kris Lecture.

Marianne Rie was the youngest child of Oskar Rie, one of Sigmund Freud's closest friends in Vienna. Early in their professional careers Rie and Freud had coauthored a monograph on cerebral palsy in children (Freud and Rie 1891); Freud also entrusted his six children to Rie as their pediatrician. What is more, every Saturday evening Oskar, his

---

Paul M. Brinich is Clinical Professor (Emeritus) in the Departments of Psychology and Psychiatry of the University of North Carolina at Chapel Hill. He serves on the faculty of the Psychoanalytic Education Center of the Carolinas and is a past president of the Association for Child Psychoanalysis.

Earlier versions of this paper were presented to the Association for Child Psychoanalysis (as the annual Marianne Kris Lecture) at its meeting in Santa Fe, New Mexico, in May 2012 and to the Chicago Psychoanalytic Society in Chicago, Illinois, in February 2012.

The Psychoanalytic Study of the Child 67, ed. Claudia Lament, Robert A. King, Samuel Abrams, A. Scott Dowling, and Paul M. Brinich (Yale University Press, copyright © 2013 by Claudia Lament, Robert A King, Samuel Abrams, A. Scott Dowling, and Paul M. Brinich).

brother Alfred, and their brother-in-law Ludwig Rosenberg (the father of future child analyst Anny Katan) gathered to play cards with Sigmund. In this tightly knit circle Marianne was first a five-year-younger playmate of Anna Freud, then a student in the *Kinderseminar*, organized by Miss Freud, Siegfried Bernfeld, Willi Hoffer, and August Aichhorn (Cohler 2008); then a fellow refugee in London; and finally a fellow editor and colleague, friend, and confidante of Miss Freud.

Marianne Rie married Ernst Kris in 1927; the two of them were active in the growth of psychoanalysis in Vienna until 1938, when they escaped to London with their children Anna and Anton. In 1940 the family moved again, this time to New York, where Marianne resided until her death.

Marianne Kris had a substantial impact on the development of child psychoanalysis in both America and England. In America she encouraged a new generation of analysts to enter the field; what's more, she included within her students and supervisees many "lay" analysts. At the same time she solicited financial support for the Hampstead Child Therapy Course and Clinic, Miss Freud's training program for child analysts. Following the death of her husband Ernst, who was one of the founding editors of *The Psychoanalytic Study of the Child*, Marianne served as a senior editor of this journal for nearly a quarter century, from volume 13 (1958) through volume 36 (1981).

Despite her activity as an editor, Marianne Kris published only four psychoanalytic papers (Kris 1932; 1944; 1957; Kris and Ritvo 1983). Two of these papers focused on the impact of siblings and parents upon intrapsychic development. However, her psychoanalytic generativity extended beyond the printed word: Both of the Kris children became psychoanalysts, and Anna Kris Wolff, like her mother, became a child analyst.

In 1950 Marianne Kris was a participant in the First Stockbridge Congress on Child Analysis and, in the years that followed, was one of the leaders of a group within the American Psychoanalytic Association (APsaA) that advocated for the inclusion of lay (nonmedical) child psychoanalysts within APsaA. When this effort failed, Kris—with the support of Anna Freud—proposed the creation of a professional home for child analysts, the American Association for Child Psychoanalysis—now the ACP. Marianne Kris was elected the first president of the organization and presided over its first annual meeting in Topeka in 1966.

Marianne Kris was involved with the development of child analysis at the personal, professional, and organizational levels from her birth in 1900 until her death in 1980 while visiting Anna Freud in London. The ACP inaugurated the Kris Lecture in 1982 to honor her memory.

The theme of this year's meeting of the Association for Child Psychoanalysis is "The Analytic Path to Progressive Development." In keeping with that theme, I have opted to take a developmental perspective on our field of child psychoanalysis, a field that has grown over time, gradually incorporating new perspectives. In this paper I will describe (1) where we've come from, and (2) how our understanding of child analysis has broadened and continues to evolve. My hope is that such a developmental approach to our field will help us to perceive and define (3) how child psychoanalysis will continue to develop in the twenty-first century.

I originally built my paper around the metaphor of a fabric, woven from many strands or threads. This seemed particularly appropriate, as weaving (along with knitting) was one of Anna Freud's favorite hobbies. Child psychoanalysis has been woven slowly and gradually for more than a century now, first accenting one strand, then adding another and another and another. The resultant fabric includes some elements already visible in the first years, but it has become much richer and more multidimensional than it was at its beginning.[1]

Here I am applying this metaphor of a fabric to the development of our field, not to the individual development of a child. The latter is never entirely smooth and always includes some discontinuities as well as important transformations. Of course, one might argue that our field's development has also had its share of discontinuities and transformations. At times the addition of a new perspective has led to a substantial rethinking of matters of theory and technique. Thus the fabric of our field has its nubs and gaps and weak areas. But on the whole, it has developed a recognizable structure and pattern.

As I continued to work with the ideas in the paper, I found that I needed to expand my metaphor to include the loom upon which any fabric is woven. As you will hear when we reach the end of the paper, we now must create contemporary structures—looms—that are able to support a new generation of child analysts and the continued elaboration of child psychoanalysis—the fabric that is the raison d'être of our organization.

The First Strand in the Fabric of Child Psychoanalysis: Unconscious Drives

Hermine Hug-Hellmuth, one of the first women to receive a Ph.D. from the University of Vienna (in physics, in 1906!), learned of Sigmund

---

1. I am an admirer of Fred Pine's (1990) approach to our field and his flexible, multimodal approach to clinical phenomena.

Freud's work through her family physician, Isidor Sadger (who later became her analyst). A schoolteacher, Hug-Hellmuth first looked for ways in which Freud's psychology might illuminate her educational work. In 1911, encouraged by Freud, she began psychoanalytic work with individual children, antedating her better-known successors, Anna Freud and Melanie Klein, by nearly a decade.

It was Hug-Hellmuth (1913) who first wrote about lines of development.[2] While her use of this concept merged the kinds of *lines* later described by Anna Freud (1965) with Sigmund Freud's concept of *phases* of libidinal development, it's clear that Hug-Hellmuth was exploring the territory Freud (1909/1955) had opened up with his "Analysis of a Phobia in a Five-Year-Old Boy" ("Little Hans").

Like many of Freud's early followers, Hug-Hellmuth was especially intent on discovering the ways in which the unconscious—and especially the various derivatives of the drives—could be seen to underlie human behavior. These analysts eagerly sought new "finds,"[3] and early volumes of our psychoanalytic journals included many articles, often just a page or two long, that described just such discoveries.

Hug-Hellmuth, like many others, hoped that making conscious what had been unconscious would lead to change. An educational system that directly acknowledged the drives and their derivatives would be radically different from the Austrian norm; it would demand less repression, and the hoped-for result would be fewer neurotic conflicts.

Although we now know that addressing unconscious contents (whether via educational interventions or via analytic work) is not *sufficient*, Hug-Hellmuth's work with children was truly pioneering. Had she not been murdered by her nephew in 1924,[4] her place in the his-

---

2. "It seems to me that where the object at stake is the obtaining of a clear general view of the mental evolution of the child, that takes place simultaneously along a number of lines of which the speech development represents but one, it is better not to emphasize the latter predominantly, but, rather, taking a hint from nature herself, to recognize the active interests definable as nursing, play and study, as dividing up the whole course of childhood into a number of periods of which these activities are mainly characteristic" (Hug-Hellmuth 1913/1919), p. xi).

3. A particularly dramatic instance of this kind of observation, involving Freud's follower Wilhelm Stekel and the eventual Nobel laureate Nikos Kazantzakis, can be found in Kimon Friar's "Introduction" to Kazantzakis' (1960) slim spiritual testament, *The Saviors of God*.

4. MacLean and Rappen's (1991) brief biography of Hug-Hellmuth describes the complications of Hug-Hellmuth's relationships with her older half–sister, Antoine, and with Antoine's son, Rudolf. Hug-Hellmuth had based some of her earliest psychoanalytic writings in part upon her observations of Rudolf's childhood development. His claims to have been her analytic patient have not been confirmed. There is, however, no doubt that Rudolf and Hug-Hellmuth had a highly ambivalent relationship that ended with Rudolf's

tory of child analysis would have been much more prominent than it has been.[5]

A side note: Hug-Hellmuth had to deal with criticism from two opposing directions. On the one hand, many of her fellow educators thought that open discussion of the drives—and especially of sexuality—with children was dangerous and would derail their educational efforts. On the other hand, many of her fellow analysts thought that the psychoanalysis of children was an impossibility, for a variety of developmental and practical reasons. The latter prejudice remains alive today; we've all heard colleagues question whether child analysis is "real" analysis.

Both of these criticisms derive some of their fuel from the forces that Don Rosenblitt (2008) described in his essay "Where Do You Want the Killing Done? An Exploration of Hatred of Children." More recently, Elizabeth Young-Bruehl (2012) has taken up some of the same ideas in her posthumously published book *Childism: Confronting Prejudice against Children*.

A SECOND STRAND: OBJECT RELATIONS (OR REPRESENTATIONS)

A second strand in the fabric of child analysis has to do with what has so unfortunately been called the "objects" of the instinctual drives—objects that usually are, of course, people. Not just people, but *important* people like mothers, fathers, and siblings. Melanie Klein (1926) was as interested as her contemporaries in discovering the contents of the unconscious, but she added to this fascination with the drives a nuanced appreciation of the part played by their targets—the so-called "objects"—and how they were represented in the mind. While some early analysts tended to view objects as relatively accidental and/or interchangeable epiphenomena associated with the drives, Klein outlined how objects and their representations and relationships contribute

---

murder of his aunt (supposedly when she would not give him money that would make it possible for him to marry). Writing in the *Bulletin of the International Psycho-Analytical Association*, Siegfried Bernfeld (1925) had this to say: "On September 9, 1924, in her fifty-third year, Frau Dr. Hermine Hug-Hellmuth, a member of the Vienna Society, of whose services, especially in the field of child-psychology, our readers need no reminder, was murdered by her eighteen-year-old nephew, Rudolph Hug. In a will made a few days before her death, she expressed a desire that no account of her life and work should appear, even in psychoanalytical publications." Hug-Hellmuth's wish to be unmentioned, odd in both its timing and content, was assiduously honored by the members of the Vienna Psychoanalytical Society, who understandably wished to avoid the scandal that surrounded her murder.

5. I do not remember Hug-Hellmuth's name being mentioned during my years in London. MacLean and Rappen's (1991) brief biography and republication of her work has illuminated a previously neglected corner of our history.

in essential ways to psychic development via the process of *ph*antasy (spelled with *ph*, not an *f*).

Klein saw child analysis as offering a unique opportunity to see early mental processes *in statu nascendi*, not yet covered-over by the sophisticated veneers that come with adulthood.

A Third Strand: The "I" and Its Mechanisms of Defense

Anna Freud's classic *The Ego and the Mechanisms of Defense* (1936) introduced a third strand into the fabric of child analysis—a strand that emphasized the defensive maneuvers used by the ego in its dealings with internal forces (instinctual drives and superego prohibitions) as well as with external, environmental factors. She was particularly attuned to the ways in which initially helpful adaptations sometimes became unhelpful encrustations.

Miss Freud's 1936 volume drew on her experience with children in her multiple roles as teacher, psychoanalytically informed observer, and child analyst. Her second landmark volume, *Normality and Pathology in Childhood: Assessments of Development* (1965), described the outline she created to summarize her evaluation of a child (the "Metapsychological Profile"). She also depicted six specific "developmental lines" that allowed clinicians to locate where a child stood in terms of various developmental phases and tasks (starting with his or her libidinal and aggressive dimensions but going on to include cognitive, affective, and other dimensions). The profile explicitly addressed and wove together two of the strands we have mentioned thus far: the status of the drives (libidinal and aggressive) and the activities of the ego (both defensive and adaptive). To these were added an assessment of the superego, completing the picture as seen from the structural perspective. Here we see Anna Freud's "synthetic function" at work, just as it was when she sat at her loom.

A Fourth Strand: The Sociocultural Environment

Fourteen years later Erik Erikson's[6] (1950/1963) *Childhood and Society* introduced a perspective on human development that took the psychoanalytic model (focused as it was on individual, intrapsychic phenomena) and immersed it in a sociocultural matrix. In this classic, Erikson laid out a series of psychosocial developmental tasks and, in so doing, added another strand to the fabric of child analysis. His classic essay "A

---

6. Anna Freud's colleague, student, and analysand.

Neurological Crisis in a Small Boy: Sam" describes how biology, individual and group psychology, and sociocultural context each contribute to specific clinical phenomena (ibid., pp. 25–38).[7]

Erikson's perspective was seen by some analysts as extra-analytic—a kind of deviation that took us away from the intrapsychic realm. However, Erikson was simply making explicit the same reality that Winnicott addressed when he famously noted (in a 1942 talk to the British Psychoanalytical Society), "There is no such thing as a baby" (1952, p. 99). Children are immersed in sociocultural matrices that mesh with and influence their intrapsychic worlds, and child analysts cannot ignore these matrices.

A Fifth Strand: Attachment

John Bowlby (1969; 1973; 1980) followed up his psychiatric and psychoanalytic work on the effects of maternal separation and loss (during and after World War II) with an excursion into ethology (in his trilogy *Attachment, Separation,* and *Loss*). Bowlby argued that the interactions between a human infant and its caretakers have evolutionary determinants that lie outside of, and are relatively independent of, the strands we have labeled as the drives, object relations, the ego, and the sociocultural environment. Bowlby and like-minded researchers (for example, Spitz and Cobliner 1966) demonstrated that the disruption of early attachment had important and predictable implications for subsequent development. This is territory that Anna Freud and Dorothy Burlingham had touched upon in their *Infants without Families* (1939–1945/1973); however, Bowlby interpreted the resultant pathology as disruptions in evolutionarily determined patterns rather than as failures in the satisfaction of instinctual drives.

A Sixth Strand: The Self

Heinz Kohut's *The Analysis of the Self* (1971) brought an additional developmental perspective to bear upon the psychoanalytic enterprise. Although Kohut was not a child analyst, his "self psychology" had some important implications for child psychoanalysis. One might say that Kohut accepted Anna Freud's long-standing interest in the synthetic function and raised her; in his hands the "self" took on a life of its

---

7. Anna Freud did not endorse Erikson's broadening of the psychoanalytic perspective. She was concerned that it would lead to a neglect of her father's fundamental insights regarding individual intrapsychic phenomena.

own, perhaps not entirely independent of the drives, their objects, the defenses, or the environment, but—and this is where Kohut added something important—with its own motives, energy, and objects. Kohut saw the development of a "cohesive self" as an achievement fraught with many normative challenges and potential pitfalls, most of which were first encountered in childhood.

A Seventh Strand: Neuropsychoanalysis

The recent work of Mark Solms and like-minded colleagues takes us back to Sigmund Freud and psychoanalysis's deep roots in neurology. Like Freud, these cross-disciplinary researchers and clinicians are trying to understand the complex relationships between brain and mind. This particular thread has not yet been woven into the fabric of child analysis, but it quite clearly builds upon Erikson's epigenetic principle (1950/1963, p. 65) and now stands as a challenge: How will our growing appreciation of the developing "brain-mind" or "mind-brain" affect our theories and practices? For example, Solms provides evidence that the phenomenon of "infant amnesia" cannot be understood fully without reference to brain maturation and to the differences between implicit and explicit memory systems (Solms and Turnbull 2002, pp. 146–49, 167–70, 175–76). In another vein, how can our growing knowledge regarding neuroplasticity be integrated into—and perhaps transform—our psychoanalytic theories and techniques?

An Eighth Strand: Mentalization

The line of thought described in Fonagy et al.'s (2002) *Affect Regulation, Mentalization, and the Development of the Self* represents an eighth strand, which we are only beginning to weave into the fabric of child analysis. Defining mentalization as "the process by which we realise that having a mind mediates our experience of the world" (p. 3), Fonagy et al. argue that Bowlby's "attachment is not an end in itself; rather, it exists in order to produce a representational system that has evolved . . . to aid human survival" (p. 2). What is more, they suggest that the assessment of a person's ability to mentalize—to imagine himself into the minds of his interlocutors and to use that imagination in his interactions with those people—provides critical data that should guide a sensitive clinician's work.[8]

---

8. This line of work first appeared in a paper entitled "Measuring the Ghost in the Nursery" (Fonagy et al. 1993) and continues to the present, with applications into areas such as

Fonagy et al. locate the genesis of mentalization in early child-parent and parent-child interchanges. There, parents echo their children's affects in ways that "mark" them as potentially comprehensible; this helps to contain experiences that otherwise might overwhelm their children's nascent psychic structures.

A Ninth Strand: Trauma

An appreciation of psychic trauma has been part of psychoanalytic thinking from its earliest days (Breuer and Freud 1893–1895/1955). However, the significance attributed to this particular strand has varied over the years, in a kind of complementary oscillation with the significance of unconscious fantasies. Initially quite prominent in the fabric of psychoanalysis, this thread later was submerged as attention shifted to other domains (for example, ego, object, self, et cetera). However, recent clinical reports and research [for example, by Bell (2005); Eth and Pynoos (1985); Novak (2004); Pretorius (2007); and Pynoos, Steinberg, and Goenjian (2007)] have brought this strand back to prominence in the fabric.[9]

A quick glance through the tables of contents of *The Psychoanalytic Study of the Child* is enough to demonstrate that child analysts have never forgotten how significant trauma can be for psychic development and structuralization.

Enough Already!

Keeping in mind "the magic number seven, plus or minus two" (Miller 1956), I will bring my list of strands to a close at nine; working memory does have its limits. However, my list could easily be expanded to include contributions from the interpersonal perspective (for example, Barish 2009), Lacanian psychoanalysis (for example, Lionel Bailly 2011; Schumacher 2011), and developmental therapy (Hurry 1998; Stern 2000), as well as issues of temperament (Chess and Thomas 1995), affect and motivation (Holinger 2008), the "representational world" (Sandler and Rosenblatt 1962), and separation/individuation (Mahler, Pine, and Bergman 1975). However, my goal here is not exhaustion but rather an appreciation of the many different strands of theory, research, and

---

clinical work with so-called "borderline" personalities (Allen, Fonagy, and Bateman 2008) as well as with children (Verheugt-Pleiter, Zevalkink, and Schmeets 2008).

9. My London colleague Sandra Ramsden Hatfield, responding to an earlier draft of this paper, suggested that it would be important to include trauma among the strands.

practice that currently contribute to the overall fabric of child analysis (K. Novick and J. Novick 2002).

So What?

During my training at the Hampstead Clinic, I saw a seven-year-old girl who had been adopted as an infant; she was referred for treatment because of both a long-standing provocative and hostile relationship with her adoptive mother and her growing obesity. Some years later I published an account of my work with "Sophie" (Brinich 1980). Looking back with more than thirty years of hindsight, I am struck by ways in which my thinking has broadened since then. And, were I to live for another thirty years, my thinking probably would have to expand as much or more.

Students at the Hampstead Clinic were expected to do a profile on every child they saw in analytic treatment—ideally one at the diagnostic phase and one at termination. The profiles emphasized

1. the drives and their development;
2. ego and superego development;
3. regressions and fixation points (which take us back to the drives); and
4. conflicts (external, internalized, and internal).

While some attention was given to the environmental matrix, the significance of self- and object-representations and their relationships was addressed only obliquely via the drives.

The fact that my paper included self- and object-representations in its title reflected some very helpful guidance provided by Philip Spielman, a now-deceased senior analytic colleague in San Francisco; he helped me to broaden my view of the clinical data in several important ways.

Three other aspects of my 1980 paper contained echoes of the multidisciplinary background that I brought to my child analytic training. (I had earned my doctorate from the University of Chicago's Committee on Human Development.) First, I made several suggestions regarding the ways in which Erikson's psychosocial tasks might be given a special twist in the development of an adopted child, adolescent, and young adult. Second, I discussed some of the ways in which issues of attachment and loss were significant in Sophie's life and in those of two other adoptees. Third, I included a brief closing section that addressed how adoption is seen in various cultures and what that information might suggest to a psychoanalytically informed observer.

In the end, my 1980 paper took up five of the nine strands I've mentioned earlier: the drives, object relations, the ego (with its various adaptive and defensive functions), the sociocultural significance of adoption, and the importance of attachment and loss. I addressed issues related to the self only cursorily, and issues related to neuropsychoanalysis or mentalization didn't cross my mind. Trauma remained quietly hidden in the background. What might these strands add to our understanding and technique?

I will take up those last four strands in a moment. First, however, I will insert a brief side-note on the limitations of analytical data.

Psychoanalysis, and child psychoanalysis in particular, cannot afford to ignore nonanalytic data. The analytic situation provides us with an unparalleled opportunity to understand what goes on in the minds of our patients; however, it has important limitations. A case in point: When I first reviewed the psychoanalytic literature on adoption (back in the 1970s) I came away with the impression that the adoption of a child was, from a psychoanalytic perspective, an almost foolhardy act: There was so much that could go wrong.

That body of literature had several weaknesses. First, every paper was based largely on work with children whose parents had brought them for treatment. That shouldn't be surprising: Analysts generally get involved only when something has gone rather seriously wrong. However, it meant that analysts had little experience with the vast majority of adoptees who were doing well. Second, the number of children involved in each study was small, and therefore the generalizability of the conclusions was limited. Third, the analytic literature never included systematic comparisons with children who were not adopted but who had experienced comparable disruptions in care.

When I returned to Langley Porter Neuropsychiatric Institute after my London years, I had access to data regarding decades of LPNI inpatients and outpatients (children, adolescents, and adults). Fortunately, the creators of the database had included whether they were adopted or not. This provided an unusual opportunity to pose a couple of questions. First, were adoptees overrepresented in the patients seen at LPNI? And second, did adoptees differ from nonadoptees in terms of their diagnoses? My wife Evelin and I (Brinich and Brinich 1982) reviewed a decade (1969–1978) of outpatient and inpatient first admissions (n = 5135) and found that adoptees were somewhat overrepresented on the children's services (roughly 5 percent of the patients, as compared with an expected incidence of 2.2 percent), but somewhat underrepresented on the adult services (1.6 percent versus the expected 2.2 percent).

Differences in the diagnoses assigned to adoptees and nonadoptees were insignificant.

Two decades later Ann Brand (a clinical psychology graduate student of mine at the University of North Carolina) and I took a careful look at a very large randomized and stratified sample of 11,840 children (ages five to seventeen) who had participated in a national health survey (Brand and Brinich 1999). Our comparison of adoptees and nonadoptees found that the vast majority of adoptees were no different from nonadoptees on measures of social adaptation; there was, however, a small group (5 percent) of adoptees whose behavior was highly problematic. This small group dramatically skewed the curve of behavior problems in adoptees. However, the vast majority of adoptees were indistinguishable from nonadoptees on the behavioral measures used in the survey.

My point is this: We must recognize the limitations, as well as the strengths, of our psychoanalytic tools. Our psychoanalytic literature has been remarkably fruitful in its exposition of what I like to call the "sticking points" in development that sometimes are associated with adoption. In doing so, however, we at times have created the impression that anyone who adopts a child is in for a lifetime of trouble. Our forte, as child analysts, is the fine-grain understanding of individuals; we should be very cautious about generalizing findings from our clinical work to nonclinical groups.

Having gotten that off my chest, I can return to my discussion of three of the newer strands that have been introduced into the fabric of child analysis since my 1980 paper. They are the self, neuropsychoanalysis, and mentalization. I also will touch briefly on the fourth, "silent" strand—trauma.

THE SELF

Despite Anna Freud's interest in the synthetic function of the ego, she found Kohut's elaboration of the self and its development a dangerous deviation from her father's insights regarding the drives and their contributions to psychic development.[10] Today, however, it is possible to take the self as an object of psychoanalytic interest (Brinich and Shelley 2002) without pulling earlier strands out of the fabric. Applying this to Sophie, we might wonder in retrospect what the effect of her adoptive mother's intolerance of Sophie's infant messiness, and her later

---

10. Although Kohut's *The Analysis of the Self* was published as Monograph No. 4 of *The Psychoanalytic Study of the Child* in 1971, it was ignored during my years in London.

abhorrence of Sophie's neediness, had upon the processes that allow for the elaboration of a cohesive self. When I described these aspects of Sophie's situation in 1980, I framed them in terms of drives, drive derivatives, and defenses; but I also suggested that Sophie's mother had adopted only part of Sophie. This left Sophie with an awful dilemma: Should she disown important aspects of her self, or should she engage in a kind of guerilla warfare with her mother that expressed precisely those aspects of Sophie's self that her mother wished to repudiate? The analytic data can be read in more than one way.

NEUROPSYCHOANALYSIS

In talking about neuropsychoanalysis as a strand in child analysis, I step out onto very thin ice: While I have found this line of work (Kaplan-Solms and Solms 2000; Solms and Turnbull 2002) absolutely fascinating, I still am quite some ways from weaving it into my clinical work, and I'm not sure how it would have affected my work with Sophie. Perhaps it would have helped me to approach the rage that Sophie directed at her adopted doll, Sarah, as a kind of neuropsychological mirror of her own experience vis-à-vis her mother. Or perhaps it would have helped me to appreciate Sophie's difficulties in the realm of affective self-regulation. This in turn might have led me to develop some practical alternative strategies for Sophie to get her developmentally appropriate needs met, as well as to manage the affective storms precipitated whenever she felt unwanted and unloved.

MENTALIZATION

In retrospect, some of my clinical work with Sophie was aimed quite specifically at improving Sophie's ability to *mentalize*, though that term had not yet entered the psychoanalytic vocabulary. Sophie and I spent hours talking about her adopted doll, Sarah, and how Sarah might feel vis-à-vis her parents—both the parents who had adopted (or stolen) her and those who had relinquished (or lost, or sold) her. Perhaps *mentalization* is just old wine in a new bottle; regardless, the term has the virtue of spotlighting an important process in development as well as providing some guidance in therapy.

TRAUMA

My work with Sophie ended when I returned to the United States at the end of my training. She continued in treatment with a woman analyst who found Sophie's frequently extremely provocative behavior just as technically problematic as I had. When my colleague later presented the case for review, Miss Freud offered her opinion that Sophie was "a seduced child who seeks only gratification" (Hatfield 2012). Seduction as a potential contributor to Sophie's problems had not been discussed during the earlier years of treatment, and I still am not sure I would agree with Miss Freud in this instance. However, it's worth mentioning that the *possibility* of a traumatic contribution to Sophie's disturbance had not been suggested previously.

DISCUSSION: SURMOUNTING THE PAST WHILE LOOKING TO THE FUTURE . . . AND THE PAST

From very early in its history, psychoanalysis has been riven with conflicts, sometimes expressed in quite nasty and personal terms; these often have spilled over into organizational and political arenas.[11]

The conflicts that have separated Kleinians from Freudians (as an example) may not be all that different from the conflicts seen in other fields (for example, surgery) that maintain themselves via an apprenticeship model. However, psychoanalysis adds to the apprenticeship model another dimension: It demands a remarkable degree of intimate self-exposure by the apprentice to the master. This creates a vulnerability that easily can veer into either idealization or paranoia if it is not respected and managed carefully. Incredibly strong allegiances are formed—especially regarding one's Training Analyst. Further, the anointing of a select few as Training and Supervising Analysts creates cohorts of pupils who are bound together in a powerful mix of loyalties, rivalries, and idealizations.

As an example of this phenomenon, King and Steiner (1991) describe the "controversial discussions" that took place during World War II between the Kleinian and Freudian camps within the British Psychoanalytical Society. Stenographers recorded who had said what to whom. The analyst Melitta Schmideberg, Melanie Klein's daughter, attacked her mother's camp:

> The Kleinians shelter behind ambiguity and vagueness. Anybody who attempts to disentangle their views is sure to be told that he misunderstood them. . . . In a manner somewhat reminiscent of Dr Goebbels [Hitler's minister of propaganda] they try to impress us by repeating time after time the same slogans, by putting forward exaggerated claims and dog-

---

11. Such conflicts antedate the institution of both certification (that most APsaA-specific method of hara-kiri) and the Training Analyst system.

matic statements, by accusing their opponents and intimidating the hesitants, by a constant play on emotions of every sort, instead of presenting and substantiating their theories according to scientific standards. (King and Steiner 1991, p. 98)

For her part, Melanie Klein felt wounded by Anna Freud; in April 1943 she wrote to Susan Isaacs:

> Not with one word has A. Freud ever acknowledged that she accepted anything from us, not even those much disputed phantasies about the attack on mother's body etc. . . . which have now been accepted for a later stage. This ungenerous or rather dishonest attitude has become very clear. . . . We are faced here with conscious and deliberate dishonesty and this must not be allowed to pass. (ibid., p. 249)

Ricardo Steiner framed the conflict in very personal terms:

> . . . on the one hand . . . Anna Freud was claiming a sort of interpretative monopoly of her father's work . . . [while on the other hand, Klein] was clearly asserting that she was, if not the most legitimate, certainly the most creative of his followers. Two daughters fighting for their father's love and possession, one could perhaps say (ibid., p. 239).

Now, seventy years later, all the participants of those discussions are gone. As Steve Jobs (2005) said in his famous Stanford commencement speech: "Death is very likely the single best invention of life. It is life's change agent. It clears out the old to make way for the new."

In contrast to the highly charged atmosphere of the "controversial discussions," in November 2011 my wife and I attended a colloquium at the Anna Freud Centre that included perspectives that ranged from "classic ego psychological" to "neo-Kleinian" to "Lacanian." We had just returned from a week of teaching in the Psychoanalytic Institute of Eastern Europe; the range of perspectives represented among the PIEE faculty was as wide as what we later heard in London. While allegiances remain, and while our tendencies toward intramural conflict have not been erased, it seems analysts now are able to listen to each other a bit better than in times past.

To the extent that we now are able and willing to add new threads to the old, and to the extent that these threads create an increasingly complex fabric that allows us to understand and help our patients, psychoanalysis—as a treatment, as a theory, and as a research method—has both broadened and deepened itself.

Ironically, this progress comes at a time when a dwindling number of people are willing to take the time or spend the resources that our services require. There has been a dramatic decline in the kind of psychoanalytic practice that was idealized forty years ago: Single-office private practice, working intensively with small numbers of relatively affluent people.

But psychoanalysis did not develop in such a rarified atmosphere. In a way we now find ourselves back where our forebears were in "*das rote Wien*" of the 1920s. Then psychoanalysis was but one element of a wide-ranging and radical rethinking of what human relationships were all about. Analysts generally were not well-to-do, nor were their patients. However, they eagerly made themselves useful in a variety of ways, across many settings. Heinz Hartmann's wife, Dora, put it this way:

> To belong at that time to the psychoanalytical movement meant that one was part of a group of young and enthusiastic rebels. This fact alone bonded people closely with each other. They believed in something, something quite different, something that was revolutionary and defined one as unconventional in relation to academia; all knew that prestige and money were not in the picture. (Dora Hartmann, quoted in Reichmayr 1990, p. 121, translated by Hamida Bosmajian)

I have in mind the analysts and activities described in Elizabeth Ann Danto's (2005) fascinating book *Freud's Free Clinics: Psychoanalysis & Social Justice, 1918–1938*. These included Siegfried Bernfeld's short-lived Kinderheim Baumgarten of 1919 and August Aichhorn's (1925) work with "wayward youth." We could add to these examples the early years of the Institute for Juvenile Research in Chicago, and Anna Freud and Dorothy Burlingham's (1939–1945) Hampstead War Nurseries.

More-recent examples of such efforts include Selma Fraiberg's (1980) "infant mental health" work in Ann Arbor, Alicia Lieberman and Patricia Van Horn's (2008) work with traumatized children in San Francisco, and Mark Smaller's (2011) Analytic Service to Adolescents Program (ASAP) in Chicago.

I also have in mind the application of psychoanalytic thought to the legal framework governing child custody (Goldstein, Freud, and Solnit 1973; 1979), Toni Heineman's analytically grounded program for foster children, A Home Within (Heineman and Ehrensaft 2006), and Deborah Luepnitz's (2005) program of psychoanalytic treatment for homeless individuals and families, Insight for All (IFA).

Our Viennese ancestors—many of them socialists, social democrats, or outright communists (Young-Bruehl 2010)—did not see psychoanalysis as a treatment only for the wealthy, and child analysis in particular was framed in very practical, down-to-earth ways that included attention to the familial and social milieu within which children were living.

The breadth and depth of thinking that such work demands is substantial; however, we have been developing just such breadth and depth over the century that I've reviewed. To take Lieberman and Van Horn's (2008) Child-Parent Psychotherapy (CPP) program as an example, it includes the following elements:

1. Support of developmental momentum
2. Reflective developmental guidance (aimed at helping child and parent to "mentalize" each other)
3. Modeling of appropriate protective behavior
4. Insight-oriented interpretations (aimed at both child and parent)
5. Addressing traumatic reminders
6. Retrieving benevolent memories ("angels")
7. Providing emotional support
8. Attending to reality—crisis intervention, case management, and concrete assistance

Lieberman and Van Horn emphasize that effective intervention in any individual case usually involves several of these modalities.

The *core* of this work lies in ". . . the therapist's ability to serve as a conduit between the child's and the parent's experience" (Lieberman and Van Horn 2008, p. 73). At times the CPP therapist must speak for the baby or the child; but at other times the translations go the other way, trying to make the parent's experience accessible to the child. Regardless of the direction, "The therapist must simultaneously hold in mind the experience of the parent(s) and of the child without rigid alignment with either" (ibid., p. 247). This means, for example, that the therapist must have the inner balance

> . . . to empathize with the mother's emotional experience without losing track of the maltreatment she has inflicted upon her child. This awareness of the different facets of a clinical situation, including the suffering that is simultaneously endured and inflicted by different family members, is a cornerstone of treatment for maltreating parents and their children. (ibid., p. 282)

Lieberman and Van Horn's model requires a combination of *well-grounded knowledge* and *personal resilience*, both embedded in and supported by *a team*.

The *knowledge base* required for this work cuts across a variety of domains: biology, anthropology, economics, politics, sociology, group and individual psychology. This is reminiscent of the breadth of studies that Freud (1926/1959) advocated in his essay, "The Question of Lay Analysis."

The *personal resilience* or "inner balance" that Lieberman and Van Horn demand of their therapists is equally essential. Anna Freud's (1966) paper "The Ideal Psychoanalytic Institute: A Utopia" comes to mind. There Miss Freud advocated for the familiar tripartite model of psychoanalytic education: In addition to seminars and opportunities for the direct observation of children, therapists must have the experience of doing intensive, psychoanalytic work with *some* children; and they must have their own personal psychoanalytic experience.

Unfortunately, we live in an era of the quick fix, where *Pharmacracy* (Szasz 2001) rules. Whether it's Red Bull or 5-Hour Energy or Viagra; whether it's Prozac, Ritalin, or Abilify; whether it's CBT (cognitive behavioral therapy), DBT (dialectical behavior therapy), or ACT (acceptance and commitment therapy); whether it's bank foreclosure or prison or military invasion, too often we intervene in ways aimed at eliminating problems without attending to their signal value or their underlying causes. Interventions like these deny the importance of Erikson's "epigenetic principle" while supporting an attitude toward human problems that is tantamount to abuse.

Amid this insanity, child psychoanalysis represents an alternative that, while currently devalued by many, will be seen by some as an important island of sanity:

- A place where the goal is to understand the mind rather than to dismiss it as ephemera produced by a brain that requires adjustment via drugs
- A place where we can appreciate and make use of the ways in which one mind affects another
- A place where the hierarchies, exclusions, and insularities that have kept psychoanalysis cooped up on Park Avenue (New York) or Michigan Avenue (Chicago) are abandoned in favor of the homes, nurseries, preschools, and schools of our local communities

The fabric of child analysis has been woven slowly yet steadily over the past century. Some older threads, initially seen as disparate or heretical, have been incorporated into the fabric while other, newer threads are still on the loom. Kerry and Jack Novick's (2005) exposition of their work with parents is a case in point; their position (with a bow to Winnicott) is that "there is no such thing as a child analysis." Child analysis can exist only if there is a framework of parents, analysts, and others to support the work.[12]

Child analysis in the twenty-first century brings to bear a range of tools (scientific, theoretical, and therapeutic) that address aspects of

---

12. The fact that early analysts sometimes analyzed their own children may have created a kind of scotoma that made it difficult for analysts to address this issue.

human development and behavior that usually are ignored by the symptom-focused perspectives popular with insurance companies and health-policy experts.

Like its subjects, child analysis has its own developmental history. And, like most developmental histories, it includes a goodly bit of conflict. As analysts we know that sometimes the residue of conflict is rigidity, a loss of flexibility, a contraction of vision. However, if we recognize our own developmental history and how it has been shaped by conflict, we are in a position to grasp the opportunities that lie before us.

Our forebears were not initially constrained by the conflicts that emerged later. They were open to all sorts of thinking and doing; they worked in all sorts of arenas, often with little pay, and often in ways that were seen as disturbing the peace.

We would do well to recapture some of their revolutionary spirit and pass it on to another generation. The Hampstead Clinic was not meant to be a museum; it was a laboratory and workshop that attracted a diversity of talented people. When Anny and Maurits Katan established the Cleveland Center for Research in Child Development, they were not creating a museum but a workshop and laboratory in which they could continue the revolutionary work they had begun in Europe.

If we return to the kind of work that characterized the child analysts of the 1920s, 1930s, and 1940s, and if we are as creative as our Viennese ancestors were in supporting the training of new child analysts,[13] the fabric of child analysis will continue to grow.

However, if the fabric is to grow, we must create new looms—looms that accommodate the many strands that make up the fabric we have inherited. Looms that can support trainees as they learn about analysis— their own personal analyses as well as those of the children they see,[14] looms that become integral parts of the communities around us.

The Hampstead Clinic was Miss Freud's loom, on which she and many others wove their version of the fabric. And there have been many other such looms: Kinderheim Baumgarten and the Jackson Nursery

---

13. According to Danto (2005), every member of the Vienna Psychoanalytic Society was expected to devote at least two hours of each working day to pro bono treatment. Those who (like Sigmund Freud) could attract patients from abroad, with their ability to pay high fees in hard currencies, were expected to contribute the fees from two such patients to the commonweal by supporting the expenses of the Ambulatorium, the free clinic sponsored by the society. At that time the usual work week was six days.

14. When I was faced with a choice between the Tavistock training or Hampstead's, the offer of a W. T. Grant Foundation fellowship made a huge difference. This covered my personal analysis (at the munificent rate of five pounds sterling per session) and my supervision expenses for four years. There was no tuition charge, so all I had to pay for were my books, housing, food, clothing, transport, and so forth.

in Vienna, the Hampstead War Nurseries, the Cassell Hospital, and the Brent Consultation Centre in London, the Child Study Center at Yale, the Orthogenic School in Chicago. While some have disappeared and others have parted from their analytic roots, still others remain: the Hanna Perkins Center in Cleveland, the Allen Creek Preschool in Ann Arbor, the Lucy Daniels Center in North Carolina.

Such looms preserve the core of our field: a personal engagement with the unconscious, with the raw power of the drives and their derivatives, in ourselves and our patients, via intensive psychoanalytic treatment.

At the same time, psychoanalysis cannot survive as a closed system; we must emulate the Roman dramatist Terence, who famously wrote, *"Nothing that is human is alien to me."*[15] The same is true of psychoanalysis, and especially of child psychoanalysis. Our looms and our work must embrace all that is human. We would do well to remember that, late in her career, Anna Freud (Sandler, Kennedy, and Tyson 1980) wrote, "There is no absolute psychoanalytic technique for use with children, but rather a set of analytic principles which have to be adapted to specific cases" (p. 199).

The fabric of child psychoanalysis must remain open to all of the strands that contribute to human development.[16] And its looms must afford our trainees the provision, protection, and participation (Young-Bruehl 2012, p. 16) required if a new generation is to be able to take up the threads that we are passing on. In doing so, we will honor Marianne Kris and the other founders of the ACP, as we preserve and expand the fabric they began.

REFERENCES

AICHHORN, AUGUST (1925). *Verwahrloste Jugend.* Wien: Internationaler Psychoanalytischer Verlag. Translated as *Wayward Youth.* New York: Viking Press, 1935.

ALLEN, J. G., P. FONAGY, AND A. W. BATEMAN (2008). *Mentalizing in Clinical Practice.* Washington, DC: American Psychiatric Publishing.

BAILLY, LIONEL (2011). *What Is Infantile in Infantile Sexuality?* Unpublished paper presented at the Anna Freud Centre, London, November 4.

---

15. In his *Heauton Timorumenos.*

16. Robert Waelder (1936) used a different but quite similar metaphor, suggesting that psychoanalysis should provide "a kind of polyphonic theory of psychic life in which each act is a chord, and in which there is consonance and dissonance" (pp. 83–84).

BARISH, KENNETH (2009). *Emotions in Child Psychotherapy*. New York: Oxford University Press.
BELL, SILVIA M. (2005). A girl's experience of congenital trauma: The healing function of psychoanalysis in the adolescent years. *Psychoanalytic Study of the Child* 60:263–91.
BERNFELD, S. (1925). Vienna Psycho-Analytical Society. *Bulletin of the International Psycho-Analytical Association* 6:106–7.
BOWLBY, JOHN (1969). *Attachment*. New York: Basic Books.
——— (1973). *Separation*. New York: Basic Books.
——— (1980). *Loss*. New York: Basic Books.
BRAND, A. E., AND P. M. BRINICH (1999). Behavior problems and mental health contacts in adopted, foster, and nonadopted children. *Journal of Child Psychology and Psychiatry* 40 (8): 1221–32.
BREUER, JOSEF, AND SIGMUND FREUD (1893–1895/1955). Studies on hysteria. In James Strachey, ed., *The Standard Edition of the Complete Psychological Works of Sigmund Freud*, vol. 2, pp. 1–305. London: Hogarth Press.
BRINICH, PAUL M. (1980). Some potential effects of adoption on self and object representations. *Psychoanalytic Study of the Child* 35:107–33.
BRINICH, P. M., AND E. B. BRINICH (1982). Adoption and adaptation. *Journal of Nervous and Mental Disease* 170:489–93.
BRINICH, PAUL M., AND CHRISTOPHER SHELLEY (2002). *The Self and Personality Structure*. Milton Keynes, UK: Open University Press.
CHESS, STELLA, AND ALEXANDER THOMAS (1995). *Temperament in Clinical Practice*. New York: Guilford Press.
COHLER, BERTRAM J. (2008). Child analysis and education: The contributions of Anna Freud and the *Kinderseminar*. *Annual of Psychoanalysis* 36:31–44.
DANTO, ELIZABETH A. (2005). *Freud's Free Clinics: Psychoanalysis & Social Justice, 1918–1938*. New York: Columbia University Press.
ERIKSON, ERIK H. (1950/1963). *Childhood and Society*, 2nd ed. New York: W. W. Norton.
ETH, SPENCER, AND ROBERT PYNOOS (1985). *Post-Traumatic Stress Disorder in Children*. Washington, DC: American Psychiatric Press.
FONAGY, P., G. GERGELEY, E. JURIST, AND M. TARGET (2002). *Affect Regulation, Mentalization, and the Development of the Self*. New York: Other Press.
FONAGY, P., M. STEELE, G. MORAN, H. STEELE, AND A. HIGGITT (1993). Measuring the ghost in the nursery: An empirical study of the relation between parents' mental representations of childhood experiences and their infants' security of attachment. *Journal of the American Psychoanalytic Association* 41:957–89.
FRAIBERG, SELMA, ED. (1980). *Clinical Studies in Infant Mental Health: The First Year of Life*. New York: Basic Books.
FREUD, ANNA (1936/1968). *The Ego and the Mechanisms of Defense*. London: Hogarth Press.
——— (1965). *Normality and Pathology in Childhood: Assessments of Development*. New York: International Universities Press.

——— (1966). The ideal psychoanalytic institute: A utopia. In A. Freud, *Problems of Psychoanalytic Training, Diagnosis, and the Technique of Therapy, 1966–1970*, pp. 73–93. New York: International Universities Press, 1971.

FREUD, ANNA, AND DOROTHY BURLINGHAM (1939–1945/1973). *Infants Without Families: Reports on the Hampstead Nurseries, 1939–1945*. New York: International Universities Press.

FREUD, SIGMUND (1909/1955). Analysis of a phobia in a five-year-old boy. In James Strachey, ed., *The Standard Edition of the Complete Psychological Works of Sigmund Freud*, vol. 10, pp. 5–149. London: Hogarth Press.

——— (1926/1959). The question of lay analysis. In *Standard Edition*, vol. 20, pp. 179–258.

FREUD, SIGMUND, AND OSKAR RIE (1891). *Klinische Studie über die halbseitige Cerebrallähmung der Kinder* [Clinical study of cerebral paralysis in children]. Vienna: Moritz Perles.

GOLDSTEIN, JOSEPH, ANNA FREUD, AND ALBERT SOLNIT (1973). *Beyond the Best Interests of the Child*. New York: Free Press.

——— (1979). *Before the Best Interests of the Child*. New York: Free Press.

HATFIELD, SANDRA RAMSDEN (2012). Personal communication.

HEINEMAN, TONI, AND DIANE EHRENSAFT, EDS. (2006). *Building a Home Within: Meeting the Emotional Needs of Children and Youth in Foster Care*. Baltimore, MD: Brookes Publishing.

HOLINGER, PAUL (2008). Further issues in the psychology of affect and motivation: A developmental perspective. *Psychoanalytic Psychology* 25:425–42.

HUG-HELLMUTH, HERMINE (1913/1919). *Aus dem Seelenleben des Kindes: Eine psychoanalytische Studie*. Leipzig und Wien: Franz Deuticke, 1913. Translated by James J. Putnam and Mabel Stevens as *A Study of the Mental Life of the Child*. Washington, DC: Nervous and Mental Disease Publishing, 1919.

HURRY, ANNE, ED. (1998). *Psychoanalysis and Developmental Therapy*. Madison, CT: International Universities Press.

JOBS, STEVE (2005). Unpublished commencement address, Stanford University, Palo Alto, CA, 12 June. Accessed online at http://is.gd/BNP7fB, on 8 January 2012.

KAPLAN-SOLMS, K., AND M. SOLMS (2000). *Clinical Studies in Neuro-Psychoanalysis: Introduction to a Depth Neuropsychology*. New York: Karnac Books.

KAZANTZAKIS, NIKOS (1960). *The Saviors of God: Spiritual Exercises*. New York: Simon & Schuster.

KING, PEARL, AND RICARDO STEINER, EDS. (1991). *The Freud-Klein Controversies, 1941–45*. London: Tavistock/Routledge.

KLEIN, MELANIE (1926). The psychological principles of infant analysis. In Melanie Klein, *Contributions to Psycho-Analysis, 1921–1945*, pp. 140–51. London: Hogarth Press, 1948..

KOHUT, HEINZ (1971). *The Analysis of the Self*. New York: International Universities Press.

KRIS, MARIANNE (1932). The use of a fairy tale in child analysis [Ein Märchenstoff in einer Kinderanalyse]. *Journal for Psychoanalytical Pedagogy* [*Zeitschrift für psychoanalytische Pädagogik*] 6:437–41.

——— (1944). Child analysis. In S. Lorand, ed., *Psychoanalysis Today*, pp. 50–63. New York: International Universities Press.

——— (1957). The use of prediction in a longitudinal study. *Psychoanalytic Study of the Child* 12:175–89.

KRIS, MARIANNE, AND SAMUEL RITVO (1983). Parents and siblings: Their mutual influences. *Psychoanalytic Study of the Child* 38:311–24.

LIEBERMAN, ALICIA F., AND PATRICIA VAN HORN (2008). *Psychotherapy with Infants and Young Children: Repairing the Effects of Stress and Trauma on Early Attachment.* New York: Guilford Press.

LUEPNITZ, DEBORAH (2005). Orwell, Winnicott, and Lacan: Notes of a psychoanalyst from Project H.O.M.E. *Psychoanalysis, Culture & Society* 10:328–34.

MACLEAN, GEORGE, AND ULRICH RAPPEN (1991). *Hermine Hug-Hellmuth: Her Life and Work.* New York: Routledge, Chapman and Hall.

MAHLER, M. S., F. PINE, AND A. BERGMAN (1975). *The Psychological Birth of the Human Infant: Symbiosis and Individuation.* London: Hutchinson.

MILLER, GEORGE A. (1956). The magical number seven, plus or minus two: Some limits on our capacity for processing information. *Psychological Review* 63 (2): 81–97.

NOVAK, B. J. (2004). From chaos to developmental growth: Working through trauma to achieve adolescence in the analysis of an adopted Russian orphan. *Psychoanalytic Study of the Child* 59:74–99.

NOVICK, K. K., AND J. NOVICK (2002). Reclaiming the land. *Psychoanalytic Psychology* 19:348–77.

——— (2005). *Working with Parents Makes Therapy Work.* New York: Jason Aronson.

PINE, FRED (1990). *Drive, Ego, Object, and Self: A Synthesis for Clinical Work.* New York: Basic Books.

PRETORIUS, I. (2007). Repeating and recalling preverbal memories through play: The psychoanalysis of a six-year-old boy who suffered trauma as an infant. *Psychoanalytic Study of the Child* 62:239–62.

PYNOOS, ROBERT, ALLAN STEINBERG, AND ARMEN GOENJIAN (2007). Traumatic stress in childhood and adolescence: Recent developments and current controversies. In Bessel A. van der Kolk, Alexander C. McFarlane, and Lars Weisaeth, eds., *Traumatic Stress: The Effects of Overwhelming Experience on Mind, Body, and Society,* pp. 331–58. New York: Guilford Press.

REICHMAYR, JOHANNES (1990). *Spurensuche zur Geschichte der Psychoanalyse* [Seeking clues in the history of psychoanalysis]. Frankfurt am Main: Fischer TB.

ROSENBLITT, D. L. (2008). Where do you want the killing done? An exploration of hatred of children. *Annual of Psychoanalysis* 36: 203–15.

SANDLER, J., H. KENNEDY, AND R. L. TYSON (1980). *The Technique of Child Psychoanalysis: Discussions with Anna Freud.* Cambridge, MA: Harvard University Press.

SANDLER, J., AND B. ROSENBLATT (1962). The concept of the representational world. *Psychoanalytic Study of the Child* 17:128–45.

SCHUMACHER, BEATE (2011). *How Do You Remember the Name of the Father? On the Oedipal Development of a Single Mother's Daughter.* Unpublished paper presented at the Anna Freud Centre, London, November 4.

SMALLER, MARK (2011). In the streets and out in the world: Being a psychoanalyst in 2010. *International Journal of Psychoanalytic Self Psychology* 6:124–26.

SOLMS, MARK, AND OLIVER TURNBULL (2002). *The Brain and the Inner World.* New York: Other Press.

SPITZ, RENE, AND W. G COBLINER (1966). *The First Year of Life: A Psychoanalytic Study of Normal and Deviant Development of Object Relations.* New York: International Universities Press.

STERN, DANIEL (2000). *The Interpersonal World of the Infant: A View from Psychoanalysis and Developmental Psychology.* New York: Basic Books.

SZASZ, T. S. (2001). *Pharmacracy: Medicine and Politics in America.* Westport, CT: Praeger Publishers.

VERHEUGT-PLEITER, A. J. E., J. ZEVALKINK, AND M. G. J. SCHMEETS (2008). *Mentalizing in Child Therapy: Guidelines for Clinical Practitioners.* London: Karnac Books.

WAELDER, R. (1936). The principle of multiple function: Observations on overdetermination. *Psychoanalytic Quarterly* 5:45–62.

WINNICOTT, D. W. (1952). Anxiety associated with insecurity. In D. W. Winnicott, *Collected Papers: Through Paediatrics to Psycho-Analysis,* p. 99. New York: Basic Books.

YOUNG-BRUEHL, ELIZABETH (2010). *Psychoanalysis and Socialism.* Inaugural Freud Lecture presented to the Psychoanalysis Unit, University College London, 13 October 2010. Available online at http://is.gd/9bdXPZ. Accessed 29 April 2012.

——— (2012). *Childism: Confronting Prejudice against Children.* New Haven, CT: Yale University Press.

"There Has Never Been Anything Like a Classical Child Analysis"

Clinical Discussions with Anna Freud, 1970–1971

AVA BRY PENMAN

This paper reports on a series of clinical discussions with Anna Freud, faculty and trainees at the Hampstead Clinic in 1970–1971. Anna Freud's comments are published here for the first time. The meetings concerned the nature and use of relationships in work with children who do not have a well-defined neurosis. If parochial borders are erased among the domains of upbringing, education, and psychoanalysis, potential therapeutic fertility and strength can increase. The clinical material in the paper makes it possible to explore the old and new aspects of the treatment relationship, such as the transferential, the externalization of the

---

Ava Bry Penman is on the faculty of the Child Psychiatry Department of the Cambridge Health Alliance, Harvard Medical School; faculty of PINE Psychoanalytic Center; and in private practice in Brookline, Mass.

Anna Freud contributions reproduced by kind permission of the Marsh Agency Ltd on behalf of the Estate of Anna Freud.

For reading the entire volume of material upon which this paper is based, and for interesting and useful discussions, my warm thanks go to Judith Chused, M.D.; Ehud Koch, Ph.D.; Veronica Maechtlinger, Dr.Med.; Jack Novick, Ph.D.; and Inge Pretorius, Ph.D. Thanks to the editorial readers for cogent observations and comments. Peter Fonagy, Ph.D., and Mary Target, Ph.D., directors of the Anna Freud Centre, gave valuable support and permission to publish this material. Finally, my special thanks to the late Anne Hurry for years of friendship.

An earlier version of this paper was presented at the Anna Freud Centre on November 1, 1995, at a Wednesday meeting in the week celebrating the centenary of Anna Freud's birth. After Anna Freud's death the Hampstead Clinic was renamed the Anna Freud Centre.

The Psychoanalytic Study of the Child 67, ed. Claudia Lament, Robert A. King, Samuel Abrams, A. Scott Dowling, and Paul M. Brinich (Yale University Press, copyright © 2013 by Claudia Lament, Robert A King, Samuel Abrams, A. Scott Dowling, and Paul M. Brinich).

self-representational, the developmental, and so forth. This is a personal account of a formative experience during training.

INTRODUCTION

IN 1970, AS A FOURTH-YEAR STUDENT IN FULL-TIME TRAINING AT the Hampstead Clinic, then in my mid-twenties, I longed to hear Anna Freud talk about specific clinical interactions with particular children, what she would have done or said, and why. I wished to add to the three wonderful years of listening closely to Miss Freud's extraordinary case discussions and summaries, and I wanted to learn more about work with children whose difficulties strained certain ideas of what was technically possible or useful in child analysis. Miss Freud accepted an invitation to attend new meetings for interested staff members and students.

Between October 1970 and July 1971, there were seventeen meetings. Five clinical cases were discussed, two to four times each. Two meetings focused on reconstruction. Discussions centered on clinical material and the presenting analyst's questions, which followed a brief developmental and family history and a word about treatment context. With Anna Freud's agreement, the meetings were transcribed from recorded cassette tapes; I was thus able to prepare introductions for each meeting and link issues and questions as we proceeded. My presentation here draws exclusively from more than 320 pages of introductory remarks and discussion transcripts, unless otherwise noted. Anna Freud's comments comprise about 70 pages of the text. The meetings were called "Treatment of 'Atypical' Children," and this was a purely descriptive use of the word *atypical*; no reference is meant to the way other analysts may have used the word. For the sake of clarity, sometimes I have taken the liberty to quote Anna Freud from several meetings when she spoke about the same point. At this time, the complete record of these meetings is at the Anna Freud Centre in London; the volume is entitled *Clinical Discussions with Anna Freud, 1970–1971*.

In the meetings, I wished to provide a forum for the discussion of clinical details outside the precious and necessarily protected privacy of supervision. Open discourse had seemed elusive at this level of clinical specificity. I hoped we could relegate our particular theoretical orientations and formulations to the background and instead, follow the particulars of what happens. I felt that discussion of children whose difficulties were not entirely neurotic would offer the chance, in fact, to talk about almost any child in the clinic and give permission to raise questions that might seem too rudimentary in other contexts. I saw that we would learn of the thoughts we wished we had had and the better quality of work that might have been attained (by someone else perhaps) in simply hearing and responding to the child's feelings. We went ahead, knowing we would risk feeling unwise; and feeling unwise is very hard, especially when working with children.

In this paper, I will try to give a glimpse into Anna Freud's clinical thinking about the treatment relationship in work with children without a well-defined neurosis. Central questions with each patient-therapist couple included: What was the general nature of the treatment relationship? How do we understand its myriad aspects? Which ones might be explored and beneficially used? From examining the material it will be possible to note instances of the clinical exploration and use of old and new aspects of the treatment relationship, for example, transferential, externalizations of self and self-representations, developmental object, real object, and so on. The discussions tended to focus on very specific details in a manner that was quite intimate and perhaps revealed, more nakedly than usual, the questions, dilemmas, fears, and quests that clinicians faced. Anna Freud's comments, in response, were personal and direct. Her deep concern for each child erased strict (parochial) borders among the domains of upbringing, education, and analysis—thus increasing potential realms of therapeutic fertility. This attitude encouraged (in me at least) freedom for intuitive exploration and thoughtful reflection. These "border lands" were not fully conceptualized at the time; some details of the material presented here and more of them in the transcripts themselves offer the possibility for further understanding and conceptualization. (Rose Edgcumbe [2000] and Anne Hurry [1998] have conceptualized related aspects of Anna Freud's thinking, drawing in part from the material in *Clinical Discussions with Anna Freud, 1970–1971*.)

My plan is as follows:
- I will give further background to these meetings—specific to our topic of the nature and use of the treatment relationship.
- I will give one case description and quote Anna Freud's reactions to selected aspects.
- Then I will give a little material from two other cases, with Anna Freud's comments.
- Finally, I will conclude with an appreciation and some observations and questions about the nature of Anna Freud's contributions to this arena of work.

A NOTE ON THE PRIMARY MATERIAL

The volume of material of the seventeen meetings is organized as follows: There is a chapter for each meeting containing all remaining records, and comprised of two sections: (a) my introductory remarks and/or the material the presenter provided, and (b) the transcribed discussion with Anna Freud. In the text of this paper, the number following the # indicates the meeting number (#1–17), and section (a) or (b); the page number refers to the discussion transcript within the designated section. I have included several quotations from published articles by Anna Freud where useful, and these will be clearly noted; the others are exclusively from Anna Freud's remarks at these meetings.

Background to Meetings, Overview of Topic

At Anna Freud's request, I delineated what I had in mind for the discussions. I will quote from my note sent to her before the meetings began:

> Dear Miss Freud,
> Questions regarding the treatment of children whose difficulties are not entirely neurotic are difficult to formulate. Perhaps we can safely say . . . that we meet daily the need to do something with these children other than, or alongside, what we have come to understand as "classical analysis" . . . much of this other work lies in the area of relationships. I have listed some points that might be interesting to discuss. . . .
> . . . What do we offer children who come without an ability to put words to feelings—who are confused in a basic sense as to what makes them feel good (safe) and who are limited to feelings of primitive pleasure when somehow "attached," aroused or fed, and un-pleasure when out of such a state (hurt, loss)?
> . . . How do we help a child feel safe [being separate]? [That is,] What kind of internal regulation would we like to see develop, and what would be the process leading to that result? If we believe such regulation (a kind of structuralization) occurs during and as a consequence of an enduring relationship, what is the nature . . . of the relationship we provide?
> . . . What is the effect of this [so-called] "other work" on the more usual aspects of analytic treatment?

On October 21, 1970, Anna Freud opened her comments on the first case by framing the broad issues. She spoke spontaneously, and her usual fluency is matched by an unusually free reach. She said:

> I'll begin by saying that the question of treating a child without an infantile neurosis, a child who is not a borderline child, but an underdeveloped child is a new experience for Miss Bry and has therefore confronted her with quite a number of questions. I would like to say that these are in reality questions which I have turned over in my mind for

"Classical Child Analysis" 177

a number of years; but I could never find anybody in the Clinic who was really interested in them and therefore I am quite surprised at the amount of interest there is shown today.

... My feeling for quite a considerable time now is that certainly it is the function of this clinic to teach the student child analysis. I wouldn't call it classical child analysis because *there has never been anything like a classical child analysis.* ... (italics added). There is a classical analysis, and child analysis is a modification of it according to the nature of the child. We are still working at the method of child analysis, to improve it, to complete it. We are still even with purely neurotic children uncertain in many directions which the best technical means are—but still, child analysis is a method which we have built up over the years.

In our dealings with children, we need something in between what we do in the nursery school . . . and analysis which is purely individual. . . . [In analysis,] . . . the educational influence on the child (even though it runs alongside it) is a by-product of the method . . . there are quite a number of children who fit into neither of these categories. They are not ready for group education . . . nor are they fit for analysis. . . . (#1b, pp. 1–2)

The method of child analysis aims very definitely at the child's ego, tries to show the ego: you've done that wrong, let us try together to do it right . . . and furnishes the ego with the possibility to do so by widening its scope of power within the personality . . . which means adding the forgotten parts, the repressed elements to the ego's knowledge, thereby helping the child to better solutions. Not altering the problems, but altering the solution of the problems. Well, that's what we call child analysis. (#1b, p. 2)

I would say that in child analysis we have learned a great deal about normal child development and about the desirable influences which help a child to develop normally. If I were to give you a short survey of them, I would say it begins with the bodily care, it goes from the bodily care to mental care for that child, to the constancy of both cares, the intimacy of a relationship in which object relations develop. (. . . the need for affection . . . for mutuality in affection. [That is] not only that the child has somebody to love, but in reverse that he is an important person to somebody. . . . [#7b, pp. 3–4]) We know that these object relations will later turn into identifications, internalizations and quite finally into the superego. We know the role of the superego. We know the role of verbalization and clarification [especially] . . . for the feeling states of the child. We know the role of reassurance which is part of the auxiliary ego role in child development. We know the necessity for stimulation—stimulation of the intellect, stimulation of fantasy, stimulation of beginning sublimations. . . . (#1b, p. 5)

Now here we have an armament from which we can choose . . . we can try to assess where the greatest needs of the child lie . . . and from this armament, we would then choose to lay emphasis on the one or on the other . . . [that is] on the intimacy, on the auxiliary ego, on the reassurance [etc.]. . . . We would have it all at our disposal; including verbalization, clarification and interpretation . . . this can be maneuvered and used skillfully to bring about the desired effects. (ibid.)

CASE: ALICE, A WAIF IN THE NURSERY SCHOOL

Alice attended the Hampstead Clinic Nursery School. She wandered around most of the time, sadly looking for a lap to sit on, unable to focus on any activity. She drooled continuously; she was unable to care for or about herself; she seemed endlessly forlorn and wanting; she seemed strikingly oblivious to what was going on.

Alice was the fifth of six children from a poor family. Many children slept in one bed, making it impossible to know who wet the bed and who did what to whom. An older brother was delinquent; an older sister poured hot water over Alice. Father was in prison. Mother was overwhelmed but good with children as babies. Mother permitted Alice to have analysis in the context of the nursery-school setting and calendar. She was unable to come to the clinic for meetings, and so occasional home meetings were arranged.

BEGINNING TREATMENT: GRATIFY AND LIMIT—VERBALIZE, CLARIFY, IMAGINE

I met Alice in the nursery school and formed a relationship with her there. I became a special friend by joining her in the group, watching (and narrating for her) what I saw going on, joining her in classroom activities where possible, and finding small ways for us to be together (for example, doing special jobs for the class, and so on). In the subsequent intensive individual treatment, I aimed to deepen an attachment and to learn more about Alice's states. My first approach was to gratify and verbalize Alice's incessant demands for getting or doing things, now focused on me. That is, I got the crayons and the paper and the tape, and such. On demand, I had an ever-ready lap. At that time, verbally describing these interactions constituted the activity of treatment. With time, she became very comfortable . . . but nothing else changed.

The technical challenge was to find and tap a developmental tendency in Alice. With this, she would move from my lap. Then we could understand more about her demands, as these were the main active features of her behavior.

I see now that I was repeatedly re-presenting in words our interactions in treatment at that time. In addition, there were other interventions.

For example, there was picture making; I marked paper with lines to show patterns and tracks of the asking-and-getting. In doll play, I used two dolls to enact the asking-and-getting, again and again. Thus, there were many ways I tried to convey to Alice what I noticed. With each, it was a re-presentation—and my presentation, another representation—of what I will call "The Story of What Alice Is Doing." She was very interested in these efforts.

Then we focused only on trying to clarify and verbalize feelings of the moment. In answer to scores of demands, I verbalized her wanting—wanting to have me, and wanting to have me do whatever she says. I slowly limited the gratification. I explained that no matter what I did she still wanted more and so I had to stop so we could find out what else she wanted. And I said, "It feels bad if I don't obey. . . . You feel then I don't care. . . ." When she saw me as having nothing and giving nothing, she angrily cried, "You're mean! I hate you! I'll never see you again!" She felt empty and forlorn. Then all she could feel was more wanting, now angry, and demand, "Just get it!!" Eventually, I could wonder about why she had to arrange so little independence for herself. Why not do things she could do, like getting the crayons . . . ? She was angry at this "forced independence"—feeling pushed away and abandoned.

In all, I tried to clarify her moment-to-moment feelings within our relationship. For us, the central, very explicit questions in treatment were Who cares for whom? When and why? When not? Why not? Further, How much love does a person have? Can it last beyond anger—hers and mine? Can her love (for herself and me) and my love (for myself and her) last beyond Alice's growth away, physically and mentally?

Following a long period of work with these issues, Alice was able, for the first time, to keep trying when first attempts didn't suit her; that is, her work was not and did not become rubbish. She spoke more—about different events of her current life in school and home. Also, she became somewhat relaxed, self-contained, and content in her play.

With time, Alice seemed relieved of her vigilance, her concerns about my opinion or supply of love at each moment. My lap was used much less. Generally, there was a new sense of organization and direction and perhaps a center to move from. Sometimes, now, there were dolls in her newly developed play. They were fed, bathed, and rocked; they went to sleep with ease. Sometimes, they would want to hear about these conversations just described, or would join in. Prior to this, dolls were carried, dragged, left, dropped, ignored; at that time, they seemed to be too far away to be cared about.

Throughout this, I was imagining her feelings and saying what they might be—an effort to wonder and speculate about her feelings, what kinds of names they might have. The activity of imagining was crucial to what I offered, I believe. In this, I accepted my imaginings about her and about us—and I took it as natural to the particular "human couple" of a grown-up and a child, and natural to what a grown-up can give a child. I now believe that central to her initial development in treatment was that I could imagine *that* she felt; and then, I could imagine *how* she felt. I cared about both and made that clear—whether the feelings were good or bad. Further, this was intrinsic to our relationship, to its ongoing-ness and to its growth. When imagining, I was always thinking of her; and this may have been especially nice and useful for the fifth of six children in her family.

Anna Freud's observations and inferences about development:
[Alice's] relationship to the mother . . . was . . . the primitive kind . . . , when the child was in distress, the mother was able to offer some contact, to take her on her lap. She was not able to sort things out for her, to understand, to have even an inkling what was wrong with the child. . . . So the bodily care which was minimal enough . . . did not [go] into what I call the mental care, the auxiliary ego care. (#2b, p. 7)

[In the nursery school] . . . Alice was ready to relate to anybody who came into the room on the basis of bodily care. It didn't matter who it was, man or woman, stranger or known person, she would climb on to their lap and hug them and want to be hugged. . . . So this was indiscriminate. . . . (ibid.)

. . . We . . . predicted that if nothing happened to help her therapeutically—she would be promiscuous later in life. . . . She'd be seduced very early because [she would take on] the first man who offered her the body care. . . . (#2b, pp. 7–8)

. . . And this is what I mean by one kind of early defect: not taking the step or not experiencing the influence that leads from the body care to the mental relationship. . . . This remains a danger point in the personality. (#2b, p. 8)

Anna Freud on technical implications—reversibility of experience, building structure:
Can [basic experiences] be undone . . . and which of them can be undone, which can't and perhaps to what age can they be undone. Of course we would like to think they can all be undone. I am pretty convinced that they can't . . . and I don't know . . . which can be undone, which only leave consequences, which can be influenced later on. (#2b, p. 2)

. . . When we analyze a person . . . the whole process is really aimed at that person's ego—to widen the scope of influence of the ego . . . to help that person . . . deal with . . . internal conflicts . . . left from the earliest experiences. . . . (ibid.)

"Classical Child Analysis" 181

... Can we apply that formula to the building up of the very structure which we expect later on to do the task, namely the ego defects? ... it would be for us, in practice, to find out where one can do so and where one can't. ... Now this ... runs counter to a different analytic theory which says if you only revive the early experiences in the transference ... you can then, in the very revival, modify the consequences. I don't believe that, not for the earliest ones, not for the basic ones. But that's for many people ... an open question. (#2b, pp. 2–3)

If you try to help [Alice] by making the past alive once more, you don't help her, because partly the past is alive anyway, much too alive ... and partly, there is no power inside her strong enough to deal with the past. ... (#1b, p. 3)

Anna Freud on how human beings are open to influence in their upbringing, in therapy, and beyond:
There is the borderline [border land?] between therapy and upbringing ... which has never been fully characterized by anybody ... [M]uch happens in therapy which also happens in upbringing and certain things happen in upbringing that also happen in therapy ... with the help of experiences gained in child analysis ... [we have] to ... review all the influences on a child ... the effective ones that change a child or a human being altogether apart from therapy. ... (#2b, p. 3)

... Where are [adult or child] character structures open to influence? ... we know they are open to many influences, because there are many people who never have therapy and who still undergo quite extraordinary personality changes during their lifetime, according to what one calls object experience ... in relationships ... sometimes experience through frustration, sometimes through satisfaction, sometimes through a new world opening up to them. And this is largely an unexplored field, but very worthwhile to explore from what we know, what we see happen in child analysis. (ibid.)

Anna Freud framing the treatment challenge:
And the question is: how could we gear these ways in which human beings are open to influence to what happens in the treatment [of children] with these early defects ... ? (ibid.)

NATURE, USE, AND ANALYSIS OF
EXTERNALIZATION AND PROJECTION

Another body of work centered around Alice's defense mechanisms of externalization and projection. In our relationship as in all others, Alice's self-esteem rested on making someone else the owner and director of her impulses. I had numerous chances to deal with these defenses.

Alice was interested in what I said, revealing an openness and, perhaps, hunger for contact, newness, growth. Whether angry, sad, or eager, she made clear her involvement, her contact with me. What follows is a clinical sampling of what happened, drawn together here, in this way, to convey the spirit and details of such interactions.

On many occasions, Alice did something like this: Alice took juice she got from the receptionist, brought it to the office, and skillfully poured a small puddle on the office table and said: "Ava, you spilled the juice! Ha, ha!" I would comment, "What? Me?—No, Alice, I didn't: You spilled the juice. But maybe I understand something: You want me to be the yucky spiller. Then you feel good and then people will like you (and not yucky me). You can feel nice on your own. I think we can know about your spilling yucky feelings, and I can help you with them. I know yucky feelings aren't fun. . . ."

I tried to confront her with the facts and explain how she changed them because she thought they made her into a bad person. At the beginning, her love for herself as well as her love for me depended on this organization. These mechanisms had made us interdependent and inseparable. I said no to participation in this organization, and thus I dismantled it: Alice had "less to love me for." She let me know how hard it was and how mad she was, saying "Shut up! It isn't true! I really didn't spill the juice! You did! You're lying! You're lying and you know it. It's bad to tell a lie. I'll tell my mother on you!" Then she moved to: "You made me do it. It's your fault. I couldn't help it." When she could tolerate an image of herself as spiller, but not as one who wishes to spill, she said that I was bad and made her do those nasty things, like make her drop a full cup. Alice and I could then address this aspect.

There was now much mental pain felt in relation to me (in the transference) and this certainly related to the mystery of who wet the bed, and the known hot water pouring by her older sister. She was left without me and with her awful bits. The analysis of them was quite a wrench for her. Dolls sometimes helped us address the feelings; Alice would listen carefully as I spoke to a doll and would ask for repetitions when she wanted to hear more. She was hurt at having to face having those aspects of herself. She was angry at her sudden powerlessness; she was angry at having to take ownership for her bad bits, her actions, and motives.

The analysis of these defenses following the limitation of gratifications helped Alice delineate her internal world. She could tolerate within herself some of both, the good and the bad. She was relieved and made many forward moves showing me her independence and freedom. She was better able to observe herself, and we could proceed with trying to further understand her feelings of sadness and worthlessness.

Anna Freud commented on Alice's use of these defenses and their analysis at the first meeting:

> How does one really see ... Alice's tendency to overuse projection and externalization? ... My answer to that would be that we have no direct influence on the defense mechanisms. We can neither teach them ... nor impute them on the child. What we do is we do other things to help every development ... and it's the ego, then, that alters the defense mechanisms. ... An ego on a different level will use different defense mechanisms. So there the influence is an indirect one, not a direct one. (#1b, p. 6)

At the second meeting, Anna Freud highlights the ongoing family situation as an environmental seduction, as follows:

> Just like a child of two would say ... No I haven't wet it; teddy has done it. ... [Alice] just didn't develop further. ... (#2b, p. 5)
>
> ... In that family ... up to 3 children slept ... in one bed and one never knew who wet the bed. Some of them were bed wetters and some were not. And I think that this must have played quite a part in the early toilet training of these children ... that when the bed was wet, somebody else had done it ... there were so many bad people in that family—the sister who threw hot water over Alice ... the father who was in prison ... there was always another bad person who could serve as the one who had done the bad thing. ... This was, partly ... an environmental seduction, to remain on that level ... instead of becoming an individual who knows when she's wet and dry. (ibid.)

The analysis of the defense itself was not unusual. The centrality (and ubiquity) of the defense in the child's organization was crucial, and thus the ramifications for further development were great. Anna Freud states:

> It's not that ... [Alice's use of this defense pattern] is one point in an otherwise higher personality who, if you confront her with it, would say, "Of course it's me; I am quite wrong to say that." But it's a low level of ego development where this is quite appropriate to her. ... The ego has to change so as not to be satisfied any more with that ... let's take another point—that the mother was able to relate on the bodily level, but not to extend the bodily care to mental care. (#2b, p. 7)

Surprisingly, comments regarding these defenses of Alice's were seamlessly embedded in Anna Freud's initial general remarks about the treatment relationship. I think Anna Freud saw how this defense-analysis worked to help Alice arrive at and get into the domain of mental care necessary to further development. Somehow, Alice's tie to me and her readiness to grow were sufficiently strong for her to "experience the influence that leads from the body care to the mental relationship"—to quote Miss Freud again.

I showed Alice how her wish to be a good girl and her wish to be loved led her to certain ego organizations that couldn't be had. I refused to agree to "false" attributions. I explicitly accepted her as a whole person, with all aspects of her states—that is, with the good bits and bad bits to be within her. She did not have a "whole-child" self-representation to which to refer. Further, I tried to give Alice's accusations and attributions affective coherence in terms of her inner world, her feelings; thus, I tried to make some kind of sense of the whole situation for her, in the current conscious experience of our relationship. In this, references to and links with the ongoing confusions in her home, with her siblings, and her mother and father increased. The transference links clarified and substantiated what was occurring in each place.

Alice made gains in independence, and these showed at home and school. Mother was pleased about Alice's forward developmental moves. Crucially, Mother did not pathologically require Alice to be a lap-baby forever.

In later periods of her treatment, the defenses of externalization and projection were not pervasive but arose only at times of special anxiety and regression. Alice's worries arose around object loss, narcissistic supplies, and states of feeling deeply sad and bad. As they arose, primitive anxieties could be examined in their conflictual aspects as well, and gradually around the aggressive, destructive wishes and associated fears.

PRIDE—A SMALL EXCHANGE WITH ALICE, AND WITH ANNA FREUD

After Alice told me that she had read a lot in her school one day, I commented that she must be proud of herself. To this she asked, "Ava, how do I be proud of myself?" I replied that that happened when she was happy with herself. Excitedly, she went on to tell me about a series of classroom privileges she had won. With each, there was a burst of pleasure; with each, I said, "That is being proud of yourself!" Clearly I took great pleasure in Alice's ability to feel so good about herself, in her pleasure with the work she accomplished and in her eagerness to tell me all about it. Anna Freud stated that she would have replied to Alice differently. Anna Freud would have said,

> That's a very difficult question, but I think when I am proud of you and when you like me, you will certainly be proud of yourself. And I think thereby you would have described how it's your pride in her that [she] takes in. (#1b, p. 6)

With characteristic clarity Anna Freud delineated the details of a process, placing the action squarely between herself and the child. She added

> You do not teach a child to be proud of herself, but through a new relationship [with someone who] appreciates her, she would suddenly feel proud . . . there we have to distinguish between the step that can be taught and those that can only be brought about in an indirect way. (ibid.)

Later, I asked Miss Freud what she might have said to a neurotic child who asked the same question. Immediately she simply stated,

> Tell me, can you think of someone in your family who was once proud of you? (#3a, p. 4)

In my interaction with Alice I did not put words to the process itself—and in that sense I did not answer her question. I had the feelings; Alice had the feelings; I named the feelings; and this led to more examples and more of the feelings felt and not to somehow conceptualizing it or describing how it worked to feel pride. I found the differences in approach fascinating.

TREATMENT RELATIONSHIP COMPONENTS

How do we understand Anna Freud's views on the nature and use of different aspects of the treatment relationship—and her views on their relations and interactivity, especially as it informs diagnosis and intervention?

To understand children such as Alice, Anna Freud preferred a descriptive frame of reference, that of minimal developmental needs, which had to be met within an enduring relationship. These needs included bodily care, affection, stimulation, support, and included the "whole auxiliary ego question." Anna Freud stated,

> We have never taken the next step . . . [to] attribute to the neglect of each of these needs a pathological outcome—we could do it from need to need . . . [and] have a scheme [to] divide these outcomes . . . from the neurotic outcomes. (#12b, p. 14)

This would clarify paths for work with children. Each child we discussed had a different problem in relationships and thus presented a different challenge in treatment. In our meetings, questions arose about how treatment could and should address such deficiencies with limit setting, instruction, advice, clarification, support, new kinds of play, and so on. I was struck with the implicit question concerning affection, if and how it might be involved in the interventions of advice and support. I wondered how and why this was an issue. Also, we asked if the child actively used the therapist as a new object and for developmental help; and regarding cultivating these aspects, we needed to know which, how, why, and when. And then, what about the potential interference with transference? To respond, we now look at a bit of the discussions of two other children.

Case Vignette: Brad

Brad was referred at age nine for antisocial, bizarre behavior. He attacked his two younger brothers and stole from shops. In his earliest years, he was neglected and frequently badly hurt. His mother locked him out of the house in the cold; his father savagely hit him. In discussing this terrorized terrorizer, Anna Freud stated:

> [We can] . . . emphasize the points of difference between the technique needed with such a case and . . . [that] needed with our neurotic children. . . . With neurotic children, we try to facilitate the transference, which means a repetition of the past . . . whereas with a child like [him], you deliberately interfere with the transference and thereby try, if possible, to correct the past. . . . And there is an enormous difference between the two actions and the two viewpoints underlying them. . . . (#3b, p. 10)
>
> There are many moments in child analysis . . . [in work with neurotic children] where one, perhaps less deliberately . . . shows the child that one is different from the parents, merely by understanding, by reacting differently to something the child says or does. That's an element which is very often neglected, which we call the analyst as a new object. A new object is an interference with the transference, whether people want to have it that way or not. (#3b, p. 13)

With this child, there was evidence of an emerging positive, if primitive, relationship with his analyst. A question was raised whether the deliberate cultivation of this relationship would "interfere with the transference and thereby . . . correct the past." Anna Freud said:

> What one will wait for, and [what will then] give the possibility for interpretation, [is] when the disturbance has come into this good object rela-

tionship. . . . [What] would need interpretation . . . is the . . . "[disaster]-fantasy" . . . which turns up even in situations where no disaster is . . . expected and can only be interpreted in situations where it's fantastic and not real. . . . [Further,] making conscious . . . the very first disasters will have to come very gradually. . . . (#5b, p. 8)

. . . Another difference of this type of work with the purely analytic work, I feel that in the purely analytic work one comes in with an interpretation at the moment when the material is nearest, at a crisis moment really. In this kind of work as one does in educational work, one doesn't bring it in at the moment when it's at a high point; one waits for a quiet moment and brings it in then, which means viewing it from a distance; it is very much more effective than viewing it at the moment of being experienced. With him at the moment when one is in very good contact with him and when he is very peacefully inclined, one could refer back to one of his stories. . . . (#5b, p. 9)

I think with a neurotic child, even at the moment of tension, except when it's a full anxiety attack or temper tantrum, there is still enough, ego left to accept what one interprets . . . whereas with a child like that one does [what one does] automatically in the upbringing of children—one waits for a moment of special and peaceful contact where the willingness to understand and to work through something and to approach . . . a disagreeable fact is greatest. (#5b, p. 10)

Let us look at one instance. A problem arose with Brad around the question of papering over a crack in the office ceiling early in treatment. Brad was disturbed by the crack and picked at it, announcing that he would do this until he could make the house (clinic) fall down. The therapist reported that Brad was relieved when he heard she wished to make the office safe; he was further relieved when she covered the crack with wrapping paper. However, he then did something sadly characteristic of him, demonstrating that this safety was not to last. Brad hit his therapist and hurt her.

In our group, much discussion ensued. In covering the ceiling's flaw, was the therapist presenting herself as a new person with unrealistic omnipotent potential? This was bound to fail and disappoint the child. After all, Brad's inner ceiling was falling down and there was nothing to be done externally about that. Or, in the papering-over, was the therapist offering a communication to the child about her interest in the whole subject of the child's safety—physically, mentally, and the safety of their relationship and of the treatment? Further questions, implied at that time, include: what kinds of symbolic actions suit a child of this age with such difficulties? What is the meaning to the therapist of her efforts? And, what is the therapist's intent and hope?

Anna Freud viewed this papering action as the therapist's clear attempt to show herself as different from the parents; in it, the therapist was interested in the child's safety, in the treatment ceiling not falling down upon him. Further, this was a token of evidence that the therapist would follow through on her promise to provide safety in all aspects of the treatment context.

Brad hurt his therapist, and this is just such a "disaster" that warranted analytic attention within the relationship at some point in time. Eventually, we would want to understand and help him understand what he does with the good experience with the therapist; we would note how he takes over, ruins it, and appropriates some kind of "control"—presumably to not be taken over, destroyed, and lost himself. For Brad, relations are disastrous, always—and unless he is helped to understand the unconscious wishes and fantasies, he would be doomed to be stuck.

CASE VIGNETTE: CRAIG

Craig's parents were unable to hear (congenital) or speak (as a related condition). He and his two younger siblings were normal biologically, as was an adult relative living with the family. Craig entered analysis in early adolescence because of great temper tantrums and impulsive hitting. His general negativity was aimed especially at his mother. With peers, he was friendless or fighting. Craig made and spoiled relations with teachers; even the most devoted gave up on him in despair. Craig couldn't fall asleep and had nightmares when he did. Craig did poorly at school; in sports, he failed because he ran any which way on the football field and jumped in the swimming pool before the whistle blew. His therapist thought school problems arose, at least in part, due to nonpractice of ego functions, a kind of lack of experience in trial action, for example. Discussion began with this aspect of his problems.

Craig was discussed after four years of treatment. Anna Freud thought through the diagnostic question as follows:

> [Craig] is an excellent case for thinking about the differences between defects, arrests and conflicts. The description . . . [given here] tended in seeing his malfunctioning as an example of underdeveloped or arrested functioning . . . [in] his inability to think—in general and abstract terms. . . . (#8b, p. 1)
>
> It seemed to me that the functions are there [and] are developed. They are interfered with from the side of the emotions. . . . I tell you where I get this reasoning from. [There was] the good history project that was one event, not then repeated by him. I am also thinking of the

good intelligence test. Again one moment not repeated. If it really was an absence of function, he couldn't have either. (ibid.)

If one could, by some miracle, remove the inhibition which comes from . . . the dissatisfaction with the object, from the disappointment in the object, from the battle with the object . . . I think, in spite of nonpractice, his intellect . . . would function. . . . (#8b, p. 2)

. . . He suffered . . . from developmental interference on every stage . . . these parents looked at from a sensible point of view are helpless, inefficient, defective and unsatisfactory . . . [and yet] assume all of their parental rights . . . are strict . . . critical and punishing in their attitude. . . . Also they depend on him . . . for hearing, but don't [respect] him as a helper and I think that this combination is an especially pernicious one for a child. (#8b, p. 4)

. . . I think much of his confusion in object relationships . . . anger, mistrust, non-expectation of help, non-tolerance for help comes from this very unhealthy mixture [in relations with his parents]. . . . (ibid.)

. . . I wonder whether the interference with intellectual functioning doesn't come more from that and not so much from the actual lack of stimulation and responsiveness that normally goes on. (#8b, pp. 4–5)

Recalling the diagnostic discussion four years earlier, Anna Freud reflected on her thoughts of the treatment implications at that time:

I remember . . . the diagnostic discussion . . . thinking one should treat his neurosis first . . . [which is] a much later production of the personality . . . and then give him certain things afterwards [pertaining to unmet needs] . . . [and then I thought—] Will we learn that it has to be the other way around? Should we consider these outcomes first and then treat the neurosis? (#7b, pp. 3–4)

Although a huge and interesting question, it was not addressed further at the time. At our next meeting, Anna Freud responded to the clinical material presented. She said, "[Craig] . . . asks for help . . . [It is given and he responds positively] and then he is unable to make use of it. . . . [Working with him then] . . . one first gives the help, and [then analyzes why he can't make use of it.]" (#8b, pp. 3–4)

At the subsequent discussion, the therapist reported Craig's wish to become a killer. Anna Freud said:

On the basis of what went on at the beginning of the hour . . . [helping him think through school responsibilities] . . . he offers you a fantasy of being a killer; he had a moment of sharing something with you and so he shared the next important thing, the killing fantasy. . . . [Addressing the therapist: . . .] You complain about the necessity to take the role of clarification and education . . . which disturb the analytic role, but to me you keep to that role also where he offers you a piece of real material; and [where there is] no need for you to go on playing that role. I think, on the basis of what went on at the beginning of the hour [discussion of how he contributes to problems at work, and therapist's advice for success . . . and further discussion of a movie] . . . he offers you a very important piece, his wish to be a killer. . . . Why not allow him, as one does in analysis, to develop the killing fantasy . . . he offers you the opportunity that he could now unfold to you his fantasy of being a killer . . . whom to kill, how to kill, probably also his sadistic fantasies . . . at the moment it's a marvelous idea to be a killer. (#9b, p. 2)

At the final meeting regarding this child, Miss Freud stated:

> In his whole development, the negative feelings always went against the people who tried to give him ego help. So I don't see that by giving him help you prevent the negative feelings. It would seem, rather, that you bring the very situation into the analytic relationship which is of such disadvantage to him outside—namely, that he does not allow people to fill the gap [left by his parents]. (#10b, p. 2)
>
> You raise the question whether . . . one should have foreseen [and arranged] that he [gets] . . . auxiliary ego help and then analytic help, but that would leave the problem that he cannot accept it. The help can only become acceptable in a situation where he can at the same time express and analyze his hate feelings. (#10b, p. 3)

For Anna Freud, I believe the issue was not whether to give the extra help to these deprived and abused children, whose background and current situation contained and created such a mixture of problems. Her message seemed to me to be "Give it, of course. And then see what happens. And use your interpretive capacities, as necessary." Anna Freud said:

> My feeling is . . . if I fantasy about it wildly . . . if he were allowed to be a killer he would plan his killing with a lot of abstract thinking, and we would suddenly find him on a very different level of functioning. You [the therapist] say he cannot plan the telephone conversation that deals with his employment, but I am sure he could plan how to capture somebody, or to torture him. . . . Couldn't he? (ibid.)
>
> . . . Whatever intervention . . . serves to clear up the diagnostic picture here . . . would serve the purpose . . . [of selecting the level and nature of approach]. (#10, p. 4)

CONCLUSION

How should I conclude this presentation and do justice to the intensity and complexity of my thoughts and feelings relating to my formative experience as a student so very many years ago? I struggled with how to pull my experiences together, knowing I wanted to stay close to the material. I needed a way to reach a conclusion, my conclusions, or at least a stopping point. Various attempts failed. . . . I found myself inventing a letter I would write to Anna Freud at this time.

Dear Miss Freud,

After reviewing all material of the seventeen meetings, I felt your comments had a free immediacy and inclusive quality reminiscent of certain of your early writings, for example, the wonderful lectures for teachers, on upbringing, on children's groups, and on war-made "artificial orphans," and so on. . . . One beautiful example of that early writing comes from the last paragraphs of *War and Children*:

> The ability to love—like other human faculties—has to be learned and practiced. Wherever, through the absence of or the interruption of personal ties, this opportunity is missing in childhood, all later relationships will develop weakly, will remain shallow. . . . It is this first love of the child which education makes use of. Education demands from the child continuous sacrifices. . . . [The child] is ready to pay this price if he gets his parents' love in return. . . . (Freud and Burlingham 1943, p. 191)

Can something similar be operative in psychoanalytic work, especially with children suffering from early and deep difficulties? In fact, perhaps this relates to an aspect of precisely the kind of "learning and practice" that Craig needed. It would involve the careful study and exploration of the formation, de-formation, and re-formation of relationships within the treatment relationship, in the moment and over time. Further, it would serve efforts to study this in development in the normal variations.

Rather naturally, that leads to the area of our relations, as analysts, to our child patients. Some therapists found work with such difficult children especially taxing, precisely because of the demands (on the analysts' minds) to relate to children whose problems entail such cruel, acute, and dramatic shifts. This was not directly addressed at the meetings. However, a few years after the meetings, you counseled:

> . . . every child to be dealt with . . . [should] be regarded by the professionals as an important representative of his own species . . . [It is] our task to arouse this type of interest in all the people who work with children. No love, for which there is not real basis, but an insatiable curiosity to learn more about the problems of child development seems to me the appropriate bond which ties the professional workers to the child in their care . . . (1982/1977, p. 299)

Treatment relationships have their own natural breadth, depth, and vicissitudes of affection. Might it be that certain kinds of curiosity on the part of the therapist link to certain kinds of love in the treatment process itself?

Regarding clinical work in general, you gave stature to a spectrum of efforts in treatment. We realize there is nothing vague or sentimental when you stated:

> It's a method, the whole thing we are discussing here . . . a method of trial and error, which doesn't go by the rules . . . so you try first what is natural in such a situation. Before you have tried . . . you don't know how a particular child will react—so one makes one's mistakes and learns from that reaction. (#4b, p. 13)

This is liberating, invigorating, and challenging. You caution against anything simplistic, as with a diagnostic:

> It's a mistake to look at [an evaluation of a child] from a single aspect [for example, considering object relations]. . . . There can be a very warm and intimate relationship with the mother [which has] constancy—and then, at the same time, be a complete absence of stimulation or of moral support . . . later on. And [then], the whole thing will go wrong. . . . It's a mixture where every ingredient is of great importance (#1b, p. 8). It's terribly important . . . that we hold no brief for either [one diagnosis or another]. (#8b, p. 16)

Regarding parents, questions arose as to how to help a child deal with very troubled parents, being wrongly accused or basically unwanted, as with Brad. The issue arose if work should address directly such awful truths; children know the unconscious of their parents well, and need help facing, bearing, and dealing with such truths. More clinical discussion is necessary, as there seemed to be discomfort and disagreement among participants, and this matter is commonly pressing with just such children.

Finally, you give further support for work with such children and account for the fact that we mustn't "expect it to be easy. . . ."

> It takes more than the child analyst's usual courage and therapeutic optimism to approach cases whose development is incomplete in one or the other essential direction. . . . On the other hand, only the therapeutic attempts made by such analytic pioneers hold out the promise that we may learn to fill the gaps in our present insight into developmental problems. . . . (1981/1974, p. 81)

You gave us broad views strongly outlined and richly colored. Of course, we will always wonder about how you would have reacted specifically. Perhaps you assumed we would search for the necessary ways to proceed, those natural to each of us individually. The discussion about replying to Alice's question about how to be proud of herself was a little example of how interesting, complicated, and instructive a few details can get! In fact, I just want to go on talking with you, and actually that is what this letter is about.

Really, though, you gave so much to so many; you gave enough. Now I simply want to thank you. My years at the clinic you created were extraordinary in countless ways; four years of immersion with others in psychoanalytic studies gave me invaluable experiences in asking, discussing, and learning. The past is present in that the whole experience endures; daily and variously, it inspires and affects my work and my life.

BIBLIOGRAPHY

CLINICAL DISCUSSIONS WITH ANNA FREUD, 1970–1971. Volume of unpublished transcripts of seventeen meetings held at the Hampstead Child Therapy Course and Clinic (now the Anna Freud Centre), London, UK. Meetings convened and moderated by Ava Bry Penman.

EDGCUMBE, ROSE (2000). *Anna Freud: A View of Developmental Disturbance and Therapeutic Techniques*. London: Routledge.

FREUD, ANNA (1981). *The Writings of Anna Freud*. Vol. 8: 1970–1980. Chap. 5: "Beyond the Infantile Neurosis" (1974), and chap. 19: "Concerning Relationships with Children" (1977). New York: International Universities Press.

FREUD, ANNA, AND DOROTHY T. BURLINGHAM (1943). *War and Children*. New York: Medical War Books.

HURRY, ANNE, ED. (1998). *Psychoanalysis and Developmental Therapy*. London: Karnac Books.

TRAUMA

What Becomes of Infantile Traumatic Memories?

An Adult "Wild Child" Is Asked to Remember

LENORE C. TERR, M.D.

A severely traumatized child, acting like a wild animal, was removed from her parents at thirteen months of age when her three-week-old sister was found, bitten and shaken to death. (Her father was later convicted of manslaughter and imprisoned.) The older child was also covered with bite marks. When she was twenty-nine months old, this child, whom I call "Cammie," was brought to me from miles away by her foster parents for once-monthly psychotherapy. I have treated her, stressing abreaction, context, and correction, once a month ever since. When she was five years old Cammie's foster family adopted her. She is now twenty-two. I call her the "wild child" because of the growly voice, vomiting at will, grabbing at the genitalia of strangers, and cruelties to animals that she exhibited after her rescue. Presently she attends college and is training to be a preschool teacher or an aide to pediatricians.

I have taken notes on what Cammie says and does during the twenty years she has come to me. In the spring of 2011, I was asked to speak later that year about infantile memories at the Margaret Mahler Symposium, Columbia University, New York. With the organizing committee's approval, I accompanied Cammie and her adoptive mother to the October 1, 2011, meeting and asked her in front of the psychoanalytic audience to recount her oldest remembrances. She, her mother, and I spoke about the

---

Lenore C. Terr, M.D., is a Clinical Professor of Psychiatry at the University of California San Francisco School of Medicine.

The Psychoanalytic Study of the Child 67, ed. Claudia Lament, Robert A. King, Samuel Abrams, A. Scott Dowling, and Paul M. Brinich (Yale University Press, copyright © 2013 by Claudia Lament, Robert A King, Samuel Abrams, A. Scott Dowling, and Paul M. Brinich).

nonverbal manifestations of her memory as well. I had briefly prepared Cammie and her mother for our presentation at the Mahler Symposium, but for the most part, it was spontaneous and unrehearsed. Their comments are quoted in this article.

At twenty-two the "wild child" reports no verbal memory from her first year. On the other hand, her behaviors, attitudes, and perceptions over the years have reflected what occurred to her and indicate very active nonverbal memories of the traumatic experiences. Fragments of verbal memory that she recounted in therapy between ages two and three have entirely slipped away. Several kinds of behavioral reenactments of the abuses she received as an infant have been reversed into altruism. Other attitudes and behaviors have remained unaltered, however. Under the influence of street drugs or anesthetics, her infantile memories have been reawakened in the form of illusions, delusions, and condensation. Following a disaster in Japan, a shard of infantile memory was retrieved in the form of a repeated nightmare.

Single cases like Cammie's inform us about the course of traumatic memories through childhood. Such cases may lead us to follow larger groups of infants for extended periods of time. We must try to further understand the effects of early trauma on the brains and minds of young children. This is of crucial importance to the future of psychiatry and psychoanalysis and to our duties to society.

INTRODUCTION

HOW DOES A YOUNG ADULT CONSCIOUSLY REMEMBER TRAUMATIC events from infancy? Can a psychiatrist or psychologist recognize the unconscious traces of very early traumatic experiences? Sometimes a single case begins to answer such questions. In fact, sometimes a single case brings us something unique enough to inspire a clinical series, a new technology, or a piece of significant research. This might eventually be the outcome of the case of "Cammie Brooks," my false name for a twenty-two-year-old college student who has come to me from a small town miles away for an hour of psychotherapy once a month since she was twenty-nine months old. When she was fourteen, I published a paper about her treatment (Terr 2003), emphasizing three principles of psychodynamic psychotherapy I consider critical to working with trauma—*abreaction* (emotional expression), *context* (cognitive understanding), and *correction* (positive behavioral or fantasized change). I called her the "wild child" in that first publication, as an homage to Jean Marc Itard, the eighteenth-to-nineteenth-century psychiatrist who tried to treat an untamed, animal-like boy who had emerged from the woodlands of France (Itard 1801; Humphrey and Humphrey 1932; Lane 1979; Truffaut 1970). Cammie was removed from her home and her birth parents when she was thirteen months old. She had been traumatized by parental biting, shaking, sexual abuse, and by witnessing the killing, by biting and shaking, of her three-week-old sister. She had acted like a little beast of the forest at the time she was rescued by the police. It took years of great foster parenting, mixed with monthly psychotherapy, to bring her behavior around. My main purpose in this paper is to consider Cammie's adult memory of those very early events, all of which totally ceased a month after her first birthday.

Methods

I have treated Cammie once every four weeks, keeping careful notes, up to the present time. Early in 2011, I was invited to make a presentation later that fall about "memory of early trauma" at the Margaret Mahler Symposium, Columbia University, New York. With the organizing committee's approval, I accompanied Cammie and her adoptive mother to the October 1, 2011, meeting and asked her memory questions directly in front of the analytic audience. In advance of that meeting I briefly prepared Cammie and her mother twice, for five to ten minutes, in August and September. I then asked her the questions for the first time in public. For the most part, our presentation was spontaneous and unrehearsed.

Cammie allowed her real identity to be revealed in 2012 in order to appear on CBS national news (the broadcast became an Emmy Award finalist). The news producer had read my book (Terr 2008) in which Cammie is featured in disguise. He asked me if she and her parents would be willing to "go public" with their story. After a discussion with me about the pros and cons, Cammie and her mother asked to meet the producer. Since that broadcast, mother and adult "wild child" have appeared under their own names at two annual meetings (the Academies of Pediatrics and of Child/Adolescent Psychiatry). They continue to give talks to foster care and pediatric organizations. Both work diligently at these presentations. Their motives are entirely altruistic. I, however, have let them know that I will do no further joint appearances with them. Cammie continues to see me as a patient once a month. She and her mother have read and approved the draft of this paper.

The reader of this paper will find its organization unusual. I will stop the flow of my prose to quote the questions I asked in New York City (under the initials *L.T.*) and then their answers (either cited as *Mother* or *Cammie*). The materials I cite on Cammie's nonverbal memories come from my notes over a twenty-year period. It made no difference to my patient whether I used her real name or not, but to keep other publications about her clear and consistent (Terr 2003; Terr 2008), I will call her "Cammie."

What is particularly interesting about tracing Cammie's infantile memory is that she was continuously and hideously traumatized in her first year of life, and then it all totally stopped. Any memory residuals she had were retained directly from infancy—or had otherwise been suggested to her later (Loftus 1993). The sexual abuses were verified through gynecological and urologic surgeries at age five. The biting injuries were verified through examination of Cammie's skin upon her delivery into foster care. The shaking injuries were partly verified through her attention deficit hyperactivity disorder (ADHD), an important finding in "shaken baby syndrome." Her baby sister's autopsy revealed biting injuries all over the child's trunk and extremities, and shaking injuries of the brain. One bite mark on the dead infant was from an adult female. All other bite marks matched Cammie's father's dental chart.

At thirteen months, when placed in the Brookses' foster care, Cammie growled. Her speech, as it developed, became a succession of deep basso grunts, delivered in short explosive bursts. From the beginning of her life with her new parents, she hissed, snarled, sniffed, screamed, gurgled, and vomited at will. She bit herself and others. She squeezed animals and sometimes threw them around. Clinging to her foster mother, she followed her as if she were the only safety zone in a battleground. She was terrified of men (including her foster father), of Hispanics, of strangers. She tried to catch the odor of any adult who approached her and often grabbed at their genitals or breasts. Under the age of three, she was psychologically tested at two different institutions and was diagnosed both times as mentally retarded. Despite these dire findings, Cammie's foster parents formally adopted her when she was five. By the time she grew to maturity, it was clear that her intelligence was superior.

I will be writing here mainly about Cammie's "episodic" (also known as "event" or "autobiographical") memory. I will also allude to three fluidly active processes of memory—*perception* (including *encoding*), *storage*, and *retrieval*. Because I am limiting myself to an infant with a highly immature brain, who experienced a number of traumatic events, I will be referring to many of Cammie's memory retrievals as metaphors, symbols, play, drawings, behaviors, attitudes, and fears (Terr 1988).

It is well nigh impossible for a baby under eighteen months to produce a full verbal narrative of an occurrence. Even little incidents from home or the park on the very day they happened are beyond relating with a beginning, middle, and end (Fivush 1992). Infantile amnesia is not only psychological, it is the physiological and developmental result of incomplete human brain development. With unpleasant events—even below twelve months—there may be fragments of the event evident in the child's words. But a full verbal narrative of episodes from before the age of eighteen months cannot ordinarily be formed without help from someone else who knows, or thinks they know, what happened. Thus, when an adult narrates a fully realized tale from his or her infancy, part of it most likely comes from another observer.

In recent years a number of "lab" experiments have been done on infants, using nontraumatic stimuli in the form of action sequences that are played out for the babies. The aim is to find out whether they remember, through watching the youngsters, for an immediate response or for deferred imitation. They do remember, it appears (Nachman, Stern, and Best 1986; Bauer 2007). Another type of experiment has been aimed at young children's verbal memory. In one study of two-year-olds, the toddlers demonstrated an ability to use newly acquired color labels to describe a lab event they had witnessed before they knew the words for colors (Morris and Baker-Ward 2007). Though fascinating, these experiments may not relate with linearity to a case like Cammie's. They were nontraumatic laboratory experiments.

We must deal with the possibility of suggestion whenever we consider a child's memory. The younger the child, the more amenable he or she is to suggestion (White, Leichtman, and Ceci 1997; Saywitz et al. 1991). In the case of their little "wild child," Cammie's foster parents made a conscious decision not to talk directly to her or in her presence about her first year of life. This guaranteed nothing about her memory, of course. Others could have talked. Familial slips may have occurred. But holding back about her first year was a decision with which I concurred. In my office, I tried not to suggest any new memory twists to Cammie's old experiences. I told her nothing about her past unless her parents agreed first to my talking about it. Of course, my behavior was not foolproof, either.

We must also deal with the question of the stress commensurate with a young child's memory. When young children's memories of ordinary pediatric examinations, for instance, were compared to children's memories of voiding cystourethrograms (VCUG examinations), their memories of the unusual and uncomfortable procedures were recalled with more detail and accuracy (Merritt, Ornstein, and Spicker 1994). Cammie's experiences were not comparable to this type of study, because they were so much more extreme in terms of the stress she endured, and they had happened at such an earlier stage of development. But the idea should be kept in mind.

In this article, I will clinically categorize Cammie's memories as follows: (1) verbal expressions of memory; and (2) nonverbal expressions (behaviors, attitudes, and perceptual returns). I will begin by considering Cammie's memories as a two-year-old child up to the time of entering kindergarten. I will then consider her school-age and adolescent memories, again breaking them down into verbal and nonverbal expressions. Finally, I will describe Cammie's adult memories, again considering the subheadings I have listed above, and especially emphasizing a group of nonverbal memories recently impelled back into consciousness. The reader may note that my old designation "behavioral memory" (Terr 1988) has been changed to "nonverbal memory," and then it has been subdivided into the three subcategories mentioned above—behaviors, attitudes, and perceptions.

Results

Memories from Age Twenty-Nine Months to Kindergarten

Verbal Memories

> L.T. to Cammie: *What do you remember inside your head from before you were thirteen months old?*
> Cammie: *Nothing.*
> L.T.: *Do you remember anything from my office—about us from before you were five or six?*
> Cammie: *Just playing Little Red Riding Hood.*
> (L.T: Red Riding Hood was played from Cammie's age five to seven.)

At age twenty-nine months Cammie was well prepared for her first psychiatric visit and related to me in a friendly, unfrightened fashion. But her little eyebrows were knit in grim concentration. Her arms and legs were covered with toddler-sized bite marks and scratches. Stimulated by the toys she saw, she threw out growly remarks about them, representing bits of verbal memory from her terrible first year. Of a fleecy pair of sheep on my desk she said, "Sheep die. Die, sheep." At that time, I thought she was referring to her baby sister's murder, but when she was eight, I learned otherwise from her mother.

> L.T. to Mother: *Repeat the story you related to me years ago of your encounter with Cammie's distant cousin through her birth parents.*
> Mother: *Cammie's cousin saw me at an educational conference and asked if I was Cammie's mom. She then remarked that her grandparents, who had lived in the same house with Cammie's birth parents, slaughtered sheep. They also tortured*

What Becomes of Infantile Traumatic Memories? 203

and shot stray cats. In fact, they bragged about it. They did this stuff in front of the kids.

On Cammie's first visit to my office, she looked at but would not touch, a baby doll I keep in my toy cabinet. She commented, "Baby die. Die baby." This was a verbal memory. Later, in reluctantly handling a family of dollhouse dolls, she said of the mother, "Got boobies. Trow [throw] away." She then hurled the mother doll onto the floor. Glancing around my room she spotted a traditional nutcracker. "He bite," she intoned in her eerie basso voice. Seeing a painted wooden Zuni snake, she said, "Snake huut [hurt]." These comments, though metaphoric, were verbal infantile memories that reflected segments of a fuller but unexpressed mental picture from before thirteen months.

Nonverbal Memories

Behavioral Expressions

At about age three, Cammie enucleated the eye of a small stoneware cat that was sitting on my desk. I immediately inked in the cat's eye to prove that I could repair things (like little girls' minds).

> L.T. to Mother: *Could you tell me once again about the poodle Cammie injured when she was three?*
> Mother: *She suddenly threw our family dog against a wall. He was paralyzed for a day. We gave him to another family because we couldn't guarantee his safety anymore.*

Cammie feared my baby doll and at first refused to play with it. I helped her invent a series of pretend tea parties with police and "big guhs [girls]" in attendance in order to keep the baby doll "safe." We played this for two years. Eventually my whole office—even Nutcracker and Snake—were allowed to come to tea because we had corrected each of their behaviors, one by one.

At eighteen, after reading my manuscript of *Magical Moments of Change*, which follows Cammie's life up to that age (Terr 2008), she asked to see my toy cat with the enucleated eye. She didn't remember doing the deed—or even remember the cat itself—but she requested that I keep it more obviously on my desk. She has inspected it several times since.

Attitudes

> L.T. to Cammie: *Tell me about Hispanic men and fat people.*
> Cammie: *For the first time in my life I have two friends who are Hispanic. I've always been scared of Hispanic guys. I stay away from fat people, but now I'm okay with some heavy women, especially my sister-in-law, who I love to pieces.*

Perceptions

During her early years I did not see evidence of perceptual returns in my office. Cammie liked our staff and did not react fearfully or inappropriately to people in the waiting room. However, her mother saw several examples.

> *L.T. to Mother: Could you give me a few illustrations of returning perceptions during Cammie's preschool years?*
> *Mother: One night when Cammie was three she screamed that her birth mom was "living in the walls." I figure there must have been mirrored closet doors near her crib and her mom came out of the mirrored door and frightened her. Cammie never could stand musty smells, especially the smell of a doll her birth mom sent her. I had to throw it out. It smelt pretty bad.*
>
> *I guess the most dramatic perception was of a house in our town. We'd occasionally pass that house in our car. Cammie would always growl, "Bad house." I finally drove up the Central Valley (alone) to her original home. It was exactly the same kind of house.*

MEMORIES FROM KINDERGARTEN TO HIGH SCHOOL GRADUATION

Verbal Memories

Cammie attended kindergarten twice—first, because she wasn't socially ready, and second, because she was having tiny "absence" seizures twenty or more times a day. The pediatric neurologist at UCSF needed to conduct an electroencephalogram (EEG) of the child under general anesthesia. Emerging from unconsciousness, Cammie clawed and screamed at her newly adoptive mom. "You bad! Trow [throw] away!" She growled, even though years before, a gifted speech therapist had helped her to correct all the growling. Here was a partial verbal return of painful infantile memories of "Mother." But they had now become condensed with other memories of a much better mother (Kris 1956). The old memory had become reactivated through the influence of anesthetics. I went to the hospital that day; Cammie's new mother was completely thrown by her little girl's confusion. But Cammie had already calmed down.

> *L.T. to Cammie: Do you remember what happened that time at UCSF?*
> *Cammie: No.*

At five and a half, after celebrating her adoption with a real tea party at my office, Cammie did not ask to play imaginary "tea" again. Instead, she started her own version of Little Red Riding Hood. In Cammie's version, everybody but the wolf was ultimately eaten. We played and talked enough about the victims' feelings that it helped the little girl develop meaningful emotions on behalf of people in bad straits. But Cammie's pessimistic narrative did not change for two years. Then one day as we played I suddenly thought to ask her something that—I believe—evoked a bit of verbal infantile memory.

L.T. to Cammie: Wouldn't a wolf rather eat deer meat than human beings?
Cammie to L.T.: Yes. But this wolf wants girls!

The latency-age child—through thinking about an imaginary wolf—suddenly realized that the family of her infancy was weird. They were outliers.

There was a little pause. Then came a partial resolution to Cammie's infantile memory:

Cammie to L.T.: How does wolf soup taste?

The child had put her old memories into transition.

L.T. to Cammie: Delicious, I bet!

We had shared the memory verbally, but only in metaphoric form. This memory return was inspired by a contextual discussion in therapy (Terr 2009), and it led to a turning point in the little girl's progress.

Nonverbal Memory

Behavioral Expressions

From the very beginning Cammie shook her entire body several times a day. During her latency years it became obvious that she was shaking herself to orgasm. To do this, she usually looked at picture books about animals. Her adoptive parents called this her "shaking habit." But it was clearly a behavioral memory of the parental shaking that had aroused her during infancy.

When Cammie switched from private to public school at the age of nine, a kindergartner named "Andy" latched on to her in the school bus, suggesting they have "sex." She was curious and thought they just might try. But when she told me about it, I got parental permission to discuss with her the "facts of life" and the "facts of love." Her new perspective on what sex could mean helped her to get rid of Andy. She also spontaneously decided to hand over the animal books she had shaken to. Gradually afterward, the shaking habit entirely stopped. And parenthetically, Andy's mother told Cammie's mother that they had adopted him following an early childhood marked by repeated sexual abuse.

Attitudes

After Andy, Cammie started liking boys.

> *L.T. to Cammie: Describe the types of boys you like.*
> *Cammie: Blond, blue-eyed, fair-skinned.*
> *L.T.: But you know you are Hispanic, right?*
> *Cammie: Right!*

Cammie's choices in girlfriends impelled me to say at one time, "With friends like that, who needs enemies?"

> *L.T. to Cammie: Can you comment on your girlfriends?*
> *Cammie: I haven't always been lucky. But I have a couple of good ones now.*

Perceptions

A nonverbal memory return—terrible gloom—descended on Cammie when she turned nine. First, a little girl down the street (whom she did not know) was raped and murdered by an itinerant handyman. Cammie heard the story in her neighborhood. Then her birth father was released from prison. Suddenly strangers parked their cars outside the adoptive family's property at all times of night. There were phone threats. A dead rat showed up in Cammie's father's office mailbox. For her own protection we were forced to show her a recent picture of her biological father, with warnings to run if she ever saw him. We were eventually able to arrange a modification in her birth father's parole rules to include staying away from Cammie and her family. But it took a while.

> *L.T. to Mother and Cammie: Would either of you comment on this period in your lives?*
> *Mother: It was pretty awful.*
> *Cammie: I don't remember much of that time except for my birth dad's picture. That I remember!*

Dreams are a kind of perception one has during sleep. Following my discussions with Cammie about sex and love, she began telling me about a dream she had been having repeatedly since, she said, her early childhood. It was a nightmare about a dark opening that expanded hugely, terrifying her. It sounded to me like a birth she might have witnessed. In checking old medical records, I found that Cammie's baby sister had been born in a delivery room. Was it an aunt who lived nearby and had a baby half Cammie's age? Or could it have been one of the animals Cammie's grandparents had tortured and killed? When she turned fourteen, with her parents' okay I offered Cammie my speculation about her dream. I described childbirth, as seen from the bottom of an obstetrical table. I also showed her a picture she had drawn when

What Becomes of Infantile Traumatic Memories? 207

she was three years old. It was of an adult stick figure with huge "boobs" (her language) and red stuff between the legs. ("Not talk 'bout dat," she had said at the time.) Perhaps she had seen something like this before she was thirteen months old. Perhaps it wasn't even a human but an animal. I wasn't sure about any of this, but we could talk about it again. Cammie listened but said little.

> *L.T. to Cammie: Did your nightmare of the expanding opening ever come back?*
> *Cammie: Nope.*
> *L.T.: Now that you're taking a human sexuality course at your college, did it reawaken any similar mental pictures?*
> *Cammie: No, it never did. And I love my human sexuality class. It's so fascinating!*

MEMORIES IN ADULTHOOD

Verbal Memories

Cammie has produced no new verbal memories. As an adult she cannot verbalize any mental pictures, symbols, or word combinations to describe her experiences up to thirteen months. The old bits and pieces uttered between ages twenty-nine and thirty-six months are now lost to consciousness.

> *L.T. to Cammie: Can you say aloud anything currently in your mind about your infancy?*
> *Cammie: No.*

Nonverbal Memories

Behavioral Expressions and Attitudes

As an adult Cammie will not declare a weakness. She has been reluctant to tell the college authorities about her learning and ADHD difficulties (untreated because of her cardiac arrhythmias). She won't tell the college about her dangerously low blood pressure and unpredictable gut (each, most likely, related to maternal use of street drugs during pregnancy). When people her age dare her to do something risky, she finds herself sorely tempted. Her bravado and self-reliance may well have helped save her life as an infant. But there has been a price to pay. She has done poorly in a few college courses because she will not ask for help.

She still feels impelled to close her closet door every night, (probably related to Mommy "living in the walls"). Her distaste for obese people (her birth mother was very fat) remains active. She still avoids Hispanic men, except for the two who have gradually become her friends.

Cammie's altruism, however, is a total turnaround from her earlier sadistic behaviors. Her cruelty to animals was curtailed by her mid-teens, probably culminating when I wouldn't let her touch the family dog for a month. Since then, she has shown nothing but kindness to pets. But even earlier than age twelve or thirteen, she began showing empathy for uncomfortable babies. She now babysits her little nephews and nieces for hours at a time and volunteers at a nursery school for impoverished children, where she is one of the youngsters' favorites. She wants to become a pediatric assistant or preschool aide and will most likely reach her goals.

Perceptual Memories

Cammie has always hated the smell of mold, oven cleaners, and slightly dirty clothes. These repulsions have been consistent, but the cause evades us.

In March 2011, at a time we celebrated our mutual birthdays, Cammie came to my office with cookies, iced tea, and a little gift. She also came with a confession. She had started having sex several months before with her steady boyfriend. "Did you like it?" I asked. "Yes," she said. "Do you still like it?" I asked. "Yes." I told her I was really glad for her. I had always been a little worried that her infantile perceptions of sexual pain and overexcitement would get in her way—and at present, we could see they wouldn't. By March, however, Cammie and her boyfriend had broken up, she told me. "He is too old, too bossy, too opinionated, and lives too far away."

Before we could talk further about sex, however, Cammie had a more-pressing business. She had smoked pot with a "kind of wild" girlfriend, along with the girl's boyfriend, who, strangely to Cammie, seemed sexually attracted to Cammie herself. The girlfriend had mentioned sexual "threesomes," but Cammie had dismissed the idea out of hand. After the marijuana, the three of them went to a hamburger joint near college, and the boy brought out some "krispy cakes" he had made. ("Boys don't bake!" I interjected, unable to stop myself. "Beware of boys who bake!") After eating some of the boy's cakes, Cammie's irritable heart started to race. "Then," she told me, "I saw an old green Japanese car pull up, and I got all paranoid. 'They're coming to get me!' I told my friends. I thought the car was loaded with Mexicans." Cammie's so-called "friends" told her that there was only one white woman, sitting all alone, in the car. Cammie immediately phoned her mother, who arrived within minutes.

At home, Cammie vomited. The smell of her vomitus was "funny"—like the old musty smells she hasn't been able to stand since babyhood.

This ended Cammie's series of birthday confessions. I asked if her mother could come into the office and join us. The following conversation ensued in March 2011:

L.T. to Mother: What color car did Cammie's biological parents own?
Mother: Green. They would pull up to the psychologist's office when we took Cammie there for appointments when she was two. But Cammie didn't see their car then. She was inside the office, and they were out in the parking lot.

At this point Cammie took over the questioning.

Cammie to Mother: Was their car small?
Mother: Yes, small.
Cammie: Japanese?
Mother: Yes.

Cammie's face lit with recognition. Under the influence of street drugs, she had visually hallucinated Mexicans and had experienced the paranoid delusion that they were coming to get her. But she had also accurately perceived the same sort of car her birth parents had owned. In Cammie's infancy, that small green car had been loaded with Mexicans, including Cammie herself.

One other perceptual memory return from the spring of 2011 deserves mention. After the earthquake, tsunami, and nuclear disaster in Japan, Cammie began a series of repeated terror dreams, focusing on the sensation of being swept away by tides while barely holding on to a pole. One night, Cammie experienced that same dream, but this time, a kindly man led her away from the tsunami.

L.T. to Cammie: Can you relate, Cammie, what the man looked like in your dream and what, if anything, he told you?
Cammie: He was older, had gray hair, and he said, "You're going to be alright."
L.T. to Mother: Are you able to describe the policeman or policewoman who initially brought Cammie to you and your husband?
Mother: It was a man. He was middle-aged, had gray hair, and was talking soothingly to Cammie.

The policeman Cammie's mother described sounded the same as the man in Cammie's dream. Cammie has always acknowledged that it was the police who saved her life. But she had not verbally or perceptually remembered her rescue. This adult dream now appeared to be an accurate perceptual memory return from infancy. The retrieval was precipitated not by drugs but by a disaster halfway across the world. Even though by the time of the memory return Cammie was a fully grown woman, her memory required a second witness—her mother—to confirm it and explain its meaning. As for what the policeman really said, we'll never know. The second witness had not heard him.

MEMORIES OF TWENTY YEARS OF PSYCHOTHERAPY

L.T. to Cammie: Cammie, what do you particularly remember, and where in time do your memories begin for the two of us?
Cammie: I remember the stuff in your office—Nutcracker, Snake. You've moved Nutcracker by the way.
L.T.: Do you want me to move it back?
Cammie: No, that's okay. I remember a fit I had with you when you told me I'd have to "sing for my supper" with my math facts until I knew them all. (I wanted her to say five math facts a night before dinner; Cammie had been around ten.) That was the worst. But mainly we've always had a good time.

It is my general observation that children do not remember their therapy well. When I see adults who were treated as children by mental health professionals, they often cannot remember their doctor's name, nor can they say much about what happened beyond, "We played."

DISCUSSION

There are a few unique points to keep in mind as I go on to discuss Cammie's memory. First, this child was horribly mistreated and then, all at once, totally removed from her home and parents (because of the murder of her infant sister). All the traumatic events stopped abruptly at thirteen months. Second, her foster family tried not to talk much or speculate at all about that horrible first year, and I attempted to follow the same rule. Third, the child, since twenty-nine months of age, has continuously been in treatment. As opposed to other cases, follow-up phone calls or interviews were not necessary. Fourth, the abuses were verified by physical examinations, surgeries, and the autopsy of a sibling. And fifth, I did not review this child's memories with her until she turned twenty-two. Only one reconstruction of a possible memory was ever attempted—at age fourteen, with regard to her repeated nightmare of an expanding opening. In the eight years that followed that reconstruction, no memories or pseudomemories of a live birth have turned up, either verbally or nonverbally. The reconstructive interpretation apparently ended Cammie's repeated nightmare.

The "wild child" gives us several points about infantile memory to think about. Here is a person traumatized brutally almost to the point of death during her first thirteen months of life (and whose father, parenthetically, murdered the four-year-old daughter of his live-in girlfriend when Cammie turned fifteen), yet Cammie can verbally remember nothing today. No matter how dramatic, horrible, and life-threatening her infantile experiences were, they have totally evaded her adult verbal memory. At two and a half she exhibited partial verbal recall with me in psychotherapy ("Sheep die. Die, sheep. . . . Baby die. Die, baby") but at twenty-two, she no longer retains even these. One might say she is "amnesic" for the events of her infancy. But she wasn't always amnesic. The verbal traces simply slipped away.

Did classical infantile amnesia in the Freudian sense blind Cammie to her earlier verbal memories—"Got boobies. Trow away," and the like? In a small clinical study of the memories of twenty children with well-verified traumas from before they were five, I found that these children's verbal memories of the traumatic events persisted through the amnesias that ordinarily accompany the resolution of the Oedipus conflict (Terr 1988). Trauma apparently overrode Freudian amnesia. Of fifteen children who had full or partial verbal memories of their early traumas, eleven were already over the usual age (approximately sixty-six months) of oedipal repression. Only two youngsters in that study, however, had been under the age of thirteen months when their traumatic events actually took place—too small of a cohort to compare to Cammie. The point nevertheless remains: Externally generated terrors do not clear from conscious memory in the same fashion and with the same timing as internally generated conflicts.

How and why Cammie's verbal snippets of experience faded away was not at all clear. Interestingly, however, another case has been reported in which a child, who had surgery at five months and—at that time—exhibited post-traumatic symptoms, reported some verbal memory to his therapist at twenty-nine months, but none at forty months (Solter 2008). There is no anatomical, physiological, or psychological group of studies that I know of to fully explain this phenomenon.

Looking carefully at the three categories of nonverbal manifestations of Cammie's infantile memory—her behaviors, attitudes, and perceptions—we can see that behaviors from Cammie's first year of life were retained into adulthood. The adult Cammie exhibits bravery to the point that she will not, cannot, admit to a weakness. This may be genetic, related perhaps to the "novelty seeking gene" that was reported by two separate groups in 1996 (Angier 1996). But it also reflects Cammie's nonverbal memories of survival. She still takes chances she shouldn't—and she is attracted to bad actors, especially the blond, slim ones. Some of her traumatically impelled behaviors were modified in the earlier phases of her life—such as her cruelties to animals and her excitements over biting and shaking. But some have remained in effect, despite anything we have done to help her.

We know that Cammie's memory traces are linked to the "old brain" on each side—the interior portions of the temporal lobes, the thalami, the ancient parts of the forebrain (Squire and Schacter 2002). Yet we don't know why she avoids certain old perceptions yet seeks others. She cannot stand certain odors, for example, although none of us understands their meanings. Hispanic men, like Cammie's father, are consistently to be shunned. Other stimuli, by contrast, such as biting and shaking, have been sought out for years. It took consistent habit training for Cammie to overcome certain self-induced perceptual returns. Yet others were as repulsive as maggots. How does an infant pick which stimulus to avoid, which to seek? Each trauma victim is different. Numbers of abused youngsters become exceedingly meek. Some become stubbornly defiant. A few become killers.

Cammie's earliest perceptual memory returns, which were reported by her mother—mommy "living in the walls," musty smells, and "bad house"—came to the child when new perceptions duplicated the infantile ones. In the year when she was six, on the other hand, Cammie's misperception of a horrible, condensed "Mother" was precipitated by hospital-administered anesthesia. In other words, different kinds of precipitants activated old sensations. These examples show that early perceptual encodings can be retained for years in unconscious but active forms. Interestingly, Cammie retained from her infancy more sight memories (cranial nerve II) and smells (cranial nerve I) than she did sounds (cranial nerve VIII) and tastes (cranial nerves VII and IX). The reason for this may have to do with the infantile nervous system's continuing development from top to bottom for months after a child is born (with corresponding development within the brain). But we'd have to observe many other cases of infantile memory before we would know this for sure.

The perceptual memory returns that occurred the spring Cammie turned twenty-two were particularly striking. Her nightmares of a Japanese flood and tsunami demonstrated that events far from home may affect the mature psyche. Cammie's dream of being rescued by a policeman was accompanied by an auditory perception of his reassurance (accurate or inaccurate?—we'll never know) and a visual description (probably accurate because her foster mother saw the man herself). This demonstrates once again that adult retrievals of early memories often require confirmation from a second observer.

The most dramatic of all the memory returns in this case report, however, is the one of the "green car." It was a perceptual return apparently based on observations Cammie made during infancy. These were observations for which—at the time they were made—Cammie had not yet learned the proper words (*Japanese* or *green*). Yet this amazingly accurate adult memory return, as confirmed by her foster mother who had seen the car, was also accompanied by gross inaccuracies—a visual hallucination (Mexicans) and a paranoid delusion (coming to get her). It was precipitated by street drugs, the exact nature of which we never learned. In most likelihood this "mini mental breakdown" condensed a number of traumatic incidents that cannot be brought to mind verbally, even today.

That particular day in March 2011, the twenty-two-year-old Cammie became sick—just as the baby, a habitual vomiter, must have repeatedly gotten sick. That particular day the adult Cammie smelled a musty smell—just as the baby, a sniffer, must have smelled similar smells. That day the adult Cammie hallucinated Mexicans—just as the baby, who had lived with brutal Mexicans for thirteen months, learned to fear her own people. That day Cammie believed that the Mexicans would take her away, just as she, the baby, knew they had taken her in every possible way except to kill her. It is a wonder Cammie survived. It is a wonder that she has become the sparkling, playful, intelligent being she is today. And it is a wonder to me—and I hope to you, the reader, as well—that she was able to retrieve from a totally unconscious memory-storage system a small old and oh-so-green Japanese car.

Epilogue

After our presentation at the Mahler Symposium, a psychoanalyst came forward to pose the following two questions to my patient. Cammie told me about it later.

> *Psychoanalyst: Weren't you embarrassed to hear your sex life discussed before an audience?*
> *Cammie: Nope. I figured most everybody in the audience had already had sex.*
> *Psychoanalyst: Well, if you had only one thing to say to the audience, what would you say?*
> *Cammie: Keep on doing what you're doing!*

REFERENCES

Angier, N. (1996). Variant gene tied to a love of new thrills. *New York Times*, January 2, p. A-1.

Bauer, P. J. (2007). *Remembering the Times of Our Lives: Memory in Infancy and Beyond*. The Developing Mind series. Mahwah, NJ: Erlbaum.

Fivush, R. (1992). Developmental perspectives on autobiographical recall. In *Child Victims, Child Witnesses: Understanding and Improving Testimony*, ed. G. S. Goodman and B. L. Bottoms. New York: Guilford.

Humphrey, G., and M. Humphrey (1932). *The Wild Boy of Aveyron*. New York: Appleton-Century-Crofts.

Itard, J. M. (1801). *Memoire sur les premier développements de Victor de L'Aveyron*. Paris: Goujon.

Kris, E. (1956). The recovery of childhood memories in psychoanalysis. *Psychoanalytic Study of the Child* 11:54–88.

Lane, H. (1979). *The Wild Boy of Aveyron*. Cambridge: Harvard University.

Loftus, E. F. (1993). Desperately seeking memories of the first few years of childhood: The reality of early memories. *Journal of Experimental Psychology, General* 122:274–77.

Merritt, K. A., P. A. Ornstein, and B. Spicker (1994). Children's memory for a salient medical procedure: Implication for testimony. *Pediatrics* 94:17–23.

Morris, G., and L. Baker-Ward (2007). Fragile but real: Children's capacity to use newly acquired words to convey preverbal memories. *Child Development* 78:448–58.

Nachman, P. A., D. N. Stern, and C. Best (1986). Affective reactions to stimuli and infants' preferences for novelty and familiarity. *Journal of the American Academy of Child Psychiatry* 25:801–4.

Saywitz, K. J., G. S. Goodman, E. Nicholas, and S. Moans (1991). Children's memories of physical examinations involving genital touch. *Journal of Consulting and Clinical Psychology* 59:682–91.

Solter, A. (2008). A 2-year-old child's memory of hospitalization during early infancy. *Infant and Child Development* 17:593–605.

Squire, L. R., and D. L. Schacter (2002). *Neuropsychology of Memory*. 3rd ed. New York: Guilford.

Terr, L. (1988). What happens to the early memories of trauma? *Journal of the American Academy of Child & Adolescent Psychiatry* 27:96–104.

——— (2003). "Wild Child": How three principles of healing organized 12 years of psychotherapy. *Journal of the American Academy of Child & Adolescent Psychiatry* 42: 1401–9.

——— (2008). *Magical Moments of Change*. New York: Norton.

——— (2009). The use of context in the treatment of traumatized children. *Psychoanalytic Study of the Child* 64:275–98.

Truffaut, F. (1970). *The Wild Child [L'enfant sauvage*, Fr.]. Film director: F. Truffaut; writers: J. Gruault, F. Truffaut.

White, T. L., M. D. Leichtman, and S. J. Ceci (1997). The good, the bad, and the ugly: Accuracy, inaccuracy, and elaboration in preschoolers' reports. *Journal of Applied Cognitive Psychology* 11:537–54.

Evolution of Traumatic Narratives

Impact of the Holocaust on Children of Survivors

NANETTE C. AUERHAHN, Ph.D.

Traumas' lessons are embedded in oral narratives of disasters that are transmitted over centuries and incorporated into historical memory; often they are woven into scripture and religious ritual; eventually they become encrypted in the collective unconscious. The story of the Holocaust functions like a map of the world for survivors' children, whose minds it both constrains and overwhelms, impacting psychological development and construction of reality. The focus in this paper is on composites of three Holocaust survivors and their daughters, who exemplify traumatic narratives' evolution as they are transmitted in fragments, sometimes silently and often nonverbally, to the second generation, who live out the stories' dictates consciously and unconsciously as they create and discover a reality into which they are born. The Holocaust lives on in survivors' current psychological lives, which occur in the wake of catastrophe, in their children's direct experiences of enduring conscious and unconscious reverberations of parental trauma, and in the children's imaginative lives as they reconstruct parental histories to decode emotional memories carried by stories parents tell that stand in place of stories that cannot be told. The paper examines daughters' interpretations of mothers' stories

---

Nanette C. Auerhahn, Ph.D., is a Clinical Psychologist in private practice in Beachwood, Ohio.

Winner of the 2011 Cleveland Psychoanalytic Center Essay Prize.

An earlier version of this paper was presented at Trauma: Intersections among Narrative, Neuroscience, and Psychoanalysis, a conference organized by George Washington University and the Washington Center for Psychoanalysis, Washington, D.C., March 4–6, 2010.

The Psychoanalytic Study of the Child 67, ed. Claudia Lament, Robert A. King, Samuel Abrams, A. Scott Dowling, and Paul M. Brinich (Yale University Press, copyright © 2013 by Claudia Lament, Robert A King, Samuel Abrams, A. Scott Dowling, and Paul M. Brinich).

as evidenced by the impact on individuation, differentiation, sexuality, the conceptualization of death, and relationships with self, mother, other, and society. Impact of the Holocaust is co-created by an amalgam of historical reality, contemporary lived experience, and fantasy, which leads children to uncover three different traumatic stories—the trauma of disaster, the trauma of the loneliness of survival, and the trauma of collateral damage to witnessing children who transmit their own versions of trauma to the third generation. Interpretative engagement and renarration, while injurious, also promote a reparative urge.

FOR VICTIMS, THE HOLOCAUST IS PERSONAL HISTORY REGISTERED and remembered as sensory experiences such as explosions, beatings, and starvation. For survivors' children, the Holocaust is family history constructed by imaginations that sift through witnessed dissociative experiences of parents and (over)heard fragmentary stories. For others, the Holocaust is reconstructed, received history known through stories. This paper examines the Holocaust's evolution from a traumatic experience of victims to a (vicarious) traumatization of their children to a tale (re)constructed by processes of storytelling and mythologizing. Not that the Holocaust is a myth, which would imply that it is fictional. Rather, it can function like a myth in that myths tell us about ancestors by way of transmitting fundamental aspects of the universe and truths we may live by. Stories of the Holocaust depict what came "before," embody values and beliefs, and serve as ever-present backdrops for survivors' families. Holocaust stories act as family myths, presenting heroes to emulate, villains to slay, evil that terrorizes, and the limits of what is possible; they shape children's historical, psychological, and ethical understandings (Zipes 1979) and serve as allegories of society and maps of the unconscious. As narratives are passed on from parents to children and from historians to others, facts combine with social and cultural theories, changing chronicles from being about survivors only, to also being about the world, death, and the meaning of life. In a similar manner, communities recorded disasters for centuries, weaving them into tales that changed with retelling, and passed down meaning to subsequent generations. Over centuries, narratives about "the great crises of history" (Barthes 1953) have incorporated customs and goals, to evolve into folktales, myths, and fables, which represent "encrypted historical memory" (Semel 2008, p. 1515). Combining with fantasy and imaginative play, these stories eventually morphed into fairy tales, which are no longer about particular people in specific places at exact times, but occur once upon a time in faraway lands to princes and princesses. In fairy tales, invaders and soldiers become witches and giants, and everyone lives happily ever after. Via a similar process, historical catastrophes were woven into scripture and biblical tales became religious tutors.

In the present, the Holocaust is incompatible with the genre of fairy tales: It has no happy ending, and its factuality resists the plasticity inherent in fairy tales. Nevertheless, the story of parents' descent into *l'univers concentrationnaire* has mythic proportions for their children, underpinning the great tasks of the first half of life: mastery of instincts and individuation-differentiation. Parents' stories guide children's journeys in search of answers to ultimate questions: Why are there death and evil in the world? and Who will ever love me? (Semel 2011) Who needs Hansel and Gretel, when concentration camps had gas chambers and ovens? Who needs vampires and monsters, when history attests to the reality of the demonic? Out of the Holocaust, self and world may be differentiated and inner and outer reality co-created. Much of what children of survivors know is often learned from the Holocaust.

Three traumas are encompassed by the Holocaust—the trauma of war, of survival, and of the second generation. Parents' past is woven into the lives of children when the first generation's current psychological life transpires in the shadow of a continuously created traumatic wake, whose reality children navigate but cannot circumvent. Holocaust survivors' traumas did not end in 1945 but lived on in a perpetual state of mourning for a people that was no more, and in the lived experiences of a second generation beset by parents' fragmented stories that had a compelling realness. The innate truth of survivors' memories constrained their children's imaginations even as their stories stimulated the children's fantasy lives, initiating transposition into a different time and place (Sam Gerson, personal communication, 2012). What was remembered and narrated became part of the consciousness of the next generation, while what was lived but silenced permeated the unconscious.

A child is born into and socialized by family tales that the child interweaves with age-appropriate fantasies and dispositional features, fantasy and personality being clinicians' usual foci. This paper highlights a less-appreciated factor in development of children's defenses, conflicts, and character—conscious and unconscious parental stories that mediate a reality constructed and found by the child. Fonagy (1999) tells us that reality is constituted by children's subjectivity and mediated by the objectivity of caretakers; relational theorists (for example, Mitchell 1988) stress the etiological role of the particular content of parent-child interactions and shared myths. For children of survivors, the Holocaust contextualized and created their minds so that they often understood inner and outer worlds according to its explanatory structure, never remembering a time when they didn't know about this primordial event.

Not that survivors' stories were ever fully told. Parents tried to protect children by silence, while children protected parents by not asking. Both generations worried that recounting trauma would injure more than heal (Auerhahn and Laub 1990). The story of collective trauma is often unwritten, eluding, as it does, victims' ability to know and to make known (Auerhahn and Peskin 2003). Interpretability is defeated when experience exceeds the ability to analyze, endure, and justify it morally (Geertz 1973). The more horrendous an event, the less people can assimilate it, and the more society forgets it. Holocaust narratives contained lacunae representing moments too disorganizing to recall, and unfolded less by deliberate reminiscences than by inadvertent nonverbal behaviors, reenactments, and body memory. Parents' internal working model of the world was transmitted as implicit relational knowledge (Bollas's (1987) "unthought known") and as unarticulated, interpersonal, and ongoing mutual understanding. Children speculated about, distorted, and filled in gaps in fragmented tales, living by tales' underlying dictates and warnings. Children heard parents' screams during sleep, witnessed parents' dissociative gaze during celebrations, and sensed parents' sadness during holidays. In this manner, parents' historical nightmare transcended time and pierced present experience, creating a need to make sense of traumas that occurred to the children, blurring not just the distinction between historical narrative and contemporary reality but also between parents' current trauma and children's witness of the incomprehensible.

Children invented Holocaust tales from parents' reenactments that evidenced disavowed qualities and from indelible visual images that they drew in their mind's eye, becoming traumatized by images' activation of affective states. By projecting themselves into narratives, stories were experienced as though partially created by the children. Historical monsters persecuted children even as they feared being monsters likewise. It was not clear to the young that the Holocaust had occurred in the past, far away. Instead, they mixed up representations of the Holocaust with their own realities, fearing Nazis crashing through doors of bedroom closets. The Holocaust magnified anxieties by the vision of parents unable to protect against life's brutalities. Traumatic history was internalized to control it and identified with instincts such as sex and aggression. The unconscious was confabulated with the external world, and both were experienced as dark, dangerous netherworlds.

Demarcation of external from internal reality is a developmental task. Given the confluence of children's imaginations with the fantastic made real in the Holocaust, the distinction between reality and fantasy blurred. The worst that could be imagined could happen, because it had. Development unfolded in the context of actualization of the demonic, which structured it. A child grapples with existential, primitive fears of rage, loneliness, and being unloved—internal conflicts embodied in the story of the Holocaust—leading survivors' children to project parts of themselves and internal objects into protagonists, who were seen as personifications of drives (which are experienced in bodily terms) and characters in the family romance. Cultural and collective beliefs, familial and individual wishes, and body memories are transmitted from generation to generation by deposit in the unconscious and by coherence around bodily experience. Survivors' embodied memories aroused reciprocal affect in their children, who experienced the affects as their own and tried on roles in parents' stories. Children imagined being victims, became villains who made victims suffer, and inflicted suffering on their selves. They internalized parents' means of blunting, changing, and otherwise defending against trauma.

Questions examined in this paper are: How does the Holocaust influence the psychological development of children of survivors? How do inner and outer realities co-create each other in the context of Holocaust narratives, which map humans' devolution to a state of disintegration that erodes each part of the individual's world—the self, the mothering other, and the stranger? Answers have emerged for the author over years of growing up in a family of survivors, working clinically with survivors and their children, consulting in Jewish nursing homes and assisted-living facilities, and interviewing survivors as a researcher with the Fortunoff Video Archive for Holocaust Testimonies at Yale University. From observation, treatment, and interviews of individuals in New York, Connecticut, California, and Ohio, the author created composite portraits to serve herein as illustrations rather than case studies. The events described are likewise composites taken from these sources; they have not been checked against historical records, because the subject under study is, in part, the power of memory whose distortions, misrepresentations, ellipses, and lacunae thwart historians but inform clinicians, not only as repositories of hidden meanings but also as inevitable, inextricable, and essential elements in the transmission of knowledge from one generation to another. The paper's structure enacts the unfolding and weaving together of facts, speculation, culture, and imagination, all of which create traumas' mythos.

THE FIRST TRAUMA: WAR

In Transylvania, twenty-six-year-old Magda lived happily with her thirteen brothers and sisters. Her nieces and nephews, including twelve-year-old Leah and sixteen-year-old Shari, spent summers on the family farm, where Magda picked baskets of lush raspberries, which she allowed the children to gorge on, always stopping them in time to prevent sickness.

One day, Magda defended her father against attack by an anti-Semitic neighbor, who took revenge by having her transported to a Polish town in the midst of a pogrom in which babies in cribs were axed to death. After months of hiding, she made her way through forests disguised as a peasant, arriving home only to be rounded up into a crowded ghetto. Unwilling to desert her parents by fleeing into a forest, she was put with them on a train to an unknown destination for days; she was beaten for requesting water. Her observant father worried about violating the Sabbath should they not arrive before then. His prayers were answered, and they reached a place called Auschwitz on Friday. The next day, Shabbat, most of the family was gassed and cremated.

When some of Magda's nephews arrived by a different train, their father, seeing fires ahead, advised his children to take off their clothes so that they would burn quickly. Amidst smoke and barking dogs, some who grasped what was transpiring committed suicide. Most arrivals were in shock, understanding nothing.

Learning that Shari and Leah had been transported to Auschwitz, Magda maneuvered their transfer to her barrack; a kapo from her school days assigned them to the Canada commando, where, the friend warned, they might be saved yet curse her for placement in a hell where Yiddish was spoken. Women in this commando staved off starvation by foraging for food while sorting arrivals' packages. Shari and Leah questioned these women: "How are you still alive?" hoping that if toothless prisoners with dog bite marks still survived, perhaps they could, too. Nevertheless, hunger quickly set in, leading Magda, Shari, and Leah to believe that their family was better off dead. Soon, they forgot everything.

The Canada commando was in an area of the camp whose workings remained secret. It contained the Sonderkommando, the ultimate secret bearers, who collected bodies from gas chambers and burned them in ovens. A tall strong man, Leah's and Shari's father had been selected for this detail. Coming upon his family's corpses, he lost his mind.

The barrack of the Canada commando had a window that faced the road from the train to the crematorium, where columns of families waited in line to enter gas chambers. People tapped on the window to ask what lay before them. Forbidden to answer, Leah watched, day and night, as flames from pits and chimneys lit up the sky amidst screams and prayers. She could never see around the building and speculated: Surely there was an exit; the building couldn't contain so many people! Eventually, she no longer fought what her eyes saw. Shari hoped that someone on the outside knew that they were missing and that tattoos meant that they were recorded and not forgotten. Seeing Jewish professionals also imprisoned, she realized that no one was out there to notify; she felt as if she had fallen *off the earth into a parallel universe. Magda took blows intended for others. She foraged in garbage cans for food for her nieces, was whipped for stealing potato peels, set upon by a German shepherd that tore people apart, and forced to clean latrines with no cloths. She was the only person trusted by many to cut the bread that constituted inmates' meager diet. On Yom Kippur, she fasted.*

In the same area as their commando was a building where medical experiments took place. Upon arrival at Auschwitz, Magda's sister Rivka was separated from her twins. Magda tried to discover if the twins were being experimented upon. No one in the family was ever able to learn their fate. (Years later, Shari was shocked to hear Rivka's wishful fantasy that they had survived by being experimented on rather than exterminated, and were living now in Europe, "lost" because they could not recall their identities.)

A man from Magda's hometown worked in the **Sondercommando.** *"Tomorrow, I die," he whispered through barbed wire. Next day, a crematorium was blown up by the men, who ran to hide among packages the women sorted. Guards shot the men and lined up the women in front of a firing squad. Several other female inmates were hanged, but the Canada commando was given a reprieve.*

One winter day, the gates of Auschwitz flew open. Emaciated inmates were marched hundreds of miles through snow and were shot if they faltered. Magda kept her family going, shouting "Get up!" if anyone fell. When a **Lager** *[German word meaning "camp"] sister could no longer walk, Magda carried her to the Ravensbrück concentration camp. When Magda found a piece of bread, she gave it to Leah, the youngest, who refused it. "You are a child. Eat!" Magda insisted with a slap. "I haven't been a child for a long time," Leah protested silently. For the last five months of the war, starvation and atrocities were so severe that the women thought about nothing else. By the time Russians arrived, Magda was sick with diphtheria, typhus, and TB. Shari was unable to rejoice and mumbled to no one in particular, "How do I pick up the pieces now that I am penniless and homeless?" There was no normal world to return to. Leah looked at the liberating soldiers and demanded, "Where have you been?" Magda, verging on death, required several surgeries and hospitalizations for a year. So long as she had felt responsible for her sister's children, she had had a reason to fight. Once a brother found them and took over, Magda no longer wanted to live, wondering, "For what purpose am I still alive?"*

Victims who survived were suspected of collaboration, of having compromised themselves, or of surviving at others' expense. Those who didn't survive were maligned for having died like sheep. Leah searched maps to locate the extermination camps, as she could not grasp where on earth they had existed. That place and time seemed like another world. Perhaps they had been on a different planet, "a lunatic terra incognita" (Kluger 2001, p. 112).

This is the story of Magda, Shari, and Leah, as reconstructed by their children. It may or may not be true in whole or in part. When Magda overheard her daughter recounting part of it to a friend, she asked in disbelief: "That *is what you think happened!?"*

The dead could not be interviewed for their versions, and the living refused to testify for fear of recurrence of nightmares.

The Second Trauma: Survival after Death

The story of the war lost by the Jews ends with the death of much of the Yiddish-speaking segment of the Jewish people. The tale has no happy ending: Justice does not prevail, survivors don't live happily ever after, and dismantling of East European Jewish culture is not undone. Instead, survival begat another trauma—a living death, as well as profound cynicism: Survivors had total lack of faith in people and in the possibility of utopia. Worse is the story's apocalyptic ending: The near triumph of evil over good lay bare civilization's impotence against evil, exposing culture as a facade that buffers against meaninglessness but guarantees neither wisdom, safety, nor morality. How does one live with such knowledge?

Leah, Shari, and Magda scattered in the United States, losing class standings by emigration. Unlike other immigrants, their families, culture, and language could not be revisited back home, making it difficult to pass on a heritage that no longer existed and family histories and recipes that no one was left alive to remember. Immigrants often live together, eating traditional food and being helped by earlier immigrants who can relate to their experiences. So few Holocaust victims survived that they lived among people who regarded them with suspicion and who didn't want to hear about incomprehensible experiences that threatened accepted worldviews. Observant Jews who believed that the righteous are rewarded and sinners punished maintained that the Shoah happened because Jews of Europe sinned. Those who believed in survival of the fittest agreed that Jews who didn't leave Europe weren't as clever as those who had. Zionists pointed to the devastation as proof that Jewish life in the Diaspora was doomed. Intellectuals explained that war is not an act of God but of man and is the price we pay for free will. Only a few individuals, out of humility, wisdom, or charity, admitted ignorance; they found the Holocaust inexplicable. Nowhere did Magda, Shari, or Leah find someone who wanted to know, knew how to ask, or understood what had happened. So much was bottled up that when Leah found a yearned-for sympathetic ear, she spoke for hours. Usually, even fellow Jews protested, "Enough already," leaving the women burdened by secret knowledge that could prevent establishment of new, normal families. They questioned how to live believing that healing was impossible. The farther away from events they got, the more they compared their experiences to normal life and to what might have been. Who should they be angry at, they wondered, when complicity had been all around—among Germans who exterminated Jews, the United States, which had not let Jews in, and Poles who had collaborated with Nazis? The main perpetrators disappeared as the world did nothing, leaving only functionaries to prosecute. In the camps, venting fury had resulted in murder. Magda, Shari, and Leah knew that if they exhibited rage now, they wouldn't be able to function, and people would shun them. With nowhere for hate to go, they held it in as it dissolved into impotence.

Leah eventually spoke publicly to churches, synagogues, and museums, to counter false attributions and to prevent history from being written by victimizers whose records superseded survivors' memories as evidence. She spoke in lieu of the dead, adding details that could only be provided by victims. Recalling Rabban Gamaliel's saying "On three things the world stands: on justice, on truth, and on peace," Leah despaired of peace or justice but testified in pursuit of a collective process of truth telling (Weine 1999), not for therapeutic purposes but as eulogy and elegy to family. There were many stories that she never shared, for they were about "experiences so demoralizing that they can only be described as a state of being outside the human" (Nutkiewicz 2003, p. 6). Even as she emphasized that despite degrading treatment, victims regarded persecutors, not themselves, as bestial subhumans, she admitted that fear generated by knowledge of what captors could do allowed attempts at dehumanization to penetrate nevertheless. To counter hopelessness, Leah highlighted Magda's extraordinary character, which had served as anchor and fulfillment of the need for someone who cared. Leah described how Magda had given comfort and protection to the young, no matter the circumstances, never betraying her respect for others, her humanity, or her family's values, distinguishing herself in a place where most sank to the lowest level. Her maintenance of civilized behavior and goodness where none existed kept alive Leah's representation of the protective, attuned, and helpful relational bond essential for creation of autobiographical narratives (Fosha 2003).

What could not be communicated was the enormity of the loss wrought by permanent eradication of European Jewish life. Its irredeemable nature underlies the lament of poet Yitzhak Katzenelson (Roskies 1989, p. 547) before his death in Auschwitz: "There was a people and it is no more."

INTERPRETATIONS OF TRAUMATIC STORIES: REVERBERATIONS OF TRAUMA

Three of a child's early representations are me, mother, and the other or stranger. The child is situated in a triad that works against fusion between mother and me and that predates the Oedipal triangle, allowing for representing good and bad parts of mother as different objects. Mother represents the caregiver who mirrors the child's affects, becoming involved to help manage difficulties. Internalization of this regulating function allows processing emotions throughout life. The undoing of this representation by catastrophe undermines verbalization, leaving a black hole where trauma is not represented. The shadow of the malevolent aggressor can contaminate the maternal representation, leaving permanent traces of malicious or indifferent responses that generate fear and aloneness and deplete survivors' emotional resources. At times, the aggressor unravels the relationship to mother and installs himself as substitute, forcing a cutting off from psychic life. This is the process underlying identification with the aggressor, which chooses the aggressor as object rather than objectlessness, for no one survives without retention of some sort of representation of a responsive other (Laub and Auerhahn 1989); this retention is a necessary but not sufficient condition for survival. The opposite of a nurturing maternal figure is not a malignant one but objectlessness: Catastrophic trauma creates a psychic hole devoid of structure and representable experience, which, if unmodified by need-mediating relationships, results in death or suicide (Cohen 1985), as illustrated by Isaiah Berlin's brother who survived torture under Stalin only to drop dead upon encountering his torturer on a Moscow street (Lewis 2007). Without a maternal representation, the life force is absent, leaving a void in which there is no life (see Gerson 2009). Attempt at reinstatement of this representation may underlie the last cry of the tortured, who, as they die, frequently cry out for mother.

Vicissitudes of warping of the maternal representation can be traced in three scenes of eating in the first traumatic narrative—that of war. During prewar times of plenty, Magda was the protective nurturer whose abundant raspberries were devoured without illness. Starving in Auschwitz, Magda was arbitrator of life and death, trusted to fairly mete out the meager rations of bread. When resources were depleted, Magda barely sustained life; her slap of Leah at Ravensbrück embodied a rupture of empathy.

As with the maternal representation, survivors' internal representation of the stranger is forever marked by trauma. Corrosion of representations of society is the unique province of collective, massive trauma. Holocaust survivors learned to be suspicious of strangers, which came to include anyone who was not a survivor. Strangers were viewed as unable to understand and as posing danger, since failure to extend empathy to Jews facilitated their dehumanization as life unworthy of life. In situations of extremity, when what is other is targeted for extermination, the individual's triad collapses into the dyad of me and not me. Few Holocaust survivors entered therapy because their representation of the outside world was so pernicious that they expected no empathy and forever walled themselves off in isolation. The message transmitted to their children was that refuge was to be found in family only: The outside world is unsafe: "They hate us and will always hate us."

The divide between survivors and others never fully healed. Their children, being different but loved, were caught in a binary opposition: When experienced as part of the self, children were cherished; when seen as belonging to the world of others, children were identified with what was rejected; not me is readily seen as an oppressor. A child's differentness embodied a rupture in continuity with the past, exiling parents in a land where the child felt at home. Although survivors generally loved their children, some were jealous of experiences they never had and yelled at children for not having suffered. Many could not relate to their children's lives and believed that the children didn't understand them, chiding, "You don't know the meaning of love"; others exclaimed, "I can't believe this thing came out of my body." Paradoxically, parents were invested in believing that their children were unaffected by the Holocaust and wanted to vicariously experience what had been denied them; they withheld information to protect children whom they loved *for* their difference. Yet when children were unhappy, some survivors taunted, "What do *you* have to worry about?" and when children were angry, some parents mocked, "What are *you* crying for? I'll give you something to cry about." Children internalize how parents regard their otherness (Faimberg 2005); many children of survivors agreed that they had no reason for unhappiness and that their problems were not worth noting. They took away the message that they had no right to their own interests and often lacked transitional space in which to establish separate identities.

Magda and Her Daughter Miriam—Aggression and Autonomy

Magda's daughter Miriam referred to herself internally as "the girl," for that is how her parents referred to her when they spoke to one another in Hungarian. To Miriam, the term connoted objectification and underlined Magda's inability (or need not to?) to recognize Miriam's distinct inner life. Magda often appeared lost in reverie, oblivious to the reactions of Miriam, who hid her individuality even from herself in an effort to neither threaten, burden, nor hurt her mother and in a bid for acceptance. Miriam internalized mother's resulting description of her as "without personality" and developed an image of herself as a "person not seen." When, as a young adult, Miriam was asked to describe herself, she could not, having internalized her perception of mother's perception of her as an empty nonbeing (Fonagy 1999). Growing up, she denied she had special talents, believing that others knew whatever she knew. Absence of mother's confirming gaze undermined the cohesiveness and coherence of identity. Miriam's presenting problem in therapy was "I have no self." It was unclear whether Magda could not recognize her daughter's traits or whether she could not tolerate difference. Both interpretations illuminate her reaction years later to learning Miriam's father-in-law's name: It was the same as that of Magda's father. Since the family followed the Ashkenazi tradition of naming children after dead, never living, relatives, Magda noted sadly, "Now *I* won't be able to name *your* son after my father" (emphases added). Miriam felt erased.

Magda clung to religion as a transitional object that preserved a link to parents and protected her pre-trauma self from retroactive disintegration by death imprints. Magda's lifeline to reconstitution of identity was a suffocating limitation for Miriam, whose assertion of autonomy by rejecting Orthodox Jewish values was viewed by mother as severing connections to the past and, hence, as a second murder of loved ones and the prewar self. Madga sought victory over Hitler by survival of her lost world into the next generation. To the extent that Miriam differed from the world that should have been, losses became final, making Miriam, not Nazis, the one who forever cut off that vanished world, giving Hitler posthumous victory. Children of survivors struggled with loyalty to a persecuted people and an eradicated culture while taking possession of their lives.

Development requires activation of aggression, which children of survivors often associated with deliberate sadism. Families' violent histories, together with parents' catastrophic reactions to anger, can make children feel like murderers when angry. Aggression and hate became too dangerous to express if they threatened the psychic equilibrium of parents whose failure to tolerate negative affects retarded integration in children and led to defenses against anger, which turned it inward, resulting in difficulties separating and self-sacrificing, masochistic tendencies. Any intense negative affect could trigger survivors' disengagement and lead to dead space. Several survivors have admitted that after the war, when their children cried, they would "see" instead infants who had starved to death in the ghettos. One child could never cry in front of his mother, unaware that while hiding, mother had killed an infant whose cries threatened to disclose her whereabouts. Development of an ability to tolerate negative affect necessitates a mother who helps manage distress without letting her reactions screen out her child's needs.

Miriam struggled with the dialectic of remaining unseen (to avoid triggering mother's disengagement and as protection from persecution) versus being heard (out of need for self-assertion and an authentic relationship). As an adult, she had difficulties promoting herself professionally. As a child, she learned not to turn to a mother whose compromised ability to reflect on emotions led to regularly being distraught rather than empathic when her daughter was distressed. The second individuation of adolescence evoked memories of separations and feelings of abandonment, as Magda's knowledge that parting can be permanent made it dangerous. This was viscerally conveyed by her haunted look when saying good-bye, which saddened Miriam and made her anxious when she parted from her own children. Miriam had no more confidence in her children's autonomy than she did in her own, and conveyed the perilous quality of separation and its potential finality to her children. As a teenager, Miriam questioned whether her wish for independence justified imposing such pain on her mother, in which case she, like Oedipus, was the murderer of her parent. How could she leave home, when Magda had stayed to care for parents rather than rescue herself? When Miriam did not want to fast on Yom Kippur, Magda's fast in Auschwitz cast Miriam's minor rebellion as violation of a religious edict for which mother was willing to die. When Miriam acted out, Magda complained, "For *this* I survived?" as if life was now meaningless. For survivors who could not reconcile generational continuity with generational difference, birth of a child's self could be a second Holocaust (Peskin, Auerhahn, and Laub 1997).

Miriam felt she had only two choices: rebellion or surrender. Submission dominated interactions with her mother and compromised the growth of self-confidence. In many relationships, rigidity retarded negotiation of conflicting needs for attachment and differentiation. Afraid of enmeshment with others, Miriam was stubborn, oppositional, and vigilant around boundaries, defending (via silent withdrawal) against permeability with anyone perceived as bent on appropriation. Adult relationships could be characterized by rage at the frustration of her yearning to be both left alone yet found as an authentic, independent person within the hiddenness with which she protectively enveloped herself. She searched for someone whom her fury could not destroy, using, valuing her therapist and husband for their strength to withstand her rage.

Miriam's resilience was impaired by keeping anxieties to herself, which caused avoidance of challenges and limitation of her emotional range to what she could contain on her own. She was flooded with anxiety, fantasizing that someone asked to focus on her needs would become enraged and kill her. Intimacy was associated with fury and disintegration. Stories about burning children left a lifelong fear of fire; she learned to light a match only as an adult. Knives and scissors were avoided, even years after she no longer remembered Magda's story about a child whose eyes were poked out. Forgotten too was her even earlier fear that her eyes might fall out. It was this fear that had generated her question if such a thing was possible, eliciting Magda's anecdote as answer. As repository of mother's nightmares and witness to mother's screams during sleep, Miriam's fears about physical integrity embodied Magda's memories of babies axed to death. Once a parent, Miriam hid knives from her children.

Magda believed that she had emerged from war as less than who she had been. Bollas (1999) calls this post-trauma self the mutational self and views it as containing the murdered pre-trauma self, the trauma, the altered self, and the caretaker self. Miriam startled when Leah described Magda's prewar laugh as deep and resonant, realizing that she had never heard her mother laugh. While Leah never told Magda how much she missed that laugh, Magda never told Leah it saddened her that the once-vibrant child had become an embittered adult. Each viewed the other as different after the war. While Magda's representation of her father was idealized, her image of a cold, distant mother, after whom Miriam was named, was retroactively tainted by the Holocaust's vanquishing of the maternal principle. Miriam envisioned her own survivor father as a corpse and Magda as a person buried alive—images that visually expressed her parents' loss of a capacity for pleasure as described by Charlotte Delbo, a survivor: "Looking at me, one would think that I'm alive. . . . I'm not alive. I died in Auschwitz, but no one knows it" (quoted in Moorehead 2011). In the recesses of the family, the survivor's child encounters the parent's ghost. "Why am I not enough to make her happy?" Miriam wondered, wishing to imbue Magda with a feeling of aliveness by investment in real, not dead people (Green 1983). The wish was to be loved by a mother who took pleasure in her daughter and who allowed both of them to be fully alive. Miriam fought against a similar feeling of deadness, expressed in her conviction that she would never live past the age of thirty. Years later, she realized that her mother had left Europe at thirty.

Miriam wondered, "Where does mother go when [mentally] absent?" The good-enough mother is available to the child to be used. Magda was lost behind a veil in a world Miriam could never access. Miriam experienced her mother's unavailability as signifying lack of interest in her, while Magda may have deliberately absented herself at times to protect Miriam from contamination by her fears and anxieties, in which case what appeared to be abandonments were instead intentional acts of devotion. To Miriam it seemed that the present constituted an unbearable absence for her mother, while what was absent fully engaged her mother's presence; Magda's past appeared to be the only reality inhabited by life, so Miriam followed the trail into the Holocaust, developing a lifelong vulnerability to depression that served as vehicle for a fantasied connection with her otherwise inaccessible, depressed mother (see Mitchell 1988). As a child, Miriam wondered if her father had survived by collaboration, which would have explained his absent tattoo, his silence about the war, and the emotional distance between her parents. She fantasized that she had been born during the war to her father's first wife, who was murdered. This personal myth of origin, that she was her father's daughter, not Magda's, was her version of the Oedipal complex and the family romance, as well as an explanation for Magda's disappointment in her. Miriam's lack of resemblance to Magda's relatives was bemoaned by her mother perhaps because it belied a reparative fantasy of continuity and rebirth, and a frustrated yearning for (re)attachment, a need not met in a marriage founded on devotion and obligation but not love.

Magda's dissociation and decathexis of the present led to blankness in Miriam that represented her own lifelessness when her mother turned attention elsewhere. "Where did you just go?" a supervisor asked, after Miriam experienced his lack of attunement as repetition of her mother's failure to remain present. Miriam regularly asked, "Are you listening?" before speaking to others, to ensure that she not address a void; the empathic listener was never taken for granted (Laub and Auerhahn 1989). She lacked the confidence that arises from unconscious knowledge of being held by a parent about whom one need not think but who always keeps one in mind. On vacation, she would fantasize mailing her therapist a postcard, so that at the moment of reading, she would exist in his mind. His offhand comment one day about having thought about their work together was regarded as a gift, as was Magda's parting words before death: "You think that I don't love you, don't you?" Miriam experienced the accuracy of her mother's insight as indication that in that moment, her mother saw her as she was, unfiltered and separate, an intentional person in her own right. Ability to distinguish a child's needs from one's own protects against intergenerational transmission of trauma, as it creates in the child a representation of existing in the heart and mind of the mother as one is, a separate being (Fosha 2003).

Shari and Her Daughter Sue—Sex and Death

Shari believed that information about the Holocaust should not be passed on, so as not to jeopardize her children's optimism; her silence was less to protect herself than to protect her daughter Sue from having to live with those memories (Nutkiewicz 2003). Shari felt that the events were unbelievable, not realizing that silence, in concert with nonverbal Holocaust associations and embodied affects, restricted Sue's ability to mentalize the past (Peskin 2010) and to trust her own perceptions. Shari never acknowledged her unspoken reminiscences, condemning Sue to live with imagined horrors, free-floating anxiety, and dread whose source she could not identify. For example, when a young mother, Shari would dress Sue up for an annual exam by a highly regarded pediatrician with a German last name. His mysterious, forbidding office, with its antique grandfather clock, dark wood paneling, and Persian rugs, saddened Shari, who, unbeknownst to Sue, was reminded of her family's home. Only years later did Sue recognize that her sense of foreboding at those visits arose from Holocaust imagery, leading her to wonder if associations to Dr. Mengele and camp selections had been hers alone or her mother's as well.

Sue absorbed her mother's unarticulated grief and identified it as her own, suffering periods of desolation without identifiable triggers or verbal content. She recalls a day in childhood when she sat next to her mother, who was listening to a concert on the radio. Sue became flooded with despair and rushed to her bedroom to sob unseen, forever after avoiding similar music to stave off waves of sadness. Only as an adult did she wonder if the affect had been her mother's. Indeed, the more dissociated was Shari's affect, the more likely Sue was to experience it. Once a social worker, Sue sometimes was filled with sadness during sessions without knowing why. She eventually realized that, directed to attend to affect at those times, patients would often cry and inevitably acknowledge defending against despair, at which point her desolation would leave. She came to understand that she could be inundated by another's unmetabolized affect and cease to feel it when the other owned and verbalized his or her feelings. Fonagy described this process:

> The dissociated core of the self is an absence, rather than genuine psychic content. It reflects a breach in boundaries of the self, creating an openness in the self to colonization by mental states of the attachment figure.... This is not a process of identification as it is not a modification of the self-representation to match the established representation of the other. The dissociative core permits direct transmission of unconscious traumatic fantasy from mother or father to child. (1999, p. 22)

Without being verbalized, secrets were transmitted via affect contagion, nonverbal indicators, unconscious communication, and witnessed dissociative states. As a child, Sue had no conscious idea what these secrets were. Obeying the tacit dictate of silence, she refused to discuss Holocaust fantasies in therapy for fear of being judged crazy or being held responsible for them. The first time she viewed a Holocaust film, she was relieved to see private imagery existing externally. The first time she heard a survivor describe being forced to hang a relative, something which she had visualized as a child, she thought, "So I didn't make it up." Believing that the image had originated with her, she had wondered, "What kind of person thinks of such things?" She hid her frightening inner world by leaving secrets submerged (Rashkin 2008) and feared making the Holocaust real by acting as if it had happened. Sue demurred when a relative offered to detail Shari's Holocaust experiences. When a friend insisted on the value of not only hearing but also recording an oral history of her mother's war experiences, Sue resisted even as her friend persisted, until finally, bursting into tears, she explained, "Don't you realize that if I tape what is said, that will mean that it really happened?"

Growing up, Sue imagined that she could wind up in the Holocaust. In movie theaters, she noted exits so as not to be trapped in a fire. In elevators, she worried doors might open onto concentration camps. She thought that camp inmates were kept naked and wondered if her mother had been raped or experimented on, a fear "confirmed" by Shari's scar from a C-section, Shari's inability to have more children, and Shari's reassurance during Sue's own pregnancy that the newborn would be healthy: "Even after the camps where we were given chemicals to prevent our periods, I never worried that anything would be wrong with my children." As a child, Sue regarded a painful medical procedure as torture, and being held down by Shari for it as collusion and betrayal. She thought treatment of a childhood vaginal infection was sterilization; mother's hysterectomy years later precipitated nightmares about Nazi doctors experimenting on her. Sue sensed Shari's discomfort with sexuality, as Shari could not accept in her child what she could not integrate into her own life. Shari's nascent sexuality had been stamped by Auschwitz's pornographic horrors, which were defended against by distance from the body, which in turn left her unable to help Sue process physical experiences and excitement. Shari's disapproving reaction to Sue's early sexualized behavior was a harsh "What do you think you are doing?" A child must internalize mother's calm processing of arousal, so as not to become frightened and associate it with disintegration. Precipitating mother's dissociation, stimulation was experienced by Sue as a danger heralding loss of emotional contact (Fonagy 1999), and was shut down. In the glare of what Sue viewed as Shari's condemnatory gaze, Sue experienced the body as the site where cruelty could be actualized. Her mother's scarred body frightened her; her own sexuality incorporated her perception of her mother's perception of sex as disgusting.

Disruption of Sue's identification with Shari was complicated by barriers to narration. It was difficult to articulate an experience not her own nor residing in memory, yet part of her identity, as if the most important events of her life had happened to others, before she was born (Bukeit, 2002), in cities where she had lived but never visited, yet remained haunted by. Disconnection from her own experience underlay her habitual reference to murdered family as *"my mother's* [never *my*] relatives," and her denial as an adult when her therapist, startled by Sue's acute grief at the death of an acquaintance's son, asked if she had ever lost a child or sibling. Only years later could Sue recognize that *she* had lost a brother (her father's son) and numerous cousins in the war and that she had been nursed with the invisible tears of her parents for dead children. Absence of parental and societal acknowledgment that the Holocaust had impacted her had invalidated her grief.

The Holocaust's status as private family memory rather than shared collective history arose from it being neither taught nor commemorated publicly during Sue's childhood, imbuing events with shame. A professor's request that Sue present her genogram in a college class met with refusal, out of Sue's fear that she would burst into tears; without a social context or collective framework, she would or could not explain her refusal and sadness. Society's silence, like that of parents, reinforced the feeling of being alone with unspeakable knowledge. She never shared that her association to a therapist's mention of a grandmother was, *"You had a grandmother?!"* For Sue, as with many children of survivors, the Nazis' deliberate targeting of aged Jews meant that a grandparent was a rare, exotic being whose presence reinforced difference. The barrier between home ("us") and community ("them") was more impermeable than that between Sue's present and Shari's past, resting as the former did on the self-other distinction, which was reinforced by survivors' distrust and society's disregard. Although past and present could not be integrated as they transpired in different worlds, the present normal world was interpenetrated by associations to the Holocaust, which continued to have a parallel existence (Laub and Auerhahn 1989). As incapable of integration as Shari's two worlds (of "before" and "after") were, both were saturated with traumatic affects and bridged by reenactment and memory. In addition, Sue's immersion in an Orthodox Jewish world at home and at school meant that she was taught two parallel histories that she never integrated. Jewish history was taught in Hebrew, American history in English. Neither mentioned the Holocaust. While

American history had clear dates and periods, the history of Jewish persecution and martyrdom was imbibed as outside of time—ever present, ongoing, and imminent.

To master fear of impending death and to be close to mother, Sue wanted to know what it felt like to anticipate death in a gas chamber. As a child, she extrapolated from experiences of letting go, overstimulation, and loss of consciousness, regarding falling asleep and feeling overwhelmed as death equivalents. She both played with and guarded against these states, even as death eluded her ability to imagine it. She tried to simulate mother's death encounter without succumbing to it, just as she closed her eyes in front of a mirror and then opened them quickly to see what she looked like with eyes shut. The dialectic involved getting close enough to death to understand nothingness while protecting against death to avoid nonbeing. She wanted to experience death and live to tell about it years before her mother recounted lining up to be executed by a firing squad.

During childhood, Sue overheard adults speculating about Rivka's twins. She pulled Miriam and Leah's daughter aside to share a distorted understanding of the twins' fate. A few years later, the cousins huddled around another frightening secret—sex. More than the facts of life, whisperings about the twins' torture remained etched in memory as horrific knowledge they did not want. When Miriam became pregnant with twins, each of the cousins admitted to a childhood fantasy of recovering and reuniting family by bearing twins; each girl had wondered which one of them would be the hero. (Childless after the war, Rivka gave a childhood ring of hers to Magda to pass on to a future daughter. During Miriam's pregnancy, inhabitation by ghosts who lived through her was made concrete with her epiphany that she wore the ring of the mother of twins, that is, Rivka/Miriam.)

Sue was haunted by a dream of a quiet unblinking girl of about five, sitting in midair as if suspended outside a window, looking in. She semi-recognized the room as her parents' bedroom and years later realized the girl resembled her appearance in an old photo that had fascinated her. In the photo, the seriousness of her five-year-old face contrasted with the serene smile of her mother who held her. The dream's eerie stillness evoked the stillness she had always experienced listening to mother's stories. Sue had felt that she must not add anything of herself when mother reminisced and must wait until alone to cry.

One evening Shari looked in on Sue upon returning upset from a wedding where an old friend mistook her for a sister murdered in Auschwitz. The man had believed that it was Shari who had died. Sue was unable to grasp Shari's distant, disturbed affect and wondered,

"What does mother want from me? Why is she waking me to tell this story?" There was something about doubling and substitution of one sister for another that caused Sue to speculate for years about the sisters' relationship and to wonder how her aunt had died. She resolved to name a future daughter after the rarely mentioned aunt.

Three scenes gesture at adult children of survivors' struggles with knowing and not knowing: (1) The adult Sue dreamt that she was high in a stadium, looking down upon a horrific scene of shrieking people being shredded by beasts. She struggled to look while looking away, until the arena and she were torn apart. She woke with a scream. (2) While going through her deceased mother's belongings, Miriam discovered letters from Rivka written in Yiddish, which Miriam could not read. She ripped some up until stopped by the thought that they might contain information about her mother's past; she put them in an antique chest where they remain, untranslated. (3) Upon his mother's death, a child of survivors tore up her apartment searching for a letter he believed she had hidden, but found nothing. Many children of survivors harbor a lifelong fantasy that information exists somewhere that explains the parent, even while they simultaneously dread the information as well as the possibility of its nonexistence. The parent is viewed as inherently unknowable but infinitely sought.

Children's feelings of paralysis, terror, and fascination, coupled with a partial grasp of parents' histories, evoke the primal scene (Hoffman 2004), which likewise immobilizes children who watch what they cannot comprehend and who are both absorbed in and excluded from parents' worlds. This evocation reinforces the Holocaust's centrality as an alternative primal scene that provokes frightening questions comparable in bewilderment to questions arising from the primal scene—not Where do babies come from? but Where do they go? What happens to babies who are burned alive, cut to pieces, or experimented upon? Sue wondered but never asked: What happened to family members? How many children were there? What were their names? Questions often were unspeakable and neither processed nor integrated into the lives of survivors' children.

Leah and Her Daughter Lily—Standing Guard against Self and Society

Leah's belief that she had learned the truth about human nature led to valuing institutions while regarding leaders and government pronouncements cynically. She viewed the world as ruled by selfish instincts of people who were easily led astray by charismatic leaders, and believed that our potential for evil required hypervigilance to protect liberties. Daughter Lily's sense of who she had to be for her mother led to becoming a lawyer who championed the wish to buttress justice. Aware of potential for self-delusion and self-righteousness, Lily never fully trusted neither herself nor others and constantly examined motives and actions, trying never to go along with others without scrutinizing assumptions. Aware of potential for hysteria, she felt endangered in crowds. Recognizing cruelty in herself, she felt ashamed when compromising values to gain acceptance. In middle school, she equated herself with a Nazi when she courted acceptance by not defending a bullied friend. When her firstborn child failed to gain weight for a while after birth, causing Leah to accuse her of starving her infant, Lily missed her scheduled therapy session, subsequently explaining, "I couldn't bring myself to tell you that I was a murderer."

Leah never stopped anticipating loss. When Lily reached a murdered sister's age, Leah disappeared without warning in a park they were in, to see how Lily would handle being suddenly alone, a reenactment that left Lily confused as to why her mother deliberately abandoned her. She felt vulnerable in the face of Leah's enumeration of life's uncertainties and clung to a mother whose status as survivor bestowed paradoxical strength that Lily felt she herself lacked. Lily's model for relatedness necessitated attachment to idealized others for guidance and protection, even at the cost of confidence in her own thinking and pleasure at her own resources (Mitchell 1988). To calm anxiety when flying, Lily relied on her mother's merits to prevent a crash, believing that God recognized the "too-muchness" of Leah's losses and would not cause any more. Implied is Lily's belief that she lacked value before God. (Was she no different than all those murdered children?) A second defense against anxiety was forged as a young adult in therapy with a non-Jewish therapist unfamiliar with details of the Holocaust. Lily harbored the fantasy that as a non-Jew, her therapist existed in a normal world in which massive trauma did not occur. As his patient, she reasoned, she too existed in this world and so was safe.

During this period, Lily came upon an elderly man in their neighborhood who could not recall where he was staying. Her mother happened to drive by and insisted that Lily get in the car immediately, leaving Lily confused as to what could be dangerous about helping a lost old man. Her disorientation arose from the nascent separation from a mother who continued to live in a Holocaust world in which paranoia was the appropriate response. While at that point Lily understood that she lived in a world different from her mother's, she nevertheless could still not discount Leah's alarm as signaling a real danger in the present world. The incident represented a confusing breach between her mother's traumatic world and a newer one that Lily was struggling to represent.

Lily stood guard against the stages of isolation, degradation, and murder that led to the Holocaust by working for progressive causes out of a belief that any minority group could be the canary in the mine that heralds genocide. She regarded groupthink as dangerous, and was wary of organized groups' potential to subordinate individual will to the collective's. She distrusted the tendency to fall into line with winners; when let go at work, she equated colleagues' support for her employer with identification with the aggressor. Friendship and trustworthiness were determined by her answer to the unasked question Would you hide me during the Holocaust? By interpreting life in Holocaust language, she saw Nazis everywhere. Periodically, her husband protested that he had to prove to her that he was not a murderer.

Lily was preoccupied with Leah's yearning to learn details, historical and political dimensions, and the larger picture hidden from Jews during the war. She traveled to European archives to research who had arranged trains and what had occurred in different countries, seeking to answer her and Leah's festering questions: Why had nations breached civilization by enabling mechanized killing on a level never seen before? How could murder have been perpetrated not by strangers but by neighbors and, in places like the Ukraine, face-to-face? Who tries to wipe out a race in this manner, killing old people and children? Who murders for no reason an entire people who have no army, land, or power?

Lily grew up encircled by a circumference of sorrow that put into question whether life had a purpose. Leah's conviction that childhood dreams are not realized encased her daughter in a reality that weighed down flights of fantasy and grandiose illusions. Lily knew that surviving trauma brings a loneliness that children cannot heal, and that morality and civilization are facades that, when stripped away, reveal who we really are. As if by osmosis she knew that survival depends on cooperation, mutuality, reciprocity, and running away from danger; she strove to never be a victim, victimizer, or bystander (Yehuda Bauer in Landau 1992). Inability to heal her mother left her feeling defeated. Belief that she had to justify her existence led to rejection of professionally studying the humanities ("How can you save the world by being an anthropologist?") and to choosing law as a career, engendering resentment that she could not be carefree. Seriousness bleached satisfaction from achievements and left her feeling guilty when happy. Her happiest moments were conceiving children—life-affirming experiences that briefly silenced reproaches of being a murderer. Lily sought permission to be happy and forgiveness for her mother and herself (Hillel Klein in Nedelmann 2005), as she strove to go beyond Leah's frozen survival to learn how to live.

THE THIRD TRAUMA: SECOND-GENERATION WOUNDS

Centrality of the Holocaust and transposition into it is reinforced by the Jewish tradition of identifying with past catastrophes. Judaism is based on rabbinical interpretations of biblical tales of murder, rape, and massacres; its history is comprised of centuries of persecution memorialized in liturgical stories involving sin, retribution, and restoration (Roskies 1989). Jewish collective memory is recorded in a literature of catastrophe that reinforces belief, casting Jewish identity as beleaguered but triumphant. The master plot of Jewish holidays has been satirized as "They tried to kill us. We survived. Let's eat." On first glance, the Holocaust is the penultimate example of Jews' master narrative. In actuality, it represents a subversive rupture in history that undermines belief. It attests to God's absence or lack of interference with history and recasts Judaism, in the minds of some children of survivors, as a religion and identity for which one dies. ("Jewish history has prepared me to die like a Jew," noted one. "How do I live [that is, engage life] as a Jew?")

Fracture of the pairing of destruction with redemption renders connection with the vanished world essential for survival (Klein and Kogan 1986). Magda rebuilt her lost world by locating it in religious observance and by identifying with family to neutralize internalization of the aggressor. Leah resurrected family by memorialization through teaching, realizing the wish that victims be recorded and not forgotten. Writers substituted texts as the Jewish homeland. Cultural Jews used tradition to rebuild a world of values. And therapists have valorized witnessing as secular consolation. God may not be listening, but perhaps readers, intellectuals, and future generations are.

In the myth of Philomela, a rapist cuts out the tongue of his victim, who weaves tapestry to expose the crime. The primordial trauma that was the myth's impetus echoes through centuries of atrocities that motivate its retelling. The myth is both archetype and testimony that prefigures an atrocity at Ravensbrück in which women's tongues were cut out (Saidel 2004) and contextualizes the resistance of Major Alexis Casdagli who, in a Nazi POW camp, cross-stitched samplers that contained secret subversive messages. Storytelling as accusation is an act of resistance and homage that undoes attempted erasure of victims by inscribing them into history. It is an assertion of power and affirmation of faith—not in God, but in truth.

Survivors' stories change with retelling by subsequent circles of witnesses. When Miriam, Sue, and Lily renarrated their parents' war stories, they followed with a second traumatic narrative—that of survival after death in an unrecognizable world. While the girls voyeuristically overheard and imbibed the first trauma after the fact, they were accidental participant observers in the second, which occurred not in memory but in vivo, before their eyes. Unacknowledged by both generations was a third trauma, recounted in this paper: wounding of children who were inadvertent, collateral damage from unresolved trauma filtered through their imaginations. This last wound was not witnessed, because the first generation was invested in believing that children were unaffected by the Holocaust, while the second generation felt it had no right to grievances that paled in comparison to survivors'. Both generations lived out an internalized injunction to be silent and to resist pathologizing in order to deny perpetrators' realization of their pernicious and persisting devaluation.

How to Tell a Holocaust Story: Implications for Healing

Survivors reject traditional notions of survival, guilt, heroism, and resistance. Survivor guilt presupposes that survival was a blessing; in reality, it was often regarded as a curse. Magda wondered why God punished Rivka with surviving after the death of her children and husband, not out of guilt, but from a perspective that privileges connection over individual survival and argues that aggression against a whole people protects them from self-blame. That is one reason why survivors often talk about "we" and describe many group traumas, but few sexual assaults; the latter were experienced not as targeting Jews as a whole but individuals who were generally raped when alone (Hedgepeth and Saidel 2010).

The Holocaust undermined faith that individual initiative usually meets with success and that hardship strengthens character, since good guys often lost, suffering served no purpose, and events showed that life is not about us. During extremity, survival of the self was not an essential aim of heroism; a different kind of resistance was a necessary but insufficient condition for survival: The minute one stopped resisting conditions that made life impossible, he or she died; still, survival most often was a matter of chance. The true aim of futile rebellions like those at Treblinka and Auschwitz was not defeat of the Third Reich but defeat of the Holocaust world (Fackenheim 1982). They were fought without expectation of success but, like the Warsaw Ghetto diaries, were undertaken in commitment to future Jewish life (ibid.). In resistance to the Holocaust world, a man about to be hung kissed the hand of the prisoner forced to execute him (Buergenthal 2009), and mothers chose to accompany children to their deaths to prevent their dying alone. Under conditions that rendered physical survival impossible, heroism aimed at spiritual survival, even in death.

Individual trauma should not be conflated with collective trauma; psychic reality should not be privileged over external reality. While nonindulgence is a precondition for treatment of overstimulation, and detached neutrality is necessary for uncovering psychic reality, active engagement is crucial if survivors are to face traumatic objective reality and dehumanization (Peskin 2010). While child abuse occurs secretly in private space, often engendering shame that filters rather than represses memory (Nutkiewicz 2003), collective, public abuse elicits neither secrecy nor shame but shifts trauma from personal to political and social realms, engendering rage and compulsion to tell a story that eludes signification. Testimony by itself is not healing but can lead to reexperiencing, reenactment, and suicide without presence of an empathic other; "witness" is a misnomer for the internal/external listener who must go beyond recording facts to understanding and integrating them in meaningful ways. Establishing conditions for narration of trauma by survivors' children in therapy requires appreciating that the therapeutic alliance is easily breached by what might appear to be minor misunderstandings or differences that highlight the chasm between "us" and "them" of which parents forewarned and into which therapists, as "others," may fall. When a parent's emotional availability is damaged by deliberate social trauma, harmonious dyadic affect regulation is not adequately internalized (Fosha 2003) and all others are suspect. To be able to disclose trauma, patients must trust therapists' ability to organize chaos and ward off flooding while helping to contain, explain, and integrate fragments. Because of prohibitions against speech in survivor families, therapists would do well to initiate discussion of the Holocaust while mindful that survivors' memories were not coded in English, a language devoid of their early affects and disconnected from their traumas. For their American children, English is the language in which injunctions against disclosure were codified and enacted. In an act of denial indicating a failure, or wish not to know, accounts of their therapies rarely detail families' violent histories (Faimberg 2005). Silence is readily equated not only with the parent-child pact not to ask nor tell, but also with parents' disregard (and hence acceptance) of children's suffering that is hidden in passive listening. Silence may reprieve bystanders' collusion during war and society's neglect and disdain of survivors after. It is recommended that therapists listen actively, going beyond including the Holocaust in case formulations to including it in treatment (Peskin 2010), demonstrating that this too can be talked about. The sharing of reactions by therapists who are neither overwhelmed nor deadened confirms that they too see the evil, thereby positioning themselves alongside children who are no longer alone with trauma, allowing it to be faced. Listening must not be static but imbued with connection to life.

Knowledge of massive psychic trauma constrains and overstimulates fantasy simultaneously. The Holocaust can become the primal myth in which questions about forbidden knowledge are framed. The Oedipal complex is the traditional version of how children's understanding of sexuality and their place in the generational order is constituted (Auerhahn and Laub 1998). For survivors' children, the primal narrative of origin may be the Holocaust, the primal scene one of atrocity. The myth of Oedipus, like the Holocaust, presents enigmatic scenes in which the child is absent; the former is a myth of beginnings, the latter a vision of endings. In both, children experience too much and know too little. Both narratives contain scenes of instinctual overstimulation, which children cannot understand, are curious about, and feel implicated in yet shut out of. Both stories contain secrets, infants targeted for murder, and questions children know not to ask. Horrified fascination with gas chambers and firing squads may fuse with speculation about parental bedrooms; a sexualized primal scene of violence can necessitate reworking of a primal scene of sex that is fantasized as violent. Fears of castration may signify and defend against objectlessness.

Since massive collective trauma structures representation of the social world, healing must include acknowledgment of its historical and political dimensions, whose importance is unique and specific to collective psychic trauma and not present in the same way in individual abuse and accidents. Trauma perpetrated by a nation and sanctioned by a government cannot be worked through via introspection alone; it requires construction of a historical narrative as well as a collective process of truth telling if the relationship between self and society is to be repaired (Bohleber 2010). Inclusion of trauma in shared collective memory reinforces its actuality. Advancing beyond tyranny of the internalized story to establish what is real, when clinicians share reactions to the facts, they lend external reality to atrocity for survivors' children *for the first time*, as from the beginning, it comingled with their minds. Making events real teases them apart from psychic reality, which then can be examined as fantasy *only*, and alleviates self-accusations, since children hold themselves responsible for what they create (Oliner 2006). Failure to make events real may lead children to refuse to talk, so as not to be blamed for the evil. For them, self-accusation as murderers is *not* a metaphor. As with survivors, the Holocaust is never used metaphorically; many survivors and their children evince absoluteness, concreteness, and need for conviction with little ability to look at possibilities, to play with facts, and to consider alternatives. Certainty sustains a sense of control, which does not establish genuine control but only control through authoritarianism (Scott Dowling, personal communication, 2010). Rigidity and concreteness arise, too, from the viselike grip in which external reality held internal reality during the Holocaust, as well as from survivors' fierce attempts to hold on to what remained after having lost too much. Their children's self-condemnation awaits interpretation *and* negation by ferreting it out from shamed silence in which it hides and by differentiating it from identification with the aggressor, as their shame signals the opposite of the shamelessness which marked aggressors' dehumanization (Peskin 2010). Therapists, like good-enough mothers, must go beyond mirroring, interpreting, and cognitive restructuring to transform affect by emotional engagement and by linking and differentiating psychic reality and historical experience to create safety, mutuality, and trust, if trauma is to be symbolized, shared (cf. Laub and Bodenstab 2007), and integrated into "normal" life. Therapy should be characterized by an element of play that counteracts rigid parental expectations and threats of entrapment, permeability, and being swallowed up, to establish itself as a transitional space that supports spontaneous fantasy and co-creation of stories about the children that are not eclipsed by stories they carry for parents (Auerhahn and Prelinger 1983). Reworking parental representations can be experienced as a threat to parents who are held internally to preserve their psychic existence. Attachment to survivor parents can seem life sustaining when parents appear too fragile to be separated from and when children internalize a sense of imminent annihilation, in which case the child, in differentiating, risks abandoning the parent and being abandoned by him, like those murdered loved ones who are never mentioned and appear to be forgotten. Children may use therapy as a place where they can protect against colonization while testing the dangers of autonomy. Defenses against permeability may lead to avoidance of fusion and render interpretations threatening if regarded as misappropriations. The yearning is for separation and freedom to express anger with someone who can withstand both. Only then will defenses against aggression be eased, allowing externalization in the service of healing.

The irony of the simultaneity of dwindling numbers of survivors with the public's mounting interest in the Holocaust and increasingly sophisticated trauma theories reinforces their children's cynicism that after the last survivor's death, society will know how it should have treated them.

Passing the Story On: The Third Generation

Magda and her nieces would observe Passover together without ever sharing with their children that they had been rounded up on Pesach, making the holiday that celebrates liberation the last holiday shared with their families and the *yahrzeit* (anniversary) of their families' captures and deaths. So similar are themes of enslavement, death, and liberation that weave through both stories (albeit in reverse order), that many Passover Haggadahs reference the Shoah. For example, the Haggadah of the Sholem Community Organization (1992, p. 11) includes Binem Heller's poem "Pesach Has Come to the Ghetto Again," which contains the line "the cup of the Prophet Elijah awaits, but the Angel of Death has intruded instead." Sitting at the seder table, Magda, Shari, and Leah celebrated their people's transformation from slaves into free men while mourning their families' dehumanization as objects and ash; they would wonder aloud why God had not redeemed the Jews of Europe like He had the slaves of Egypt, and they would reminisce about the war. Their daughters' representations of Passover became imbued with a melancholy that was inextricably intertwined with these remembrances.

After their parents' deaths, Miriam, Sue, and Lily celebrated Passover together. As they sang the last song in the Haggadah, "Chad Gadya," which recounts how in every generation an enemy arises who attempts to annihilate the Jews, Holocaust stories hung unspoken in the air. To provide positive principles upon which to base Jewish identity and to prevent transgenerational transmission of despair, Miriam ended the seder with a legend that posits a primal scene of creation that predates the primal scene of atrocity and has the last word.

Legend—The Primal Scene of Creation

Mystics believe that since God is everywhere, creation of the world began with an act of contraction by which God withdrew into Himself, leaving a space into which was projected a ray of divine light called Zohar, which constituted the material world. Man was created to complete and elevate this world that existed in the space of God's absence. It came to pass in the middle of the twen-

tieth century that Man created Hell. In the midst of barbarism, some humans showed compassion to others. The smallest functional unit of mankind is not the individual but the dyad, and the unit of value is not individual beliefs but actions. Acts of kindness release sparks of divine light that still cling to material reality. These splinters together can re-form Zohar. The density of the black hole called Shoah was illuminated by the purest of lights, kindled by acts of mercy, justice, and caring. These actions prevented the world from being destroyed by the void of Nothingness and re-created God, who inquired about His people. When God learned what had happened, He rent His garments and sat alone amidst mountains of ashes, weeping. After a period of mourning and lamentations, during which God was visited by martyrs who tried to console Him, He gathered these souls around Him, arose, and declared, "Let us begin again."

Biblical stories, like that of Exodus, locate God in miracles. Post-biblical narratives, like that of Purim, imply that God works through history. In modern times, survivors' stories mark sites where God was not but might yet be (see Gelernter 2009). Where was God in Auschwitz?—In the doomed Jew's kiss of his unwilling hangman, in the Yom Kippur fast of the starving Magda, and in the sharing of food between famished prisoners. These stories warn us to cultivate morality and empathy to bind aggression, to change how power is wielded, and that knowledge of the Divine must be approached through human activity (cf. Greenberg 1988). While suffering destroys more than it ennobles, it can elicit a reparative urge, which is the one thing children of survivors hold in common and which the second generation tries to transmit to the third.

REFERENCES

AUERHAHN, N. C., AND D. LAUB (1990). Holocaust testimony. *Holocaust and Genocide Studies* 5 (4): 447–62.

——— (1998). The primal scene of atrocity: The dynamic interplay between knowledge and fantasy of the Holocaust in children of survivors. *Psychoanalytic Psychology* 15:360–77.

AUERHAHN, N. C., AND H. PESKIN (2003). Action knowledge and interpretative action in work with Holocaust survivors. *Psychoanalytic Quarterly* 72 (3): 615–58.

AUERHAHN, N. C., AND E. PRELINGER (1983). Repetition in the concentration camp survivor and her child. *International Review of Psycho-Analysis* 10:31–46.

BARTHES, R. (1953). *Writing Degree Zero*. Trans. A. Lavers and C. Smith (1968). New York: Hill and Wang.

BOHLEBER, W. (2010). *Destructiveness, Intersubjectivity, and Trauma*. London: Karnac Books.

BOLLAS, C. (1987). *The Shadow of the Object.* New York: Columbia University Press.
———— (1999). Dead mother, dead child. In *The Dead Mother: The Work of Andre Green*, ed. G. Kohon. New York: Routledge.
BUERGENTHAL, T. (2009). *A Lucky Child: A Memoir of Surviving Auschwitz as a Young Boy.* New York: Little, Brown.
BUKIET, M. J., ED. (2002). *Nothing Makes You Free: Writings by Descendants of Jewish Holocaust Survivors.* New York: Norton.
COHEN, J. (1985). Trauma and Repression. *Psychoanalytic Inquiry* 5:163–89.
FACKENHEIM, E. (1982). *To Mend the World: Foundations of Post-Holocaust Jewish Thought.* Bloomington, IN: Indiana University Press.
FAIMBERG, H. (2005). *The Telescoping of Generations: Listening to the Narcissistic Links between Generations.* London: Routledge.
FONAGY, P. (1999). Attachment, the Holocaust, and the outcome of child psychoanalysis: An attachment based model of transgenerational transmission of trauma. Paper presented at San Francisco Psychoanalytic Institute and Society, February.
FOSHA, D. (2003). Dyadic regulation and experiential work with emotion and relatedness in trauma and disorganized attachment. In *Healing Trauma: Attachment, Trauma, the Brain, and the Mind*, ed. M. F. Solomon and D. J. Siegel. New York: Norton.
GEERTZ, CLIFFORD (1973). *The Interpretation of Cultures.* New York: Basic Books.
GELERNTER, D. (2009). *Judaism: A Way of Being.* New Haven, CT: Yale University Press.
GERSON, S. (2009). When the third is dead. *International Journal of Psychoanalysis* 90:1341–57.
GREEN, A. (1983). The dead mother. In *On Private Madness.* Madison, CT: International Universities Press.
GREENBERG, I. (1988). *The Jewish Way: Living the Holidays.* New York: Simon & Schuster.
GUBKIN, L. (2007). *You Shall Tell Your Children: Holocaust Memory in American Passover Ritual.* New Brunswick, NJ: Rutgers University Press.
HEDGEPETH, S. M., AND R.G. SAIDEL, EDS. (2010). *Sexual Violence against Jewish Women during the Holocaust.* Waltham, MA: Brandeis University Press.
HOFFMAN, E. (2004). *After Such Knowledge: Memory, History, and the Aftermath of the Holocaust.* New York: Public Affairs.
KLEIN, H., AND I. KOGAN (1986). Identification processes and denial in the shadow of Nazism. *International Journal of Psycho-Analysis* 67:45–52.
KLUGER, R. (2001). *Still Alive: A Holocaust Girlhood Remembered.* New York: Feminist Press of the City University of New York.
KOHON, G., ED. (1999). *The Dead Mother: The Work of Andre Green.* London: Routledge.
LANDAU, R. S. (1992). *The Nazi Holocaust.* London: I. B. Tauris.
LAPLANCHE, J. (1987). *New Foundations for Psychoanalysis.* Trans. D. Macey (1989). Oxford, UK: Blackwell.

LAUB, D., AND N. C. AUERHAHN (1989). Failed empathy: A central theme in the survivor's Holocaust experience. *Psychoanalytic Psychology* 6:377–400.

LAUB, D., AND J. BODENSTAB (2007). Book review: Psychoanalysis and trauma: History beyond trauma: Whereof one cannot speak, thereof one cannot stay silent. *Journal of the American Psychoanalytic Association* 55:335–41.

LEWIS, J. D. (2007). Trauma, repression and regression: Towards a unified theory of trauma and its consequences. Paper presented at the Annual Conference of the International Federation for Psychoanalytic Education, Toronto, October.

MITCHELL, S. (1988). *Relational Concepts in Psychoanalysis: An Integration*. Cambridge, MA: Harvard University Press.

MODELL, A. (1993). *The Private Self.* Cambridge, MA: Harvard University Press.

MOOREHEAD, C. (2011). *An Extraordinary Story of Women, Friendship, and Resistance in Occupied France*. New York: Harper / Harper Collins Publishers.

NEDELMANN, C. (2005). No reconciliation, but self-searching in the sense of rapprochement: Hillel Klein's Holocaust research in Germany 40 years after. *International Journal of Psychoanalysis* 86:1133–42.

NUTKIEWICZ, M. (2003). Shame, guilt, and anguish in Holocaust survivor testimony. *Oral History Review* 30 (1): 1–22.

OLINER, M. M. (2006). The externalizing function of memorials. *Psychoanalytic Review* 93:883–902.

PESKIN, H. (2010). Disorders of dehumanization: From anti-Semitism to the Holocaust in clinical psychoanalysis. Paper presented at the International Association of Relational Psychoanalysis and Psychotherapy (IARPP), San Francisco, February.

——— (2012). Man is a wolf to man: Disorders of dehumanization in psychoanalysis. *Psychoanalytic Dialogues* 22:190–215.

PESKIN, H., N. C. AUERHAHN, AND D. LAUB (1997). The second Holocaust: Therapeutic rescue when life threatens. *Journal of Personal and Interpersonal Loss* 2:1–25.

RASHKIN, E. (2008). *Unspeakable Secrets and the Psychoanalysis of Culture*. Albany, NY: State University of New York Press.

REISNER, S. (2003). Trauma: The seductive hypothesis. *Journal of the American Psychoanalytic Association* 51:381–413.

ROSKIES, D. (1989). *The Literature of Destruction: Jewish Responses to Catastrophe*. Philadelphia: Jewish Publication Society.

SAIDEL, R. G. (2004). *The Jewish Women of Ravensbrück Concentration Camp*. Madison, WI: University of Wisconsin Press.

SEMEL, N. (2008). *And the Rat Laughed*. Trans. from Hebrew by M. Shlesinger. Melbourne, Australia: Hybrid Publishers.

——— (2011). Lecture presented at the College of Jewish Studies, Beachwood, OH, March.

SHOLEM COMMUNITY ORGANIZATION, ED. (1992). *Sholem Family Hagadah for a Secular Celebration of Peysakh*. Los Angeles: Sholem Community Organization.

WEINE, S. M. (1999). *When History Is a Nightmare: Lives and Memories of Ethnic Cleansing in Bosnia-Herzegovina*. New Brunswick, NJ: Rutgers University Press.

WINNICOTT, D. W. (1971). *Playing and Reality*. New York: Penguin.
ZIPES, J. (1979). *Breaking the Magic Spell: Radical Theories of Folk and Fairy Tales*. Lexington, KY: University Press of Kentucky.
——— (1983). *Fairy Tales and the Art of Subversion: The Classical Genre for Children and the Process of Civilization*. New York: Routledge.

CLINICAL AND THEORETICAL CONTRIBUTIONS

The Internal/External Issue

What Is an Outer Object? Another Person as Object and as Separate Other in Object Relations Models

ANDERS ZACHRISSON, FIL. LIC. (PH.D.)

The question of what we mean by the term outer object *has its roots in the epistemological foundation of psychoanalysis. From the very beginning, Freud's view was Kantian, and psychoanalysis has kept that stance, as it seems. The author reviews the internal/external issue in Freud's thinking and in the central object relations theories (Klein, Winnicott, and Bion). On this background he proposes a simple model to differentiate the concept of object along one central dimension: internal object, external object, and actual person. The main arguments are: (1) there is no direct, unmediated perception of the actual person—the experience of the other is always affected by the perceiver's subjectivity; (2) in intense transference reactions and projections, the perception of the person is dominated by the qualities of an inner object—and the other person "becomes" an external object for the perceiver; (3) when this distortion is less dominating, the other person to a higher degree remains a separate other—a person in his or her own right.*

Clinical material illustrates these phenomena, and a graphical picture of the model is presented. Finally with the model as background, the author comments on a selection of phenomena and concepts such as unobjectionable transference, "the third position," mourning and loneliness.

Anders Zachrisson is Associate Professor, Department of Psychology, University of Oslo and Training Analyst, Child Analyst, and Former President of the Norwegian Psychoanalytic Society.

The Psychoanalytic Study of the Child 67, ed. Claudia Lament, Robert A. King, Samuel Abrams, A. Scott Dowling, and Paul M. Brinich (Yale University Press, copyright © 2013 by Claudia Lament, Robert A King, Samuel Abrams, A. Scott Dowling, Paul M. Brinich).

> The way that the internal colours and distorts the external is of course a central preoccupation of psychoanalysis generally. (Spillius et al., 2011, p. 326)

The Basic Assumption in Object Relations Theories

It is a fundamental assumption in object relations models that the self stands in relation to internalized objects. Such objects are representations of important persons in infancy and childhood. When these persons are internalized, they function as objects for the self in the inner world. The relations between self and object representations are called "object relations," and they are charged with specific affects. A feared father can be internalized as a harsh father object standing in a threatening relation to a guilty, an anxious, or a shameful aspect of the self. An alternative formulation is sometimes proposed. We internalize object relations not objects. This variation doesn't change the essential point in object relations models; object-affect-self representations are building stones in the individual personality.

This assumption is based on Sandler's concept of representation and his conceptualization of the representational world (Sandler and Rosenblatt 1962). The difference between the general term *inner world* and the somewhat more specific *representational world* is not generally accepted among object relation theorists. When I nevertheless leave these differences of opinion aside, it is because I do not consider them to affect the general argument in this paper.

We have to see the use of the term *object* in light of the history of the concept and of the dynamics working in the relation between one person (the self) and a second person being object for the first. Freud's "object" was mainly an object for a drive (that is, for the needs and strivings of an individual). The object relations models gradually grew out of these first conceptualizations of psychoanalysis; the term *object* was kept, but its connotation was changed and became much more complex. The inner object is not a "subject" related to the self, it is an "object." And in the model I'm going to propose, it will be clear that the external object is not a subject related to the self. The recognition of the subjectivity of the other is a result of development. Only to the degree that the other is perceived as a separate person will his subjectivity be recognized and appreciated.

Actually, the latter is a crucial step in the experience of the other, and a central component in the capacity to mentalize. Without this development, the other remains an object. Bollas hints at this quality of experience, naming it "normotic" (1987). Based on an observation by

Winnicott, he uses this term to connote a defensive attitude akin to the false self-state. Both self and the other are experienced as objects, as surfaces without mental, subjective depth. The person presents himself as all too normal, *abnormally normal* in Bollas's expression (ibid., p. 136).

The question I will consider in this paper is the following: What is an external, or outer, object, and what is the difference between a "person" and an "outer object." As a background for my discussion, I briefly review the ways Freud, Klein, Winnicott, and Bion thought about and conceptualized the psychic/external dimension. I then present clinical material illustrating the phenomena at stake. At its basis, this question concerns the way psychoanalysis understands the relation between inner and outer reality. Let us start there, with the psychoanalytic theory of knowledge.

The Epistemological Stance of Psychoanalysis

Psychoanalysis has kept the epistemological stance expressed by Freud in his early writings. The philosophy of German-speaking Europe in the late nineteenth century had returned to Kant's critical philosophy. Liebmann (1865) and Lange (1866) spoke for a rational, empirical methodology as the only scientific way to knowledge, and they rejected the possibility of absolute, metaphysic knowledge of the world. Freud was in line with these thoughts: "The unconscious is the true psychical reality; in its innermost nature it is as much unknown to us as the reality of the external world, and it is as incompletely presented by the data of consciousness as is the external world by the communications by our sense organs" (Freud 1900, p. 613).

For neo-Kantian philosophy, as for Freud, the way to knowledge was through experience elaborated by rational thinking.[1] And the truth of reality could only be approached; it could never be reached. This critically realistic stance has been varied and shaded off during the twentieth century but has kept a strong position in psychoanalysis and in science in general.

A consequence of such a view on knowledge is that persons also are beyond direct, "true" perception. So, how can we know another person? And, in psychoanalytic thinking, what is the connection between person and object? Reading contemporary psychoanalytic papers, we soon are struck by the many different uses of the term *object:* inner or internal, outer or external, real, actual, living, separate, good, bad, persecuting, and so on. As a rule these different types get no further specification,

---

1. For a detailed discussion of this point see Tauber 2009.

as if the meaning were self-evident. Especially confusing is the terminology concerning the relationship to other persons and the use of the term *outer object*. Often the terms *person, object,* and *outer object* seem to be synonymous and interchangeable. So we have to ask when a person is a "person" and when an "object"; and whether a mother always is an "object" or if she sometimes is just a "mother."

ELASTICITY OF TERMINOLOGY AND CONFUSION IN THINKING

One problem has to be noted in an investigation of a concept like "object." The term has different connotations within different analytic models. And we have to find a balance between two partly contrary factors in concept formation—the need for a quantum of clarity and precision and the need for flexibility and elasticity. We have to face the question of how *elastic* a concept we need and ask if there is a point where useful elasticity turns into unclear thinking and muddy confusion (Sandler 1983). Freud reflected on this issue in his paper on narcissism: "Empirical interpretation . . . will not envy speculation its privilege of having a smooth, logically unassailable foundation, but will gladly content itself with nebulous, scarcely imaginable basic concepts, which it hopes to apprehend more clearly in the course of its development" (Freud 1914, p. 77).

Freud introduced the concept of "object," but in a meaning different from what it later received in the object relations models. First, his "object" was a drive-satisfying object in a model where man was primarily pleasure seeking (Sandler and Sandler 1998). In *Mourning and Melancholia,* though, the notion is more complex. The object is related to the ego and is affecting the self-experience. In contemporary object relations models, this conception is elaborated to full-blown models of personality.

DILEMMAS CONNECTED TO THE INNER/OUTER ISSUE

Hämäläinen (2009) has discussed the inner/outer issue in psychoanalysis. He initially states the triviality of the questions he asks, and notes how the apparent clarity dissipates at a closer look. And he wonders whether we should refrain from asking such questions, to avoid destroying the potential space (referring to Winnicott 1953). He ends his discussion by formulating a dilemma with three aspects:

> How do we recognize another's subjectivity and remain genuinely conscious about it and . . . avoid sinking into ultra-realism?

How can we retain transitional phenomena and the associated omnipotence without sinking into fundamentalism?
And how can we interact with another, genuinely separate subject . . . ?
(Hämäläinen 2009, p. 1295)

These three questions are closely connected to my theme: How can we know another person? The danger of ultrarealism is, as I see it, to perceive the other as a surface or as a thing in the world, without an inner life (Bollas's "normotic" attitude). The danger of fundamentalism seems to refer to ideological and religious systems belonging to transitional space; where truth, in Hämäläinen's reading of Winnicott, is omnipotently determined, like the child's relation to its transitional object. If the beliefs of a system or an individual get the status of undisputable truth and reality, they have turned fundamentalistic. The last question concerns the very possibility of interaction with the other as a separate being, when our perception of the other is affected by our inner reality.

Hämäläinen also notes that these questions have been avoided in psychoanalytic thinking, and offers the hypothesis that a reason for this is that they confront us with "existential anxiety awakened by the threat of the essential aloneness of man" (p. 1277).

My project is to look into the basic structure of the relation between one person (me, myself) and another person in object relations theories. In doing so, I will try to elucidate Hämäläinen's questions and indicate ways of thinking about them.

In line with the epistemological stance of psychoanalysis referred to above, the assumption is that there cannot be a direct (true or objective) relation between me and another person. The relation is always mediated, in one way or another, by the inner, object world of the perceiver. I will propose an example of how this mediation can be conceptualized. But let us first have a brief look at the development of psychoanalytical thinking about the "psychic reality/external reality" issue.

PSYCHIC/EXTERNAL: A SKETCH OF PSYCHOANALYTIC CONCEPT FORMATION

FREUD

As we have noted, Freud was from the start concerned with the relation between psychic and external reality. And, as we saw in the quotation above, his view was that neither psychic nor external reality could be known completely. In chapter 7 of *The Interpretation of Dreams* he introduced the concepts of *"perceptual identity"* and *"thought identity,"* which together form the basis for the distinction between primary and secondary process thinking and its connection with the pleasure and reality principles (1900, pp. 597–603). In the absence of a drive-satisfying object in the external world, the (hungry) child first perceives (hallucinates) the memory of the satisfying experience (perceptual identity). This, however, leaves him unsatisfied, and a secondary process instead creates a mental image of the experience by establishing a thought identity with it. This is the dawn of conscious thinking and of contact with external reality.

In later papers he developed his thoughts about primary and secondary processes (especially in connection to dreaming and unconsciousness) and about the pleasure and reality principles (Freud 1911). In Freud's thinking, the ego becomes the agent in the mind, which is in contact with external reality, and "negotiates" the tensions and conflicts between id (drives), superego (moral demands), and the constraints and possibilities of external reality. The movement from perceptual to thought identity marks the start of this development in the ego and makes way for the function of the *delay* and the *detour* mechanisms, hallmarks of ego functioning and the individual's adaptation to reality.

One highly pregnant seed for the development of the object relations models—and for the argument in this paper—is Freud's paper on mourning and melancholia (1917). A crucial element in the paper is the individual's tolerance for psychic pain. A *benign* cycle predominates when the individual has the capacity to tolerate and contain loss and sorrow. This cycle includes several steps: accepting (the reality of) death and loss; mourning, which is a process of libidinal detachment from the lost object; gradually coming to grip with reality; and, finally, remaining in contact with reality, including future losses. It is fair to say that life is a continuous cycle of forming relationships and dealing with losses, of attachments and mourning.

If this capacity to accept reality is insufficient, we may be faced with a *malign* cycle: (the reality of) death and loss is denied; a mourning process doesn't start; the self becomes poor and empty (by narcissistic and ambivalent identification with the lost object instead of libidinal detachment); and reality (the other person) remains deformed by projected object representations (Freud 1917).

Mourning is the "normal" reaction to death. Melancholia, however, is a mourning gone astray. In Freud's words, when the reality of death is denied, "the shadow of the object . . . [falls] upon the ego, and the latter . . . [can] henceforth be judged by a special agency, as though it were an object, the forsaken object" (ibid., p. 249). In Freud's paper, we can recognize two contrary ways of facing the challenges of life. One way is to turn one's eye to reality, accepting it as it is; this stance makes mourning possible. The other is to turn a blind eye to reality and deny it. The consequence of this stance is that thinking is replaced by magic and omnipotent control, and a process of mourning will never start.

KLEIN

In Klein's object relations model, the main emphasis is on the inner, object or part object, world.[2] So, the importance of external reality as a factor and agent in psychic life is played down in Kleinian analysis compared with the Freudian model. However, in Klein's view, the self's interaction with reality, notably the experience of frustration, was a significant factor in psychic development. Frustration amplifies the death drive and is connected to the internalization of bad objects (Spillius et al. 2011). And in her distinction between the two positions, we can note the oscillations between the more-subjective part objects of the paranoid-schizoid position and the more-"realistic" whole objects of the depressive position. The part object is often a heavily distorted version of mother's breast, and projective and introjective mechanisms and splitting play central roles in the paranoid-schizoid position. In the depressive position, the objects integrate and represent whole persons, closer to reality. This is a result of the gradual development of the ego:

> Integration, consciousness, intellectual capacities, the relation to the external world and other functions of the ego are steadily developing. . . . The relation to the mother as a person, which has been gradually developing while the breast still figured as the main object, becomes more fully established and identification with her gains in strength when the child can perceive and introject the mother as a person. (Klein 1952, p. 72)

And later in the text she has an observation connecting directly to our theme: "The continued experience of facing psychic reality, implied in the working through of the depressive position, increases the infant's comprehension of the external world. Accordingly the picture of his parents, which was at first distorted into idealized and terrifying figures, comes gradually nearer to reality" (ibid., p. 74). In the depressive position these internal representations of the parents become more realistic, and the parents themselves may be objects of reparation, concern, and love.

---

2. Consider the joke about the musing of the Kleinian analysand after arriving late to a session: I know it is my unconscious, but the bus was also involved in a traffic incident.

What Klein described here is the infant's mental development in the first year of life. Her "positions" are, however, not phases in a development where one is passed and the other reached; they are *potential positions* that can be activated at any time. Thus, they continue to play a role in psychic reality all through life.

WINNICOTT

Winnicott's main contribution to the question of psychic/external is the conceptualization of an intermediate area of experience, which is neither totally internal nor totally external. He named it "potential" or "transitional" space, and in the child's world it is inhabited by transitional objects. Such an object is, in Winnicott's view, possessed by the child in a way that makes it possible to preserve an illusion of omnipotent control over it; it is modeled on the illusion of control that the infant feels it has of its mother, who tries to adapt as best she can to the infant's needs.

> From birth . . . the human being is concerned with the problem of the relationship between what is objectively perceived and what is subjectively conceived of, and in the solution of this problem there is no health for the human being who has not been started off well enough by the mother. The intermediate area to which I am referring is the area that is allowed to the infant between primary creativity and objective perception based on reality-testing. (Winnicott 1953, p. 11)

Winnicott stated that there is no possibility for the infant to proceed from the pleasure principle to the reality principle and to establish such an intermediate area without the help of a good-enough mother who "makes active adaptation to the infant's needs, an . . . adaptation that gradually lessens, according to the infant's growing ability to account for failure of adaptation and to tolerate the result of frustration" (ibid., p. 10).

Here Winnicott anticipated Bion's model, wherein the mother's containment of the infant's anxiety is necessary for the development of the capacity to tolerate frustration and of an apparatus for thinking (Bion 1962a; 1962b).

In Winnicott's thinking, the potential space plays a crucial role in man's development of culture (1953). And he underlined its paradoxical nature: "The baby creates the object, but the object was there waiting to be created and to become a cathected object" (1971, p. 89). This formulation beautifully adds to the complexity of Freud's epistemological position. It corresponds closely to the critical stance of neo-Kantian philosophy and to Bion's notion of "pre-conception" (see below).

The development in the infant's mind of an external world and of persons as external beings is in Winnicott's thinking a movement *from* (1) *relating* to objects *through identifications, to* (2) *using* objects (1971). In the relating through identification with the object, the child experiences the object as a part of itself, a part that can be omnipotently dominated. In the use of an object, the child gives the object an independent existence, and in that way moves it toward external reality (that is, in the direction of a "real" person).

Bollas has commented on the role assigned to projective identification in the perception of other persons. He noted that the problem is that in projective identifications, the interest is in the projections of the self, not the qualities of the other. And he added:

> Working exclusively from this [projective identification] theory of perception, identification, empathy and critical appraisal risks destroying the integrity of the object itself. It is hard to escape the ironic realization that a theory meant to identify how we perceive the other by mental entry may result in the replacement of the other by the self. (Bollas 2006, p. 713)

This observation is in line with the dilemmas Hämäläinen noted in his discussion (2009). As an alternative, Bollas offered the concept "perceptive identification," based on the self's ability to perceive the other as a separate other.[3] With this ability, the self can enjoy the other's qualities, be nurtured by his or her integrity, and celebrate the other as a different being. Very much in the mentality of Winnicott,[4] he concluded: "This model presupposes a *jouissance* of difference (not similarity) and implicitly appreciates the difference of the object. . . . Perceptive identification allows us to love an object" (Bollas 2006, p. 714).

BION

Bion (1962a) has elaborated Freud's model into a more-detailed theory of thinking. His point of departure is distinctly Kantian. He classified thoughts by their developmental history into pre-conceptions, conceptions (or thoughts), and concepts. The pre-conception is an inborn disposition to experience an important piece of reality. As an example, he used the infant's expectation of a breast. When a pre-conception (of the breast) meets a realization approximating it (the actual breast),

---

3. Here Bollas uses the expression "as a thing-in-itself." In the rest of the paragraph he talks about "object" or "object-in-itself." In line with the argument in this paper, I use "other" or "separate other" instead.

4. In the present, quite narrow internal/external issue Bollas supplements Winnicott. In other areas, his contributions are, of course, highly independent.

the result is a conception. He referred to the pre-conception as a priori knowledge of the breast and also as an "empty thought." These are Kantian notions. They connote knowledge, or truth, which is not dependent on experience; knowledge that exists a priori of the experience (of the actual breast).

Kant's epistemology attempts to secure the possibility of true and exact (that is, scientific) knowledge via logic (Kant 1781). Bion has applied Kant's system to Freud's sketch of a theory and formed a psychological theory about the development of thinking. His points of departure are threefold: the child's *basic needs,* its *inborn mental capacities,* and its *tolerance of frustration* when needs are left unsatisfied.

Bion let the infant and the breast serve as the model that gives him a language for his thinking. He described four "combinations" or "constellations" for pre-conception, realization, and tolerance of frustration. The first occurs when pre-conception mates with its realization: The infant is hungry and the breast is there. The result is a conception. Conceptions therefore are intimately conjoined with an emotional experience of satisfaction (Bion 1962a, pp. 306–7).

The other three constellations concern cases in which the hungry infant doesn't get the breast. Bion wrote, "The model I propose is that of an infant whose expectation of a breast is mated with a realization of no breast available for satisfaction. This mating is experienced as a no-breast, or 'absent' breast inside" (ibid., p. 307).

This situation, however, is ambiguous. Has the infant the capacity to handle the frustration of an absent breast or not? "If the capacity for toleration of frustration is sufficient the 'no-breast' inside becomes a thought, and an apparatus for 'thinking' it develops" (ibid., p. 307). This is the second constellation. The breast is not there, the frustration is tolerated, and the result is a thought and the development of an apparatus for thinking. The way Bion pictured the emergence of a *thought* corresponds to Freud's notion of *thought identity* and his model of ego development. When the ego tolerates the frustration of not being mated with the satisfying object and starts "thinking the breast" (thought identity), it can adapt to reality (by delay and detour mechanisms). This is the Freudian "reality principle."

If the capacity for toleration of frustration is inadequate, the infant has two alternatives to handle the bad internal "no-breast" situation: (1) evasion, and (2) modification of frustration. When the infant is incapable of handling the frustration, the result is neither a conception nor a thought but an evasion. (This is an addition to Freud's model. Freud didn't discuss the situation where the child is unable to tolerate the "no-breast" frustration, although he hinted at it in 1917.) Instead of producing a thought, the negative realization without tolerance for the frustration will result in a bad object (β-element, *thing-in-itself*), fit only for evacuation. And further, evacuation disturbs the development of a thinking apparatus; projective identifications take its place (Bion 1962a).

What happens if the frustration is subject to modification? This is the fourth constellation that Bion discussed. Modification refers to the process whereby an intolerable frustration is made tolerable. A crucial factor in the child's experience of frustration is mother's *reverie;* the way the mother modifies the infant's intolerable inner states (the infant's *nameless dread*) into tolerable feeling states. This process makes the establishment of a "K-link" possible (1962b). A K-link is Bion's term for a piece of knowledge about reality (a thought). So, in contrast to evacuation (the aim of which is to deny reality), modification aims at knowing the no-object (the object whose absence triggers the frustration). This process corresponds to Bion's α-function, whereby sensory states become mentally meaningful. He connected the K-link and the α-function with curiosity about reality, while β-elements refer to sensory states remaining meaningless. And because they are meaningless, they cannot be subject to mental work; they can only be evacuated the way we can observe, for example, in psychosomatic processes.

Considering Bion's theory, we have to ask if the case wherein the child is able to tolerate the frustration is an ideal one, or rather an end product of a developmental process. Can the infant ever manage its inner states without mother's presence and containing function? We are prone to think that mother's containing function is a necessary facilitating element in the infant's development, and that formation of conceptions and thoughts are processes beyond the infant's ability without this assistance. This means that Bion's second constellation is a special (ideal) instance of the fourth, a notion closely in line with Winnicott's model.

It is also striking to note the correspondence between Bion's model and Fonagy's *mentalization* model. In the latter, the capacity for mentalization, that is, to reflect on one's own and other people's mental states, is related to the child's attachment to its parents (Fonagy et al. 2002). So both Bion and Fonagy consider the quality of the child's psychic environment, especially the way the child's anxiety is handled, as an essential element in the development of a capacity for thinking and mentalization.

Bion's theory specifies conditions for the development of an apparatus for thinking and of conceptions and thoughts concerning external reality. He noted how this development can be disturbed and how the individual's capacity to learn from experience can be severely impaired, when the infant is left unsupported and unable to handle inevitable frustration and anxiety.

SUMMING UP

Freud based his conception of external reality and its place in psychic reality—the distinction between the pleasure and the reality principles—on the notions of perceptual identity and thought identity. Klein and Winnicott developed their own concepts to handle the same dynamics. Klein's model contains detailed descriptions of how perceptions of reality are distorted—by projective identification, by splitting, and by denial. Her two *positions* point to a distinction between a more-distorted perception of reality and a less-distorted one. This distinction also concerns the perception of other persons.

Winnicott, both in his concept of transitional space and in his distinction between relating through identifications and use of an object, has given precise formulations of the infant's move from omnipotent primary process thinking to a more-realistic experience of other persons. And he underlined the importance of the mother's emotional holding of the child, helping it to develop the capacity to tolerate frustration and face reality.

Bion explicitly departed from Freud's model and elaborated it into a more-detailed theory of thinking. He also elaborated Winnicott's notion of tolerating frustration, first hinted at in Freud's paper on mourning and melancholia. The relative capacity to tolerate frustration when the need-satisfying object is absent is the pivot of his model. This capacity is connected to the alternatives of denying reality on one side and accepting reality and developing an apparatus for thinking about it on the other. In Bion's language the alternatives are between evasion of β-elements, that is, meaningless sensory impressions, by projective identification on one side and forming K-links and producing α-elements, that is, meaningful sensory impressions, on the other.

Bion bridged the gap between Freud and the object relations models, between Freud's *object for a drive* and Klein's and Winnicott's *object relations as building-stones for personality*.

These four models approach the issue of inner/outer in psychoanalysis from different angles. In my view, however, they share a common, central conceptualization of the infant's contact with external reality and the infant's development of the reality principle.

The Experience of Another Person

In the last section I reviewed the inner/outer issue in three object relations models (Klein, Winnicott, and Bion) on a general level. No clear differences in epistemological stance came to the fore. So when we turn to the specific question of the perception of other persons, the main argument is common for the three models.

In the inner world, representations of the self stands in relation to internalized object representations. Now what about the relationship between one person and another person in the real world? As we have noted, the relations of the self to real persons are never direct relationships. The perception of the person "out there" is always colored by internal object relations activated by specific elements in the situation. This means that one person's (my) relationship to another person is invested by qualities of the (internal) objects that this other person activates in me. In other words, an emotionally important person in actual time becomes associated with an object in my inner world, and for that reason takes over the emotional charge of this object. In the example above, the internalized father object can be actualized in later meetings with authority figures, and thus color and distort the perception of these persons. This also implies that our patients' descriptions of their parents are not "objective" descriptions. We get descriptions of the object representations of their parents, and these are, in specific ways, "distorted" descriptions. And in the course of an analytic process, as a result of transference analysis and working through, the parent descriptions are modified, more "normal," and become, as it seems, less distorted by projections (see also Klein 1952, p. 74).

If the distortion is strong, as we can see in intense transference reactions and projections, the perception (experience) of the person and the relationship to him or her is dominated by the object's qualities and the activated affects. In such cases, the experience of the person becomes, to a considerable degree, fixed in its meaning for the self. In the mind of the perceiver, the person "becomes" the object, and this person functions as an *external object* for the perceiver.

So we have objects in the inner world and persons in the outer world. In addition, we can talk about the relationship to a person as a relation to an outer or external object. Outer objects are persons misperceived due to projected or transferred emotional charges from (inner) object relations. The person is not perceived and treated "realistically," but as if he *were* the other (Zachrisson 1998). The person "behind" the object is "transported" into the actual person—conferring the concept *transference!* The term *outer object* is a condensation of this thought.

CLINICAL VIGNETTE

The following material serves as an illustration of the dynamics we are considering. The analysand was a thirty-year-old musician, B. He was passionately involved with his family members (mother, father, and younger brother). In B's description, his father was a split person; intelligent, strong, and violent; at the same time he could be very kind and self-sacrificing. B felt that his father was devoted to his sons, but he could also be rough and condescending.

Separation anxiety and inhibition of aggression are central elements in B's character. The session notes are taken from the last months of his first year in analysis. They illustrate how the transferred object representations strongly affected the experience of the analyst.

NOTES FROM SESSIONS

In a waking nightmare, B saw his father in the bed beside him, lying on his back, arms stretched out, head aside, crucified, dead. It was horrible. He turned and looked at his wife and then again at his father. He was awake, yet he saw father twice before he realized that a sheet and a blanket formed the body and arms. The head was a wastebasket on the floor. This dream occurred while B was preparing his father's birthday celebration, doing everything he could to please him. At the same time, B felt rage over his father's humiliating attitude toward him. His image of father oscillated between the boundlessly kind and the brutally devaluating father.

A line of associations evolved: Father drew B across the street in spite of a red traffic light. He did it in a rough way, irritated. B was seven, the memory so clear, the impression so strong; father transgressed the laws. He thought of himself stealing a pornographic magazine in his teens, escaping trembling, confused, almost in a trance. And then a deeply shameful thought was paralyzing him; he imagined that I was masturbating behind him, full of contempt. And he felt deeply humiliated. The condescending father was transferred to the scornful analyst looking down upon him from behind.

Nevertheless, B was submissive and deeply grateful to be listened to and accepted by me. To disagree with me was unthinkable: He adjusted to me even if he disagreed. A compound picture of this dynamic gradually emerged in our work. His submissiveness concerned his relationship to mother and, in fantasy, its purpose was to prevent her rejection of him; the humiliation emanated from father and triggered frustration and (unconscious) rage. Both these elements were in the transference and could be described to him: his anxiety to be left by mother and humiliated by father without means to defend himself—and how this scenario repeated itself in many of his relationships (including in his analysis).

One morning B didn't come to his session. At our next appointment he described how he was afraid of oversleeping and had woken up several times during the night and checked that the alarm clock was activated. The last time he had happened to deactivate the clock, he had woken up after his appointment. He said that the treatment put him under heavy, sometimes almost unbearable, pressure. But no blame was allowed to fall on me. He himself was to blame. He would get an extra alarm clock.

On his way to the next session, B imagined that it was my first session for the day and that I would have preferred to stay in bed with my wife. He became enraged. Then the image changed; he saw me alone and unhappy, my wife had left me, and he was seized by compassion. However, the murderous rage had the upper hand in his mind. Authority figures passed through his mind: teachers, military officers, his father, and me; meanwhile contradictory impulses pulled him to and fro. He became afraid of what he could do. He imagined himself attacking me with a hammer—and then he saw my look, crushing him in contempt.

This drama—played out in his internal object world—distorted his perception of both past and present situations. His contradictory experiences of father's depression and dependency on his sons, father's kindness, contempt, and explosive anger clashed in his mind and put him in an emotional vise. And these scenarios, activated in the analysis, were transferred to his analyst.

A bit later I had to cancel a session. B's first reaction was to object; he would not subject himself to my arrangements. Then violent, destructive images emerged. He imagined himself banging his hand down on the table, striking an ax into the table. He imagined that I was sitting behind him with a sardonic smile on my face. He felt that I looked at him and thought how ugly he was. And there he lay, exposed and humiliated.

I suggested that the canceled session reminded B of the fact that I have relationships with other people. He cut me off and said that he thought I was planning to start seeing a new patient. Furthermore, he thought I had told the new one that I soon would have some additional sessions available—his sessions.

Here we can see how B's rage derived from several sources: (1) the humiliation he felt on the couch, (2) the thought that he would be forced to leave his place to a new patient, and (3) the thought that I was being deceitful with him. But still he felt it would be disastrous to criticize me. If he ever so slightly gave his small finger to the rage, it would create a catastrophe. He noted that I had described such thoughts and feelings before and he hadn't understood my thinking. Now, however, he could feel that these were at the heart of the matter.

Toward the end of the next session, he felt a rage that took his breath away. He was afraid he would lose control and attack me physically, and he started to apologize. Suddenly, however, he stopped himself and said, "Now I am tired of having to apologize all the time!" I felt that he, in a glimpse, saw the difference between his father and me, and that he, as a result of our work on his transferences, began to see me more in my own right.

B's intense father transference had distorted his experience of me; I had become *an outer object,* transformed by the highly complex, ambivalent, sometimes split image of his introjected father object. This had been in the center of our work for more than a year, in my efforts to make the dynamics clear and his work to see and accept these forces in his mind. Now, our efforts begin to bear fruit. His statement that he was tired of having to apologize was a first tiny step out of this transference, a first step whereby I gradually became less "father" or "mother" and more "real" in his mind. When he returned after the Christmas holidays, his experience of me was somewhat changed; his murderous rage and separation anxiety were less conspicuous in his mind, and other themes entered our work.

The Analyst as a Separate Other

Let us now consider the case, the beginning of which we saw at the end of the vignette, when the relation to the person becomes less dominated by internal object qualities. B's perception of the other (me) then became less rigid. It was not dominated by transferred object qualities and the person (me) could stand out more as a separate *other.* B began to perceive his analyst more as an individual, related to him as a being separate from B himself. This other, because he was perceived as a *person,* was invested with interest, even curiosity and concern, and the relationship became open to change and development. This experience of the other had a more-pronounced presence and richness and a more-spontaneous nature than had been the case in the other, prior position.

I see this development as an accumulated effect of analytic work: (1) the analyst's registration of transference qualities, his containment of the patient's feelings and projections, and his efforts to clarify and interpret the dynamics; and (2) the patient's work to understand the dynamics and to let these insights affect his self-understanding and perception of the analyst. All these elements take part in the process. This kind of development is not very often a sudden jump to a new level of function, but is usually a small step, forth-and-back movement, where repeated working through is essential.

There is a striking similarity between the conceptions of this model and those of the open and closed systems of self-regulation developed by Novick and Novick. They write:

> Our . . . work on sadomasochism and its underlying defensive omnipotent beliefs has led us to the view that there are two distinct kinds of solutions to conflicts throughout development. One is attuned to reality and is characterized by joy, competence and creativity. The other avoids reality and is characterized by sadomasochism, omnipotence and stasis. (2001, p. 96)

Novick and Novick relate these two systems of self-regulation to a dual-track model of development. And the quality of the environmental response to the phase-related challenges from fetal life to adolescence plays a part in the individual's developmental track; how the parents can tolerate their own and the child's pain and anxiety through childhood. We note the convergence of this thinking with the views of Winnicott and Bion already described. We also note the correspondence between the closed and the open systems on one side and Klein's paranoid-schizoid and depressive positions on the other. Actually, such conceptual convergences should not surprise us if we keep in mind that these different conceptions address closely connected or sometimes even the same phenomena.

An Attempt to Draw a Comprehensive Picture of the Model

Summing up this line of reasoning, we get the following simple notions. (We have to keep in mind that our focus is restricted to one aspect of the object concept, its position on an inner/outer dimension.) Internal object relations are affective relations between aspects of internalized objects and self-representations. External objects are internal objects externalized onto a person by projection or transference. When a person is perceived in relative freedom from projections, he can be experienced as a separate other. The difference between *external object* and *separate other* is a relative difference. External objects are "colored by" or "invested with" qualities of the projected internal object. This means that they are controlled by the self, and in that way have a fixed meaning for the self; it works like a closed system. In the clinical material, we could see how B's perception of his analyst was distorted by the transference of internalized representations of both of his parents, making the analyst appear to be deceitful, rejecting, and full of contempt. In contrast to this, when a person is perceived as a separate other, he or she is free—to a higher degree—from the dominance by an externalized object relation. The other can be subject to curiosity, and the experience is open to changes.

We have to conceive of these two ways of relating to a person as two positions, which are potentially activated. In the first position we have the self in relation to a projected or transferred "outer" object, which to a degree is undifferentiated from the internalized object. In the second position we have a fairly realistic perception of, and relationship to, the other person. The perception will never be completely free of "distortions" from the internal object world, but free enough to allow the other person an "independent existence" in the mind of the perceiver and to open up a space for mutual relating, concern, interest, learning, and knowledge.

In the course of development, the child will oscillate between these positions. When a child, or a patient, moves from relating to "the other" to relating to "an outer object," it is a loosening of the grip on reality, like a movement from depressive to paranoid-schizoid position (Klein's conception), or like a shift from the open to the closed system of self-regulation (the conception of Novick and Novick). We may think of it as a regression, but it is a regression involving a shift of position or track, not primarily a backward movement along one developmental line. Clearly, this relates to a normative feature of growth. Such oscillations between more-mature and less-mature positions are characteristic of human development and endemic to how people change.

In the illustration the model is presented graphically (see fig. 1). Two positions from which a self can experience another person are represented. The left hand side (I) presents the dynamics when the object dominates the experience of the other, and the right hand side (II) presents the dynamics when the other is perceived more "in his own right," relatively free from projections.

QUALITIES OF EXPERIENCE DISTRIBUTED IN THIS MODEL

In a provisional way, we can distribute qualities of experience to the two positions of the figure. Roughly, we can locate the more-projective and "subjective" elements on the left hand side (position I), and the more "real," perceptive elements on the right hand side (II), corresponding

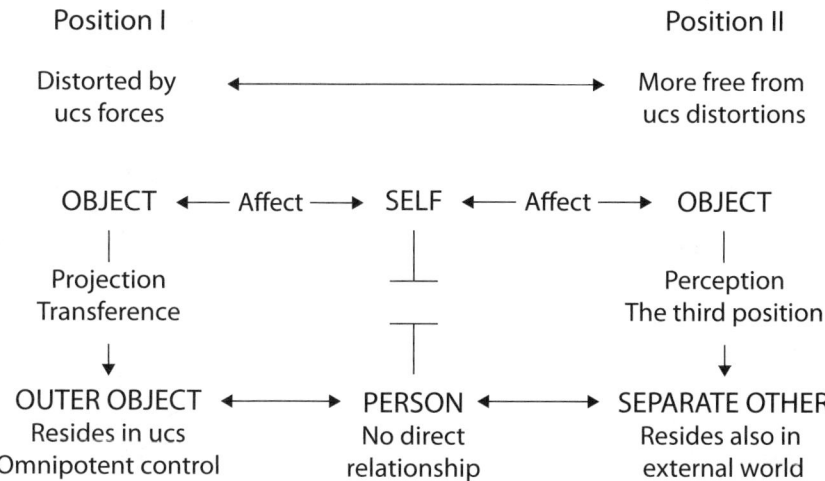

Fig. 1. Experience of another person as outer object and as a separate other.

to Freud's pleasure/unpleasure and reality principles (see fig. 2). This is, of course, only one way of several to represent the positions of the concepts and thus to indicate aspects of their connotation.

The outer object resides in the subject's inner world. In the extreme, it belongs to a closed system of experience, unaffected by reality (Novick and Novick 2001). In the other (third) position, the subject recognizes the otherness of the other and gives the separate other an existence in reality, independent of the self. The other is recognized as a subject in his or her own right. And this independence arouses curiosity and interest about who the other one *is*. It is in this position that it is possible for the individual to *learn from experience*.

Winnicott's *transitional space* has its place in between inner and outer world, with a paradoxical existence, being neither outer nor inner yet both of these at the same time (Winnicott 1953). Transference in its nonpsychotic form has the same paradoxical residence in transitional space, both inner and outer, both past and present at the same time (Freud 1915; Zachrisson 1998). The unobjectionable transference (Freud 1912) refers to the patient's positive experience of the analyst, where the transferred "deformation" of him or her doesn't work as a resistance. The concept has played a role in the discussions of the concepts of therapeutic and working alliance and of the conditions for productive analytic work (Evans 1976; Stein 1981). In the model, it belongs to the open system (II), the third position, where therapeutic change

I		II
Outer Object	Intermediate Space	Separate Other
Closed system Externalization Projection Fixed meaning	"Normal" transference Transitional space	Open system The third position Perception Curiosity, interest
"Psychosis" Loneliness? Emptiness?	"Neurosis"	"Normality" Fellowship? Relatedness?

Fig. 2. Schematic outline of qualities of experience in the model.

takes place. It may even be that a benign "projection" of aspects of the self into the other makes the way for an empathic understanding of the other; that such a process, as a mutual phenomenon, allows nonverbal communication and understanding to take place.[5] Over time this mutual relation in combination with transference analysis can step-by-step free the analyst from the "distortions" of transferences and projections. This movement is not easy to illustrate clinically. Gradually, the patient's withdrawal of projections opens up for a more-empathic perception of the analyst and a more-pronounced mutuality in the experience of the analytic relationship. One feature of what we could call a "good" analytic process may be such a "benign circle."

My view differs from Winnicott's at one point. His child has an illusion of omnipotent control over its transitional object. In my view, this illusion belongs to the "outer object" dynamics, and the transitional space has an intermediate position, between illusion and perception.

The extreme outer object is a psychotic experience (Britten 2007). The extreme at the other end, a perception totally without projection (subjectivity), is a virtual, "ideal" position, just as "normal," in the sense of completely nonneurotic, is an unreachable, ideal state. Most of our patients are in the intermediate area, retaining at least some space for interest in and curiosity about reality and other persons. Thus they may engage in a

---

5. I owe this last point to one of the reviewers of this paper.

"normal" transference relationship to the analyst, and a working through of internal object relations and resistances can take place. The result is a more-clear distinction between inner and outer reality—and probably a more-creative use of the possibilities in potential space.

Hämäläinen reflects on the anxiety that these questions confront us with, an anxiety awakened by the threat of existential aloneness of man (2009). Let us look at the three seminal analytic texts on loneliness. For Winnicott (1958), the capacity to be alone in the presence of another was both the result of a crucial developmental step and a sign of maturity. In contrast, Fromm-Reichman (1959) described the deep, painful experience of loneliness she encountered in her schizophrenic patients—a feeling state beyond words, an unbearable anxiety. Klein investigated the source of the inner sense of loneliness and thought of this state as "the result of a ubiquitous yearning for an unattainable perfect internal state" (1963, p. 300). She connected it to paranoid and depressive anxieties and, like Fromm-Reichman, saw loneliness as a part of schizophrenic and/or depressive illness. These views seem to coincide: In one form or another, loneliness is a general human experience. However, it becomes more malignant and painful in severe psychopathological states.

The argument in this paper invites us to an additional reflection. In one position we have the self in relation to a projected or transferred "outer object," undifferentiated from the internalized object. This experience may be connected to a state of deep loneliness because the relationship isn't a mutual, real relationship but a pseudorelationship, more like a psychotic state. In this view, the deepest loneliness belongs to the "outer object" dynamics. In the other position the experience of the other (as a person) is marked by separateness, but it is a separateness that includes a potentiality for relationships and thus for an alleviation of loneliness.

COMMENTS ON SOME THEORETICAL CONCEPTS IN RELATION TO THE MODEL

It is illuminating to compare the line of thinking in this paper with other models and conceptual distinctions. As long as the models share the epistemological basis and give transference and projection a role in the individual's perception of the world, we can expect convergences in points of view and concept formation. This is actually self-evident; the perspectives may differ, the phenomena, however, are the same.

In Segal's *symbolic equation* (1957), there is a breakdown of reality testing. The symbol or the word is equated with the thing it represents.

Thoughts are not distinguished from reality. To mention the name of a thing is to make it real; to have a wish is the fulfillment of it. In such an inner state, thought is omnipotent, exerting magical control of reality, like in the "outer object" position.

There is also a close connection between the two positions I have described and the two patient attitudes referred to by Steiner (1993): the need to be understood (by the therapist) and the wish to understand (oneself). This is not surprising: The wish to understand is the very expression of curiosity and of efforts to face reality. The same seems to go for Killingmo's (1989; 1995) distinction between conflict- and deficit-based psychopathology. In the former the therapeutic aim is the uncovering of unconscious conflicts by interpretations. This corresponds to position II in the model (figs. 1 and 2). In deficit-based pathological states, the therapeutic aim is different. The validation of meaning in self-experience (affirmation) has to precede the interpretation of unconscious conflicts. These patients have to be understood before they are able to be curious about and develop a wish to understand themselves.

Britton's "the third position" closely resembles my position II (fig. 1). Britton (1989) used this term to connote the child's capacity to observe the parents' relationship as a witness and not a participant and tolerate his feelings of love and hate in doing this.

> If the link between the parents perceived in love and hate can be tolerated in the child's mind, it provides him with a prototype for an object relationship of a third kind in which he is a witness and not a participant. A third position then comes into existence from which object relationships can be observed. Given this we can also envisage *being* observed. This provides us with a capacity for seeing ourselves in interaction with others and for entertaining another point of view whilst retaining our own, for reflecting on ourselves whilst being ourselves. (Britton 1989, p. 87)[6]

We note that Britton echoes the importance of tolerating one's feeling states, a point underlined by both Winnicott and Bion. And the last sentence in the quotation clearly anticipates a central element in the mentalization model (Fonagy et al. 2002).

Some Consequences of the Model

With this model as background, a central aspect of the psychoanalytic task becomes clear. We try to assist the patient in a movement from

---

6. For a recent discussion of the relation between oedipal dynamics and the conflict over knowledge (quest for self-knowledge and denial of reality), see Zachrisson 2013.

a state of fixed relations to a state of more-realistic relations, that is, from relations with persons as outer objects (distorted by projections of dominating inner object relations) to relations with persons who are separate and independent others. We can conceive this as a movement from a transferred "ghost of the past" to a relationship in its own right, with new possibilities of experience and learning (a "new object"). This ability to perceive the separateness and subjectivity of the other is strengthened by transference analysis and working through. It has been formulated as a process where the projections are taken back by the patient.

A side effect of this reflection is the observation that one aspect of "the third" position is the ability to differentiate between the (inner) object and the (actual) person. Thus, the third position establishes an interest in, and a curiosity about, reality and about the other as a real person in the mind of the perceiver. This formulation clarifies the function of the third position as a prerequisite for reality testing and for the capacity to learn from experience. Thus, the third position echoes the reflecting part of the empathic/reflective listening that is a crucial element of the analytic attitude (the analyst's evenly distributed attention).

We have to note the distinction between a "normal" and a "psychotic" transference. In the normal transference the analysand maintains an "as if" quality in the experience of the analyst. The analyst is invested with qualities of the object but is not (completely) identified with it. This kind of transference places the analyst in potential space, akin to Winnicott's transitional object. In contrast, when the patient *identifies* the analyst with the object, that is, when the analyst becomes an outer object for the patient, the "as if" quality of experience is lost, the patient enters a delusion, and reality testing breaks down.

Also in Freud's *Mourning and Melancholia*, we have recognized two contrary ways of facing the challenges of life. To turn one's eye to reality, embracing it with curiosity and interest, and to learn from experience—that is what makes mourning possible. The other way is to turn a blind eye to reality and deny it. As a consequence, thinking is replaced by magic and omnipotent control, and a process of mourning will never start. Thus, mourning plays an essential part in the movement of the self toward perception of reality: in the reintegration of split off parts of self and in the renouncement of the denial of separation and death, that is, accepting reality as it is (Caper 1992; Steiner 1996).

With these reflections in mind, I will return to the beginning of the paper and comment on the dilemmas that Hämäläinen formulated as a conclusion of his paper on the inner/outer relationship in psychoanalysis: How do we recognize another's subjectivity and remain genuinely conscious about it without succumbing to ultrarealism? How can we retain transitional phenomena and the associated omnipotence without succumbing to fundamentalism? And how can we interact with another, genuinely separate subject (2009, p. 1295).

The questions may sound esoteric and hairsplitting but are actually quite important. If the foundation of our thinking is unclear or ambiguous, the whole edifice remains unstable. Conceptual elasticity is necessary. So too is a quantum of clarity, and efforts to reduce muddy concept formation definitely have their place in psychoanalysis.

The ability to recognize the other's subjectivity and not see him as only an "objective" surface, the avoidance of fundamentalism (that is, the omnipotent illusion of knowledge of absolute truth), and the ability to perceive the other as a genuinely separate subject—all three of these abilities seem to depend on the perceiver's position in relation to other persons, his or her ability to perceive them as separate others. In contrast, when projection heavily distorts the image of the other person, we find ultrarealism (perceiving the other as a surface or a thing in the world), fundamentalism (truth is omnipotently determined by the self), and an inability to perceive the other's subjectivity. These follow from a deficient recognition of the other person as a separate other. Without a quantum of such recognition, the other is not perceived as a human being in his or her own right. The other remains an outer object, without autonomy and subjectivity.

REFERENCES

Bion, W. R. (1962a). A theory of thinking. *International Journal of Psycho-Analysis* 43:306–10.

——— (1962b). *Learning from Experience.* London: Karnac.

Bollas, C. (1987). *The Shadow of the Object.* London: Free Association Books.

——— (2006). Perceptive identification. *Psychoanalytic Review* 93:713–17.

Britton, R. (1989). The missing link: Parental sexuality in the Oedipus complex. In *The Oedipus Complex Today: Clinical Implications,* ed. R. Britton et al., pp. 83–101. London: Karnac.

——— (2007). *IPA Congress,* Berlin, July 27.

Caper, R. (1992). Does psychoanalysis heal? *International Journal of Psycho-Analysis* 73:283–92.

Evans, R. (1976). Development of the treatment alliance in the analysis of an adolescent boy. *Psychoanalytic Study of the Child* 31:193–224.

Fonagy, P, G. Gergely, E. Jurist, and M. Target (2002). *Affect Regulation, Mentalization, and the Development of the Self.* New York: Other Press.

FREUD, S. (1900). The interpretation of dreams. *Standard Edition*, vol. 5: 509–621.
——— (1911). Formulations on the two principles of mental functioning. *Standard Edition*, vol.12: 213–26.
——— (1912). Dynamics of transference. *Standard Edition*, vol. 12: 99–108.
——— (1914). On narcissism: An introduction. *Standard Edition*, vol. 14: 73–105.
——— (1915). Observations on transference-love. *Standard Edition*, vol. 12: 157–71.
——— (1917). Mourning and melancholia. *Standard Edition*, vol. 16: 24–258.
FROMM-REICHMAN, F. (1959). On loneliness. In *Psychoanalysis and Psychotherapy*, pp. 325–36. Chicago: University of Chicago Press.
HÄMÄLÄINEN, O. (2009). The relationship of inner and outer in psychoanalysis. *International Journal of Psychoanalysis* 90:1277–97.
KANT, I. (1781). *Critique of Pure Reason*. Trans. N. Kemp Smith. London: Macmillan, 1929.
KILLINGMO, B. (1989). Conflict and deficit: Implications for technique. *International Journal of Psycho-Analysis* 70:65–79.
——— (1995). Affirmation in psychoanalysis. *International Journal of Psychoanalysis* 76:503–18.
KLEIN, M. (1952). Some theoretical conclusions regarding the emotional life of the infant. In *The Writings of Melanie Klein*, vol. 3, pp. 61–92. London: Hogarth Press, 1975.
——— (1963). On the sense of loneliness. In *The Writings of Melanie Klein*, vol. 3, pp. 300–13. London: Hogarth Press, 1975.
LANGE, F. A. (1866). *Geschichte des Materialismus*. Leipzig: J. Bædeker, 1877.
LIEBMANN, O. (1865). *Kant und die Epigonen*. Erlangen: H. Fischer, 1991.
NOVICK, J. N., AND K. K. NOVICK (2001). Two systems of self-regulation. *Psychoanalytic Social Work* 8:95–122.
SANDLER, J. (1983). Reflections on some relations between psychoanalytic concepts and psychoanalytic practice. *International Journal of Psycho-Analysis* 64:35–45.
SANDLER, J. AND B. ROSENBLATT (1962). The concept of the representational world. *Psychoanalytic Study of the Child* 17:128–45.
SANDLER, J., AND A.-M. SANDLER (1998). *Internal Objects Revisited*. Forward by O. Kernberg. London: Karnac Books.
SEGAL, H. (1957). A note on symbol formation. *International Journal of Psycho-Analysis* 38:391–97.
SPILLIUS, E. B., J. MILTON, P. GARVEY, C. COUVE, AND D. STEINER. (2011). *The New Dictionary of Kleinian Thought*. London: Routledge.
STEIN, R. (1981). The unobjectionable part of the transference. *Journal of the American Psychoanalytic Association* 29:869–92.
STEINER, J. (1993). Problems of psychoanalytic technique: Patient-centred and analyst-centred interpretations. In *Psychic Retreats: Pathological Organisations of the Personality in Psychotic, Neurotic and Borderline Patients*, pp. 131–46. London and New York: Routledge.

——— (1996). The aim of psychoanalysis in theory and practice. *International Journal of Psychoanalysis* 77:1073–83.
TAUBER, A. I. (2009). Freud's dream of reason: The Kantian structure of psychoanalysis. *History of the Human Sciences* 22:1–29.
WINNICOTT, D. W. (1953). Transitional objects and transitional phenomena. In *Playing and Reality*, pp. 1–25. London and New York: Routledge, 1971.
——— (1958). The capacity to be alone. *International Journal of Psycho-Analysis* 39:416–20.
——— (1971). The use of an object and relating through identifications. In *Playing and Reality*, pp. 86–94. London and New York: Routledge.
ZACHRISSON, A. (1998). Transference: Polarities and paradoxes. *Scandinavian Psychoanalytic Review* 21:183–98.
——— (2013). Oedipus the king: Quest for self-knowledge—denial of reality. Sophocles' vision of man and psychoanalytic concept formation. *International Journal of Psychoanalysis* 94:313–31.

Commentary on Zachrisson

OLAVI HÄMÄLÄINEN, M.S. (PSYCH.)

This piece is a discussion of Anders Zachrisson's paper "The Internal/External Issue: What Is an Outer Object? Another Person as Object and as Separate Other in Object Relations Models." In this paper, Zachrisson referenced three questions that I had posed in a previous paper. Here, I clarify and elaborate on the terms internal object, actual person *and* illusion. *Zachrisson's and Winnicott's depictions of the capacity to be alone are compared and contrasted.*

ANDERS ZACHRISSON HAS WRITTEN A CLEAR AND IMPORTANT ARTICLE on the internal/external issue, which I believe to be a fundamental issue in psychoanalysis. He refers to the three questions from the discussion section of my paper "The Relationship of Inner and Outer in Psychoanalysis":

> How do we recognize another's subjectivity and remain genuinely conscious about it and . . . avoid sinking into ultra-realism?
> How can we retain transitional phenomena and the associated omnipotence without sinking into fundamentalism?
> And how can we interact with another, genuinely separate subject . . . ?
> (Hämäläinen 2009. p. 1295)

Since these questions arise from my paper as a whole, they could be difficult to understand without reading it. Therefore I would like to add some clarifications:

Ultra-realism is a life without a transitional world, without illusions of any kind, a completely rationalistic view of the world and other people. In my paper I wrote, "It would appear indisputable that, for our work, it is of vital importance that we do not impose our own experiential

---

Olavi Hämäläinen is Training and Supervising Analyst, Finnish Psychoanalytical Society.

The Psychoanalytic Study of the Child 67, ed. Claudia Lament, Robert A. King, Samuel Abrams, A. Scott Dowling, and Paul M. Brinich (Yale University Press, copyright © 2013 by Claudia Lament, Robert A King, Samuel Abrams, A. Scott Dowling, and Paul M. Brinich).

world on the other and that we always respect the other's separateness, leaving the final criterion for truth to him or her" (p. 1292).

This would be the realistic view of our patients. But in order to avoid being ultra-realistic:

> At the same time, we must nevertheless continuously rely on our own internal world, our own fantasies, our own feelings—or in Bionic terms, our reverie experiences—in order to be able to assist the analysands in their self-perception. This, then, demands that we pay particular attention to keeping in mind that we are always dealing with our own internal world. (ibid.)

In my paper I also depicted *private and common fundamentalism* as a situation in which we view our illusions as objective and singular truths—thus transforming illusions to delusions. This is the danger with illusions. But illusions are also needed in order to have potential space and to be able to be creative and empathetic.

Zachrisson writes, "Hämäläinen also notes that these questions have been avoided in psychoanalytic thinking, and offers the hypothesis that a reason for this is that they confront us with 'existential anxiety awakened by the threat of the essential aloneness of man'" (p. 1277).

Here I am not referring especially to these three questions in my discussion, as the reader might understand, but to the inner/outer issue as a whole.

FURTHER TERMINOLOGICAL CONSIDERATIONS

Zachrisson suggests the terms *internal object*, *external object* (sometimes *outer object*), and *actual person* (sometimes *other*) to differentiate the concept of object. In my article I was only differentiating between object and other. In my terminology object is always referring to the inner world, and other to the outer world. This other refers to *actual person* in Zachrisson's terminology. It is important to notice that Zachrisson's term *external object* also refers to the inner world, though it does not seem so; as Zachrisson writes, "External objects are internal objects externalized onto a person by projection or transference."

Thus an external object is the experience of the other disturbed by the internal object. Keeping this in mind, this becomes a very illustrative and clear way of differentiating between the other (the actual person) and an object.

Zachrisson writes, "My view differs from Winnicott's at one point. His child has an illusion of omnipotent control over its transitional object. In my view, this illusion belongs to the 'outer object' dynamics, and the transitional space has an intermediate position, between illusion and perception."

I have some difficulties understanding this statement. What is the difference between Zachrisson and Winnicott here? Is not an illusion a transitional phenomenon happening in a transitional space in Winnicott's thinking? And is not a transitional space in the intermediate position between inner and outer in his depiction? It is difficult to place transitional phenomena in the inner/outer distinction by their very nature, as I demonstrated in my paper (Hämäläinen 2009, pp. 1285–86). They belong to the field of experience and are therefore in fact internal (and belong to the outer object dynamics in Zachrisson's terminology). Most psychoanalysts are inclined to accept Winnicott's statement of these phenomena as being in intermediate position between the inner and the outer, because this depicts their true nature so well (Winnicott writes that the question about them being inner or outer should not be asked).

Zachrisson also asks how we can think about loneliness. "In one form or another, loneliness is a general human experience. However, it becomes more malignant and painful in severe psychopathological states." Winnicott writes about the capacity to be alone as a positive sign of maturity (1958).

I think that separateness leads to a challenge of existential loneliness. It can be tolerated if one has true contact with the separate other—not only with the outer object, if we use Zachrisson's terminology. And loneliness is possible to tolerate if one can miss others when one is alone engaging in psychic work on these feelings. This requires object constancy. This is the capacity to be alone as a mature achievement.

In my earlier paper I wrote:

> I think that when someone has enough capacity to be alone he can enjoy solitude but experience loneliness when left alone. He can also experience feelings of longing and needing as well as anger without losing the integrity of the self: He has a feeling that his unconscious part is taking care of him. He can also accept his separateness and the illusionary nature of complete sharing.
>
> On the other hand, when this capacity is not developed enough or is temporarily or permanently deteriorated by regression one cannot enjoy solitude, and when left alone, experience loneliness as a horror in the way Fromm-Reichman (1959) pictures it. She describes real loneliness as an experience where the fact that people existed in one's past, or may be present in one's future, is outside the realm of possibility. I imagine that this is an intolerable feeling for anyone and that it leads to defenses against needing anyone, which has the tendency to turn to paranoid

anxiety, where the fusion of aggressive and needing feelings creates an experience of threatening objects in the environment. The own, unconscious part is experienced as threatening, making attacks from within. (Hämäläinen 1999, p. 42)

Zachrisson writes, "For Winnicott (1958), the capacity to be alone in the presence of another was both the result of a crucial development step and a sign of maturity."

Winnicott actually writes, "The basis of the capacity to be alone is the experiencing of being alone in the presence of someone. In this way an infant with weak ego organization may be alone because of reliable ego support" (Winnicott 1958, p. 36).

An infant gets this ego support from his mother in the situation where he is alone in the presence of his mother. This forms the *basis* for this highly sophisticated capacity—as opposed to Zachrisson's reading of it being the consequence—which is closely related to emotional maturity.

Despite these notions Zachrisson's article is an important and clear statement in discussion about internal/external issue, and I enjoyed reading it. It was easy to read despite the difficulty in the terminology in this area, and for that reason I could recommend it for psychotherapy and psychoanalytic training programs.

REFERENCES

HÄMÄLÄINEN, O. (1999). Some considerations on the capacity to be alone. *Scandinavian Psychoanalytic Review* 22:33–47.

——— (2009). The relationship of inner and outer in psychoanalysis. *International Journal of Psychoanalysis* 90:1277–97.

WINNICOTT, D. W. (1958). The capacity to be alone. *International Journal of Psycho-Analysis* 39:416–20.

The Interface between Cyberspace and Psychotherapeutic Space

Relationship Avoidance and Intimacy in Adolescent Psychotherapy

ETZIONA ISRAELI, M.A.,
ZEHORIT ASULIN-SIMHON, M.A.,
AND RUTH SHARABANY, PH.D.

This paper documents one aspect of an adolescent boy's psychotherapy, as a basis for discussion of the theoretical issues for introducing cyberspace communication into psychodynamic therapy. The patient's "blogging" serves as a platform for consideration of several seemingly contradictory functions. It is an avenue for the patient to reveal himself while

---

Etziona Israeli is a Lecturer and Supervisor in the Postgraduate Program of Psychoanalytic Psychotherapy and former Chair of the Child-Adolescents track in the University of Haifa, Israel. She is a Clinical Psychologist at the outpatient clinic in Tel Aviv for adolescents in boarding schools, and is in private practice.

Zehorit Asulin-Simhon is a Clinical Psychologist in private practice. She is also a doctoral student in "Psychoanalysis and Discourse" at Bar-llan University, Rammat-Gan, Israel.

Ruth Sharabany is Associate Professor, Department of Psychology, University of Haifa, Israel, as well as former Chair of the Postgraduate Program of Psychoanalytic Psychotherapy and former Associate Editor of the *Journal of Social and Personal Relationships*.

The authors would like to acknowledge the important contribution of the reviewers to this paper.

An earlier version of this paper was presented at the conference of the International Association for Relational Psychoanalysis and Psychotherapy, Madrid, Spain, June–July 2011.

The Psychoanalytic Study of the Child 67, ed. Claudia Lament, Robert A. King, Samuel Abrams, A. Scott Dowling, and Paul M. Brinich (Yale University Press, copyright © 2013 by Claudia Lament, Robert A King, Samuel Abrams, A. Scott Dowling, and Paul M. Brinich).

maintaining comfortable control and also avoiding direct contact with the therapist and diluting communication. The blog writing allows for the regulation of emotions to some degree as well as an experience of solitude with an imagined audience. This therapy is in the context of the adolescent roller coaster—loss, anger, distancing while yearning for intimacy, and acting out. Changes in the therapy are mirrored by vicissitudes in the function and content of the blog. Cyberspace communication is a hallmark of the present generation. The implications of introducing it into adolescent therapy as well as refraining from it need to be considered. We attempt here to examine the role of this new space with regard to the patient, the therapist, the therapeutic relationship, and the course of therapy.

REALITY, THE INNER WORLD, AND THE "CYBERSPACE" BETWEEN THEM

PSYCHOTHERAPY IS CONCERNED WITH AN INDIVIDUAL'S INNER WORLD, his reality, and the interface between them. Technological developments have produced a third world for the individual—cyberspace. Cyberspace encompasses many different forms of communication these days, via e-mails, blogs, instant messages, the Web, and interactive games. These forms of communication present complex interferences within the therapy session, but also opportunities. They introduce new settings for psychotherapy in ways that require new regulations. We will discuss in what way exposure of the therapist to the virtual world of the patient can facilitate the therapeutic process by opening an additional channel of communication. At the same time, an invitation to view the virtual cyber world of the patient may reflect an impasse in the therapy, diverting the therapeutic encounter and serving as a defense mechanism—a way of avoiding direct contact with the therapist. Lingiardi (2008) provides two examples of the role that cyberspace plays within therapy. One example is of a patient who sent her therapist e-mails when he went on vacation. This example demonstrates how the use of e-mail facilitated therapeutic work on separation and loss and enabled the therapist to experience the intense anxiety that the patient was feeling. The second example serves to demonstrate how the use of the computer in therapy became like a shield that protected the patient from psychic pain. It cushioned the patient from the experience of painful contact with people in general and especially with the therapist. The example we bring here somewhat differs in that the therapist was only exposed to the patient's blog while regular therapy sessions continued, and there was no therapeutic communication via the Web.

Adolescents are often very familiar with cyberspace and have a better understanding of it than their therapists do, and it seems that they are as much involved emotionally there as in the real world (Steinberger, 2009). A 2010 U.S. survey reported that about 93 percent of teenagers between the ages of twelve and seventeen use the Web for different purposes (Lenhart et al., 2010). The virtual world influences the emotional development of adolescents in that they feel that it is not just an instrument or tool but also an object that influences their way of seeing the world, the way they think, and the nature of their relationships (Turkle, 2004).

We ask: In what ways is dwelling in cyberspace a defensive move on the part of the patient? Is it about avoiding direct contact with the therapist, using remote communication, and at times diluting the communication by making it public? Alternatively, to what extent does it facilitate progress within the therapy and serve as an invitation to the patient's internal world? Introducing cyberspace may facilitate the patient opening up and relating what is hard to convey face-to-face—a mode open to presenting personal matters and uncovering unconscious issues.

Emotional Maturation in the Cyberspace Age

We have to be reminded that adolescence is viewed as a stage in the cycle of life reminiscent of developmental disturbance (A. Freud, 1969; Kernberg, 1978). One window to the adolescent turmoil reveals the complexities in developing youth that are resolved in various ways as the adolescent matures. Separation-individuation processes are a window to adolescent developmental tasks and the kernel of adolescent maturation (Blos, 1967; Levy-Warren, 1999).

The road to the golden stage of an adolescent's separation from his primary objects—becoming an individual in his own right, yet not substituting isolation and coldness for closeness and intimacy—is a bumpy one. In search of this balance, alongside a progressive wish to separate and disengage from infantile ties of dependence, the adolescent deals with a regressive desire to unite with the object. These contrary desires fluctuate between the internal world, represented by object and self, and the actual relationship with parents and adults. In a traumatic context, such as the sudden loss of a parent at a young age, this process has additional burdens, as in the case presented here.

The therapist-adolescent relationship is caught up in these core developmental conflicts. While the therapist hopes to build intimacy and closeness in order to facilitate the therapy, the adolescent fears that intimacy is a slippery path toward dependency and identity loss.

Thus, while motivated to cooperate, the patient also strives to gain appropriate distance and reacts by canceling appointments and becoming antagonistic and silent (Esman, 1985). In the midst of this tumult, cyberspace enters the arena.

What is the role of cyberspace in this scenario? Does cyberspace open up new channels through which the adolescent may grow and deal with developmental burdens, or does it merely further complicate his life? In our modern society the computer occupies an important place for most of us and for adolescents in particular. It has changed how we experience ourselves, the people around us, and the world in general (Turkle, 2004). For regular users the computer has become an extension of themselves, like a new organ—it is their mind and memory, the door to social relationships (ibid.).

Interacting in cyberspace provides functions that are particularly relevant and useful to the adolescent. It can provide an arena for working on conflicts through role play while communicating on some level with other surfers, or as a way to connect with virtual communities that have the potential to help shape and define both the youth's identity and his/her relationships (Malatar, 2007).

Cyberspace offers an opportunity for immediate accessibility to others online, creating partnerships that can support and promote development. On the constructive side, an adolescent who suffers from social anxiety may find that a virtual community accepts him, makes him feel secure within it, and, for a while at least, that he is free of this anxiety. Finding a community that shares his interests and provides a social circle may change how the adolescent views himself. This experience can lead to actual changes in his behavior in the "real" world, be it to a greater isolation or a newfound social confidence. Cyberspace may provide users who feel lonely with a sense of belonging, and at times, can be a rehearsal space for social communication. However, it may also encourage a direct and immediate discharge of aggression, explicit sexual communication, and so on, thus hindering internal psychological processing that is conducive to maturity. Adolescents may find communities that provide them with detailed and dangerous information about drug abuse and suicide that support their emotional fluctuations. Thus, cyber communication provides opportunities for better and for worse.

The case presented in this paper raises a multitude of therapeutic dilemmas relating to the patient, the therapist, and the therapy process itself. We have chosen to focus on a single aspect—the patient-therapist relationship—as it unfolded in psychodynamic therapy when cyberspace entered the process. We do not propose treatment techniques but rather share the experience of the encounter between cyberspace and the therapeutic space and raise the questions based on what the therapist needed to deal with in her sessions with the adolescent.

BLAME, PAIN, AND HELPLESSNESS

At the age of fourteen Dan was referred to the therapist due to his outbreaks of anger and aggression toward his family and friends. He was described as an intelligent and excellent student who had an attention deficit and a history of attending psychotherapy throughout childhood.

During the first session Dan expressed a strong conviction that his home did not meet his needs. Dan's father was killed in an accident when he was three years old; his sister was born approximately two months after the death of his father; and when he was five years old his mother remarried a widower who introduced his own three children into Dan's home. Dan felt that he was living with someone else's family. Although the therapist could sense Dan's pain, she had difficulty feeling any closeness to him. He complained about his family and accused his mother of not knowing how to be a mother; he claimed that his stepfather did not know how to relate to him; he blamed the other children as they too suffered from an array of emotional difficulties, and the attention they required made him feel that they had ruined his life. Dan described a home, family and friends that had no order or logic. He jumped from subject to subject, which prevented the therapist from following his train of thought. He avoided connecting to his own pain, to which the therapist reacted with feelings of helplessness. The therapist found herself attempting to draw a picture of the events in his life and his emotional experiences but without success. She sensed that he was in great distress, which was expressed at home through aggressive behavior, but she felt shut out emotionally. Her own countertransference was a mix of pain and compassion, incoherence, and an aching rejection. Is this what he brought by way of his transference? And how much were the therapist's reactions the consequence of her own issues, her own sensitivities?

During the course of the therapy sessions, Dan became more and more introverted. He entered the room, sat down, and kept silent. While expecting the therapist to lead the conversation, he rebuffed her attempts scornfully, providing merely brief responses. Opposite the therapist sat a youth who was becoming increasingly angry. It seemed to her that he felt misunderstood. Their mutual frustration increased as their sessions were marked by lengthy periods of silence and a shared feeling of entrapment within them. Was he reproducing with the therapist the experience he was having with his family? The therapist had no entry at this stage and only attempted to survive, endure, and contain.

Absent-Present, Separate-Connected

During the summer holidays the sessions ceased. Dan attended a youth-leader course following which he planned to spend some time with his paternal grandmother.

In one hour, he explained that the reason for this visit was because his girlfriend, whom he had met during the course of therapy, had gone on vacation and he felt lonely without her. He surmised that he might feel better if he himself went away. The therapist was excited by his openness and his associating the separation from and missing his girlfriend with visiting his grandmother. Perhaps this had created an opening for them to explore his emotions. At this point Dan closed his eyes and pretended to have fallen asleep. Although the therapist experienced this as defiance and disinterest in the session, she also began to wonder about the separation from his girlfriend, herself, and the therapy, and his reconnecting with his paternal grandmother. She had been mourning the death of Dan's father, living with this painful loss every day. Dan's bond with his grandmother also seemed linked to their never-ending yearning for the same man. Dan's simulated sleep evoked within the therapy a strong sense of both presence and absence. Paradoxically, Dan was very present in the room during his "sleep." In that hour the therapist wondered silently if she too was both present for and absent from him, like his dead father. Shutting his eyes was not merely avoidance and defiance; now the therapist realized that this behavior was pregnant with meaning. In hindsight, could this have been an act of death but also of birth? Annihilating the world? Turning inward? There is an allusion to such symbolic behavior in poetry. For example, Sylvia Plath (1953) describes how one's closing of the eyes is like annihilating the world, while reopening them is like renewing everything, realizing that this very subjective experience feels like ending and creating the whole world.

Be-Logged: Belong to My Blog

Whilst the therapist was deep in thought, Dan opened his eyes, straightened himself in the chair, and said, "I open my blog every day and write in it." He said that while visiting his grandmother he would maintain contact with his friends, who read and responded to his blog. Surprised by this unexpected development, the therapist became curious; the room lit up and she was filled with hope that a new channel of communication had opened. It promised a means of escape from the frozen and frustrating therapy room to a more-vital space. As he described his blog, something in Dan changed and he transformed from dozy and depressed to excited and alive. The therapist was aware of the transformation in the room and was hopeful that something new was evolving that would perhaps allow them to achieve collaborative therapeutic work.

Now, as their session was drawing to a close, Dan, who was going to miss several meetings, asked the therapist for her e-mail address in order to send her his blog. She felt unable to refuse this request. She did not yet understand its meaning but sensed its importance and decided to give him her address. After the session the therapist was left with questions and reflections: Why did she immediately agree? Did she violate the therapy setting? Did her own countertransference of worrying about him and wanting to keep in touch take over at that moment? Was she attempting to circumvent a resistance issue that is so common in adolescent therapy? What would have been the meaning, and how might he have reacted had she refused his request in this last session before the break? And what had prompted Dan to invite her to read his blog at the last meeting before the vacation? Did it awaken his early feelings of the traumatic departure of his father when he was three years old? How was memory structured for him as the meaning of the past loss would have shifted in early adolescence? Did closing his eyes and not seeing the therapist, draw him closer to her? Did the moment of her own quietude in the hour remind him of his blog and open up the possibility of sharing it with her? Perhaps via the blog forum they would both experience the presence and absence of the other. Meanwhile, he had created a communication bridge, a transitional space between him and her to fill the time that he would be absent from therapy. Indeed, the request was made after he closed his eyes. They both agreed that once Dan had posted a new blog entry, the therapist would confirm that she read it by private e-mail. They would then discuss it at their next therapy hour.

The Transitional Space

Dan's blog was revealed to the therapist while he was on vacation. He relayed that he was missing his girlfriend and was making her a gift—a hammock to hang in her garden and relax in. From reading in his blog about his yearning for her and the hammock he was weaving, the therapist could see the two parallel tracks—his defiant, isolated, and silent self, which was evident in the therapy, while the more-hidden, tender feelings toward his girlfriend were quietly developing at the same time. The creation of the hammock and Dan's writing revealed gentleness and replaced with yearning what was missing in his life; the "web" of cyberspace was the "net" from which he was weaving his newfound close relationships.

The Interface between Two Spaces

When Dan and the therapist met after the break, they reflected upon Dan's blogging. They agreed that during the forthcoming therapy sessions they would discuss his writing. In his blog, Dan candidly described his relationships with his parents, siblings, and girlfriend. His harsh descriptions were filled with violence. The therapist was exposed to a powerful anger that had never before surfaced. It seemed that blogging gave him license to show his rageful feelings. In one of the following sessions, Dan spoke offhandedly of the physical harm he had inflicted upon himself. He rolled up his sleeve and showed the therapist his cuts and wounds. It seemed that cyberspace had opened a door to Dan's wounded world and enabled him to allow his therapist to touch his "painful lesions." What had arisen originally in cyberspace—written in a blog and e-mailed to all his readers—had now been introduced into the therapy room. He now faced a living person who showed concern and compassion for the wounds to his arms and the pain in his heart. The therapist gathered that he had described the events in his blog as they were happening in real time.

His writing was an attempt to communicate the feelings that were flooding him; it appeared to help him regulate their mixed and intense affect and block his impulsive acts of self-mutilation. His self-directed rage now found an outlet in his writing. He wrote:

> Anger. A lot and right now. . . . And unfortunately there is nothing else for me to do but to write and wait for it to pass. It's been a long time since I was angry. Not simple anger but real anger. Anger that creeps under the skin, under the flesh, the muscles, to the veins, the blood. . . . Anger which makes you grind your teeth. Anger which I have never been able to describe in words and which, naturally, ends in a fight. I could kill right now. I will get organized and go for a walk to pass the time. Maybe I will go to karate earlier tonight.

The therapist learned from his blog that what appeared to be his unwillingness to talk was actually his inability to articulate his moments of fury; perhaps an attempt to protect the therapist from his anger. They discussed his attempts to find ways to express his anger in less-harmful ways—by going to karate lessons rather than cutting himself, or leaving the house in order to avoid any temptation to hit someone.

THERAPEUTIC ISSUES OF INTEGRATING CYBERSPACE AND THERAPY

Nothwithstanding some of the advantages of Dan's blogging, the therapist found herself bewildered by other issues within their relationship. Who initiated the discussion of his blog, her or him? What could be done with the considerable amount of information contained within them? What needed to be talked about, and what could be set aside? To whom was he writing? Did he write indirectly to specific people, to the therapist? Did he imagine the therapist reading what he wrote, and imagine her reaction? Maybe he believed that by her reading his blog the therapist would understand what was happening in his life—that she was online with him all the time, following his life and his distress. Possibly, he saw the therapist like his father, whom he wanted to believe was with him and constantly watching over him. Did controlling the cyber communication with the therapist give him a sense of what he missed since the loss of his father? Perhaps Dan had invited the therapist into his virtual space in order to get closer to her, to minimize her misunderstanding of him. Perhaps the safe distance of cyberspace enabled them to become closer.

ANGER AND FURY AS MASKS FOR PAIN, MOURNING, AND LONGING

Later, they attempted to uncover some of the sources of his anger. The range of emotions in the room changed: Anger was replaced by melancholy and his fits of rage by a deep sadness. The fury disintegrated, and the underlying deep sorrow appeared in its stead. In one blog entry, Dan described the memorial service for his father at the cemetery. He wrote of how, when standing by the grave, he desperately tried not to cry. However, when his grandmother hugged him, his tears flowed without hesitation. He spoke about the sadness that had become his permanent companion, his envy of those who had a father and a normal family, the loss of his father and a family like the one everyone else had and for which he yearned so deeply. At this stage in the therapy, Dan worked on two parallel emotions—the difficulty for him to express his feelings of anger and rage without acting on them, and the difficulty for him to experience feelings of sadness and longing.

Rather than remaining dull and empty, the sessions became infused with more feelings of sadness, but they were also more alive as he was uncovering the realness of his psychic pain. The therapist wondered silently whether his writing represented his search for his dead father. It seemed that touching on his emotional pain and loss in the therapy stimulated powerful cravings for intimacy and even fusion. What prompted these speculations was Dan's expectations that his therapist follow him online at all times in order that she might respond immediately to his blogging. However, the therapist read the blog in her own time, and she responded privately and in confidentiality to his private e-mail address and not, as he had requested, in the public blog. Each time the therapist received his e-mail alerting her to a new posting, and perused it, her only response was: "Thanks. I read it. We'll discuss it in our meeting."

During this time Dan came to sessions early and eagerly. He talked about the therapy in his blog and even mentioned his therapist in positive terms. He also described how he was dealing with his anger and his desire for change, asking his friends for help. He apologized for his aggressive behaviors toward them and asked for their understanding. Dan wrote that he felt closer to his therapist and that therapy was helpful. He described a meeting in which he had managed to tell the therapist about his anger at his family, saying: "I took out all my anger . . . at my parents on the psychologist!"

Dan realized the significance of the therapeutic alliance and its contribution and managed to express it in his blog. When the therapist acknowledged that she had read the blog and understood that these meetings were important to him, he was embarrassed and said, "It was nothing." However, the urgency for the therapist to recognize the importance of therapy in his life was evident. From this session she understood that the plea to his friends for help and support was also addressed to her. She wondered openly to him about this possibility. Gradually, Dan was becoming more in touch with his need for others. At the same time, it awoke within him an accompanying anxiety: While Dan was becoming closer to the therapist, his fears and anxieties were increasing as he began to realize that the very person he was beginning to trust—the one who "had been found"—could also be lost.

The Downfall: Too Close, Not Close Enough

The therapist's interpretation that Dan's plea to his friends for help may also have been a sign that he was ready to accept help from her, was followed by a sharp change in his emotional state. He became extremely anxious and then disappointed. He felt that the therapist was not helping him make the change he so desired and needed. He was also frustrated that she did not respond to his blog publicly. (The therapist continued only to acknowledge, via a private e-mail, that she had read his latest posting.) He did not consider their talks in her office to be sufficient, and he attributed this to her indifference. He began to describe their therapeutic alliance as a business relationship only. In hindsight, the negative impact of the therapist's comment on his public plea for her help made him defensive, drove the therapeutic relationship downhill thereafter, and culminated in a suicidal threat.

Did the therapist prematurely vocalize what the patient needed to be kept in cyberspace—the place of unspoken words, where feelings are expressed, heard, and witnessed but are not directly acknowledged? The adamant demand that the therapist respond publicly to his blog was followed by the therapist's interpretation that he was asking for her help. Was this a trigger for his angry and resolute need to have more control over their exchange? The therapist's refusal to respond to him in a public space was viewed as abandonment, akin to an estrangement of family. Dan's need for the therapist to be online, watching and protecting him—perhaps like a good father—among other possible meanings was unfulfilled. He seemed to want an immediate response in order to feel her presence. Any attempt to understand and express what he needed from her did not placate his disappointment. His frustration and anger were expressed in his blog by a diminution of the value of the therapy and the therapist. His writing expressed open defiance. Dan referred to the therapist by name, describing his meetings with her as boring and useless. In ridicule, he wrote that he had dozed off in a session, causing the therapist pain. However, mentioning his dozing off also reminded her that it had happened right before his holiday, following which he had invited her to connect to his blog. The therapist interpreted this as a mixture of his intense need for her presence and his destructive fury.

Reading his blog during this period was uncomfortable and confusing for the therapist. She felt that Dan's impressions of her as weak and flawed were also being exposed to his readership. Their intimacy was being violated and their therapeutic relationship was being marred by the inclusion of anonymous others. During this period Dan did not show up to the sessions, usually without notice or explanation. He did not respond to the therapist's attempts to make contact by telephone or e-mail. In her desperate hope to save the therapy, the therapist reconsidered responding to his request to write in his public space but decided against it.

In his blog Dan described his emotional state in harsh terms, and in one of his reports he clearly expressed suicidal thoughts. The therapist was faced with an excruciating dilemma. The best course of action would have been to wait for their next session and discuss the blog at that time. However, she was very concerned for his welfare and was not certain that she could wait the few days until the next session, or if he would even attend the next session. The therapist found it impossible to assess the degree of seriousness of his suicidal intentions. Dan continued to refuse to respond to her calls and e-mails. The therapist left him a message that there was an urgent matter she needed to speak to him about, and if he did not respond, she would have to speak to his parents. Again, Dan did nothing. Consequently, the therapist informed his mother of her concerns.

Dan came to their next meeting angry with the therapist for informing his parents of the contents of his blog. He announced that he would probably not continue with therapy and, if he did, he would not talk. That same day, before disconnecting her from his blog, he wrote: "Whoever is wondering why I have changed the address of my blog, it can be summed up by stating that there are some people who I do not wish to read it." The therapist felt that the message was directed specifically at her and sensed a strong feeling of banishment and the closure of the window that had allowed her a glimpse into Dan's world.

Dan's parents were not successful in persuading him to attend the sessions, and he came for only one last farewell meeting. The therapist realized that their fourteen months of weekly meetings were coming to an end. During this session he expressed his contempt for the therapist and the therapy, claiming that all his needs were being met by activities and people that excluded her: "Karate is fun, I have regular contact with my friends, and my need to write is fulfilled by my blog." The therapist felt a deep sadness that this course of therapy had come to such an abrupt end. She contemplated whether this was how a child felt when his father suddenly died, believing it was because he had not been good enough. Was she living Dan's experience when he suddenly lost his father? Or was this construction simply her own way of trying to place a contextual framework around an ending that she felt was out of her control, one in which she felt some responsibility? Was her sadness simply her sadness, belonging to her and her alone within the context of losing a patient?

Discussion

Naturally, there was a sense that Dan's course of therapy terminated abruptly, and perhaps a different kind of intervention would have produced a more-positive outcome. One cannot ignore the context of adolescent therapy, and engaging adolescents in psychotherapy is a notorious issue (Meeks and Bernet, 1996). It is generally accepted that there is a 40–60 percent dropout rate for this age group in outpatient psychotherapy (Kazdin, 1995; Wierzbicki and Pekarik, 1993; Midgley and Target, 2005).

Various questions and dilemmas are present in this type of therapy: family issues; working with loss, aggression, and self-harm; the assessment of suicide risk; abrupt termination; and so on. However, in this case, while examining the impact of the blog, we have tried to focus only on the fluctuations between distancing and avoidance versus more intimacy that cyberspace afforded. The role of cyberspace is dual— enabling and facilitating an arena for therapy while potentially also distancing, defaming, and sabotaging the therapy itself.

Dealing with cyber communication raises a central issue of confidentiality, and the present case had specific features. While Dan was posting his own private thoughts and details on events as well as his relationship, for better or worse, with the therapist, there was no public breach by the therapist. She read the blog when he invited her to read it, and only acknowledged receipt via his private e-mail. Her acknowledgment contained only one sentence, leaving no opportunity for any content to be copied and pasted to the blog. Following the therapist's refusal to acknowledge or respond to the blog publicly, Dan expressed a central frustration that communication was one-sided. The therapist considered the blogging in some way as breaching the privacy of the therapy by the patient, and of course did not participate in the public domain of blogging. While we are focusing on the therapy processes and considering the in-depth meaning of the patient's wish and frustration, current literature about youth and cyberspace claims that the expectation for an immediate response is the norm of youth cyber communication (Mesch and Talmud, 2010; Mesch, 2013).

Dan had an issue with the loss of his father at an early age. This traumatic separation from a parent may have set the stage for special difficulties in dealing with separation. Of course, it is possible that Dan may have experienced problems with separation despite the death of his father. Given that dealing with separation is a central part of adolescence and growing up, dealing with the vacation-separation is particularly sensitive. Dan's blogging served a variety of complex and contradictory functions. He used blogging to bridge a separation gap and to keep a connection, while using it later to express and cause hurt, and then to cut himself off. He sat alone and expressed his emotions in writing. Yet, he was proclaiming his feelings to a wide audience of peers. Dan avoided the verbalization of his feelings to his therapist, whereas he let her read about them. He was able to connect to the anger and hurt he felt toward his family and later toward his therapist. Meanwhile, this very activity served to regulate his emotions. Thus, vicissitudes in the therapy process occurred and were being mirrored through the blog.

The therapist's reading of Dan's blog and the discussion of its contents during the therapy sessions gave him the feeling that he had a partner to his pain, that he was understood and not alone in his distressful and stormy world. For a while, he let someone recognize his pain and suffering. In fact, he once wrote in his blog that without the therapy his parents would never have known about his self-mutilation. His fits of anger and acting out lessened, and more space, both via the blog and in the therapy room, was devoted to his emotional pain. By the patient revealing his personal blog to the therapist, he entertained the idea that she knew him more intimately and understood both him and his world. The absence of the therapist's facial expressions and reactions supported the projection of being understood, not being separate, and avoided the anxiety of being misunderstood. The patient may have indulged in an illusion of synchronization and harmony between himself and his therapist.

For a significant chapter in the course of Dan's therapy he increasingly showed progress in his capacity to identify his own emotions and connect them to his actions. He dared to express publicly his positive feelings toward his therapist and the significance of therapy in his life. By acknowledging where he came from, via the blog, the therapist grew closer to the patient. Through his blog and their discussions about his writings, the therapist could see beyond his resistance. Dan opened a window to his experiences, his difficulty in controlling his urges, his fear of his impulses, the pain over the loss of his father, his fear of intimacy, and his suffering. All of this happened during the therapy period. Some of it was dealt with verbally and explicitly (for example, mourning, missing his father, not being able to know him, and so forth); some of this happened in his life (like being able to cry for his father, calling for help, and so on).

Nevertheless, the blog created unique challenges to the treatment. It may have created an abrupt move toward a personal and intimate closeness for both the patient and therapist. For Dan, revealing his dependency and neediness might have been premature. Overwhelmed, he denied altogether his need for a relationship and therapy. The shortcut to his internal world affected the therapist as well. She found it difficult to assess the risks of the suicidal intentions expressed in his blog. She became worried and reacted by intervening and contacting his parents.

Perhaps having had a more-solid emotional partnership between them could have enabled him to bear the renewed experience of his childhood—the loss of the father and, in turn, the confusion of depression and mourning. The blogging enabled them, at least to some extent, to deal with the storm of his anger. Yet, it was not sufficiently effective to support his neediness, depression, or suicidal threats.

Cyberspace combined with therapy enabled the patient's anger to find a secure outlet where he could express, understand, process, and uncover many affect states, including his sadness. However, both spaces—cyberspace and therapy—failed to maintain the delicate balance between the anger and yearning for dependence and the need for someone to fulfill his needs in the exact form the teen expected. The process of transforming the pain to a tolerable level might have required the live presence of the therapist. Perhaps without it, a sense of alienation and insecurity took hold. The opportunity for mutual dialogue, assessment, and revision was shut down.

The safe distance from the therapist that might facilitate free expression and the projected illusion of a comforting constant presence runs the risk of upending it into a sense of absence and loneliness, which happens unbeknownst to the therapist.

For Dan, cyberspace might have been a way to maintain an illusion of the total presence of his therapist in his life. Giving the therapist access to the blog, the patient protected himself from any sense of frustration resulting from the pain of one session's conclusion and waiting for the next—that is, he protected from absence, separation, and loss. When Dan did feel frustrated by his therapist, he used the blog to undermine the therapy, to try to embarrass and injure the therapist, and to remove himself from any potential help the therapist could give.

The written word has particular validity, evidence, and recognition, more so than the spoken word. While speaking to a therapist, one cannot be sure of being understood. A blog, directed specifically at the therapist, can be seen by the writer as a more-accurate recording of his emotions, without requiring him to actually acknowledge the existence of the therapist. Most important, writing the blog enables the maintenance of the paradox of having total intimacy while being avoidant. The adolescent gains a sense of personal control over the closeness on the one hand and maintains avoidance on the other, both of which are elusive.

Communication in cyberspace is also a hallmark of a generation gap. Introducing it into adolescent therapy may be compared to a family emigrating to a new country. The adolescent may become more easily acculturated than his adult therapist. The adolescent uses cyberspace as a new, intriguing, and enjoyable world to explore. Meanwhile, the therapist, like an immigrant parent, often lags behind and learns the language of the Internet and its twists and turns at a slower pace (Sharabany and Israeli 2008). In terms of countertransference, the therapist needs to work in a new and unfamiliar world. He or she is required to relinquish safe ground while at the same time is invited to participate in a "young" world. The therapist is at risk of being tempted into an illusion of youth devoid of the restrictions of place and time provided by cyberspace. He or she shares with the patient the illusion of creating an intimate relationship without any associated emotional pain.

Specifically in this case, the willingness of the therapist to read the blog exposed her to raw expressions of emotion and an in-depth familiarity with the youth's internal world. This dual sense of presence and absence, closeness and remoteness was experienced by the therapist, which sometimes confused and, most likely, reflected the experience of the patient. The question remains: To what extent was this feature prominent and specific to this therapy or is it one of the defining features of cyber communication?

Cyberspace has distinctive features that complicate and confound the therapeutic relationship: It is a virtual world, without physical presence; it can secure anonymity; the object and the subject are concurrently present while physically absent; one can imagine the other being totally present and freely projecting his reactions while remaining in total isolation and introversion. Cyberspace provides an invitation to securely reveal everything.

The introduction of cyberspace into therapy raises many dilemmas concerning the setting, the transference, the countertransference, and the management of the therapy. What is the emotional significance of a request to communicate over the Internet? What is the significance of the refusal or acceptance of this form of communication? Does the use of cyberspace promote or obstruct communication and express a desire to defend oneself from direct personal contact? To what extent is it a modern expression of resistance to therapy, or is it a new channel of communication that may support the therapy? What situations may help or harm the therapeutic process?

Once cyberspace finds its way into the course of therapy, a multitude of new decisions have to take place. How is the link between the two spaces managed? Who initiates what is to be discussed? How is the subject matter selected or ignored, assuming both patient and therapist know the content? How is the exposure of the therapist to old information that was there prior to therapy dealt with? Should it be ignored?

CYBERSPACE—THE PLAYGROUND OF THERAPIST-ADOLESCENT RELATIONSHIP VICISSITUDES

When the patient refers the therapist to his writings on the Internet, the therapist may consider this an expression of the patient's resistance and acting out. However, it may also be the search for an alternative facilitated communication enabling the expression of blocked emotions (Blos, 1963; Meeks and Bernet, 1996). It might be an easier means of communication, enabling the expression of emotions that the patient is struggling with and cannot articulate during a therapy session. Introducing blogging into therapy is infused with meaning that reflects the emotional and relational state. The use of the blog by the patient may protect the therapist and the therapeutic relationship. Cyberspace may provide the patient with a direct means of expression until such time as he feels more secure in speaking about these issues in the therapist's office and is able to process and integrate thought, emotion, speech, and action (Gabbard, 2001).

Judging from the way the therapy and blogging evolved in Dan's case, cyberspace was called upon initially to provide a transitional space to bridge the vacation-separation period. It then evolved into a security blanket for the patient, protecting him from acting out his urges and, for a period, even enabling him to bring and discuss these issues face-to-face in therapy. Dan's treatment presented an opportunity to follow his feelings and their vicissitudes in this cyber context. It filled a separation gap, offered a transitional and facilitative mode of communication, and prevented, for a while, a premature termination.

From this case and its multiple dilemmas, the need to consider new ground rules and definitions of setting emerge. In Dan's case, the issue of privacy took place in a specific way. While Dan's messages were public, the therapist made efforts to maintain privacy by only confirming that she had read the new posting via private e-mail. In the collaborative stage of the therapy, issues expressed in the blog were the basis for discussion in the session. The therapist then had to withstand the extended demand that she respond to the blog publicly. Dan actualized his own wish: He made public various aspects of the therapy (the name of the therapist, his feelings toward the therapy—first positive, then negative, and so on). Situations where the adolescent patient tells his circle of friends all about the therapy and the therapist are not uncommon. A significant difference may be that in Dan's case the therapist was invited and exposed to this content and she confirmed that she had read it. Under regular circumstances the therapist may or may not be aware of this breach of privacy. Thus, the issue of privacy may have various aspects. One can imagine a full continuum of degrees of public-private cyber communications of patient-therapist, each affording specific considerations.

Therapists in the twenty-first century cannot ignore technological developments and their place in the human experience. The question of whether to blog or not to blog (or to use other cyberspace options) is likely to present itself in therapy and to the therapist. The topic of cyberspace has arrived on our therapeutic shores and is here to stay.

REFERENCES

BLOS, P. (1963). The concept of acting out in relation to the adolescent process. *Journal of the American Academy of Child Psychiatry* 2:118–36.

——— (1967). The second individuation process of adolescence. *Psychoanalytic Study of the Child* 22:162–86.

ESMAN, A. H. (1985). A developmental approach to the psychotherapy of adolescents. *Adolescent Psychiatry* 12:119–33.

FREUD, A. (1969). Adolescence as a developmental disturbance. In *Adolescence*, ed. G. Caplan and S. Lebovici. New York: Basic Books.

FREUD, S. (1905). Three essays on the theory of sexuality. In *The Standard Edition of the Complete Psychological Works of Sigmund Freud*, ed. J. Strachey. Vol. 7, 136–243). London: Hogarth Press.

GABBARD, G. O. (2001). Cyber passion: E-rotic transference on the Internet. *Psychoanalytic Quarterly* 70:719–37.

KAZDIN, A. (1995). Bridging child, adolescent, and adult psychotherapy: Directions for research. *Psychotherapy Research* 5:258–77.

KERNBERG, O. F. (1978). The diagnosis of borderline conditions in adolescence. *Adolescent Psychiatry* 17:298–319.

LAUFER, M., AND E. LAUFER (1984). *Adolescence and Developmental Breakdown*. London and New York: Karnac Books.

LENHART, A., K. PURCELL, A. SMITH, AND K. ZICKUHR (2010). Social media and mobile Internet use among teens and young adults. Available online at http://pewinternet.org/Reports/2010/Social-Media-and-Young-Adults.aspx. Accessed May 4, 2013.

LEVY-WARREN, M. H. (1999). I am, you are, and so are we: A current perspective on adolescent separation-individuation theory. *Adolescent Psychiatry* 24:3–24.

LINGIARDI, V. (2008). Playing with unreality: Transference and computer. *International Journal of Psychoanalysis* 89 (1): 11–127.

LITOWITZ, B. E., AND R. A. GUNDLACH (1987). When adolescents write: Semiotic and social dimensions of adolescents' personal writing. *Adolescent Psychiatry* 14:82–111.

MALATAR, E. (2007). Caught in the web: Patient, therapist, e-mail, and the Internet. *Psychoanalytic Review* 94 (1): 151–90.

MEEKS, J. E., AND W. BERNET (1996). *The Fragile Alliance*. Melbourne, Australia: Krieger Publishing.

MESCH, G. S. (2013). Media and peer sociability. In *Routledge International Handbook on Children, Adolescents and Media*, ed. D. Lemish. New York: Routledge.

MESCH, G., AND I. TALMUD (2010). *Wired Youth: The Social World of Adolescence in the Information Age*. New York: Routledge.

MIDGLEY, N., AND M. TARGET (2005). Recollections of being in child psychoanalysis: A qualitative study of a long-term follow-up project. *Psychoanalytic Study of the Child* 60:157–77.

PLATH, S. (1953). Mad girl's love song. Available online at http://allpoetry.com/poem/8498479-Mad_Girls_Love_Song-by-Sylvia_Plath. Accessed May 4, 2013.

SHARABANY, R., AND E. ISRAELI (2008). The dual process of adolescent immigration and relocation: From country to country and from childhood to adolescence—Its reflection in psychoanalytic psychotherapy. *Psychoanalytic Study of the Child* 63:137–62.

STEINBERGER, C. B. (2009). Cyberspace: The nodal self in the wide world—Adolescents signing-on. *Psychoanalytic Review* 96 (1): 129–44.

TURKLE, S. (2004). Whither psychoanalysis in computer culture. *Psychoanalytic Psychology* 21:16–30.

WIERZBICKI, M., AND G. PEKARIK (1993). A meta-analysis of psychotherapy dropout. *Professional Psychology: Research and Practice* 24:190–95.

Acute Onset of the Sinking Feeling in the Elderly

A Case Report and Addendum to an Article Published in This Annual in 1984

JOHN HITCHCOCK, M.D.

During a recent review of S. Freud's "Elisabeth von R.," the author experienced a forme fruste of the sinking feeling he had described in this annual in 1984. He avers that his current reaction promoted a more-nuanced analysis, and advocates the rereading of classic psychoanalytic literature.

THE CONTEXT: WHILE (RE)READING FREUD'S EARLY CASE HISTORIES for a study of the particular responsibilities of the psychoanalyst, a work in progress, the author "happened" across the following. Freud's patient Frau Cäcilie M. described a sensation in her throat, preventing a response when she had felt insulted. Simultaneously she had the thought, "I shall have to swallow this." Freud goes on to express his conclusion that the mechanism in conversion reactions is based on symbolization (Freud 1892). I made no reference to this passage in my 1984 article.

Précis: My article "The Sinking Feeling" (Hitchcock 1984) defines the event as a brief sensation akin to a transitory depression located most commonly in the abdomen. The thought "Oh, no!" often accompanies the feeling. Focusing attention on the circumstances preceding the event may elucidate the precipitating dynamics. Freud's paper "Negation" (Freud 1925) and Anthony's paper on screen sensations (An-

---

Dr. Hitchcock is a retired psychoanalyst. He was a Training and Supervising Analyst and Supervisor in child and adolescent analysis in the Pittsburgh Psychoanalytic Institute.

The Psychoanalytic Study of the Child 67, ed. Claudia Lament, Robert A. King, Samuel Abrams, A. Scott Dowling, and Paul M. Brinich (Yale University Press, copyright © 2013 by Claudia Lament, Robert A King, Samuel Abrams, A. Scott Dowling, and Paul M. Brinich).

thony 1961) provide a framework for exploring the sinking feeling as a phenomenon in which the subject feels both forced to and capable of "swallowing" a previously denied aspect of reality. The clinical psychoanalytic context offers a particularly felicitous opportunity to integrate the past, present, and transference aspects of the sinking feeling.

Although my immediate response on recognizing a work having particular relevance, even priority, to my contribution, was awareness of a brief gut reaction, my next thoughts bespoke a "higher" order of a defensive posture.

> 1. Was this simply an instance of *lapsus memoriae*, propelled by the blind ambition of youth (anything under eighty)? Was I *really* aware of Fräulein Elisabeth? Of course I had read the case studies, probably more than once, and I have always been drawn to metaphorical constructs. I use the specific imagery of having to swallow something in my article (1984, p. 325).
> 2. Could all those psychoanalytic luminaries in my list of credits have failed to remind me? And what of the editors and reviewers of the annual (outsourcing responsibility)?
> 3. Does my strong negative reaction to plagiarism reflect a suspicion that I am susceptible?

As I was "brought up short" at my discovery of what I hadn't known that I knew, I reflected on my vulnerability to this dynamic over the course of my lifetime, many such instances dating from earlier than three years of age through young adulthood. That I could not possibly have integrated these things at the time, due to the associated affect, seems perfectly reasonable now.

A bonus to this bit of self-reflection was afforded by Erikson when he says, "The resulting compulsive preoccupation with the repetition of meaningful memories—rather than being only symptomatic of mere helpless regressions may well represent a 'regression in the service of development' in Peter Blos's (1980) term: for, in fact, there are now new age-specific conflicts for the sake of which the old person's sense of 'I' must become free" (1984, p. 162).

I conclude that once again a careful mining of Freud's writings continues to yield riches, even for the octogenarian.

BIBLIOGRAPHY

ANTHONY, E. J. (1961). A study of "screen sensations." *Psychoanalytic Study of the Child* 16:211–45.
ERIKSON, E. H. (1984) Reflections on the last stage—and the first. *Psychoanalytic Study of the Child* 39:155–65.

FREUD, S. (1892) Case histories (5): Fräulein Elisabeth von R. In *Standard Edition*, vol. 2: 135–81.
FREUD, S. (1925). Negation. In *Standard Edition*, vol. 19: 235–39.
HITCHCOCK, J. (1984) The sinking feeling. *Psychoanalytic Study of the Child* 39:321–29.

Index

Abnormally normal, 251
Abrams, S., 86, 88, 89, 91, 93
Abreaction, 198
Abuse and neglect. *See* Child abuse and neglect
Acceptance and commitment therapy (ACT), 166
ACP (Association for Child Psychoanalysis), 150, 151, 168
ACT (acceptance and commitment therapy), 166
ADHD, 200, 207
Adler, A., 17, 67
Adolescence: aggression during, 282, 283; body identity of females, 47–48; developmental tasks of, 59, 103, 105, 106, 129; emotional maturation during, 281–83; father's role during, 129; individuation/separation issues during, 281–82, 291–92; killing fantasies of male adolescent, 188–90; parent–adolescent relationship, 59; peer relations during, 59, 61–63; romantic relationships during, 115–16; self-harm during, 286–87, 291; sexuality during, 59, 63; sibling trauma during, 9, 42–49, 59–64; and suicidal feelings, 118–19, 122, 282, 289–90, 292–93. *See also* Adolescent psychotherapy; Concurrent work with parents of adolescent patients; Cyberspace communication
Adolescent psychotherapy: absent-present, separate-connected issues during, 284, 293–94; advantages of cyberspace communication in, 295; anger of male client during, 283, 286–90, 292, 293; blame, pain, and helplessness of male client during, 283–84; challenges in use of cyberspace for, 292–96; clinical example of, 283–93, 295; confidentiality in, 291; countertransference in, 294; cyberspace communication in, 279–96; dropout rate for, 291; and emotional maturation, 281–83; mourning by male client during, 287–88, 291; privacy issues in, 288–90, 295–96; questions on use of cyberspace with, 285, 287, 289, 294; self-harm by male client in, 286–87, 291; termination of, 290; and therapeutic alliance, 288–90, 292, 295–96; transitional space in, 285–86, 295
Adoption, 158–62
Adults: changes in sibling relationships in adulthood, 49; and impact of Holocaust on survivors' children, 215–43; memories of infantile trauma by adult female, 207–10, 211, 212–13; and sibling trauma, 41–49, 73–82
Affect, 157
Affect Regulation, Mentalization, and the Development of the Self (Fonagy), 156–57
Agger, E., 39, 49–50
Aggression: during adolescence, 282, 283; assertion versus, 120–22; S. Freud on, 36; A. Freud on, 36; and Holocaust survivors' children, 225–29, 241; Klein on, 38; of toddlers, 58, 59. *See also* Anger
Aichhorn, A., 150, 164
Ainslie, R. C., 37
Akhtar, S., 37
Alice case, 178–85
Allen, J. G., 157n8
Allen Creek Preschool, Ann Arbor, 168
American Psychoanalytic Association (APsaA), 150
Analysis. *See* Adolescent psychotherapy; Child psychoanalysis; Countertransference; Termination; Transference
"Analysis of a Phobia in a Five-Year-Old Boy" (S. Freud), 152
Analysis of the Self, The (Kohut), 155–56, 160n10
"Analysis Terminable and Interminable" (S. Freud), 88
Analytic Service to Adolescents Program (ASAP), Chicago, 164

Index

Anger: of adolescent males in psychotherapy, 111, 118, 126, 283, 286–90, 292, 293; of analyst, 46; of children in psychoanalysis, 179, 182, 189; of fathers, 110, 121, 133, 263; of Holocaust survivors and their children, 222–23, 225, 226, 241; of parents, 133; and sibling trauma, 9, 43–44, 46, 48, 60, 70, 94. *See also* Aggression
Angier, N., 211
Anna Freud Centre, 163, 174
Ann case, 73–76, 79–82
Anthony, E., 298–99
Anxiety: of adolescents, 114–17; of mothers, 114–17, 119
APsaA. *See* American Psychoanalytic Association (APsaA)
Arlene case, 41–49
ASAP. *See* Analytic Service to Adolescents Program (ASAP), Chicago
Assertion versus aggression, 120–22
Associaton for Child Psychoanalysis (ACP), 150, 151, 168
Ast, G., 22n5
Asulin-Simhon, Z., 279–97
Attachment, 155, 156, 159, 241
Attachment, Separation, and Loss (Bowlby), 155
Attention deficit hyperactivity disorder (ADHD), 200, 207
Auerhahn, N. C., 215–34
Autism, 68
Autobiographical memory. *See* Episodic memory
Autonomy of Holocaust survivors' children, 225–29, 241

Bailly, L., 157
Baker-Ward, L., 201
Balsam, R., 6–8, 35–52, 86, 90
Bank, S., 37
Barish, K., 157
Barrie, J. M., 56
Barthes, R., 216
Basil case, 118–22
Bassin, D., 86, 90
Bateman, A. W., 157n8
Bauer, P. J., 201
Bauer, Y., 236
Becca case, 61–64
Bell, S. M., 157
Benedek, T., 105
Benjamin, J., 10, 11, 37, 67, 70–72, 89, 90
Benson, R., 130
Bergman, A., 157
Berlin, I., 224

Bernet, W., 291, 295
Bernfeld, S., 150, 153n4, 164
Best, C., 201
Bethany case, 76–82
Bion, W., 31, 38, 256, 257–60, 270
Biringen, A., 90
Birth order of siblings, 17, 92–93, 95
Blog writing. *See* Cyberspace communication
Blos, P., 59, 281, 295, 299
Bodenstab, J., 241
Body identity, 47–48, 58
Bohleber, W., 240
Bollas, C., 218, 228, 250–51, 253, 257, 257nn3-4
"Borderline" personalities, 156–57n8
Bosmajian, H., 164
Bowlby, J., 155, 156
Brad case, 186–88, 192
Brand, A. E., 160
Brazil, 20
Brent Consultation Centre, 168
Breuer, J., 157
Brinich, E. B., 159, 163
Brinich, P. M., 149–72
British Psychoanalytical Society, 162–63
Britton, R., 268, 270
Brothers, 28–29, 28n6, 71. *See also* Siblings; Sibling trauma/experience; Sisters
Buergenthal, T., 239
Buhler, C., 23–24
Bukeit, M. J., 232
Burlingham, D., 37, 155, 164, 191
Byatt, A. S., 39

Cammie ("wild child") case, 197–213
Caper, R., 271
Cassell Hospital, 168
Castration complex, 16, 25, 26, 28
CBT (Cognitive Behavior Therapy), 114, 117, 166
Ceci, S. J., 201
Charcot, J.-M., 4, 15
Chess, S., 157
Child abuse and neglect, 186–88, 192, 197–213, 239
Child custody, 164
Childhood and Society (Erikson), 154
Childism: Confronting Prejudice against Children (Young-Bruehl), 153
Child-Parent Psychotherapy (CPP), 165
Child psychoanalysis: additional strands of, 157–58; assumptions underlying, 128; and attachment, 155, 156, 159; of children without a well-defined neurosis, 173–93; clarification and verbalization

in, 178–81; conflicts within, 162–63; construction and reconstructive fantasy in, 46; decline in clients for, 163–64; developmental history of field of, 149–67, 166n12; doll play in, 179, 182; and ego and mechanisms of defense, 154; externalization and projection in, 181–84; and A. Freud, 106, 130, 131, 152, 168, 173–93; goals of, 106, 131, 139, 166, 270–71; importance of therapeutic alliance, 130; and Klein, 130; knowledge base of, 165; Loewald on fantasy character of, 45; and mentalization, 156–57, 159, 161; multimodal techniques for, 107; music metaphor for, 168n16; and neuropsychoanalysis, 156, 159, 161; and nonanalytic data, 159–60; and object relations (or representation), 153–54; parent-child dyad as unit of assessment and unit of treatment, 104; personal resilience needed by therapists for, 165–66; practical applications of, 164; and pride in self, 184–85; regression in, 49–50, 60; and self psychology, 155–56, 159, 160–61; and separation anxiety, 61; and sociocultural environment, 154–55, 159; suggestions on development of, 166–68; theater metaphor for, 8, 35, 40; and trauma, 157, 159, 161–62; and unconscious drives, 151–53, 159; weaving metaphor for, 149–68. *See also* Adolescent psychotherapy; Concurrent work with parents of adolescent patients; Countertransference; Termination; Transference

Children of Holocaust survivors. *See* Holocaust
Child Study Center, Yale University, 168
China, 20
"Chinese Lobster, The" (Byatt), 39
Chodorow, N., 70, 90
Christina case, 127
Cleveland Center for Research in Child Development, 167
Clinical Discussions with Anna Freud, 1970-1971, 173–93
Cobliner, W. G., 155
Cognitive Behavior Therapy (CBT), 114, 117, 166
Cohen, D., 58, 59, 88
Cohen, J., 224
Cohler, B. J., 150
Coles, P., 19n3, 37
Colonna, A. B., 35, 37
Computers. *See* Cyberspace communication

Conceptions, 257, 258–60
Concepts, 257
Concurrent work with parents of adolescent patients: affects/anxieties of parents in, 108; alliance tasks for parents in, 108, 130; assumptions underlying, 105–6, 128–29; beginning phase of, 108–9, 112–15, 119; and centrality and importance of parents, 133; and confidentiality issues, 105, 112, 132–33; and developmental point of view, 127–29; and developmental task of parents, 103, 106–7; difficulties of, 124; and divorced parents, 126–27, 145; evaluation phase of, 108–12, 119; and family history, 125–26; and father's role, 129; with female adolescent, 114–17, 127, 143, 144, 145; full range of therapeutic techniques used in, 130–31; goals of, 106, 109, 131–32, 137–39, 142–45; importance of therapeutic alliance in, 130; with male adolescents, 110–14, 117–26; middle phase of, 108–9, 115–20; parenthood-phase components in, 109; predetermination phase of, 108–9, 120–22; and privacy versus secrecy, 112, 132–33, 144–45; reasons for, 103–10; resistances/defenses of parents in, 108, 124–25, 144; and separateness versus separation, 103, 106, 108–9, 112, 139–40; summary chart on, 108–9; technical recommendations on, 130–33; termination phase of, 108–9, 122–24; therapist's techniques, interventions, and goals in, 109, 141–45; transference-countertransference complexities in, 137, 141–45; transformation in, 103, 106, 108–12, 114, 117–20, 126–29, 133, 137, 140–41
Confidentiality: and cyberspace communication, 290, 291; and parent work, 105, 112, 132–33
Conflict-based psychopathology, 270
Constructions versus interpretations, 32
Continuity fallacy, 85
Conversion reactions, 298
Countertransference: in adolescent psychotherapy, 294; Agger on, 39; and cyberspace communication, 294; misconception of, 85; in parent work, 137, 141–45; sibling countertransference, 54; theater metaphor for, 8, 35, 40
CPP (Child-Parent Psychotherapy), 165
Craig case, 188–90
Crisis of nonuniqueness. *See* Sibling trauma/experience

Cyberspace communication: and absent-present, separate-connected male adolescent, 284, 293–94; in adolescent psychotherapy, 279–96; adolescents' use of, 281; advantages of, in adolescent psychotherapy, 295; blogging as, 284–93, 295; challenges in use of, for adolescent psychotherapy, 292–96; clinical example of, 283–93, 295; and confidentiality, 291; and countertransference, 294; as defense mechanism, 280, 281, 291, 293; distinctive features of, 294; e-mail as, 280; and emotional maturation during adolescence, 281–83; and generation gap, 294–95; privacy issues in, during adolescent psychotherapy, 288–90, 295–96; questions on use of, in psychotherapy, 285, 287, 289, 294; and therapeutic alliance, 288–90, 292, 295–96; as transitional space, 285–86, 295; types of, 280

Dan case, 283–93, 295
Dann, S., 29
Danto, E. A., 164, 167n13
DBT (dialectical behavior therapy), 166
Death instinct, 36
Defenses: cyberspace communication as, 280, 281, 291, 293; A. Freud on, 143–44, 154, 183–84; S. Freud on, 143; and trauma generally, 159
Deficit-based psychopathology, 270
Delay mechanism, 254
Delbo, C., 228
De Marneff, D., 58
Denial, 143, 144, 232, 239, 260
Dent, V., 39–40
Detour mechanism, 254
Developmental theory, 157
DeVito, E., 106, 142
Dialectical behavior therapy (DBT), 166
Differentiation: clinical examples on, 73–82; definition of, 66, 69; and Oedipus complex, 69; relationship consequences of, 69–70; sibling differentiation, 10, 37, 66, 69–70; sibling recognition of differentiated identity, 72–73
Disposition, 12, 84–86, 88–89, 93–96
Dissociation, 16
Divorce, 126–27, 145
Dowling, S., 137–45, 241
Dreams and nightmares: of children of Holocaust survivors, 231, 233, 234; in Craig case, 188; S. Freud on, 16, 253–54, 254; of Holocaust survivors, 222, 228; and infantile trauma memories, 198, 206–7, 209, 210, 212; and sibling trauma, 17, 19n3, 21, 56, 63; as symptom of trauma generally, 22; waking nightmare, 262
Drives, 151–53, 159, 250, 252, 254

Eddington, A., 15
Edgcumbe, R., 175
Edward, J., 37
Ego: and child psychoanalysis generally, 157, 159; A. Freud on, 154, 155, 160, 177, 180–81; S. Freud on, 252, 254, 258; Klein on, 255
Ego and the Mechanisms of Defense, The (A. Freud), 154
Ego psychology, 36, 38, 40
Ehrensaft, D., 164
Elderly, 298–300
Ellman, S., 38n1
Emde, R. N., 90
Environmental seduction, 183
Envy, 30, 48, 93
Epigenetic principle, 156, 166
Episodic memory, 200–213
Epistemological stance, 251–52, 253, 256, 258, 269
Erikson, E., 127, 154–56, 158, 166, 299
Eros, 36
Esman, A. H., 282
Eth, S., 157
Evans, R., 267
Event memory. See Episodic memory
Externalization, 181–84
External objects. See Internal/external issue

Fackenheim, E., 239
Faimberg, H., 225, 239
Falsifying trends, 86
Fantasies. See Incest fantasies; Murder fantasies
Father-child relationship: and adolescent females experiencing sibling trauma, 59–62; and adolescents generally, 129; and adult female with younger sister, 41, 43, 47–48; and anger of father, 110, 121, 263; and "Law of the Father," 7, 26, 29, 40; male adolescent's mourning for father's death, 287–88, 291; as outside of mother-infant dyad, 70–71; and separation process, 40. See also Concurrent work with parents of adolescent patients; Mother-child relationship; Parent-child relationship
Fenichel, O., 36
Fivush, R., 201

Fonagy, P.: on dissociated core of the self, 230, 231; on mentalization, 156–57, 156–57n8, 259, 270; on pretend mode, 57; on reality as children's subjectivity mediated by caretakers' objectivity, 217, 225
Fortunoff Video Archive for Holocaust Testimonies, Yale University, 219
Fosha, D., 229, 239
Fosshage, J., 40
Foster children, 164
Fraiberg, S., 164
Frank case, 117–18, 125–26
Freud, A.: on adolescence, 281; on Alice case, 178–85; and American Association for Child Psychoanalysis, 150; on attachment, 155; on Brad case, 186–88, 192; on child analysis, 106, 131, 168, 173–93; child analysis by, 130, 152; on childhood disturbance, 89; childhood of, 150; on concentration-camp children, 29; and conflict between Kleinians and Freudians, 162–63; on Craig case, 188–90; on death instinct, 36; death of, 144; on defenses, 143–44, 154, 183–84; on developmental lines, 93–94, 152, 154; on developmental process, 86, 87–88, 93–94, 152; on disposition, 86, 89, 93–94; on ego, 154, 155, 160, 177, 180–81; on environmental seduction, 183; on Erikson, 155n7; on goal of child analysis, 106, 131; and Hampstead Clinic, 150, 158, 167; and Hampstead War Nurseries, 164, 168; hobby of, 151; on hysteria, 17; on Kohut, 160; and M. Kris, 150; "Metapsychological Profile" by, 154, 158; on object relations, 177, 186–87, 189; on openness to influence, 181; on psychoanalytic education, 165–66; on sex and aggression, 36; on "Sophie" case, 162; on superego, 154, 177; on treatment of children without a well-defined neurosis, 173–93
Freud, S.: on aggression, 36; on brothers, 28–29; on castration complex, 16, 28; on cerebral palsy in children, 149; on children between ages of two and four, 23; on constructions versus interpretations, 32; on conversion reactions, 298; on death instinct, 36; on defenses, 143; on developmental process, 87, 88, 152; on disposition, 12, 85, 88–89; on drives, 250, 252, 254; on ego, 252, 254, 258; epistemological stance of, 251, 256; on Eros, 36; fees charged by, 167n13; friendship between Rie and, 149–50; on genital stage, 38, 38n1; grandson of, 30, 31; on hysteria, 16; on infantile phobia, 24, 152; on infantile sexuality, 25; on infants, 28, 30, 31; Klein compared with, 38, 38n1; Lacanian and Marxist readings of, 36; on lay analysis, 165; on "Little Hans" case, 15–16, 24, 28, 152; on mother-child relationship, 104; on mourning and melancholia, 254–55, 260, 271; on narcissism of minor differences, 14n1; on nature-versus-nurture debate, 127, 128, 140; and neurology, 156; on object for a drive, 250, 252, 260; on Oedipus complex, 17, 35–36, 38n1; on parent-child axis, 7, 8; on perceptual identity and thought identity, 253–55, 258–59, 260; on phases of libidinal development, 152; on pleasure and reality principles, 254, 260, 266–67; on pride in self, 184–85; on "seduction theory" of trauma, 16, 17; on separation of sexuality and reproduction, 25, 27; on sexual difference, 25; on siblings, 17, 26; on superego, 254; on theory versus observation, 15; on transference, 267; on transformation of puberty, 140; on trauma, 31–32, 157; on unconscious, 251, 254. *See also specific works*
Freud's Free Clinics (Danto), 164
Friar, K., 152n3
Fromm-Reichman, F., 269
Fundamentalism, 253, 272, 275, 276
Furman, E., 105

Gabbard, G. O., 295
Galasinski, D., 90
Garcia, J., 130
Geertz, C., 218
Gelernter, D., 243
Gender: feminine-based associations to word *sibling*, 5–6, 90, 91; feminist view of, 27; and gender role identity, 89–90; internalized gendered family discourse, 46–49; meaning of, 25–26; and phallocentrism, 3–5, 11, 12, 84–86, 90, 91, 96; sibling trauma and gendering, 24–28; toddler's awareness of, 58
Gender distinction, 26
Gender role identity, 89–90
Gergely, G., 86
Gerson, S., 217, 224
Ghana, 20
Giedd, J., 128
Gilmore, K., 7, 8–9, 53–65, 85, 86

Goals: of concurrent work with parents of adolescent patients, 106, 109, 131–32, 137–39, 142–45; of psychoanalysis, 106, 131, 139, 166, 270–71
Goenjian, A., 157
Goldstein, J., 164
Graham, I., 54
Green, A., 228
Greenberg, I., 243
Grubrich-Simitis, I., 17, 31–32
Guilt, 42

Hämäläinen, O., 252–53, 257, 269, 271–72, 275–78
Hampstead Clinic, 150, 158, 167, 167n14, 173–93
Hampstead Clinic Nursery School, 178–86
Hampstead War Nurseries, 164, 168
Hands, 41, 42, 47–48
Hanna Perkins Center, Cleveland, 168
Hartmann, D., 164
Hartmann, H., 36, 38, 85, 86, 88, 164
Hatfield, S. R., 157n9, 162
Hedgepeth, S. M., 238
Heineman, T., 164
Heller, B., 242
Hendrick, I., 85
Herzog, J., 40
Hitchcock, J., 298–300
Hoffer, W., 150
Hoffman, E., 234
Holinger, P., 157
Holocaust: and absence of grandparents of survivors' children, 232; and aggression and autonomy in survivors' children, 225–29; demarcation of external from internal reality in survivors' children, 218–19; healing in telling stories of, 238–42; and identification with the aggressor, 224; impact of, on survivors' children, 215–43; interpretations of traumatic stories of, 223–37; lacunae in stories of and survivors' silence about, 218, 229–32, 239–40; and Leah and her daughter Lily, 219–24, 228, 234–38, 242; and Magda and her daughter Miriam, 219–29, 233, 234, 237, 238, 242, 243; and maternal representation of survivors, 223–24; and Passover Haggadah, 242; as primal myth compared with Oedipus complex, 240; resistance to, 237–39; and sexuality of survivors' children, 231–32; and Shari and her daughter Sue, 219–23, 229–34, 238, 242; and standing guard against self and society, 234–37; stories of, as family myths and as allegories, 216–17; survivors' attitudes toward their children, 225; and survivors' internal representation of the stranger, 224–25; third generation following, 242–43; and trauma of second generation, 217, 237–38; and trauma of survival, 217, 222–37; and trauma of war, 217, 219–22; and understanding of death by survivors' children, 233–34
Homeless, 164
Hug, R., 152–53n4
Hug-Hellmuth, H., 151–53, 152n2, 152–53nn4-5
Humphrey, G., 199
Humphrey, M., 199
Hurry, A., 157, 175
Hyman, S., 127–28
Hysteria: Charcot on, 4; S. Freud on, 16; A. Freud on, 17; infantile hysteria, 18–19, 21; male hysteria, 17; Mitchell on, 3–5, 39; phallocentrism in theories on, 3–5; and sibling trauma, 4–5

Id, 254. See also Drives
"Ideal Psychoanalytic Institute: A Utopia" (A. Freud), 165–66
Identification, 66, 69, 257, 260
Identification with the aggressor, 224
Identity: clinical examples of adult females' yearning for recognition of elder sisters, 73–82; configuration of, within sibling matrix, 9–11, 66–82; gender role identity, 89–90; and identification, 66, 69; mutual recognition of sameness and difference within sibling relationships, 10, 37, 67, 70–71; and parent recognition, 80–82; questions on formation of, 11; and sibling trauma, 68–69. See also Body identity
Incest fantasies, 16, 23, 24, 26, 91, 92, 93
Incest taboo, 4, 5, 6, 7, 25, 26, 29, 36, 54
India, 20
Individuation/separation, 157, 281–82, 291–92
Infancy: Bion on, 257–58; S. Freud on, 28, 30, 31; memory in, 200–201; mother's survival of infants' aggression, 70; nervous system development in, 212; play during, 57; toleration of frustration in, 258–59. See also Mother-child relationship; Toddlers
Infantile amnesia, 211
Infantile hysteria, 18–19, 21. See also Sibling trauma/experience
Infantile phobia, 24, 152
Infantile sexuality, 25

Infantile traumatic memories: in adulthood, 207–10, 211, 212–13; from age twenty-nine months to kindergarten, 202–4, 211; and attitudes, 203, 206; and behavioral expressions, 203, 205, 207–8, 211–12; and brain structure, 212; discussion of, 210–13; and dreams, 206, 209, 210; and encoding, 200; introduction to, 198–99; from kindergarten to high school graduation, 204–7, 212; methods for, 199–202; nonverbal memories, 203–13; overview of, 197–98; and perceptions, 200, 204, 206–10, 212–13; and retrieval, 200; and storage, 200; verbal memories, 202–5, 207, 211

Infants without Families (A. Freud and Burlingham), 155

Inner/external issue. *See* Internal/external issue

Institute for Juvenile Research, Chicago, 164

Internal/external issue: and analyst as separate other, 264–65, 271; and assumptions in object relations theories, 250–51; Bion on, 257–58; clinical example of, 262–64; consequences of model on, 270–72; definition of outer object, 261; dilemmas connected to, 252–53; and epistemological stance of psychoanalysis, 251–52, 253, 256, 258, 269; and experience of another person, 261; and external objects versus separate others, 265–66, 276; S. Freud on perceptual identity and thought identity, 253–55, 258–59, 260; graphic presentation of model, 267, 268; Hämäläinen on, 252–53, 257, 271–72, 275–78; Klein on, 153–54, 255–56, 255n2, 260; and loneliness, 269, 277–78; model of, 265–72; overview of, 249–50; qualities of experience in model of, 266–69; and symbolic equation, 269–70; theoretical concepts on, 269–70; and "third position," 270, 271; and transference, 262–65, 271; Winnicott on, 256–57, 260, 276–77, 278

Internet. *See* Cyberspace communication

Interpersonal perspective, 157

Interpretation of Dreams (S. Freud), 253–54

Isaacs, S., 163

Israeli, E., 279–97

Itard, J. M., 198–99

Jackson Nursery, 167–68

Jealousy: envy distinguished from, 30, 93; and sibling trauma/experience, 16, 19n3, 20, 24, 30, 48, 93

Jews. *See* Holocaust; Judaism

Joan case, 21
Jobs, S., 163
Jones, E., 25
Judaism, 237, 242–43. *See also* Holocaust

Kaempferrt, W., 15n2
Kahn, M., 37
Kant, I., 251, 257, 258
Kaplan-Solms, K., 161
Kapp, Y., 20, 24
Katan, A., 150, 167
Katan, M., 167
Kazantzakis, N., 152n3
Kazdin, A., 130, 291
Kennedy, H., 37, 168
Kernberg, O. F., 281
Kevin case, 110–14, 124–25
Kieffer, C. C., 37, 39
Killing fantasies. *See* Murder fantasies
Killingmo, B., 270
Kinderheim Baumgarten, 164, 167–68
King, H., 4
King, P., 162–63
Kinship rights, 27
Klein, H., 237
Klein, M.: on aggression, 38; and amalgamation of parents and siblings, 18; child analysis by, 130, 152; and conflict between Kleinians and Freudians, 162–63; on death instinct, 36; on depressive position, 38, 38n1; on ego, 255; S. Freud compared with, 38, 38n1; influence of, 144; on loneliness, 269; on object relations, 153–54, 255–56, 255n2, 260; on Oedipus complex, 38n1; on "only child," 19, 19n3; on phantasy, 154; on projective identification, 257, 260; on transference, 261
Kluger, R., 221
Knight, R., 89, 90
Kogan, I., 237
Kohut, H., 155–56, 160, 160n10
Kramer, S., 37, 90
Kris, E., 150, 204
Kris, M., 37, 38, 67, 88, 149–50, 168
Kuba, S., 37

Lacan, J., 7, 24, 29, 31, 36, 157
Lachmann, F., 40
Lament, C., 3–13, 37, 84–99, 137–45
Lampl-De Groot, J., 85
Landau, R. S., 236
Lane, H., 199
Lange, F. A., 251
Langley Porter Psychiatric Institute, 159–60

Language, 23, 31
"Lateral" relations. *See* Siblings; Sibling trauma/experience
Laub, D., 218, 224, 227, 229, 232, 240, 241
"Law of the Father," 7, 26, 29, 40
"Law of the Mother": and ability of mothers to give birth, 27; Balsam's clinical example of, 7–8, 43–46, 48–50; Mitchell on, 7, 24, 26, 27, 29, 35, 40–41; and socialization of siblings, 7, 26, 29, 40–41. *See also* Mother-child relationship
Layton, L., 90
Leah/daughter Lily story, 219–24, 228, 234–38, 242
Leichtman, M., 37, 201
Lenhart, A., 281
Levin, C., 37
Levy-Warren, M. H., 281
Lewis, J. D., 224
Lichtenberg, J., 40
Lieberman, A. F., 164, 165
Liebmann, O., 251
Lingiardi, V., 280
"Little Hans" case, 15–16, 24, 28, 152
Loewald, H., 8, 35, 40, 45
Loftus, E. F., 200
Loneliness, 269, 277–78
Lowenstein, R. M., 38
Lucy Daniels Center, North Carolina, 168
Luepnitz, D., 164
Luke case, 122–24

MacLean, G., 152n4, 153n5
Magda/daughter Miriam story, 219–29, 233, 234, 237, 238, 242, 243
Magical Moments of Change (Terr), 203
Mahler, M., 37, 157
Malatar, E., 282
Malinowski, B., 6, 25
Marciano, P., 130
Mauthner, M., 24–25
Mayer, E. L., 47
Mayes, L., 58, 59, 88
McCleod, B., 130
"Measuring the Ghost in the Nursery" (Fonagy et al.), 156–57n8
Meeks, J. E., 291, 295
Meissner, W. W., 90
Melanesia, 6, 25
Melinda case, 114–17
Memory: of infants, 200–201; and possibility of suggestion, 201; processes of, 200; and stress, 201–2. *See also* Infantile traumatic memories
Mentalization, 156–57, 159, 161, 259, 270
Merritt, K. A., 201

Mesch, G. S., 291
Middle child, 93
Midgley, N., 291
Miller, George A., 157
Mitchell, J.: on absence of siblings from theoretical superstructure, 3, 15–18, 28, 36, 39, 53–54; on differentiation, 69–70; on disposition, 12, 84; on gendering in sibling trauma, 24–28; on hysteria, 3–5, 39; in identification, 69; on "Law of the Mother" versus "Law of the Father," 7–8, 24, 26, 27, 29, 35, 40–41, 48–50; on love and hate between siblings, 48, 87; on nonlinear perspective of developmental process, 11–12, 84, 87; on Oedipus complex, 4, 39, 49; on "only" child, 18–20, 93; origins of interest in siblings, 4, 15, 39; on phallocentrism, 3–5, 11, 12, 84–85, 91; on seriality, 7, 35, 40, 50; on sibling trauma, 4–5, 12, 16–32, 35, 36, 39, 40, 47, 53–58, 64, 67, 91–93, 95–96; on social world of sibling trauma, 28–32
Mitchell, S., 217, 229, 235
Modification of frustration, 258–59
Moorehead, C., 228
Morris, G., 201
Moses and Monotheism (S. Freud), 28, 31–32
Mother-child relationship: of adolescent females experiencing sibling trauma, 59–63; and adult females with elder sisters, 75, 77–81; and adult female with younger sister, 41–49; in Alice case, 180; and anxiety, 116–17, 119; Bion on, 256–59; and child's relational attitudes and behavior, 90–91; daughters of Holocaust survivors, 225–37; and family seriality, 7, 35, 40, 50; S. Freud on, 104; and gender role identity of child, 90–91; and impact of Holocaust on survivors' children, 215–43; and infant's aggression, 70; and maternal representation, 223–24; mother as child's "object," 30; and mother as gold standard of childbearing creativity, 27, 46, 48; mutual recognition within, 70; and siblings, 7–8, 29, 40; and subjectivity of mothers, 70; Winnicott on, 104, 155, 166, 256–57, 260, 276, 278. *See also* Concurrent work with parents of adolescent patients; Father-child relationship; "Law of the Mother"; Parent-child relationship
Motivation, 157
Mourning and Melancholia (S. Freud), 252, 254–55, 260, 271
Murder fantasies, 7, 23, 24, 26, 91, 92, 93, 96, 188–90

Mutational self, 228
Mutual recognition: clinical examples of adult females' yearning for recognition of elder sisters, 73–82; and father, 70–71; of mother and child, 70–71; and negotiation of difference, 71; and shared third, 11, 71; of siblings, 10, 37, 67, 72–73

Nachman, P. A., 201
National Research Council, 106
Nature-versus-nurture debate, 127–28, 140
Nazism. *See* Holocaust
"Negation" (S. Freud), 298
Neubauer, P. B., 37, 49, 88, 89, 91, 93
"Neurological Crisis in a Small Boy: Sam" (Erikson), 154–55
Neuropsychoanalysis, 156, 159, 161
Neuroscience, 127–28, 130, 140
Newman, L. M., 35, 37
Nightmares. *See* Dreams and nightmares
Nonlinear perspective of developmental process, 11–12, 84, 85, 87–88, 93–94, 96
Normality and Pathology in Childhood (A. Freud), 154
"Normotic" attitude, 250–51, 253
Novak, B. J., 157
Novick, J., 103–45, 158, 166, 265, 266, 267
Novick, K. K., 103–45, 158, 166, 265, 266, 267
Nutkiewicz, M., 223, 230, 239

Object relations: basic assumptions in, 250–51; Bion on, 257–58; and different connotations of term "object," 251–52; and experience of another person, 261; A. Freud on, 177, 186–87, 189; S. Freud on object for a drive, 250, 252, 260; S. Freud on perceptual identity and thought identity, 253–55, 258–59, 260; internal/external issue in, 249–72, 275–78; Klein on, 153–54, 255–56, 255n2, 260; mother as "object" for child, 30, 70; and "Sophie" case by Brinich, 159; Winnicott on, 256–57, 260, 276–77; younger sibling as "other-object," 30. *See also* Internal/external issue
Obsessive-compulsive disorder (OCD), 117
Oedipal Sibling Triangles (Sharpe and Rosenblatt), 56–57
Oedipus complex: and child's understanding of sexuality, 240; compared with Holocaust as primal myth, 240; and differentiation, 69; dominance of, 25; S. Freud on, 16, 17, 35–36, 38n1; Klein on, 38n1; layering of sibling trauma and, 60–61; Mitchell on restrictive nature of, 4, 39, 49; sibling trauma as distinct from, 23, 29–30, 55, 56–57
Olesker, W., 89, 90
Oliner, M. M., 241
"Only" child, 18–20, 19n3, 93
Ornstein, P. A., 201
Orthogenic School, Chicago, 168
Outer object. *See* Internal/external issue

Panic attacks, 114–17
Paranoia, 39–40
Parent-child relationship: centrality and importance of, 133; as constant pillar in child's familial relationships, 92; parent-child dyad as unit of assessment and unit of treatment, 104; and transgenerational transmission of sibling trauma, 9, 59. *See also* Concurrent work with parents of adolescent patients; Father-child relationship; Mother-child relationship
Parents of adolescent patients. *See* Concurrent work with parents of adolescent patients
Parent Trap, The, 62
Parthenogenesis, 27
Passover, 242
Patriarchy, 5. *See also* Phallocentrism
Peer group, 59, 61–63
Pekarik, G., 291
Penis envy, 26
Penman, A. B., 173–93
Perceptive identification, 257
Perceptual identity, 253–55
Peskin, H., 218, 227, 230, 239, 240, 241
Peter Pan, 55–56, 63
Phallocentrism, 3–5, 11, 12, 84–86, 90, 91, 96
Phantasy, 154
Pharmacracy (Szasz), 166
Philomela myth, 237
Piaget, J., 87
Pine, F., 151n1, 157
Plath, S., 284
Play, 57
Play therapy, 179, 182
Pleasure principle, 254, 260, 266–67
Potential space. *See* Transitional space
Prall, R. C., 90
Pre-conceptions, 256, 257–58
Prelinger, E., 241
Pretorius, I., 157
Privacy versus secrecy, 112, 132–33, 144–45, 288–90, 295–96
Projection, 181–84, 261, 268, 271
Projective identification, 257, 260

Provence, S., 37
Pruett, K., 129
Psychoanalysis. *See* Adolescent psychotherapy; Child psychoanalysis; Concurrent work with parents of adolescent patients; Countertransference; Termination; Transference
Psychoanalytic education, 165–66
Psychoanalytic Institute of Eastern Europe, 163
Psychoanalytic Study of a Family, 37
Psychoanalytic Study of the Child, The, 150, 157, 160n10
Psychogenic fallacy, 85
Purim, 243
Pynoos, R., 157

"Question of Lay Analysis, The" (S. Freud), 165

Rangell, L., 86
Rappen, U., 152n4, 153n5
Rashkin, E., 231
Reality principle, 254, 260, 266–67
Recognition. *See* Mutual recognition
Regression: in analytic situation, 49–50, 60; Blos on, 299; of toddler at birth of sibling, 23, 24, 57–58
Reichmayr, J., 164
Reiss, D., 104
Rembar, J., 130
Representational world, 157, 250. *See also* Object relations
Reproduction versus sexuality, 25, 27
Rie, A., 150
Rie, O., 149–50
Ritvo, S., 37, 67, 150
Robinson, J. L., 90
Rosenberg, L., 150
Rosenblatt, A., 56–57, 67
Rosenblatt, B., 157, 250
Rosenblitt, D. L., 153
Roskies, D., 223, 237

Sadger, I., 152
Safer, J., 37
Saidel, R. G., 237, 238
Salberg, J., 123
Sandler, A.-M., 250, 252
Sandler, J., 157, 168, 252
Saywitz, K. J., 201
Schacter, D. L., 212
Schizophrenia, 269
Schlesinger, H., 123
Schmeets, M. G. J., 157n8
Schmideberg, M., 162–63

Schore, A. N., 130
Schumacher, B., 157
Scott, J., 25
Secrecy versus privacy, 112, 132–33, 144–45, 288–90, 295–96
"Seduction theory" of trauma, 16, 17
Segal, H., 31, 269–70
Self-harm, 286–87, 291. *See also* Suicide
Self psychology, 40, 155–56, 159, 160–61
Self-regulation, 265, 266
Semel, N., 216, 217
Senet, N. V., 58
Separateness versus separation, 103, 106, 108–9, 112, 139–40
Separation anxiety, 61–63
Separation/individuation, 157, 281–82, 291–92
Separation trauma, 20, 21–22, 31
Seriality, 7, 35, 40, 50
Sexual abuse, 199, 200
Sexual difference, 25–26
Sexuality: during adolescence, 59, 63; S. Freud on infantile sexuality, 25; of Holocaust survivors' children, 231–32; Hug-Hellmuth's discussion of, 153; Oedipus complex and child's understanding of, 240; reproduction versus, 25, 27
Shaken baby syndrome, 197, 199, 200
Sharabany, R., 279–97
Shared third, 11, 71
Shari/daughter Sue story, 219–23, 229–34, 238, 242
Sharpe, S., 56–57, 67
Shelley, C., 160
Sholem Community Organization, 242
Sibling rivalry, 12, 86, 90, 91
Siblings: absence of, from theoretical superstructure, 3, 15–18, 28, 36, 39, 53–54, 67; birth order of, 17, 92–93, 95; changes in sibling relationships in adulthood, 49; and differentiation, 10, 37, 66, 69–70; feminine-based associations to word *sibling*, 5–6, 90, 91; S. Freud on amalgamation of parents and siblings, 17; Graham on, 54; identity configuration within sibling matrix, 9–11; jealousy of, 16, 19n3, 20, 24, 30, 48, 93; love and hate between, 5, 21, 40, 48, 59, 69, 87; of middle child, 93; minimal difference between, 14, 68, 72; mother's role with, 7–8, 29, 40; and mutual recognition of sameness and difference of, 10, 37, 67, 72–73; recent theoretical analysis of, 36–37; recognition of differentiated identity by, 72–73; and seriality, 7, 35, 40, 50; of sick or handicapped children,

37, 62; "static sibling," 49; timing of births of, 92–93; of twins, 37, 57, 62, 92; younger sibling as "other-object," 30. *See also* Brothers; Sibling trauma/experience; Sisters

Sibling trauma/experience: adolescent's experiences of, 9, 42–46, 59–64; of adult females' yearning for recognition of elder sisters, 73–82; of adult female with younger sister, 41–50; and aggression, 43–45, 58, 59, 96; clinical examples of, 41–50, 59–64, 73–82; dispositional features of, 12, 84–86, 88–89, 93–96; environmental considerations on, 94–95; and gendering, 24–28, 58; Gilmore on, 8–9, 53–64; and identity, 68–69; and jealousy, 16, 19n3, 20, 24, 30, 48, 93; Lament on, 11–12; layering of Oedipus complex and, 60–61; Mitchell on, 4–5, 12, 16–32, 35, 36, 39, 40, 47, 53–58, 64, 67–68, 91–93, 95–96; nonlinear perspective on, 11–12, 84, 85, 87–88, 93–94, 96; Oedipus complex distinguished from, 23, 29–30, 55, 56–57; phallocentric biases on, 3–5, 11, 12, 84–86, 90, 91, 96; regression of toddler at birth of sibling, 23, 24, 57–58; in social world, 28–32; and splitting, 31; symptoms of, 23; toddler's experience of, 8–9, 18–24, 29–30, 55–58, 72, 79, 93; transgenerational transmission of, 9, 59; universality of, 4–5, 19, 53, 55, 57, 67–68, 91–92, 91n1, 95–96; Vivona on, 67–69

Sinking feeling, 298–300

Sisters: clinical example of adult female with younger sister, 41–50; clinical examples of adult females' yearning for recognition of elder sisters, 73–82; conflicts and aggression between, 43–45; guilt of successful older sister, 42; intimacy between, 43; Kuba on role of, in female development, 37; Mauthner on "sistering," 24–25; relationship of adult sisters, 49. *See also* Brothers; Siblings; Sibling trauma/experience

Smaller, M., 164
Sociocultural environment, 154–55, 159
Solms, M., 156, 161
Solnit, A. J., 37, 88, 164
Solter, A., 211
Sonia case, 59–61
"Sophie" case, 158–62
Spence, D. P., 88
Spicker, B., 201
Spielman, Philip, 158

Spillius, E. B., 250, 255
Spitz, R., 155
Splitting, 16, 31, 57, 255, 260
Squire, L. R., 212
Stalin, J., 224
"Static sibling," 49
Stein, R., 267
Steinberg, A., 157
Steinberger, C. G.
Steiner, J., 270, 271
Steiner, R., 162–63
Stekel, W., 152n3
Stern, D., 157, 201
Stollor, R. J., 89
Strachey, J., 88
Strangers, representation of, 224–25
Suicide, 118–19, 122, 282, 289–90, 292–93
Superego, 154, 177, 254
Survivor guilt, 238
"Symbolic," 31
Symbolic equations, 31, 269–70
Szalita, A., 39
Szasz, T. S., 166

Talmud, I., 291
Target, M., 57, 291
Tauber, A. I., 251n1
Tavistock Clinic, 167n14
Temperament, 157
Terence, 168
Termination, 108–9, 122–24, 290
Terr, L. C., 197–214
Theater metaphor for analytic situation, 8, 35, 40
Thing-in-itself, 257n3, 259
"Third position," 270, 271
Thomas, A., 157
Thought identity, 253–55, 258–59
Three Essays on the Theory of Sexuality (S. Freud), 27
Todd, V., 105
Toddlers: aggression of, 58, 59; body identity of, 58; gender awareness of, 58; imaginative world of, 57; sibling trauma of, 8–9, 18–24, 29–30, 55–58, 72, 79, 93; transitional language of, 31. *See also* Infancy; Mother-child relationship
Toleration of frustration, 258–59, 260
Totem and Taboo (S. Freud), 28, 29
Transference: of adult female with elder sister, 75–76, 78–79; of adult female with younger sister, 43–46, 43n3; Agger on, 39; in Alice case, 182; S. Freud on, 267; and internal/external issue, 262–65, 271; Klein on, 261; misconcep-

Transference (*continued*)
tion of, 85; multiple transferences, 40, 49–50; normal transference relationship, 267–69, 271; and outer object, 261; in parent work, 137, 141–45; psychotic transference, 268, 271; sibling transference, 54; theater metaphor for, 8, 35, 40; and transitional space, 267

Transformation: assumptions underlying, 140; S. Freud on, 140; in parent work, 103, 106, 108–12, 114, 117–20, 126–29, 133, 137, 140–41

Transgendering, 27

Transitional space: cyberspace as, 285–86, 295; Winnicott on, 252, 256, 259, 260, 267, 268, 276–77

Transitivism, 23–24, 30

Trauma: abreaction in psychodynamic psychotherapy for, 198; Charcot on, 4; and child psychoanalysis generally, 157, 159, 161–62; clinical reports and research on, 157; context in psychodynamic psychotherapy for, 198; correction in psychodynamic psychotherapy for, 198; evolution of traumatic narratives, 215–43; S. Freud on, 16, 17, 31–32; and identification with the aggressor, 224; infantile traumatic memories, 197–213; and mutational self, 228; and "Sophie" case, 162; symptoms and expressions of, 22–23; violence of, 22; Winnicott on separation trauma, 20, 21–22. *See also* Sibling trauma

Trobrianders, 6, 25
Truffaut, F., 199
Tuch, R., 88
Turkle, S., 281, 282
Turnbull, O., 156, 161
Twinning reaction, 57
Twins, 37, 57, 62, 92
Tyson, P., 89
Tyson, R., 89
Tyson, R. L., 168

Ultra-realism, 252–53, 272, 275–76
Unconscious, 251, 254. *See also* Drives
University of Chicago, 158
University of North Carolina, 160

Van Horn, P., 164, 165
Verheugt-Pleiter, A. J. E., 157n8

Vertical relations. *See* Father-child relationship; Mother-child relationship; Oedipus complex; Parent-child relationship
Vienna Psychoanalytic Society, 153n4, 167n13
Vivona, J., 7, 9–11, 37, 59, 66–83
Volkan, V. D., 22n5

Waelder, R., 168n16
Wagonfeld, S., 89
War, trauma of, 217, 219–22, 224
War and Children (Freud and Burlingham), 191
Watson, J., 86
Weine, S. M., 223
Weiner, A. B., 28n6
Weinstein, L., 88
Weisz, J., 130
Westen, D., 85
White, T. L., 201
Whitley, E. M., 130
Wierzbicki, M., 291
"Wild child" case, 197–213
Wineman, I., 37
Winnicott, D. W.: and Bollas's term "normotic," 250–51; on child's reactions to brother's birth, 94; on Joan case, 21; on loneliness, 269, 278; on mother-infant relationship, 104, 155, 166, 256–57, 260, 278; on mother's survival of infant's aggression, 70; on object relations, 256–57, 260, 276–77; on potential or transitional space, 252, 256, 259, 260, 267, 268, 276–77; on separation trauma, 20–23, 31; on splitting and dissociation, 16–17; on toleration of feeling states, 270
Wolff, A. K., 150

Yale Longitudinal Study, 37
Yale University, Child Study Center, 168
Yale University, Fortunoff Video Archive for Holocaust Testimonies, 219
Yanof, J., 104
Yom Kippur, 221, 227, 243
Young-Bruehl, E., 36, 124, 153, 164, 168
Zachrisson, A., 249–74
Zevalkink, J., 157n8
Zipes, J., 216